# *The Optina Elders Series*

Vol. 1 ELDER LEONID OF OPTINA
    *by Fr. Clement Sederholm*
Vol. 2 ELDER ANTHONY OF OPTINA
    *by Fr. Clement Sederholm*
Vol. 3 ELDER MACARIUS OF OPTINA
    *by Fr. Leonid Kavelin*
Vol. 4 ELDER AMBROSE OF OPTINA
    *by Fr. Sergius Chetverikov*
Vol. 5 ELDER NEKTARY OF OPTINA
    *by I. M. Kontzevitch*
Vol. 6 ELDER SEBASTIAN OF KARAGANDA
    *by Tatiana V. Torstensen*
Vol. 7 ELDER BARSANUPHIUS OF OPTINA
    *by Victor Afanasiev*

# ELDER AMBROSE OF OPTINA

ST. AMBROSE OF OPTINA
From the collection of I. M. Kontzevitch.

# ELDER AMBROSE
## *of Optina*

by
FR. SERGIUS CHETVERIKOV

ST. HERMAN OF ALASKA BROTHERHOOD
2009

Copyright 1997, 2009 by the
St. Herman of Alaska Brotherhood

*Address all correspondence to:*
St. Herman of Alaska Brotherhood
P.O. Box 70
Platina, California 96076

www.sainthermanpress.com

*Front cover:* Icon of St. Ambrose of Optina, painted in 1988 by M. N. Sokolova, Moscow, for St. Ambrose's canonization.

First English Edition 1997

Second English Edition 2009

Translated from the Russian edition: *Opisanie Zhizni Blazhennoi Pamyati Optinskago Startsa Amvrosia [Description of the Life of Optina Elder Ambrose of Blessed Memory],* published by the Kazan-Ambrose Shamordino Convent, Kaluga Province, 1912. This Russian edition was reprinted by the St. Herman of Alaska Brotherhood, Platina, California in 1980.

---

Publishers Cataloging in Publication

Chetverikov, Sergius, Archpriest (1867–1947)
    Elder Ambrose of Optina.
    Translated from the Russian.

Library of Congress Control Number: 96-068651
ISBN: 0-938635-60-3
ISBN-13: 978-0-938635-60-4

Dedicated to the memory of
an Optina disciple,
ARCHIMANDRITE AMBROSE
(KONAVALOV) (†1971)

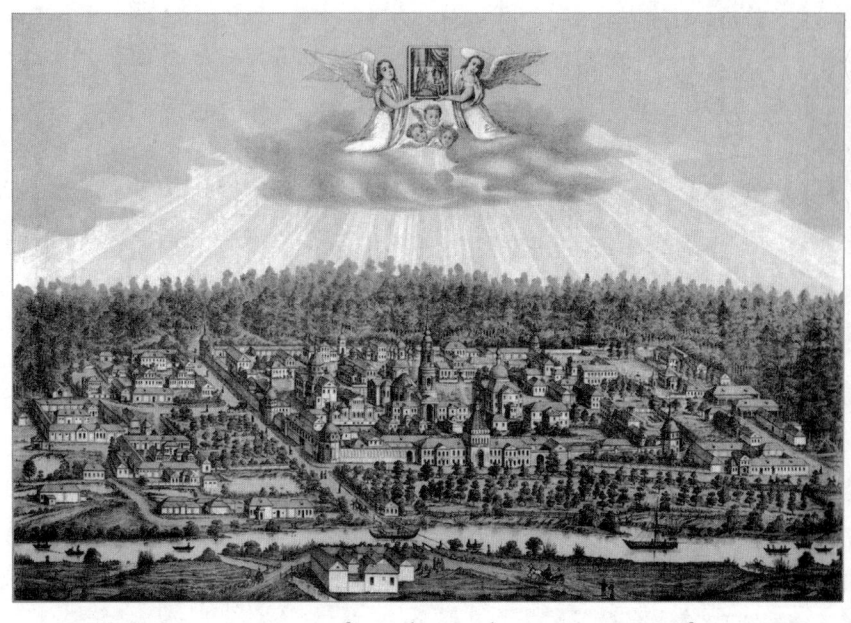

Optina Monastery as seen from the northwest. Engraving from 1887.

# CONTENTS

INTRODUCTION . . . . . . . . . . . . 11
CHRONOLOGY . . . . . . . . . . . . 31
THE LIFE OF ELDER AMBROSE OF OPTINA
  1. The Eternal Truth of Orthodoxy . . . . . . . . 33
  2. A Profile of the Spiritual Make-up of Elder Ambrose 39
  3. The Youth of Elder Ambrose . . . . . . . . . 43
  4. The Call of God . . . . . . . . . . . . . . . 49
  5. Optina Monastery—A Grace-Filled Corner of the
     Russian Land . . . . . . . . . . . . . 59
  6. Optina Monastery and the Remarkable Monastic
     Movement . . . . . . . . . . . . . . . 75
  7. The Spiritual Growth of Elder Ambrose . . . . 107
  8. The Eldership of Hieroschemamonk Ambrose . . . 135
     Early Years of Eldership . . . . . . . . . 135
     Fr. Ambrose's Correspondence . . . . . . 157
     The Cell of Fr. Ambrose . . . . . . . . . 197
     The Elder's Pastoral Care . . . . . . . . 214
  9. The Last Podvig of Love of Elder Ambrose . . . . 295
 10. The Last Days of Elder Ambrose . . . . . . 341
 11. The Special Manifestations of the Grace-filled
     Power of God in Elder Ambrose . . . . . . 373
CONCLUSION . . . . . . . . . . . . 435
AKATHIST . . . . . . . . . . . . . 441
GLOSSARY . . . . . . . . . . . . . 459
SELECT BIBLIOGRAPHY . . . . . . . 463
INDEX . . . . . . . . . . . . . . . 465

Elder Ambrose of Optina.

# INTRODUCTION

## 1. THE GLORIFICATION OF ST. AMBROSE

Over the decades since his repose, St. Ambrose of Optina has come to personify the nineteenth-century revival of eldership and the study of patristic wisdom in Russia, first initiated by St. Paisius Velichkovsky during the eighteenth century. Thousands of believers, from simple peasants to members of the aristocracy and renowned personalities such as author Feodor Dostoyevsky,* sought and found solace and divinely inspired wisdom in the humble "hut" of Elder Ambrose in the St. John the Forerunner Skete of Optina Monastery.

In June of 1988, as part of the celebration of the one-thousand-year anniversary of the conversion of ancient Russia to Orthodox Christianity, the Holy Synod of the Russian Orthodox Church resolved to number Elder Ambrose in the choir of the saints. That year many Russian people began to awaken to their lost heritage and sacred calling after a long period of Communist repression. Large numbers of people were baptized, churches began to be reopened and renovated, and it became common for people to identify themselves as Christians.

In preparation for the jubilee celebrations in Russia, Optina

---

*Dostoyevsky used Elder Ambrose as a model for the character of Elder Zosima in his novel *The Brothers Karamazov*. The writer recounted Elder Ambrose's counsel to him over the loss of his son in the chapter of the same book called "Peasant Women Who Have Faith."

Procession with the relics of Elder Ambrose on October 10/23, 1988, the Saint's first feast day after his canonization.

INTRODUCTION

Monastery, which had been designated as a museum by the Communist authorities for many years and was by then in a dilapidated state, was returned to the Church on November 17, 1987. Before long, more and more men began to join the Optina brotherhood, and repairs were swiftly begun. At the present time, all the original churches and buildings have been restored, as well as those of the Forerunner Skete. Likewise, the monastery has revived its literary work, and numerous spiritually edifying books have been published there. The Lives of the Optina Elders have become increasingly popular among believers, not only in Russia but in other lands as well.

In April 1990, the Russian Orthodox Church Outside of Russia glorified the entire Synaxis of Optina Elders. In 1996 they were locally canonized by the Moscow Patriarchate, and then in 2000 there followed their Church-wide glorification in connection with the glorification of the New Martyrs and Confessors of Russia.

The present book, the fourth volume of the Optina Elders Series, is one of two widely known Russian hagiographical works on the great Elder Ambrose. The first biography was written by the Elder's disciple, Archimandrite Agapit (Belovidov) (1842–1922), and published in 1900, not long after the Elder's repose. The second biography, of which the present book is a translation, was written by the well-known author, Archpriest Sergius Chetverikov (1867–1947), and published in 1912. Fr. Sergius made use of Archimandrite Agapit's book as a major source for his own work.

## 2. IN MEMORY OF ARCHIMANDRITE AMBROSE (KONAVALOV)

The St. Herman of Alaska Brotherhood is publishing a translation of Fr. Sergius' biography at the prompting of an

Archimandrite Ambrose (Konavalov)
in one of his Canadian sketes.

Optina disciple who emigrated to North America: Archimandrite Ambrose (Konavalov). When still a seminarian, Gleb Podmoshensky, later Abbot Herman of the St. Herman Monastery, was visiting the New Diveyevo Convent in Spring Valley, New York, where he encountered Archimandrite Ambrose. Fr. Ambrose spoke to him for a long time about Optina and about his ardent desire to see specifically the Chetverikov biography re-

Archimandrite Ambrose in the cemetery of
New Diveyevo Convent in New York.

printed, which he hoped would inspire a new generation of monastics. Fr. Ambrose had often visited Optina Monastery in his youth, walking fifty miles from his home, and had known Elder Joseph, Elder Ambrose's cell-attendant and successor as Elder. He received a blessing from Fr. George Kosov of Spas-Chekriak village, another disciple of Elder Ambrose,* to enter a monastery, but before he could do so he was drafted into the army during the First World War. After the Revolution he emigrated with the White Army to Constantinople, and thence to Canada. The increase of Orthodox immigrants to Canada in-

---

*New Hiero-confessor Priest George (†1928) was glorified by the Russian Orthodox Church in 2000. See pp. 386-89 below.

spired him to begin establishing monasteries there, and he summoned his friend Monk Ioasaph (later Archbishop of Canada), with whom he founded four monastic establishments in Alberta. During the 1950s and 1960s he served in the St. Vladimir Cathedral in Edmonton, Alberta. He reposed in the Holy Trinity Monastery in Jordanville, New York, in 1971.

The St. Herman Brotherhood eventually reprinted the original Russian edition of Fr. Sergius' book in 1980, nine years after the repose of Archimandrite Ambrose, dedicating it to his memory. We likewise dedicate this English translation to Fr. Ambrose. May his memory be eternal!

## 3. ABOUT THE AUTHOR

The author of the present volume, Archpriest Sergius Ivanovich Chetverikov, was born on June 12, 1867, in a small southern Russian town to a poor, pious family of the merchant class. His mother reposed when he was two years old upon giving birth to his brother, who himself died shortly thereafter. His father soon remarried. His stepmother was a kind woman who raised him well, and became almost as dear to him as his own mother would have been. He later wrote: "My father taught me to pray, and to love the Church and church singing. Thanks to my father, the Church and its feasts, especially Nativity and Pascha, occupied the central place in our domestic life, its chief content and educational element. Every Saturday I went with my father to the All-night Vigil and came to love church singing. Without instruction or lectures the Church took possession of my soul."

Sergius' elder sister taught him to read and write. At the age of seven he was sent to school. At the age of nine his parents sent him to the preparatory class of the church school—not because they wanted him to become a priest, but because that was the only school in their town.

When he graduated primary school as the number two student, he was given a collection of the works of the Russian poet Lermontov, after which he moved to Taganrog. But these books, as he recalled, "brought me greater harm than good, which became especially evident in the higher classes of the gymnasium—the sixth, seventh, and eighth.... He [Lermontov] corrupted my soul, and it was only with difficulty that I was delivered from what he had placed in it. In Taganrog I went through the most difficult years of my life: faith was extinguished in me, and I lost the purity of my soul and body."

By God's mercy, this period of his life finally came to an end. On his summer vacation from school he went to visit his married sister in the Crimea, where he met two young women who were teachers. "Through their purity and friendship they warmed and purified my soul. There was nothing romantic between us.... My experiences in Taganrog were forgotten and died; and a new, pure, bright, spiritual life began."

Sergius moved from the Crimea to Moscow, where he attended Moscow University from 1886 to 1892, first studying medicine and zoology, and later switching to philology. But secular education did not satisfy him. He decided to go to the St. Sergius Lavra to take counsel with the young new director of the Theological Academy, Archimandrite Anthony (Khrapovitsky).* "He immediately captivated me by his warmth, simplicity, and bright, shining countenance. Our conversation lasted two hours. He advised me to transfer to the Academy and continue my education.... He supplied me with books and told me to come in August of the following year for the entrance examinations."

Sergius studied diligently. Eighty applicants, some of the best students, came for the examination. Of the eighty, only the

---

*Later first chief hierarch of the Russian Orthodox Church Outside of Russia.

The author, Fr. Sergius, at the time this book was written.

# INTRODUCTION

thirty with the highest scores could count on financial aid. Sergius passed the examination with the thirtieth highest score, and was even granted the St. Sergius Scholarship, which was only granted to one student each year in each of the four grades.

With his entrance into the Academy, Sergius' life settled down. He had found his path. "Attending the lectures of the professors, at the same time I also spent time amidst the crowds of worshipers who came from all the ends of Russia—in the Holy Trinity Cathedral at the relics of Sts. Sergius and Nikon, and in the chapel on the site of St. Sergius' cell, where the Mother of God had appeared to the saint and where, every Friday at 2 a.m., a Moleben with Akathist was served to the Mother of God and sung by the full Lavra choir. I visited Elder Herman at the Gethsemane Skete [of the St. Sergius Lavra], as well as Elder Barnabas of the same Skete, who was my spiritual father. I entered into a new life, a joyous and peaceful one, filled with theological labors which absolutely took hold of my soul and totally satisfied me. The feelings and the freshness of my youth returned to me."

During his time as a student he was blessed to attend some of the Divine Liturgies celebrated by St. John of Kronstadt, which had an important influence on him: "He served, entirely enveloped by an inward fire. I have never seen such a fiery service, either before or since. He was truly like a seraphim, standing before God."

After four years Sergius graduated the Theological Academy. He was married in 1896 to Yelena Stratonikovna Yakovleva. Soon thereafter he was ordained to the priesthood and briefly assigned to the Exaltation of the Cross Brotherhood, which had been founded by the landowner N. N. Neplyuyev in Chernigov, in connection with agricultural schools for men and women. Soon after this he was assigned to a parish in Chernigov.

He then moved on to work as a catechetical teacher, first in Saratov, and then in Poltava, where he served for twelve years as chaplain of the Poltava Military Academy, until the Revolution forced his evacuation from Russia. At this time a tragedy took place in his life. By the time of the Revolution, he and his wife had had seven children. As the time to evacuate drew near, one of his sons was ill, and Fr. Sergius' wife Yelena and their eldest daughter stayed behind to care for him. Fr. Sergius and his other four children (one had died in childhood) were evacuated along with the staff and students of the Military Academy, with the hope that the family would be reunited after the boy had recovered. Unfortunately, this was not to be—those who stayed in Russia were never able to escape. They maintained contact as much as they could over the years, but communication was very difficult during the 1920s and 1930s. It is believed that Yelena reposed in about 1937.

After leaving Russia, Fr. Sergius served as a parish priest, first for three years in rural Serbia, and then in Bratislava, Czechoslovakia, from 1923 to 1928. In 1928 Fr. Sergius was transferred by Metropolitan Eulogius to Paris, where he was assigned as priest of the Russian Christian Student Movement, specifically to care for the émigré youth who were scattered throughout Europe. This period of his life lasted ten years, and he considered this assignment to be the most important work of his life. During this period he traveled extensively throughout Europe, working with a great many members of the Movement, both youths and adults. He carried on an enormous correspondence with them, in this way guiding the Movement and forming deep spiritual bonds with a great many people.

Fr. Sergius' literary output was sizeable. In addition to the present volume, he wrote a biography of St. Paisius Velichkovsky, a book on Optina Monastery consisting of a historical essay and personal recollections, and a collection of writings

Fr. Sergius (right) at Valaam Monastery in 1939, drinking tea with Schemamonk Nicholas (left) of Konevits Skete and Hieromonk Pambo (center).

on the Jesus Prayer. He also wrote over thirty articles and essays for the magazine *Put'* (*The Way*), and for *Vestnik* (*The Messenger*), the magazine of the Russian Christian Student Movement. In addition, he authored several pedagogical articles. Thanks to his efforts the letters of Elder Anatole I (Zertsalov) of Optina were published, as well as several volumes of Elder Ambrose's letters.

In 1930, Fr. Sergius for the first time visited Valaam Monastery, which was then in Finnish territory, and was greatly touched in soul by the monastic life and the beauty of nature there. He subsequently made frequent visits there in connection with his literary work and to deepen his spiritual life. He made his last visit to Valaam in 1939, just before the start of the

Russo-Finnish War, and ended up fleeing with the monks to Finland, where he remained with them for a short time in their temporary quarters. Not wishing to burden them due to his increasing age and infirmity, he eventually settled with his son Theodosius Sergeyevich in Bratislava, where he spent his last years and reposed on April 29, 1947. Not long before his death he was tonsured into the great schema.

## 4. SILENCE, A VISION OF ETERNAL REST

In publishing this volume on the Life of St. Ambrose of Optina, we would like to present a remarkable text that was probably not known to Fr. Sergius when he compiled this book. This is the account of S. Glebov, a relative of Optina Elder Macarius (Ivanov), in which Elder Ambrose describes an event that took place in his own youth. This account sheds light on the Elder's formative years, and tells of the final impetus that compelled him to enter the monastery.* S. Glebov writes:

In the late 1860s I was traveling to various holy places of Russia with my elderly mother, who in her old age desired for the last time in her life to venerate the holy relics of God's saints at the places of their repose. We stopped for a few days in Optina Monastery in the Kaluga region with the definite intention of visiting the local ascetic Fr. Ambrose, well known for his holy life. He lived not far from the monastery in his own little desert skete, where he received weary pilgrims who came to him, some for advice, others for consolation of their sorrowing hearts.

The beauty of Optina Monastery—surrounded on all sides by evergreen forests, luxurious monastic orchards, delightful spacious ponds filled with leisurely swimming fish of various

---

*This account was first published in Russian in *Russky Palomnik* (*The Russian Pilgrim*), no. 17, 1904, pp. 286–88.

A recent photograph of the Optina Church of the Entry of the Theotokos, in which the relics of St. Ambrose repose.

kinds—never leaves the memory of a pilgrim who has been there.

Fr. Ambrose received us kindly and invited us into his log-cabin cell, surrounded by an orchard. There he usually received all of his visitors, who were always thirsty for his soul-profiting talks and spiritual instruction. Our talk with Fr. Ambrose was a very long one and highly beneficial for our souls.

Whoever saw him even once found it impossible to forget his meek face with its smooth, parchment-like white skin—a face that reminded one of something sacramental in all of his actions. Having learned about the purpose of our pilgrimage throughout Russia, the good Elder invited us to stay in Optina for ten days or so. Blessing our stay in the monastery, the holy Elder said, "In our monastery, life is as if in Paradise, and you will never be able to fill yourself to satiety—there is so much grace here. The services in our temples here are so solemnly beautiful that they draw one involuntarily to God by their holy teaching and compunctionate church singing."

Taking advantage of Fr. Ambrose's blessing, we stayed in Optina for seven days. During that time we visited the Elder several times and heard his wise evangelical teaching on life. When he learned that I am involved with various periodicals of the "secular kind," Fr. Ambrose handed me a short manuscript and suggested that I have a look at it. This was the content of the manuscript:

> It was a wonderful time in spring. I could not resist the temptation to cast myself into nature's embrace, and the springtime paradise that I chose as the place of my daily visits was the dark, thick forest situated on the high bank of a large, wide river [the Oka] that washes several central Russian provinces with its milky waters.

Icon of the Most Holy Theotokos "She Who Ripens the Grain," painted at the direction of Elder Ambrose (see pp. 328–29 below).

Giving myself over to this blessed state in the bosom of nature, I drank in its aromatic breath and delved deeply into spiritual contemplation of the Creator, Who is too immense to behold...

The surrounding world from which I had come then retreated from me to somewhere far away, and disappeared into a realm of concepts foreign to me...

I was alone. Around me there was only the slumbering forest. Its ancient giants stretched far into the skies. They searched for God. I also was in search of Him.

But suddenly I am outside of the forest, somewhere far away, in another world, quite unknown to me, never before seen by me, never imagined by me... Around me there is bright, white light! Its transcendence is so pure and enticing that I am submerged, along with my perception, into limitless depths and cannot satisfy myself with my admiration for this realm, cannot completely fill myself with its lofty spiritual feeling. All around me everything is so full of beauty. This life is so endearing ... the way so endless. I am being swept across this limitless, clear space. My sight is directed upwards, does not descend anymore, does not see anything earthly. The whole of the heavenly firmament has transformed itself before me into one bright light, pleasing to the sight... But I do not see the sun. I can see only its endless shining and bright light. The whole space in which I glide without hindrance, without end, without fatigue, is filled with white light, just as are the light and beautiful beings here, transparent as a ray of sun. And through them I am admiring this limitless world. The images of all these beings unknown to me are infinitely diverse and full of beauty.... I also am white and bright as they are. Over me, as over them, there reigns eternal rest. Not a single thought of mine is any longer enticed by anything earthly, not a single beat of my heart is any longer moving with human cares or earthly passion. I am all peace and rapture. But I am still moving in this infinite light, which surrounds me without change. There is nothing else in the world except for the white,

## INTRODUCTION

bright light and these equally radiant numberless beings. But all these beings do not resemble me, nor are they similar to each other; they are all endlessly varied and compellingly attractive. Amidst them, I feel incredibly peaceful. They evoke in me neither fear, nor amazement, nor trepidation. All that we see here does not agitate us, does not amaze us. All of us here are as if we have belonged to each other for a long time, are used to each other, and are not strangers at all. We do not ask questions, we do not speak to each other about anything. We all feel and understand that there is nothing novel for us here. All our questions are solved with one glance, which sees everything and everyone. There is no trace of the wars of passions in anyone. All move in different directions, opposite to each other, not feeling any limitation, any inequality, or envy, or sorrow, or sadness. One peace reigns in all the beings. One light is endless for all. Oneness of life is comprehensible to all.

My rapture at all this superseded everything. I sank into this eternal rest. No longer was my spirit disturbed by anything. And I knew nothing else earthly. None of the tribulations of my heart came to mind, even for a minute. It seemed that everything that I had experienced before on earth never existed. Such was my feeling in this new radiant world of mine. And I was at peace and joyful and desired nothing better for myself. All my earthly thoughts concerning fleeting happiness in the world died in this beautiful life, new to me, and did not come back to life again. So it seemed to me at least, there, in that better world.

But how I came back here—I do not recall. What

transitory state it was, I do not know. I only felt that I was alive, but I did not remember the world in which I had lived before on earth. This did not seem at all to be a dream. Actually, about earthly things I no longer had the least notion. I only felt that the present life was *mine,* and that I was not a stranger in it. In this state of spirit I forgot myself and immersed myself in this light-bearing eternity. And this timelessness lasted without end, without measure, without expectation, without sleep, in this eternal rest. Thus it seemed to me that there would not be any kind of change…

But then suddenly, the thread of my radiant life was cut off, and I opened my eyes. Around me was the familiar forest, and a beam of spring sunlight was playing on its meadows. I was seized with terrible sadness. "Why am I here again?" I thought. And that radiant, light-emanating world, which I had just experienced with all its hosts of numberless visionary beings, vividly remained impressed before my mental eyes. But my physical vision did not see it any longer. This terrible and tearful sorrow I could not endure, and I began to weep bitterly.

Only after that experience did I believe in the concept of the distinction between the soul and the body and understand what the spiritual world was. But the question of what the meaning of life is still remained a mystery for me. And in order to penetrate into this mystery, I left this world into which I was born and embraced the monastic life.

"Oh, Father, then that must have been your dream?" I asked Fr. Ambrose, pointing to his manuscript.

"I do not know whether it was a dream or whether it occurred in reality," replied the righteous Elder with concentration. "I still have not solved that problem for myself, but I believe that my spirit lives separately from my body; otherwise it could not have seen that which my physical vision does not know. After all, one cannot perceive the light of day with the tips of the fingers on one's hand. So also, I think my soul cannot visualize that which is not in God's world. And if the soul sees this world, which my eyes do not see, then it must be that it in truth exists as something real. And I believe in this absolutely...."

With these words, the Elder's thoughtful gaze rose prayerfully to the icon of Christ, and he reverently crossed himself.

Such universal mysteries filled the soul of this highly revered Optina Monastery Elder, Ambrose. With such an outlook on God's world did he direct all the believing pilgrims who used to come to him at Optina to receive a holy blessing for their lives. And precisely in this transcendent spirit he greeted all the people who were suffering in heart and soul, who sought in his holy guidance healing of their infirmities. And how many living examples there were of those who truly partook of the good counsel of Elder Ambrose and experienced a miraculous spiritual transformation....

*I knew a man in Christ ... (whether in the body, I cannot tell; or whether out of the body, I cannot tell: God knoweth). Such a one was caught up to the third heaven* (II Cor. 12:2).

The holy relics of St. Ambrose of Optina.

# *Chronology*

| | |
|---|---|
| 1812 | November 23. Alexander Michailovich Grenkov born in Bolshaya Lipovitsa, Tambov Province. |
| 1830 | Enters Tambov Theological Seminary. |
| 1839 | Troyekurovo Recluse Fr. Hilarion blesses Alexander to go to Optina. |
| 1839 | October 8. Arrives in Optina. |
| 1841 | Tonsured as a ryassophore monk. |
| 1841 | October 11. Elder Leonid reposes. |
| 1842 | November 29. Tonsured into the mantia (full monk) with the name Ambrose. |
| 1843 | January. Ordained hierodeacon. |
| 1845 | December. Ordained hieromonk. |
| 1846 | Tonsured into the schema. |
| 1848 | Begins labor of eldership. |
| 1860 | Elder Macarius reposes. |
| 1862 | Archimandrite Moses reposes. |
| 1865 | Elder Anthony reposes. |
| 1865 | Eldership firmly established in Optina. |
| 1875 | Blesses the purchase of Shamordino property. |
| 1884 | October 1. Consecration of the church and beginning of a women's convent in Shamordino by Bishop Vladimir of Kaluga. |
| 1890 | Departure to Shamordino. |
| 1891 | September 21. Final illness. |
| 1891 | October 8. Receives Divine Unction and Holy Communion. |
| 1891 | October 10. Reposes at 11:45 a.m. in Shamordino. |
| 1891 | October 13. Buried in Optina next to Elder Macarius. |
| 1988 | Canonization. |

Synaxis of All the New Martyrs and New Saints of Russia.
*Icon by Archimandrite Cyprian.*

# I

# *The Eternal Truth of Orthodoxy*

> ... *I will build my church; and the gates of hell shall not prevail against it.*
> Matthew 16:18

ORTHODOXY is the greatest sacred treasure of the Russian people, the foundation of all of its spiritual and state life. At the dawn of its historical existence, the Russian people, in the person of the great and holy Equal-to-the-Apostles Grand Prince Vladimir and his grandmother Olga, stood under the holy banner of the Orthodox Faith. During the medieval period, faith in Christ softened the enmity between the princes and placed a beginning to their unification under the rule of a single grand prince. Monasteries and their founder-ascetics such as Sts. Anthony, Theodosius, and Sergius, and adamant preachers of the Faith such as Sts. Isaiah, Leontius, and Stephen, by their labors, tears and prayers placed the precepts and ideals of true Christian life deeply into the hearts of the Russian people. The Christian Faith helped them to live through the unbearable Tartar yoke. Orthodoxy also inspired them, and the Orthodox Church blessed the overthrow of this yoke. In the Time of Troubles (1612) Russia was saved and united under the banner of Orthodoxy by the raising of the Holy Trinity-St. Sergius Lavra. The Christian Faith also helped the people to endure the burden of serfdom. In a word, wherever we look we see that

Christianity in its purest expression—the Orthodox Faith—comprised the very soul of the Russian people. However, it seems that the Orthodox Faith and the Russian Orthodox Church in particular were never subject to so many and such fierce attacks as they are at the present time.

Passing over the details of all these attacks, we will only say that they contain one fundamental error. Looking at the state of the specifically temporal and external side of church life, accusers of the Church do not notice the very essence of this life, the life-giving power of the grace of God, which exists unchangeably in the Russian Orthodox Church and is its members' most precious inheritance.

It is impossible to doubt that this life-giving and salvific power of the grace of God exists unchangeably in the Church, since the Church was founded on earth by our Lord Jesus Christ and was called, not to carry out its own work on earth, but the work of God. It is intended to be the guardian of God's saving truth on earth, to accomplish the people's moral renewal and spiritual regeneration. To assume that the Church has changed its calling, that the lamp of truth and holiness on earth, which was lit not by a human but a divine Hand, has been extinguished—is not this to doubt the power of God and to deny faith in Christ the Son of God? If the Church has lost the truth entrusted to it, if it has lost its way on the crossroads of life and lost the true path to Christ, then do not these words of the Savior seem empty: *I will build my Church, and the gates of hell shall not prevail against it* (Matt. 16:18)?

Thus, as a result of the divine origin of the Church and the task to which it is called from on high, Christ cannot abandon it, but, as in the first times of Christianity, so even now He unfailingly shines forth in it with His quiet, heavenly light; and this inner light of the Church can be seen by those who have eyes to see.

# THE ETERNAL TRUTH OF ORTHODOXY

The truth of this can be judged by the fruits of the Church's life. *A good tree cannot bring forth evil fruit, neither can a corrupt tree bring forth good fruit.... Wherefore by their fruits ye shall know them* (Matt 7:18, 20). The fruits of the universal Church are: martyrs, hierarchs, monastic saints, unmercenaries, and others whose struggles are recounted in Church history and whose moral beauty glistens as bright stars upon all mankind. The Russian Church has also brought forth these fruits. In order to see this we need only recall the Saints—Prince Vladimir; Anthony and Theodosius of the Kiev Caves; Alexander of Neva; Sergius of Radonezh; Isaiah and Leontius of Rostov; Euphrosyne of Polotsk; Stephen of Perm; Zosima and Sabbatius of Solovki; Peter, Alexis, Jonah, and Phillip of Moscow; Dimitry of Rostov; Tikhon of Zadonsk; and Seraphim of Sarov. Ever memorable also are those blessed fathers as yet uncanonized: Philaret of Moscow, Philaret of Kiev, John of Kronstadt, Ambrose of Optina* and many others. Over the course of a thousand years the Russian Church has nurtured in its bosom hosts of saints—people filled with the spirit of Christ. How could the Church have accomplished this if Christ had not been with it and if the grace of God had neither filled it nor breathed life into it? The power of the grace of God operated in every stage of the Russian Church's existence—both in the pre-patriarchal period, the patriarchal period and the synodal period.** The Russians of ancient times felt this, as do those of

---

* All of these Holy Fathers of the Russian Church have been canonized since this book was written.—ED.

** From the conversion of Russia until the early fifteenth century, the Russian Church was ruled by the Patriarch of Constantinople and presided over locally by the Metropolitan of Kiev. From the reign of Peter I to the year 1918, after the Bolshevik Revolution, the Russian Church had no patriarch, and was ruled by the Holy Synod. Since that time, the Russian Church has again been ruled by a patriarch—ED.

St. Ambrose (top right) amidst the saints canonized during the jubilee year of 1,000 years of Orthodoxy and sanctity in Russia: the Millenium of Russia's Baptism, 988-1988. *Icon by Fr. Theodore Jurewicz.*

the present day who are true, consecrated offspring of the Church. If the fruits brought forth by the Russian Church are the same as those of the Universal Church and if the Russian Church as well as the Universal Church manifests grace-filled life to its members, then it is obvious that neither Church has died and that the Spirit and life has not flown from them, despite any seemingly unfavorable outward circumstances.

# THE ETERNAL TRUTH OF ORTHODOXY

Orthodox monasteries are among the main centers of Church life, in which a constant struggle takes place for the preservation of living faith in God in all aspects of life. Within them is conducted a relentless battle against sin in the name of holiness and purity of life. The wrath of unbelievers who deny the Church is directed in particular at monasteries. It is impossible by words and objections alone to defend churches and monasteries from unjust accusations—to open the eyes of the blind and the ears of the deaf. In order to demonstrate to society the truth of the Church, it is necessary to familiarize people with the living fruits of true Church life, according to the words of the Gospel: *Come and see* (John 1:46)—see the Church's contribution to society and its priceless significance.

One of these ripe fruits of the life of the Church is Optina Elder Hieroschemamonk Ambrose, whose biographical sketch we are placing before the reader's attention. May the following biography of this remarkable Elder not only provide consolation to believers, but also disclose to nonbelievers the wealth of spirit, the power of mercy and love, and the intellectual insight that this marvelous Elder gleaned from the innermost depths of the Russian Church and universal Orthodoxy with its monasticism. He was dedicated to the Church with all his being, and he was educated and grew under its influence. Seeing this, may the faithless perceive the truth and power of Orthodoxy. May they sense the truth and beauty of the Russian Church, feel in it the power of the grace of God and, with joy in their hearts, see in the Church the bastion of God's truth on earth, the treasury of exalted, grace-filled gifts and the path to heavenly blessedness.\*

---

\*The significance of these words can be better appreciated when one considers that they were written in Russia in 1912, five years before the Bolshevik Revolution, in which the Russian Church was attacked by the faithless ones. Chetverikov wrote this book in order to convert the hearts of the godless before it was too late.—ED.

"Life-icon" of St. Ambrose showing scenes of major events in his life.
*Icon painted and treasured in Optina today.*

# 2

# *A Profile of the Spiritual Make-up of Elder Ambrose*

> *Ye are not straightened in us.*
> II Corinthians 6:12

A LITTLE under two miles from the district city of Kozelsk, in Optina Monastery, is the grave of Elder Hieroschemamonk Ambrose—"Batiushka Abrosim," as he was and is called by the simple people—a grave sacred and dear to the Russian Orthodox heart. This grave is located on the right side of the Catholicon of the Entrance into the Temple of the Most Holy Theotokos. Over the grave can be seen a small, pleasant-looking chapel, in which, on the left side, there is placed a white marble memorial with a moving inscription which precisely defines the significance of the personality and life of the Elder: *To the weak became I as weak, that I might gain the weak: I am made all things to all men, that I might by all means save some* (I Cor. 9:22).

On the walls of the chapel hang the holy icons of the Resurrection of Christ, the Kazan Mother of God (which the Elder especially revered) and St. Ambrose of Milan, his heavenly protector. Before the icons glow ever-burning lampadas. A quiet calm, a reverent prayer wafts through and around the chapel. Pilgrims love to visit this spot, to have Pannikhidas served over the grave of the Elder. They pour out their numerous sorrows and needs to him as to one living.

Many years have passed since Fr. Ambrose's repose, but the path to his grave has not become overgrown. The reverent memory of and sincere faith in him, as in a heavenly protector and helper, has not grown weak, either in the Monastery or in the people, but has rather spread further and grown stronger.

What has always attracted the heart of the people to Fr. Ambrose? It is obvious to all that the great power of the grace of God rested upon Elder Ambrose, filling his heart with inexhaustible joy and love, and his mind with wisdom and clairvoyance. He was in the true sense a Christian sage, able to elucidate the most complex and painful mysteries of life, to lead one out of the most difficult, and apparently endless, moral and material quandries. Over the course of his nearly thirty years of eldership he was a thoughtful, loving "mother" to suffering mankind. Hundreds of people of the most diverse callings and stations came to him daily, each with his own perplexity, request or sorrow. No one was turned away, no one left him without having received his affection, no one left unconsoled or uncomforted. In this small cell and around it crowded nuns, monks, peasants, merchants, landowners, priests, students of the university and theological academy, high-school boys and girls, doctors, writers, dignitaries.... Bishops and princes sought conversation with him. And each received from him an appropriate "word of profit." With all he was equally polite, simple, and clear. All felt like children before an experienced, kind and wise father.

He founded all of his relationships with the people who came to him solely on the basis of strengthening them in heeding their consciences. To him, precious above all was the eternal salvation of the soul that had entrusted itself to his care.

## THE SPIRITUAL MAKE-UP OF ELDER AMBROSE

As a result, all of his relations with people were holy, simple, unselfish and meaningful. That is why people clung to him and strove to open the very depths of their souls to him. But if one did not know how to do this, the Elder himself would help, for he had the amazing ability to penetrate into one's interior world, to read one's heart like an open book and reveal to one what that person neither understood nor noticed.

The versatility and wealth of his spirit were extraordinary. He combined in himself a living faith, an active life, strictness with kindness, seriousness with a sense of humor, concentration of spirit with gregariousness, love of solitude with sociability, magnanimity, simplicity, vast theoretical knowledge and experience of life—a life entirely with God combined with practicality.

Elder Ambrose was wise, but his wisdom was not mere book-learning or theological erudition—it was vast experience of mind and heart, sensitivity to the most profound Christian suffering, and the ability to utilize this experience and apply it to individual people and circumstances. His counsels were usually of few words, but he was able by one direct comment, by a joke, a gesture or a saying, to enter into one's pain, to encourage, console and point the way out of life's problems.

So great was Fr. Ambrose's wisdom, so great was his kindheartedness and warmth of feeling, so well could he understand each person and approach his emotional wounds, that not only simple people, who have always flocked to monasteries and elders, but even the intelligentsia itself—so often weak in faith, faint-hearted, murmuring, self-loving, impatient, worn out by doubts and sometimes even hostile toward the Church and all things of the Church—noticed him, valued him, and were drawn to him that they might warm themselves at his gentle, loving heart and be instructed by him in Christian wisdom. And they truly warmed themselves and learned!

Thus Fr. Ambrose appeared in the second half of the nineteenth century as a link between educated society, the common people and the Church. The need for such a link was felt long ago in Russian society; and Optina Monastery itself served to a notable degree in this capacity during the first half of the nineteenth century, when it sheltered on the one hand Elders Leonid, Macarius, Moses and Anthony, and on the other hand, the Kireyevsky brothers, Gogol, Shevirev and other representatives of the Russian intelligentsia of that time. This was Elder Ambrose's special service to the Russian people, to Russian history—a service in which he remains unsurpassed.

Having portrayed the general make-up of the character of Elder Ambrose, and having indicated his significance for the Russian people, let us turn to a more detailed and chronological portrayal of his life and personality.

# 3

# *The Youth of Elder Ambrose*

## AT HOME AND IN SCHOOL

*Of such is the kingdom of God.*
Mark 10:14

FATHER AMBROSE, in the world Alexander Michailovich Grenkov, was the son of a sexton in the village of Bolshaya Lipovitsa in the Tambov province: Michael Feodorovich and his wife Martha Nicholaevna. They had a large family and lived in the home of his father, Theodore Igorovich, the priest and chancellor of that village parish. On November 23, 1812, there was a large gathering of guests in the home of Fr. Theodore during a family celebration, and on this very day Alexander Michailovich was born. Recounting this later, Fr. Ambrose loved to joke: "I was born among people, and I live among people."

The Elder's parents were deeply pious. Concerning his mother, Martha Nicholaevna, he later related: "She lived piously and worked out her salvation in her own particular way." The order of family life was simple, strict, and church oriented, as was customary with the clergy of that time. Not much information has been preserved about Alexander Michailovich's early childhood. He grew up as a lively, cheerful, bright and restless child. His mother would, for example, make him rock his younger brother's cradle, but this bored him. He would wait for a minute, and when his mother had left the room, he would jump through the window and run away to play with his friends. Sasha [diminuitive for Alexander] loved his friends, loved horses and pigeons, and loved to play with his brothers and sisters in the spaciousness of the countryside. However, the strict older members of his family did not like his playfulness and restlessness, and he often had to hear reproaches from both his mother and grandmother; his grandfather sometimes even tore out a tuft of his hair. It seemed to Sasha that he was not loved by his family, and he was jealous of his brothers and sisters—but he was mistaken. They loved him, only they treated him more sternly than the others. The strict way of life in a priest's home in the old days was undoubtedly beneficial for the lively boy; it tempered his mischievous impulses and engraved in his soul an awareness of the purpose and seriousness of life. As Sasha grew, they began with God's help to teach him reading and writing. He was taught using the Church-Slavonic primer, the Horologion, and the Psalter, as was the usual custom. From his earliest youth the inspired Psalms of King David began to train the ear and permeate the heart of the future great Elder. On every feast, or perhaps more often, Sasha's father brought him to the temple of God, and he soon learned to sing and read at the cliros. The time came for Sasha to be sent away to school. School studies began relatively late for the boy; he was twelve years old when he was enrolled in the first grade of the Tambov Church School. By then his older brother was studying there, and the school authorities had given him the surname "Grenkov." This name was given to Sasha also. The old dormitory was poor, harsh and unsightly. This, however, did not affect Sasha's naturally cheerful and lively character, and he studied with great success. The dark side of dormitory life, the sorrowful spectacle of poverty and the downtrodden condition of many of his friends and their parents, only kindled more strongly the boy's characteristic compassion and pity towards all who were sorrowful and burdened. He himself knew how to value any kindness shown to him, and kindness was, in all probability, rarely expressed in school at that time. "When I was a young boy," he recalled later, "we had a school tailor. I was a tall one; he always called me Sasha, but my other friends did not address me so affectionately. I must admit that this really touched me." This seemingly unimportant event says much about the sensitive heart of the youth, which thirsted for affection and love, and about his ability, even as a child, to attract the love of those around him. Sasha was loved by his friends for his cheerfulness and kindness. On the feast days of Christmas and Pascha, Sasha would ride home with his older brother to the family village, where their older brother, who was already a psalm-reader, would ride with them on horseback through the village and provide them with simple village entertainment.

Because he was the son of a poor sexton with a large family, Sasha was able to receive the privilege of a partial scholarship. He studied so well that he graduated first out of 148 students in his school.

At the age of eighteen, Alexander Grenkov enrolled in the Tambov Theological Seminary, where he studied well, thanks to his wonderful talent. One of his friends from seminary said, "It happened that I would buy a candle with my last kopeck and repeat the assigned lesson over and over. He, however, would hardly study, then come to class, stand up and give the instructor the answer just as it was written in the textbook—better than everyone else." In the seminary Grenkov was always the center of his circle of friends. Though he loved society and was a cheerful, buoyant and clever youth, he always preserved moral

The Tambov Theological Seminary.

purity and modesty, interior austerity of spirit and profound, sincere religious feeling; perhaps this was the reason why the hearts of all were especially attracted to him. After he had already become an elder, he vividly recalled many incidents from his seminary life, accurately characterizing some of his rectors and teachers. Fr. Ambrose once told of his attempt to write poetry in the seminary. "I must confess to you," he said, "I once attempted to write poetry, supposing that this was easy. I picked a good spot, where there were valleys and mountains, and made up my mind to write there. For a long, long time I sat there and thought about what and how to write, and thus I did not write anything. This reminds me of one monk of the Kiev Caves Lavra about whom an academician wrote, who also attempted to write poetry, and this is what he wrote:

> The gentle Dnieper flows and winds,
> Monk Hesychius wrote these lines."

Although he never became a poet, when he was an elder he often liked to instruct his listeners in rhyme, in all likelihood so that the painful truth he expressed would not be so grievous to conceited hearts, and because a solution made in a joke or clever turn of phrase is more readily accepted and remains more deeply impressed in one's memory.

Elder Hilarion, recluse of Troekurovo Village.

# 4

# *The Call of God*

*There are many thoughts in a man's heart;
but the counsel of the Lord abides forever.*
Proverbs 19:21

*By the Lord are the steps of a man rightly directed....*
Psalm 36:23

Having a naturally cheerful and lively character, loving the society of people, captivated by songs and music, and even at one time dreaming about enlisting in the army, Alexander Michailovich did not even think about becoming a monk. It is clear, however, that our thoughts are not the same as those of God, and our ways are not the ways of God. "I had never thought of going to a monastery," he said after he had become an elder; "however, others for some reason predicted to me that I would live in a monastery." The fact that others foresaw in Alexander Michailovich a future monk is quite remarkable. It showed that, despite his cheerfulness and sociability, Alexander Michailovich was and appeared to be a man "not of this world." This means that already in his early youth, noticeably to all, he had no real inward attachment to the world, and was so pure in heart and so attuned to God that people could foresee no other path in life for him than the path of total dedication to God in monasticism.

Alexander Michailovich himself did not yet clearly discern his life's calling, but there were moments when this calling unexpectedly and powerfully proclaimed itself in his soul. Thus, a year before the completion of his studies in seminary, Alexander Michailovich fell seriously ill. There was almost no hope for his recovery.

"Everyone despaired of my recovering," related Fr. Ambrose; "I also had little hope for it. They sent for the confessor. He did not arrive for a long time. I said, 'Farewell, God's world.' And right then I gave a promise to the Lord that if He would raise me up healthy from my sick-bed I would without fail go to a monastery."

Never having thought about a monastery, as he himself said, Alexander Michailovich suddenly gave a vow to become a monk. It seems clear that this vow had already been ripening and dwelling in the depths of his heart for a long time without his being aware of it, having already been strongly imprinted there by all the circumstances of his past life and by his personal character traits. It lacked only an appropriate incident in which to clearly burst forth in his pious, youthful consciousness.

Thus in 1835, at twenty-three years of age, Alexander Michailovich stared into the face of imminent death and determined his life's path. Just the same, this path also frightened him. He was frightened by the great responsibility before God and man which he was preparing himself to assume, and he was terrified of the break with the lighter side of life in the world. A fierce struggle began in his soul between his decision and his involuntary doubts:

Was he suitable for the chosen path? Was his decision serious? Was he not taking this back-breaking yoke upon himself light-mindedly? Was he not falling into self-deception? He could not prevent these and similar questions from coming to mind and disturbing his soul. For four years he endured this difficult inner struggle, painstakingly hiding his state of soul from everyone and awaiting a definite indication from the Lord above.

Of course, while he was still in seminary, he could not seriously think about bringing his vow into fulfillment—he first had to complete his education. But when his seminary studies were concluded, it seemed necessary for Alexander Michailovich to determine his future path of life. Still not entirely resolved to accept monasticism, he wanted to select a societal position that would afford him the opportunity at any given moment to turn away from it to where his sense of duty called; but monasticism was a calling for which he still did not feel sufficiently mature. Therefore, he did not go to the theological academy, which would have bound his freedom all over again for a few years, nor did he particularly seek ordination. He accepted with joy the suggestion of one landowner to be a home tutor to his children. He spent over a year in this position. Here he now noticeably displayed his amazing knowledge of people and his ability to handle them, leading them in a good direction. "It happened," he later related, "that a husband and wife were fighting, and both turned to me with complaints about each other. I thought to myself, what am I supposed to do? Although they would argue, around an hour or two later they would again be reconciled! If, for example, I accepted one's side, it would have set the other against me. Thus it happened that I would only listen to their complaints, looking at them and smiling silently. Soon enough, my hosts of course would be reconciled, and I maintained a good relationship with both of them." From this story it is apparent that already at this time, when Alexander Michailovich was only twenty-five years old, people around him submitted to his influence, giving him a special place in their society and making him judge over the intimate aspects of their lives. In Alexander Michailovich the future Elder was already being formed to a certain degree by his sympathy toward people and his ability to lead them out of difficult situations. Living in the landowner's family, Alexander Michailovich was for the first time closely acquainted with worldly society, and that brought him great benefit, broadening his life's experience.

Meanwhile, in the Lipetsk Theological School a teaching position opened up. Alexander Michailovich expressed a desire to take this job and was assigned to it on March 7, 1838.

As a teacher at the Theological School, Alexander Michailovich left a sparkling impression. He was intelligent, thoughtful, observant, lively, cheerful, and extraordinarily kind; but he also possessed that particular type of strictness which develops in a man through an exalted understanding of honor and human responsibility. He was an irreplaceable educator of young souls and a wonderful member of the school staff. At that time it seemed that a smooth, serene life was before him—doing his favorite work in a circle of co-workers sincerely inclined towards him. But in reality it was not so. Insistent thoughts of monasticism, of the vow he had taken, would not abandon his heart. The transition from external activity with its many cares, and from worldly diversions in this youthful environment, to an interior conversation alone with his own conscience became more and more agonizing. His conscience implacably reproached him for not fulfilling the vow he had given and for his empty waste of time. The deeply believing Alexander Michailovich then sought consolation and peace in ardent prayer. By night, when his fellow workers, with whom he lived in one common public apartment, fell asleep, he stood before the icon of the "Tambov" Mother of God (a blessing from his parents) and prayed for a long, long time, unseen and unheard

## THE CALL OF GOD

by others, to the Mother of God to direct his path. However, his fellow workers soon found out about his nightly prayers, and some of them even inappropriately ridiculed him. Then Alexander Michailovich began to hide in the attic and there continued to pour out his prayerful feelings to the Protectress of the Christian race. Ardent solitary prayer, and in part the ridicule that he bore from his co-workers for its sake, strengthened even more the feeling of serious and profound love for God in the soul of the young man. The thought of God dominated his heart more and more, becoming much sweeter and closer to it. In order to more completely devote himself unhindered to this growing feeling of contact with God, Alexander Michailovich began to leave the city periodically. Near Lipetsk, on the other side of the Voronezh River, one can still see an enormous state forest that reminds one of the Optina forest. In his free time from class, Alexander Michailovich loved to go there for solitary strolls and divine contemplation. Once, during such a walk he chanced upon a flowing waterfall and began to listen to its babbling. In this babbling creek he clearly began to hear the words, "Praise God, hold on to God!" "I stood far away, listening to this mysterious voice of nature and was quite amazed," the Elder later related. His heart felt a more vital nearness to God; ardent prayer was kindled more strongly in him and more decisively drew him from the world to the shelter of a solitary, quiet monastic habitation.

Realizing the great importance of the life decision that had formed in his soul, Alexander Michailovich was afraid to accept it entirely on his own personal responsibility. Before taking such a decisive step, he wanted to find moral support in the strong and holy will of another who might bless him on his chosen path and free his soul from this agonizing feeling of loneliness.

The summer of 1839 arrived. Examinations in the theological school ended, and the students dispersed to their families' homes. The teachers also began their vacations. Alexander Michailovich spent the summer with his friend, the son of the priest of the village of Slansk, Paul Stepanovich Pokrovsky. Not far from the village at that time lived the well-known recluse of Troekurovo, Fr. Hilarion, to whom many turned for advice, both in person and in writing. Our friends also thought to visit the recluse, to request his counsel and blessings on their future life.

Having rested for a time in Slansk, the young men directed themselves by foot to Troekurovo, which is located eighteen miles from Slansk. Fr. Hilarion received them affectionately. Alexander Michailovich's heart deeply trembled when, revealing his thoughts and feelings to the Elder, he heard from him the words: "Go to Optina! You could have gone to Sarov, but they do not have the same kind of elders as they once did." At this point, as certain people have related, Fr. Hilarion added: "You are needed in Optina!"

Thus it seemed that the die was cast. But the prudent and cautious Alexander Michailovich still did not rush to carry out the desire of his heart—he still wanted to acquire one more blessing, the blessing of the great Abbot of all Russia, St. Sergius the wonderworker of Radonezh, the founder of monastic life in the northern regions of the Russian fatherland. Since not much time remained before classes would begin in the school, he persuaded his friend to undertake another journey, this time to the Holy Trinity-St. Sergius Lavra.

Paul Stepanovich himself felt inclined toward monasticism and, as he loved to visit the holy monasteries, he joyfully agreed. They began to get ready. Alexander Michailovich bent young branches into bows with his own hands, attached them to the back part of a simple village cart and covered them with felt and matting in order to have protection from rain and the intense

## THE CALL OF GOD

heat of the sun. Fr. Stephan Pokrovsky, Paul Stepanovich's father, who supported the young men's journey, joyfully gave them his own horse, despite the fact that this was the work season. Finally, all was ready for the journey. The weather was pleasant, and the young friends proceeded down the road happily and cheerfully, accompanied by the blessings and good wishes of their families and acquaintances.

How blithe and joyful their souls became as a light breeze refreshed them, and the wide expanses of the fields, with the boundless depths of azure skies, enveloped them on all sides! Their souls seemed to be immersed in the depths of infinity, permeated with the other world, and they felt within themselves the living presence of the Omnipotent God! In communion with nature and people, day after day passed by unnoticed for them, and finally, having avoided noisy Moscow, they arrived at the Holy Trinity-St. Sergius Lavra.

According to the established custom they stopped at the Khotkova Women's Monastery, where they venerated the graves of the parents of St. Sergius, Cyril and Maria\*. There Alexander Michailovich conversed alone with the recluse Martha for a long time, but what they said remains a mystery.

An inexplicable feeling of contrition embraced the soul of Alexander Michailovich in the Lavra. He saw before him those hills which, once covered by the thick forest, were the witnesses to the solitary prayers of the young St. Sergius. How he understood these labors, how they captivated his own reverent heart! Here was the spring which gushed forth at the prayers of the Saint! Here was that wondrous cell, now turned into a chapel, where St. Sergius sent up his ardent prayers all night long, and the threshold across which the Mother of God once stepped. In the "deep dawn" on Saturdays they celebrated with deep devo-

---

\* Cyril and Maria are themselves saints.—ED.

tion the Paraclesis in memory of this miraculous visit. And here was the very church where the incorrupt relics of the God-pleaser reposed! How many thoughts, how many great recollections, how many profound and sweet feelings flowed in the young, pure, sensitive soul of Alexander Michailovich when he fell to the earth at the reliquary of the great intercessor of the Russian land, entreating him for blessings, help and strength on his chosen life's path! Of course, his prayer was not in vain. Profound interior peace and a calm resolve descended upon his soul in this hallowed place. The young worshippers prayed, fasted, confessed and received Christ's Holy Mysteries. Finally, the days of their pilgrimage came to a close. The time arrived to set off on their return trip. With a sad but grateful feeling, full of the exalted impressions of what they had experienced, our pilgrims left the holy Monastery. They completed their return journey hardly noticing it, and at the end of the school vacation they returned to Lipetsk.

Alexander Michailovich's intention was finally resolved, and he began to await a favorable occasion for its fulfillment, or it is better to say, for the last decisive call of God. And this call soon followed. Classes commenced, and Alexander Michailovich set about his lessons.

At the end of September, Alexander Michailovich was at a party in someone's house together with his colleagues. It was especially merry. It is said that Alexander Michailovich was the life of the party; he joked, laughed, was loud and infected the guests and the host with his glee. Arriving at home, however, he still felt an unprecedented melancholy and pain of conscience. An inner voice strongly proclaimed to him: "Do it! It is time to put an end to everything. It is impossible to serve God and mammon! You need to choose one or the other! You need to cling wholly to God alone. You must forsake the world!"

The next day, having met with Pokrovsky, Alexander

Michailovich said to him discreetly, away from the others, "I'm going to Optina." He was amazed: "How can you go? After all, classes just began—they will not let you go!" "Well, what can I do," answered Alexander Michailovich; "I cannot live in the world any longer. I will leave secretly, just do not tell anyone!"

After a little time Alexander Michailovich disappeared from Lipetsk. The overseer of the school was at that time the priest Kastalsky, the head of the Lipetsk Cathedral. The disappearance of a teacher placed him in a difficult position. It was necessary to inform the seminary authorities about what had happened, but at the same time he felt sorry for Alexander Michailovich. Not knowing what to do, the overseer of the school decided for the time being to keep silent about Alexander's disappearance, awaiting further developments.

Steps leading to the main Optina Monastery.
An old pre-revolutionary postcard with the inscription:
*Greetings from Optina Kozelsk Hermitage.*

# 5

# *Optina Monastery: A Grace-filled Corner of the Russian Land*

> *How beloved are Thy dwellings, O Lord of hosts!*
> *Blessed are they that dwell in Thy house.*
> Psalm 88:1, 5

WHILE Alexander Michailovich, relying on the will of God, hastens with a joyful heart to his longed-for goal—Optina—let us say a few words about this holy Monastery.

The origin of Optina Monastery is attributed by some to the ancient pre-Mongolian time. The names of schemamonks and schemanuns, which are preserved in the commemoration books of the Monastery, show that at first the Monastery was "mixed" and that it already existed in the fifteenth century, for at the beginning of the sixteenth century mixed monasticism was abolished.

The first written mention of the Monastery is attributed to the beginning of the seventeenth century, when the Monastery consisted of one wooden church and six cells. Tsars Michael Feodorovich, Alexis Michailovich, and Theodore Alexeevich provided the Monastery with "alms."

During the eighteenth century, a difficult time for monasteries, the Monastery fell into decline as did many others; and by the end of that century there remained only three very old monks, one of whom was blind.

The rebirth of the Monastery was bound up with the well-known Metropolitan Platon of Moscow, who took over direction of the Monastery at the very end of the eighteenth century. Traveling around his diocese in the year 1796, he turned his attention to the wonderful site of Optina Monastery, found it quite convenient for desert-dwelling, and decided to take measures to order the Monastery aright. Having summoned the Superior of the Pesnosha Monastery, Fr. Macarius, a former disciple of the well-known Moldavian Elder Paisius Velichkovsky, the Metropolitan requested from him a talented and conscientious man, whom he could send to be the superior of Optina Monastery. Fr. Macarius answered, "I do not have anybody like that, holy Vladika!" Pondering, he added: "Unless you want us to give you the gardener, Abramius?" Under the pretext of making a purchase in the city, Abramius was sent to Moscow and presented to the Metropolitan. He made a favorable impression on the Bishop and immediately was sent to bring order to Optina Monastery. He reluctantly accepted this responsibility. He was very sad to part with his garden solitude, but there was nothing he could do; he had to submit. Arriving in Optina, Fr. Abramius found there an extreme state of neglect. "There wasn't a towel for the priest to use to dry his hands in the altar, and there was little help in misfortune and scarcity. I wept and prayed, and prayed and wept."

Having lived in the Monastery for two months, and seeing no help coming from anywhere, Fr. Abramius' spirits fell. He set out to Pesnosha to Fr. Macarius and began to beg his former Superior to take away from him the back-breaking burden of directing Optina Monastery.

## OPTINA MONASTERY: A GRACE-FILLED CORNER

Fr. Macarius calmed him down, and, with the help of the landowners whom he knew, he provided him with a multitude of monastery necessities and likewise gave him a few good assistants from among his own brethren. After this, matters went differently, and little by little the Monastery began to enter into good order. Fr. Abramius directed Optina for twenty years; he gave his whole soul to it and laid a firm foundation for its later spiritual and material good order.

After Metropolitan Platon, Bishop Philaret, later Metropolitan of Kiev, did much good for Optina. At this time, in 1821, when Fr. Daniel was the Superior of Optina, the founding of the St. John the Forerunner Skete began. The construction of the Skete attracted the ascetic brothers, Frs. Moses and Anthony (Putilov). Concerning the activity of these wondrous monks who brought the monastic life in the Monastery to flowering, we will speak in another section. We will move on now to a description of the Monastery's outward appearance and the impression it creates.

Optina Monastery is located on the right bank of the deep but narrow Zhizdra River, at the edge of an age-old, majestic pine forest which extends for many miles around the Monastery. From whatever direction the traveler approaches the Monastery—whether by the large post road from Kaluga, by meadow or through the forested shore from Kozelsk, or along the dark tree-lined road from the district city of Likhvin, the Monastery makes the same strong, inexplicably sweet, profoundly peaceful impression. The huge pine forest is filled with a wondrous vivifying aroma, which ascends like a vast cloud of fragrant incense to God's Altar. Under the canopy of the ancient pine trees reigns undisturbed quiet, especially on a languid summer day. Only from time to time is it disrupted by the rustling of falling branches, the flying of little birds, or the scampering of a small animal. The peacefully winding, mirror-like, silvery Zhizdra majestically streams through its emerald banks. The broad meadow extending from the bank opposite the Monastery brings joy to one's gaze by its freshness and its multitude of assorted flowers. The white buildings of the Monastery and the blue domes of the churches with their gold crosses stand out beautifully against the dark green forests. The city of Kozelsk, which can be seen from there, is picturesquely situated and imparts a liveliness to the area without disturbing its solitude.

Here amidst the undisturbed quiet of nature the soft sound of the monastery bell suddenly resounds, and something dear, close, holy and heavenly wafts into the soul of the traveler. Yes, in this Monastery all is truly in a complete and wondrous harmony—the forest, the meadow, the river, the white monastery walls, and the vast, heavenly firmament which is cast over it all. It encompasses the soul with a single, unified impression, placing it involuntarily before the Face of God and filling it with a joyful feeling of contrition!

This first impression not only does not weaken, but is intensified when one enters the Monastery itself. A slowly moving ferry manned by a calm and cordial monk takes the pilgrim from the shores of the meadow to the wooded shore of the Monastery. Coming up from the ferry, the pilgrim sees first of all to the right, affixed to a pillar, an icon of the Mother of God, who seems to bless the pilgrim's entry into the Monastery that is consecrated to her. Walking around the rather extensive orchard, the traveler approaches the beginning of a wide, tall, stone staircase, which leads to the holy gates. To the right and to the left of the staircase, outside of the monastic enclosure, stands the two-story monastery guest house. A whitewashed stone wall surrounds the Monastery in a wide rectangle. Having ascended the staircase, which has a book and icon shop located on one of its landings, the pilgrim

Optina Monastery.

enters the holy gates from the west side into the interior courtyard of the Monastery. Directly before him he sees the main church in honor of the Entrance of the Most Holy Theotokos into the Temple, with side altars in honor of St. Nicholas and St. Paphnutius the Wonderworker of Borovsk. To the right, a short distance from the Church of the Entrance, is the church in honor of the Kazan Icon of the Mother of God; and on the left, to the north of the Church of the Entrance is the church named for St. Mary of Egypt, with side altars in honor of Righteous St. Anna, the right-believing prince St. Alexander Nevsky, and St. Ambrose of Milan. This Church has a very beautiful iconostasis. To the east of the Church of the Entrance there is yet another church, in honor of the Vladimir icon of the Mother of God.

Thus these four main churches of the Monastery, together with the bell tower over the holy gates, form a perfect four-sided cross. Around the churches, along the wall, are the monastery buildings—the trapeza, the brothers' cells and others. The whole space between the churches is occupied in part by the monks' cemetery and in part by fruit trees.

If we leave the monastic enclosure, to the right, through the gates which are located on the south side of the wall, we will see the beautiful monastery infirmary with its church in honor of St. Hilarion the Great. Further to the south is the new monastery cemetery, the "potter's field," as Archimandrite Dositheus called it, with a church in honor of All Saints. Beyond this is the forest.

Leaving the monastic enclosure through the northern gate, to the left we see the new guest house, and further on is the laundry house and a farmyard, beyond which lies the monastery garden. Finally, if from the holy gates we go straight to the east, past the Church of the Entrance, and leave the Monastery through the small eastern gates, we enter straight into the thick forest, through which is a path to the Skete, located about seven hundred yards from the Monastery.

Inside the Monastery walls, one's attention is drawn, after the churches, to the monks' cemetery. Here in the gravestone epitaphs there unfolds an interesting and instructive spiritual history of the brotherhood and of the inner life of many monks and laymen who had a close spiritual relationship with it.

There is much to learn from these inscriptions, much to think about, and much that leads one to contrition!

Here, for example, alongside the grave of Fr. Ambrose is the grave of his instructor and predecessor in eldership, Hieroschemamonk Macarius (born of the Orel nobility), the inscription on which says, "By deed and word he especially taught two virtues—humility and love." Alongside the grave of Fr. Macarius is buried his predecessor in eldership Fr. Leonid (a citizen of Karachev), who "left his memory behind in the hearts of many who received consolation in their sorrows." At the feet of these great Elders are the graves of Fr. Macarius' spiritual children—Ivan Vasilievich and Peter Vasilievich Kireyevsky, so well known in the history of Russian enlightenment.* On the memorial for Ivan Vasilievich is written: *I loved wisdom and sought her out from my youth.... When I perceived that I could not otherwise obtain her, except God gave her me, ... I prayed unto the Lord and besought Him.... For they shall see the end of the wise, and shall not understand what God in His counsel hath decreed of him* (Wisdom of Solomon).

A marvelous inscription, which portrays the entire order of the spiritual life of an ascetic, is placed over the grave of Fr. Ambrose's disciple, the Skete Superior Hieroschemamonk An-

---

*Alongside the graves of the Kireyevsky brothers, at the feet of Elder Ambrose, is the grave of Elder Hieroschemamonk Joseph, the humble, meek and wise disciple of the great Elder.

atole (who was from a clerical family): *With patience I waited patiently for the Lord, and He was attentive unto me, and He hearkened unto my supplication. And He brought me up out of the pit of misery, and from the mire of clay. And He set my feet upon a rock, and He ordered my steps aright. And He hath put into my mouth a new song, a hymn unto our God* (Ps. 39:1-4). These words of the Psalmist accurately describe the entire path of the spiritual growth of a Christian—from the beginning of his existence in the mire of passions until his repose and confirmation in the Lord through purity of heart.

On the grave of Schemamonk Carpus is written: "Schemamonk Carpus, an attentive ascetic, blind and from peasant stock.... He spent the entire day in difficult obediences, and almost the entire night in handiwork and prayer. Meekness, silence with constant self-reproach, friendly disposition towards the brothers and unceasing forcing of himself towards all good were the distinguishing characteristics of this ascetic."

On the grave of the twenty-two-year-old Monk Gabriel, we read: "During his seven-year stay in the Monastery he did not grieve anyone, lived in the Monastery as a stranger, preserving stillness; he was obedient and respectful to all, meek and contrite; he practiced great abstinence with food; he was exceedingly zealous towards church; he opened his conscience before his elder in everything, unwaveringly fulfilling his counsels. He bore his illness with patience and in a good spirit. *He, being made perfect in a short time, fulfilled a long time* (Wis. 4:13-14)."

On the grave of Schemamonk Pachomius, we read: "He reposed in his ninety-sixth year, but according to the witness of some, in his one-hundred and sixth year.... From his very youth until deep old age, he led the Christian life of a wanderer according to the words of the Gospel, not having a place to lay his head (cf. Luke 9:58). In the course of his life he visited all the noteworthy Russian holy places several times, staying in them as long as he saw fit. Six years before his repose, with the weakening of his physical strength, he remained in Optina Monastery, where he quietly ended his days. He was illiterate, but he knew well the lives of all the saints and remembered well the days of their commemoration. His constant prayers were: 'Theotokos, Virgin Rejoice!' or: 'The angel cried,' and 'Shine, Shine, O New Jerusalem!' which he always sang, whether entering into houses, visiting them, or leaving them.

"He had the custom of begging alms, but he would soon afterwards give them to other poor people. He spoke very little, but his words later proved to be correct in very deed, therefore many trusted him and were inclined towards him. In him the Psalmist's words were fulfilled: *He who dwells in the help of the Most High, shall abide in the shelter of the God of Heaven. He hath set his hope on Me, and I will deliver him ...* (Ps. 90:1,14)."

Further there follow expressive inscriptions on the graves of Hieroschemamonks Pimen, Savvas, and others whom we will not list. In them lie many of life's lessons, both for the monks of the Monastery, as well as for lay people. In reading them, page by page an unknown world is revealed before one; examples of holy, God-pleasing lives preserved for the edification of the brothers.... One does not wish to tear oneself away from these pages; one does not wish to walk away from these silent instructors.

But now they have rung the bell for Vespers. We enter the church, towards which the dark figures of monks in long mantias are drawn from every direction.

The Optina churches are striking neither by their size, nor by their wealth, nor by beautiful architecture. Everything is moderate within them, everything simple and modest, but so comfortable and bright, so joyful, that one does not want to part from them. The service is celebrated in good order and enthusiastically. The priests proceed majestically through the

The bell tower over the holy gates of the Skete.

church, with their mantias trailing behind them. The hymns do not strike one either by their ornateness or volume, but in each word there breathes a living feeling that is conveyed to the worshipers. Who of the visitors of Optina during the 1890's would not remember especially Abbot Mark, an eighty-year-old Elder, who sang the stichera and irmoi with youthful enthusiasm? The distinct, clearly understandable reading and a stunning choice of instructive texts add to the beauty of the Optina Monastery services.

Let us walk now from the Monastery to the Skete.\* A rather wide little road proceeds through the dense forest and brings us from the eastern gates of the Monastery to the holy gates of the Skete, which are located beneath the small, pink bell tower. The Skete occupies a fairly significant area and is enclosed by a wooden fence with stone pillars and stone towers at the corners. To the right of the holy gates is a small house—this is the former dwelling of Fr. Ambrose. To the left of the holy gates is

---

\*For people who are unfamiliar with the order of Optina and in general with monastery life, we will note that skete life in comparison with monastery life is more strict and solitary; and there is not such a large number of pilgrims in the Skete as in the Monastery. The skete brothers themselves live in a much more isolated way than do those of the Monastery. While the Monastery has daily church services, in the Skete they are only celebrated on Saturdays and Sundays, as well as on certain feasts. On the rest of the days in the skete church there is only the reading of the Psalter with the commemoration of benefactors. The prayer rule of the skete dwellers is performed alone in the cells, in which, generally, they spend the greater part of their time in solitary divine contemplation and in the reading of spiritual books. The visitor coming to the Skete rarely meets one of its inhabitants. It leaves the impression of a deep desert. For rest, the skete dwellers occupy themselves with handiwork in their cells—weaving, making wooden boxes, lathe work, spoon carving, and calligraphy. The skete dwellers eat only fasting foods all year, except on Christmas, Pascha, and during the fast-free weeks. To check his own spiritual life, the skete dweller must turn as often as possible to an elder, confessing all of his most subtle thoughts to him.

another similar house. In it lived Fr. Ambrose's instructor, Fr. Macarius.

Isolated, surrounded on all sides by the tall forest, the Skete makes a profound impression on every visitor. This impression was conveyed thus by one visitor to the Skete: "With reverence, with head uncovered, the pilgrim opens a quiet, soundless door and steps across the holy threshold of the Skete. At some distance opposite the entrance, the modest but elegant wooden church greets one and affably invites him in.

"Barely has the pilgrim entered the Skete, when he is overwhelmed by the fragrance of flowers. Along both sides of the wide path, tidily covered with yellow sand, the flowers stand in whole families from the entrance of the Skete to the church, reaching almost to its very threshold and surrounding the church like a wreath. They are dispersed along the side paths to the refectory, to the cells, to the apiary, to the skete pond, to the cedar-lined walk, to the towers, and to the skete cemetery.

"The fresh, clean cells of the skete-dwellers are sheltered in the midst of this splendor, with clear, clean windows, and low, covered porches, their steps sloping straight down to the grass, with balconies above the porches and white wooden benches on the balconies. The order and cleanliness everywhere is amazing, and even the stillness strikes one by its austerity. Only a sigh escaping from someone's breast in this land of stillness reveals that there are living people here. The only sounds heard here are those from beyond the skete enclosure. Through the resounding forest are the melancholy moans of the cuckoo or the squeaky sound of the lonely woodpecker cutting through the icy air; and from the open windows of the church the pure, full, concentrated sounds of the church clock on the wall slowly, resonantly pour forth and then die...."

The skete church is also distinctive: "This is not an ordinary

The skete church.

The main entrance to the Optina Skete of St. John the Forerunner.

church, but resembles rather that fraternal house of the Gospels in which the Savior shared His supper with His Apostles and gave them His parting commandments.... At the entrance of the simple wooden entrance hall made of logs are a wooden bucket with water and a wooden ladle. Fragrant flowers adorn the windows. To the left of the entrance door, inside the church, is a tiny, comfortable cell for the skete altar-attendant who lives here, in front of the church. The windows themselves are built not as windows are usually built in churches: dark with iron bars on the outside, like a prison. No, these are large, remarkably bright windows which open out, as in homes. The walls, papered with white glossy paper, look so bright, so inviting. Along the walls are occasionally hung, in simple painted frames having no trimmings or unnecessary adornments, depictions of ancient ascetics, with serious but benign expressions. In general, everything in this church bears the character of a simple fraternal, homey dwelling, designated not for worldly visitors, but expressly for their own family, for solitary prayer."

Such is Optina Monastery with its Skete—this is truly a grace-filled little corner of the Russian land, and one cannot help but love it, having once visited it. However, the main significance of Optina Monastery is not its good external organization and appearance, nor its beautiful surroundings, but its fate by the will of God to be the focal point of exalted Christian spirit and asceticism of the nineteenth century, in the person of its famous Elders and Superiors—Frs. Leonid, Macarius, Anthony, Moses, Ambrose and other fathers, less known but filled with the same ascetic spirit. In order to understand the character of Optina asceticism, in order to rightly comprehend the meaning of Optina Monastery in the spiritual life of the Russian people, and finally, in order to clearly imagine the spiritual atmosphere in which Elder Ambrose grew, we must make a brief historical account of that spiritual movement which took place in Russian monasticism in the second half of the eighteenth and beginning of the nineteenth centuries, and whose central figure was the ever-memorable Moldavian Elder, Archimandrite Paisius Velichkovsky.

Optina Monastery and its saints.
Contemporary plan for reconstructing the former glory.

# 6

# *Optina Monastery and the Remarkable Monastic Movement*

> *The fear of the Lord is the beginning of wisdom;
> and all they that foster this have a good understanding.*
> Psalm 110:9
>
> *Come ye children, hearken unto me; I will
> teach you the fear of the Lord.*
> Psalm 33:11

THE CONTRIBUTION of Elder Paisius Velichkovsky consists, not in his revealing some new form of monastic asceticism, but in his reestablishing and confirming in the consciousness of his numerous disciples the true idea of monasticism, the true aim of Christian podvig, and indicating the method by which this goal is attained.

His teaching was not his own invention, but was merely the restoration of the ancient ascetical teachings of the Holy Fathers, which Fr. Paisius* extracted from the ancient books of the Holy Fathers and brought to the remembrance of his contem-

---

\* Elder Paisius was glorified as a Saint on Mt. Athos, in the Church outside of Russia and later by the whole universal Church in 1988—ED.

poraries, endeavoring to impress it in their minds and hearts by his own personal example.

Basing himself on the works of the Holy Fathers, Elder Paisius taught that the true idea of monasticism, the true aim of Christian life, lies in attaining to the likeness of God. External asceticism is valuable, not in and of itself, but only inasmuch as it contributes to the realization of the above-mentioned aim. Likeness to God is attained by a path of unceasing cleansing of the heart and the impressing on it of Christian virtues—humility, repentance, meekness, love, chastity, prayer and others. In order to succeed in this podvig and not be diverted to a false path, one must have an experienced instructor, must have regular, pure-hearted revelation of one's thoughts before him, and trusting, sincere obedience to him. If such an instructor cannot be found, then it is essential to turn to the works of the ascetic Holy Fathers and to try to find in them guidance for one's life.

Such is the teaching of Elder Paisius. That this teaching is the teaching of the Holy Fathers can be supported by the following patristic testimony:

"Every effort, the entire podvig (of a man)," writes St. Symeon the New Theologian, "must be turned so as to acquire the Spirit of Christ, and thus to bring forth fruit of the Holy Spirit; for in this consists spiritual law and well being."*

"And in the future life, a Christian will not be tested as to whether he renounced the world, whether he fasted, whether he performed vigils, ... but he will be diligently examined as to whether he has any kind of likeness to Christ, as a son to his father, as Paul says, '... My little children of whom I travail in birth again until Christ be formed in you' (Gal.

---

\* *Discourses of St. Symeon the New Theologian,* Vol. I, translation of Bishop Theophan, 1892, 2nd discourse, p. 30.

4:19). The likeness to Christ is composed of truth, meekness, righteousness, and, together with them, humility and love of men."*

St. Symeon also writes concerning "eldership": "One must with all zeal, effort and attention, and with all vigilance, guard oneself by much prayer, so as not to fall into the hands of a spiritually deluded one, or deceiver, or false apostle, or false Christ; but to find a true and God-loving guide who would have Christ within himself and would precisely know the teachings, rules and decrees of the holy Apostles and the dogmas of the Holy Fathers; or, it is better to say, who would know the will and mysteries of the Master Himself and Teacher of the Apostles—Christ. It is incumbent upon us to seek and find such a teacher who, from the beginning, would have heard all this in word and learned from those words, and who would then have been taught everything mysteriously and in truth by the Comforter Spirit Himself through activity and experience; so that he would thus have been vouchsafed to hear from Christ God Himself, Who taught the Apostles: *It is given unto you to know the mysteries of the Kingdom of Heaven* (Matt. 13:11)."**

From St. John of the Ladder we read concerning eldership: "They deceive themselves who, placing their hope in themselves, suppose that they have no need of a director."***

"As a ship which has a good helmsman comes safely into harbor with God's help, so the soul which has a good shepherd, even though it has done much evil, easily ascends to Heaven. Without a guide it is easy to wander from the road, however prudent you may be; and so he who walks the monastic way

---

\* *Ibid.*, pp. 30-31.
\*\* *Ibid.*, Homily 11, p. 98.
\*\*\* St. John Climacus, *The Ladder of Divine Ascent* (Brookline, Massachusetts: Holy Transfiguration Monastery, 1978), p. 5.

under his own direction soon perishes, even though he may have all the wisdom of the world."*

"For the man who goes (by way of the monastic path) his own way, traveling without understanding of the Gospels and without any guidance," says St. Mark the Ascetic, "often stumbles and falls into many pits and snares of the devil; he frequently goes astray and exposes himself to many dangers, not knowing where he is going. For many have endured great ascetic labors, much hardship and toil for God's sake; but because they relied on their own judgment, lacked discrimination, and failed to accept help from their neighbor, their many efforts proved useless and vain."**

From St. John Cassian the Roman we read the following: "Discernment is a gift of God which, however, must be developed and trained. How? By renouncing one's own judgment in favor of that of experienced fathers. This is the most wise school of discrimination in which even those who do not have any particular ability learn to properly discern concerning what is just...."

Abba Moses related to St. John Cassian concerning discernment: "True discrimination comes to us only as a result of true humility, and this in turn is shown by our revealing to our spiritual fathers not only what we do but also what we think, never trusting our own thoughts, and by following in all things the words of our elders, regarding as good what they have judged to be so. In this way not only does the monk remain unharmed through true discrimination and by following the correct path, but he is also kept safe from all the snares of the devil. It is impossible for anyone who orders his life on the basis

---

* *Ibid.*, Summary of Step 26, Chapters 52-53, p. 195.
** St. Mark the Ascetic, "Letter to Nicholas the Solitary," *The Philokalia*, Vol. I (London: Faber and Faber, 1979), pp. 151-2.

of the judgment and knowledge of the spiritually mature to fall because of the wiles of the demons. In fact, even before someone is granted the gift of discrimination, the act of revealing his base thoughts openly to the fathers weakens and withers them. The enemy does not like the light and, therefore, evil thoughts, as soon as they are revealed, are dispersed and annihilated. For just as a snake which is brought from its dark hole into the light makes every effort to escape and hide itself, so the malicious thoughts that a person brings out into the open by sincere confession seek to depart from him. This is confirmed by many, many examples and experiences."\*

Concerning the fruits of obedience, St. John of the Ladder writes the following in his fourth chapter: "From obedience comes humility ... from humility comes discernment ... from discernment comes clairvoyance ... and from clairvoyance comes foreknowledge. And who would not run this fair course of obedience, seeing such blessings in store for him?"\*\*

He further writes: "Those who have leaped out of obedience will tell you of its value; for it was only then that they fully realized the heaven in which they had been living."\*\*\*

From the many instructions of the Holy Fathers concerning the true aim of Christian and monastic life we have presented only a few,\*\*\*\* but from them it is clear that the teaching of Elder Paisius is founded entirely on the teachings of the Holy

---

\* St. John Cassian, "On the Holy Fathers at Sketis and on Discrimination," in *The Philokalia,* Vol. I (London: Faber and Faber, 1979), p. 103.

\*\* *Op. Cit., The Ladder of Divine Ascent,* Step 4, Chapter 105, p. 47.

\*\*\* *Ibid.,* Step 4, Chapter 123, p. 53.

\*\*\*\* Those wishing to acquaint themselves with them in more detail will find them in the works of Abba Dorotheos, St. John of the Ladder, St. Symeon the New Theologian, in *The Philokalia,* and also in the collections of the letters of Optina Elder Hieroschemamonk Macarius, especially in the fourth part, to nuns.

Fathers. However, as is shown in the biography of this Elder, he had to expend much effort and labor before he reached a clear knowledge of the truth, which by that time had been lost from the awareness of monks.

Fr. Paisius Velichkovsky was a native of Little Russia [Ukraine]. He was born in the city of Poltava in 1722, into the family of a cathedral priest, and was named Peter in the world. He received his education in the Kiev Theological School.

From his early years he was permeated with fervent love towards God and burned with a desire to consecrate himself entirely to Him. Captivated by this desire and without graduating from the Theological School, he entered the Lyubech Monastery, from which he later moved to other Ukrainian monasteries. Moving from monastery to monastery, he sought everywhere for a man who could teach him true monastic life, and, not finding such a one, he set out for Moldavia and Vlachia, where he also spent several years in different monasteries, benefitting from the counsel and guidance of the best of the Moldavian monks. His heart burned more than ever with love for God, but he meanwhile continued to feel unsatisfied, since he had not located his desired instructor in the spiritual life. Finally, he withdrew to Mt. Athos where, having visited some of the monasteries, he settled in complete solitude. He was at that time twenty-five years of age. He lived in extreme unacquisitiveness: he did not even have a shirt; he had only a cassock and a very old ryassa, covered with patches. He spent his time in prayer and in the reading of the books of the Holy Fathers, which he obtained from the neighboring monasteries.

At this time, a young monk by the name of Bessarion found him and implored him to allow him to settle with him and be his disciple. Remarkable is the answer that Fr. Paisius gave to Bessarion:

"Brother! You compel me to say something sad ... for I also, with much effort and sorrow, likewise sought an instructor and did not find one; and I endured many sorrows, and even now I bear them.... The salvation of the soul, concerning which you ask me, cannot be made easy except by a true spiritual instructor, one who forces himself first of all to fulfill all the commandments of the Lord ... for how can one instruct another on a path which he himself has not walked? He himself first of all must withstand all the passions of soul and body even unto blood, and conquer, with the help of Christ, lust and anger, pride, sensuality, love of glory and love of money, so as to learn to heal others and instruct them in the commandments of God.... Such, O brother, is the instructor we should acquire, but alas! Such are our times! Foreseeing by the Spirit of God this woeful time, our God-bearing Fathers, out of pity for us, left us their holy writings, which we must with great solicitude and with many tears study day and night!"*

Following this rule, attentively studying the works of the ascetic fathers, and implementing their instructions in very deed, Fr. Paisius by degrees attained to greater and greater experience, so that in a short time he was noticed by many seekers of Christian wisdom who, settling near him, persistently implored him to be their guide on the path to salvation. Fr. Paisius refused for a long time, but was finally forced to yield to their requests and thus there sprang up near him a company of his disciples.

After a few years he moved with his brotherhood to Vlachia and settled at first in the Monastery of Dragomirna, and later in the Monastery of Neamts, which he directed until his repose on November 15, 1794.

---

*Schemamonk Metrophanes, *Blessed Paisius Velichkovsky* (Platina, California: St. Herman of Alaska Brotherhood, 1976), pp. 84-85.

From the time that Fr. Paisius became the head of the spiritual brotherhood of monks, he directed, with all concern, the realization of the ascetical precepts of the Holy Fathers in the life of the brotherhood. He set forth spiritual growth in Christ as the aim of monastic labors, as we have said above, and as the means to attain this aim, the "path of eldership"—that is, the path of sincere revelation of thoughts on the part of the disciples, and loving guidance on the part of the instructors. According to the order established by him, each evening all the brothers had to reveal their thoughts to their spiritual fathers. If there arose among the brothers some unpleasantness, it had to be cut off that very day by reconciliation. If someone did not wish to make peace, the Elder subjected him to separation, so that he could neither cross the threshold of the church, nor say the prayer "Our Father ..." until he was reconciled.* So as to better acquaint the brethren with the true task of asceticism, Fr. Paisius considered as essential the constant and attentive study of the ascetical works of the Holy Fathers. One of the greatest contributions of Fr. Paisius, not only for Russian monasticism but for all of Russian Orthodox society, lies in the fact that with great labor and at great expense he gathered ancient Slavonic and Moldavian translations, as well as Greek originals, of the works of the Holy Fathers. He painstakingly verified them with one another, corrected them, and with great skill sometimes translated them afresh into Church Slavonic. He did not cease this labor until his very repose. When he was no longer able to arise from his bed, he surrounded himself with books on the bed; here beside him there lay dictionaries, Greek and Slavonic Bibles, Greek and Slavonic grammars, and the book which he

---

*In this prayer we ask to be forgiven as we forgive others; therefore, to pronounce it without having forgiven our brother is to condemn ourselves.—ED.

was translating. Among the books there stood lit candles. He himself, bent over, wrote for entire nights, forgetting even his bodily infirmity and his grievous sickness and difficulties.

When the Nativity Fast began, all the brethren of Fr. Paisius' monastery gathered each evening, except for Sundays and feast days, in the refectory. Candles were lit. The Elder arrived, sat down in his customary place and began reading his translations of the works of the Holy Fathers: St. Basil the Great, St. John Climacus, Abba Dorotheos, St. Theodore the Studite or St. Symeon the New Theologian. The brethren listened with deep attention. Such readings continued all winter, until Lazarus Saturday. Reading a book, the Elder at the same time interpreted it, bringing forth testimony from the Holy Scriptures, from the Old and New Testaments, and from the teachings of the Holy Fathers of the Church. He had such a gift that by his words he could animate the most despondent, console the most sorrowful, and awaken in each of them zeal for salvation. Thus the monastery of St. Paisius became in truth a school of spiritual life, where by word and deed the brethren were instructed in the rules of true Christian asceticism. The Elder paid particular attention to strengthening the feelings of brotherly love and mercy in his spiritual children. In Neamts Monastery he established an infirmary and a shelter for pilgrims. There he also placed his aged brothers and those from outside—the lame, the blind, and the enfeebled. He ordered those who labored there to serve the sick as they would the Lord; each Saturday to wash their hair and change their shirts, to look after the cleanliness of their beds and, in the summertime, to air out their clothing in the sun.

Fr. Paisius' many years of tireless labors did not remain fruitless. His name soon became known not only on Mt. Athos and in Vlachia, but even in Russia. He conducted a wide correspondence with many Russian monks and priests. A whole multitude of disciple-elders trained and educated by him set out from his monasteries for Russia, supplied with manuscripts of his translations; and these they dispersed to many monasteries, pouring a fresh, living stream into the life of Russian monasticism. His translation of *The Philokalia* aroused the interest of Metropolitan Gabriel of St. Petersburg, and by his request the Elder's disciple Athanasius obtained for him both this book and the Greek original. By the order of the Metropolitan the book was printed in St. Petersburg in 1793, and later editions were published during the time of Metropolitan Philaret of Moscow in 1822 and 1832. Besides *The Philokalia*, Fr. Paisius also translated the book of the great instructor of interior life, St. Isaac the Syrian, and those of a few others. All of these translations of Fr. Paisius were spread in manuscript among Russian monks, painstakingly recopied and studied with zeal; and they strengthened their striving for spiritual life and spiritual perfection.

Of the disciples of Fr. Paisius who lived in Russia, we will mention a few who had ties to Optina Monastery. Such are:

1) Archimandrite Theodosius of the Sophroniev Hermitage. Fr. Macarius of Optina later had contact with him.

2) Archimandrite Cleopas, who lived in the Ostrov, Tikhvin and Simonov (in Moscow) Monasteries. He left many disciples, among whom was Macarius, the particularly noteworthy builder of Pesnosha Monastery, who corresponded with Fr. Paisius and who placed in Optina his remarkable disciple Abramius, of whom we spoke earlier.

3) The monks Alexander and Philaret of Novospassky Monastery. They had spiritual contact with Fr. Paisius and exerted a strong spiritual influence on the future Optina monks Moses and Anthony (Putilov), of whom we will speak below.

4) Athanasius (a former secretary of the senate) who obtained Fr. Paisius' translation of *The Philokalia* for Metropoli-

tan Gabriel and who later labored with certain other disciples of Fr. Paisius in the Svensk Monastery, where at one time the above-mentioned Moses lived with him .

5) Another Hieromonk Cleopas and his friend Schemamonk Theodore who lived for many years with Fr. Paisius, who tonsured them and firmly established them in the spiritual life. They left for Russia in 1801. The famous first Elder of Optina—Hieroschemamonk Leo or Leonid (Nagolkin)—became friends with them and matured under their guidance.

6) Another Schemamonk Athanasius (a former commander of an imperial regiment) who lived with Elder Paisius for seven years, moved to Russia in 1777 and reposed in Ploschansk Hermitage in the Orel Diocese where, under his spiritual guidance, another Optina Elder matured—Hieroschemamonk Macarius (Ivanov).

From this short enumeration of disciples of Fr. Paisius one can see what a wide spiritual net he cast across the Russian land. This net also captured those who were destined to place the beginning of their spiritual life in Optina. Besides the above-mentioned Abramius, there were the following: Moses and Anthony (Putilov), Leonid (Nagolkin), and Macarius (Ivanov). Concerning these, we must now speak in detail.

The son of a Serpukhov merchant, Timothy Ivanovich Putilov (thus Fr. Moses was named in the world) grew up in a family distinguished by its strict piety, and was himself quite pious. At nineteen years of age he entered the mercantile business in Moscow. Here he spent all of his free time in the reading of the Holy Scriptures and loved to be with people of exalted spiritual life. The Nun Dosithea of the Ivanov Monastery exerted a strong influence upon him, as did the Novospassky monks Alexander and Philaret, who, as we have said earlier, preserved the Paisian leaven. Hearing their conversations, Timothy himself began to burn with the thirst for a life totally in God. Finally, he went together with his younger brother Jonah to Sarov Hermitage, where at that time St. Seraphim of Sarov was struggling. Jonah remained there permanently, but the Lord destined Timothy to move to the Svensk Monastery, where many of Fr. Paisius' disciples were gathered—the monks Athanasius, Seraphim, Basil and others, whom Timothy joined. Having heard that in the impassable Roslavl forests of the Smolensk Province there dwelt, in separate cells, another group of disciples of Fr. Paisius, Timothy was inflamed with the desire to share their way of life; and in 1811 he joined them. Here he received the tonsure with the name Moses, and for ten full years he lived as a hermit in a way similar to that of the ancient desert dwellers, under the guidance of Elders Athanasius, Dositheus and Dorotheus.

He passed his time in prayer, in reading, and in copying the Paisian translations of the books of the Holy Fathers. While still in the Svensk Monastery he had copied, in semi-uncial script, Fr. Paisius' translations of St. John Climacus and the Life of St. Symeon the New Theologian. With Elder Athanasius in the Roslavl forest, he found many other translations of Fr. Paisius, which he likewise hastened to employ for his spiritual edification. In 1816 his other younger brother, Alexander, came to settle with him, and he too was soon tonsured as a monk with the name Anthony.

To show the reader the kinds of thoughts and feelings that penetrated the young ascetics in their forest solitude, we present an excerpt from a letter of Fr. Moses to his brother, Alexander—then still a layman. This letter was written by Fr. Moses after his return to his forest refuge from a trip to Moscow.

"Having reached my desert nest I wished and hastened with my whole soul to quickly communicate these lines to you.... One may say that just as after labors, rest is sweet—so too at the end of traveling and of the scatteredness that accompanies it, it is quite pleasant to be in the refuge of quiet solitude. Personal experience reveals that when one is in the sphere of objects which engage the sight, taste, hearing and all the senses, one cannot be occupied so sweetly in the remembrance of God and the teaching of His holy law. When one withdraws from the world, one is freed from sensual meetings which captivate the mind and thoughts; all spiritual occupation becomes alive and sweet because the mind, freed from occasions of dispersion, begins to become collected within itself. Through this the soul begins to sense the presence of God, and pious fear and love towards Him are more noticeable.... For us, who are desirous of God's salvation but have a nature infirm and tainted by sin, there is a good, easy and effective means to repentance—withdrawal from the world. The mind becomes collected within itself through solitude and attention, seeing that which proceeds from the heart and the contrary thoughts that come to it. Seeing this, it understands its impurity and, unable to endure it, forces itself towards purification. To purge and battle against thoughts, not having strength in oneself, one discovers from experience one's infirmity and wretchedness and absolute need of the Savior Christ. Seeking the help of Christ, one appeals to His omnipotent power as one who is infirm in his own reasoning and strength. One calls upon the all-good and all-powerful Name of Jesus with sincere self-reproach and heartfelt sorrow, that He might cleanse and strengthen and extend the hand of salvation. Thus, by first recognizing one's own wretchedness and weakness, one later experiences the salvation of God, which comes to one's aid at the time of interior battle. For *the Lord is nigh unto all that call upon Him, to all that call on Him in truth* (Ps. 144:19) *and He will save the humble of spirit* (Ps. 33:18). When one experiences this salvation in the feelings of the heart, one rejoices as much for the relief from impure thoughts as in the goodness of God and His Providence, cooperating with and saving him. Through this one enters into living faith with a sure feeling, not of one's own strength but of Christ's, which is why one especially devotes oneself with sweetness of heart to the Savior and gives one's whole self over to Him, with undoubting hope in Him and love. This giving over of oneself with heartfelt hope imparts to the soul a surpassing peace and joy. This forms the interior Kingdom of God, which Christ the Savior commanded us to seek before all. And it is in truth the most complete and satisfying blessing for a man, so that all other material good things desired by the world now seem too coarse, have no meaning and are not worth seeking.

"All of this came to my mind as I began to write, not because I have become established in spirit in precisely this way, but because I have experienced in part the progress of the interior life in stillness, which attracts the soul for the purpose of true repentance...."

From this letter it is clear that the main attention of Fr. Moses was turned to the interior condition of his heart, in which connection he undoubtedly benefited from the counsel of his elders and from the instruction of the books of the Holy Fathers. He subtly noticed the distinctive features of this condition and determined the precise path that leads a man to a living knowledge of God—through a clear awareness of his weaknesses and through an awareness of obvious help from on high. In view of such a spiritual make-up, Fr. Moses was clearly sufficiently prepared even then to become a guide of others along the path to spiritual salvation. In fact, a great change in his outward circumstances soon occurred. In Optina at the beginning of the nineteenth century there lived an ascetic of exalted life, Fr. Theophan, who was also one of the disciples of Fr. Paisius. He and Fr. Moses became friends. Through Fr. Theophan, Fr. Moses became known to the Superior of Optina, Abbot Daniel. It was just at that time that Bishop Philaret of Kaluga conceived the idea of founding a skete at the Monastery, with the aim of giving the monks of Optina Monastery who desired it the possibility of a more solitary and contemplative life. The Superior proposed Fr. Moses as a person capable of serving for the realization of this matter. The Bishop received Fr. Moses quite favorably, and on June 6, 1821, a group of Roslavl hermits headed by Fr. Moses arrived at Optina. With the blessing of Bishop Philaret, they set about the founding of the Skete, which was soon established and consecrated. Fr. Moses was assigned as the first Superior.

In 1825, when the position of Superior of Optina was vacant, Fr. Moses was transferred to this post; and his brother, Fr. Anthony, was designated as Superior of the Skete. He bore this responsibility until 1839, when he, in his turn, received another assignment.* Fr. Moses remained as Superior of Optina until his repose in 1862.

As Superior of Optina Monastery and having been bred in the precepts of Fr. Paisius, Fr. Moses wished to plant there the same order of spiritual life which Fr. Paisius had bequeathed to his disciples—that is, the order of "eldership." But Fr. Moses himself, due to his complicated responsibilities as Superior of the Monastery and for other reasons, was not able to be an "elder" for his brothers. It was necessary to find such a man who, without occupying an official position in the Monastery, would by his own refined personal qualities, by his spiritual experience, and by his knowledge of the path of "eldership," be able to draw to himself the trust, love and respect of the brothers and to stand at the head of their spiritual podvig. The Lord soon sent just such a man to Fr. Moses. This was the renowned Fr.

---

*Fr. Anthony was one of the most remarkable ascetics of Optina Monastery. Concerning him see Fr. Clement Sederholm, *Elder Anthony of Optina* (Platina, California: St. Herman of Alaska Brotherhood, 1994)—ED.

Archimandrite Moses.

Leonid (Leo in schema) Nagolkin,* the first in the line of the great Optina Elders.

Fr. Leonid was born in 1768 in the city of Karachev, in the Orel Province. In his youth he was occupied with trading and traveled as a salesman to many corners of Russia, everywhere entering into dealings with people of every calling and station, so that even as a youth he had gained a great knowledge of people and experience of life.

In 1797 he left the world and entered Optina Monastery, but at this time he stayed only a short while. Soon he moved from Optina to White Bluff Monastery, under the direction of one of the aforementioned disciples of Fr. Paisius—Basil Kishkin. In 1804 Fr. Leonid was chosen as Superior of the White Bluff Hermitage. However, burdened by this position, he left the abbacy in 1808 and, together with the Paisian disciples Schemamonk Theodore and Hieromonk Cleopas, settled a little over a mile from the Monastery in a lowly cell in the deep forest, where he spent his time in solitary prayer, divine contemplation, and the study of the works of the Holy Fathers. After living here for a short time, the friends found it necessary to move to the far north. At first Fr. Theodore, and then Frs. Leonid and Cleopas moved to Valaam, where they labored for a period of six years. According to the expression of one of the local fools-for-Christ's-sake [Anthony Ivanovich] they "traded well"—that is, they were successful themselves, and they led others forward on the spiritual path. However, here a trial awaited them. Certain Valaam monks, and even the Superior himself, were exceedingly disturbed by the fact that they, being schemamonks, were conducting conversations with people all the time concerning the salvation of the soul. In their opinion,

---

* See Fr. Clement Sederholm, *Elder Leonid of Optina* (Platina, California: St. Herman of Alaska Brotherhood, 1990).

such a way of life was not befitting to schemamonks. They were also disturbed by the teaching of the Elders concerning revelation of thoughts and interior prayer. They finally sent a report to Metropolitan Ambrose of St. Petersburg accusing the Elders of preaching a heresy. An inquiry was conducted and the Elders were acquitted. But for them to remain at Valaam after this was undesirable, and in 1817 they transferred to the St. Alexander of Svir Monastery where they were noticed by Emperor Alexander I, "The Blessed." Here in 1822 Schemamonk Theodore reposed and Fr. Leonid, having lost his spiritual friend and instructor, decided to return to his native land in the south. He lived for some time in the Ploschansk Hermitage in the Orel Province, where he became spiritually acquainted with an ascetic who lived there, Hieromonk Macarius (Ivanov). Later, in April of 1829, through the invitation of Fr. Moses, Fr. Leonid moved to Optina Monastery where he lived right up to his death in 1841.

In the person of Fr. Leonid, Fr. Moses had found a true "elder" for his Monastery. Fr. Leonid became the soul of the Monastery. Not occupying any sort of administrative position, he became the spiritual director of the Optina brotherhood solely on the strength of his lofty gifts and his enormous experience of life. Without the blessing of the Elder, none of his spiritual children took a single step in their lives. Each evening the brethren flocked to his cell to open their souls to him about the day that had passed and to receive beneficial instructions or consolation. After the brethren, there followed lay people. From cities and villages all types of people began to appear—nobility, merchants, middle-class people, and peasants of both sexes. All had heard about his wisdom and clairvoyance; all believed in and had personally experienced the power of his prayer. No one was refused. The doors of the Elder's cell were not closed to anyone. All were received by the Elder with a fatherly disposition and love, and no one left his cell unconsoled.

The well-known traveler, the monk Parthenius, who visited Fr. Leonid not long before his repose, paints an interesting picture of the cell life of the Elder and his relationship to his visitors:

"Entering his cell," he writes, "I became afraid and began to tremble. Almost the entire cell was filled with individuals from various walks of life: landowners, merchants and simple folk. All were standing on their knees in fear and trembling, as if before a fearsome judge; and each one was waiting for his replies and instruction. I likewise fell to my knees behind everyone else. The Elder was sitting on his bed and braiding a belt. This was his handiwork, braiding belts, and he gave them as a blessing to his visitors....

"Among these people kneeling before him was a certain gentleman who had come to worship at the Monastery and to visit the great Elder. The Elder asked him, 'And you, what do you want from me?' With tears the gentleman replied, 'I want, holy Father, to receive instruction profitable for my soul.' The Elder asked, 'And did you do what I told you to do before?' He replied, 'No, holy Father, I am unable to do that.' The Elder said, 'Then why did you come to ask for something else, if you did not do the first?' Then he told his disciples in a stern voice, 'Toss him out of my cell.' And they removed him. I, and everyone else who was there, was frightened by such a severe action and punishment. But the Elder was not upset at all; once again he began to speak meekly with the others and to let people leave.

"The next day I came to him again, and once more he received me with love and spoke with me at length. Then the women who had been there the previous day came. The sick one was with them, but no longer ailing; she was completely well. They had come to thank the Elder. When I saw this, I was astonished; and I told the Elder, 'Holy Father, how do you dare to perform such works? Through human fame you can lose all your labors and ascetic struggles.' But in reply he told me, 'Athonite Father! I did not do this by my own power. The grace of the Holy Spirit imparted to me at ordination did this, and it happened according to the faith of the people that came; as for me, I am a sinful man.' When I heard that, I was greatly profited by his good discretion, faith and humility. Then once again the gentleman from yesterday came in and begged for the Elder's forgiveness with tears. The Elder forgave him and told him to do what he had previously been told. Then he dismissed us all."

The enormous spiritual experience and lofty authority of Elder Leonid can be seen in the following occurrences:

At the end of the 1820's or beginning of the '30's, Fr. Leonid visited the Sophroniev Hermitage. At that time Hieroschemamonk Theodosius was living there in seclusion (in the orchard). Many people considered him to be a spiritual man and clairvoyant because he had foretold the War of 1812 and several other occurrences. Fr. Leonid found his state dubious. After speaking with the recluse, the Elder asked him how he was able to foretell the future. The recluse replied that the Holy Spirit made the future known to him; and to the Elder's question about the manner in which He made this known, he explained that the Holy Spirit appeared to him in the form of some type of dove and spoke to him in a human voice. Fr. Leonid, seeing clearly in this the delusion of the enemy, began to warn the recluse that one should not believe this sort of thing. But the recluse was offended and indignantly retorted to the Elder, "I thought that you, like the others, wanted to derive profit from me, but you came to teach me!" Fr. Leonid withdrew and said to the abbot when he was leaving the Monastery:

"Watch out for your holy recluse; do not let anything happen to him." Fr. Leonid had hardly journeyed as far as Orel when he learned that Fr. Theodosius had hanged himself.

Not far from the Optina Monastery there lived a certain gentleman who boasted that, as soon as he laid eyes on Fr. Leonid, he would see straight through him. This gentleman did come to the Elder; and at the time there were many visitors. The man came in; he was tall and heavily built. Fr. Leonid had the custom that when he wanted to make a special impression on someone, he would shade his eyes by putting his left hand to his forehead as if he were examining some object in the sun. When this gentleman came in, the Elder lifted his left hand and said, "Eh, the blockhead is coming! He's come to look straight through sinful Leonid. But he, the rascal, hasn't been to confession and Holy Communion for seventeen years." The gentleman shook like a leaf and began to weep and repent that he, a sinner and unbeliever, in fact had not been to confession and had not received the Holy Mysteries for seventeen years.

There was yet another incident. There was a landowner who made donations to the Monastery but did not visit very frequently. He lived openly with one of his peasant women in his old age, even though his children by his first and lawful wife had grown up and married. After hearing about the famous Elder, Fr. Leonid, and that he received many people for confession, this landowner made overtures to Fr. Leonid through the Abbot: he would like to make his confession to him. Fr. Leonid refused, to the great offense of the landowner, who began to beg both the Abbot and Fr. Macarius to be his intercessors before Fr. Leonid. After repeated requests, the Elder against his will agreed, but stated that he would not be responsible for what might happen. The landowner made his confession; Fr. Leonid did not allow him to receive the Holy Mysteries. You can imagine the shame and humiliation of this gentleman, who looked down on everyone and who now had to humble himself before the entire Monastery like a catechumen. To his even greater shame, his married daughter who was accompanying him was preparing to thank the great Elder for his decision. Once again the gentleman asked the Abbot and Fr. Macarius to intercede. They refused out of conscience and because they knew how immovable Fr. Leonid was in such matters. What happened? The landowner returned home and after less than a month broke off his years-long relationship with his mistress, to the mutual joy of his entire family.

The two last incidents indicate to us with exceptional clarity the great significance of a true "elder" in moral education. What strength and deep faith he had to have, what independence and integrity of spirit, what firm conviction, so as to break up and melt like wax the thick and hard crust of pride and sensuality which shackled the hearts of such people as the aforementioned landowners! From the people surrounding them, from the married clergy, of course, no one would have dared even pronounce those words which the Elder boldly expressed. And if they had pronounced them, they would have made an entirely different impression. From the lips of the Elder they evoked contrition of heart, compelled them to weep, brought forth moral renewal, and awakened a deep moral conversion.

Fr. Leonid was especially close to the simple people; he took pity on them and loved them, and was warmly loved and respected by them in turn. He was always besieged by a crowd of peasants, who brought all their sorrows and needs to him.

He, if one may say so, stood at the very heart of the people, and listened to its beating, be it joyful or sorrowful. And the simple people carried word of their beloved Elder abroad, far beyond the bounds of the Kaluga Province.

Elder Leonid.

Fr. Leonid was likewise close to the nuns of many women's monasteries. Under his leadership, direction by elders was firmly established in them, and many nuns learned to have an attentive attitude towards their interior life.

However, according to the words of the Psalmist: *Many are the tribulations of the righteous* (Ps. 33:19); Fr. Leonid had to bear not a little grief in Optina. There were monks there who saw a misuse of the Mystery of Confession in the practice of the revelation of thoughts. In the reception of a multitude of visitors, especially of women, they saw the breaking of the vows of a schemamonk; and in the anointing of the sick with blessed oil, a pride-filled claim to the gift of wonderworking. And sure enough—reports and complaints flew to Kaluga, to the then-Bishop Nicholas, as well as to the consistory. Certain confessors of women's monasteries complained that Fr. Leonid, by his preaching of the revelation of thoughts to elders and eldresses, diminished the authority of confessors and was leading to novelty and even heresy.

The Bishop, desiring to put an end to the unpleasantness and murmuring, gave order to transfer Fr. Leonid from the skete apiary to the Monastery and forbade the Elder to receive lay visitors. In the women's monasteries there began a real persecution of the disciples of Elder Leonid; many of them were driven out of their monasteries as heretics, and others were taken under strict supervision, deprived of the mantia, etc. The Elder himself was forbidden to wear the schema. He greatly sorrowed over all these troubles, grieving not for himself but for his unfortunate disciples, whose courage he tried to sustain by letters.

However, at the very time that it befell Fr. Leonid to go through all these trials, the Lord granted him a great consolation—to find a close spiritual friend and helper in the person of Hieromonk Macarius (Ivanov). This was the second famous

Optina Elder, the successor of Fr. Leonid and the instructor of Fr. Ambrose, which is why we consider it necessary to relate some biographical information about him.*

Fr. Macarius was descended from the nobility of the Orel Province and was named Michael Nikolaevich in the world. He was born on the small estate of his father near Kaluga. His parents were simple people, good and pious. In his early childhood his meek and deeply believing mother had a great influence upon him. She often visited the Kaluga Lavrentiev Monastery with him, and her conversations with the then-Superior of the Monastery, Archimandrite Theophan, indelibly imprinted themselves in his child's soul. He so loved Fr. Theophan that once, attending the Liturgy with his mother, he ran to him in the altar through the open royal doors.

By nature, Michael Nikolaevich's health was rather weak; he had an impressionable, serious and deep character, receptive to all that was lofty, beautiful and holy. He loved nature very much, loved music and singing, and he himself played the violin and sang.** He received his education at first in the parish school and later at home, under the guidance of an invited tutor. When he had reached the age of fourteen, he was appointed as a bookkeeper in the District Treasury of Lgov; he occupied this position for four years. In 1806 Michael Nikolaevich's father died, and he left this position in order to take up farming in the village and to take charge of his younger brothers and sisters. Farming did not suit him. He was very kind, and could not refuse anyone anything. He was ready to give away all of his possessions to whomever asked. At this time he developed an enthusiasm for the reading of the Holy

---

*See Fr. Leonid Kavelin, *Elder Macarius of Optina* (Platina, California: St. Herman of Alaska Brotherhood, 1995).

** Subsequently he was an ecclesiarch, singer and canonarch.

Scriptures and books of spiritual content. His brothers tried to persuade him to marry. He did not decisively refuse, but when the parents of the girl that he had chosen answered that she was still young and they still wanted to think it over, Michael Nikolaevich greatly rejoiced over this answer and ceased entirely to think about marriage.

On October 6, 1810, when he was twenty-two years old, he set out on a pilgrimage to the Ploschansk Hermitage of the Theotokos in the Orel Province, and from there did not return home. He had found his true place. The Ploschansk Hermitage made an irresistible impression on him. According to his own words, when he entered the Monastery he did not know where he was—on earth or in Heaven, and all the monastics seemed to him like angels of God. Remaining in the Monastery, he zealously took upon himself the labors of a monk. His first instructor in the monastic life was the strict ascetic, Fr. Jonah, under whose guidance he spent six years. In 1815 Michael Nikolaevich was tonsured into the mantia and received a new name—Macarius.

In that same year one of Elder Paisius' disciples, Schemamonk Athanasius, who had a great influence on the future spiritual life of Fr. Macarius, came to live in Ploschansk Hermitage. According to the personal testimony of Fr. Macarius, Fr. Athanasius was not distinguished by erudition but was entirely steeped in the spirit of Elder Paisius, and he was transformed, body and soul, by his precepts. Fr. Athanasius was exceedingly simple of soul, full of deep feeling, sincerity and heartfelt warmth. He was meek, condescending, compassionate and loving. He could not see a needy person without immediately helping him. He loved to receive wanderers and supplied them with the things necessary for the road, at which he would say: "People send it to us, but where are they going to get it from?" He conversed with guests willingly, not from books but from the experience of his heart, from the wise guidance of Elder Paisius. He loved to speak about the Kingdom of Heaven, about the future torment, about mercy towards the poor, and about the fact that the present life must serve as a preparation for the future one. He said all this with such sincerity, with such humility, that it was touching to look at him, and his words involuntarily penetrated to the depths of one's soul. The humble and meek heart of Fr. Macarius had long thirsted for precisely such an instructor. He hastened to become acquainted with Fr. Athanasius and became firmly attached to him with the devoted love of a son. Finally, in 1817, with the blessing of the Superior, he moved for good into the Elder's cell and from that time remained inseparably with him, took care of him, and learned from him up to the Elder's repose in 1825. Besides his deep personal influence and his conversations about Elder Paisius and about other great ascetics, Fr. Athanasius also had an enormous significance for Fr. Macarius since he had brought with him to Ploschansk Monastery many manuscript copies of Elder Paisius' translations of the works of the Holy Fathers.

Reading these manuscripts with profound interest and attention, Fr. Macarius was gradually more and more filled with their spirit. From precisely this time, Fr. Macarius began to be spiritually conformed to that great Elder-instructor and expert of interior life, as would be revealed later in Optina. The manuscript translations of Elder Paisius were carefully preserved by Fr. Macarius and were subsequently published by him, concerning which we will speak in detail below. As he read Elder Paisius' translations of the Holy Fathers, Fr. Macarius paid particular attention to the teaching of the Holy Fathers on the mental Jesus Prayer or Prayer of the Heart—that is, the constant prayerful preservation in the heart of the Name of the Lord Jesus Christ. Fr. Macarius very much wanted to learn this exalted spiritual activity.

However, Elder Athanasius was forbidden by Fr. Paisius to touch this prayerful podvig. According to his instructions, he studied only the oral Jesus Prayer, the constant turning to the Lord Jesus verbally, and for this reason, he was unable to fulfill the desire of his disciple, Fr. Macarius; or, perhaps he did not wish to, finding this matter premature for him. Fr. Macarius, however, did not abandon his intention. In 1819, he set out on foot on a pilgrimage to Kiev. On the return trip he visited Glinsk Hermitage. Here he became acquainted with one of the disciples of Abbot Philaret (the Superior of the Monastery), Hierodeacon Samuel, who was a doer of the Prayer of the Heart, having learned this under the guidance of his Superior. Fr. Macarius greatly rejoiced over this acquaintance. They spent three days over the book of St. Isaac the Syrian, conversing about the Prayer of the Heart. However, by Fr. Macarius' own later admission, at that time on account of his spiritual level he still did not have the capacity in himself for this exalted activity and almost endangered himself by applying himself to it prematurely.

In 1825, as we have already stated, Fr. Athanasius reposed. Fr. Macarius greatly grieved over this, since he had lost in Fr. Athanasius his instructor and friend. His spiritual loneliness was painful for him, but the Lord soon consoled him. In 1828 Fr. Leonid arrived at Ploschansk Hermitage from the St. Alexander of Svir Monastery and greatly gladdened Fr. Macarius. He found in him a new instructor, even more powerful in spirit and experience than Fr. Athanasius. Having been tested in the fight with visible and invisible enemies, Fr. Leonid was also able to extend a helping hand to one who was being tempted; possessing the great gift of spiritual discernment, he freely and easily solved perplexities and gave beneficial advice. Fr. Leonid, on his part, was glad to meet Fr. Macarius. In view of his profound humility, Fr. Macarius had great spiritual experience and could thus be not only Fr. Leonid's disciple, but also his friend. Oneness of soul, oneness of upbringing, and oneness of striving soon closely bound the hearts of the Elders by mutual friendship, which no one could dissolve. And when, after some time had passed, Fr. Leonid transferred from Ploschansk Hermitage to Optina Skete, Fr. Macarius yearned with his whole soul to go there. However, not a little time passed before his wish could be realized. Only in 1834 did his transfer to Optina take place. He tearfully bade farewell to Ploschansk Hermitage, under whose roof he had lived for twenty-four years, and set out on his way. Soon after his arrival at Optina Monastery he was assigned, in 1836, to be the confessor of the entire Optina brotherhood; and in 1839, after Alexander Michailovich's arrival, he was made Skete Superior.

In concluding these brief biographical sketches of the two famous Optina Elders—the predecessors of Fr. Ambrose, we will present a description of their outward appearance. Fr. Leonid was naturally gifted with a powerful build and with unusual strength: he could lift up to twelve poods [about 420 pounds]. His face was swarthy and round, shaded by thick, long hair; in his old age this became a real yellow-gray, wavy lion's mane and reached far below his shoulders. His gray eyes were not large and looked straight ahead, penetratingly; his height was above average; his gait was very graceful—manly but light.

Fr. Macarius from his youth was weak and had a sickly build. With time he became somewhat stronger, but in old age he suffered from shortness of breath. He was of medium height, and at the time of his stay in Optina he was already completely gray. In his cell he wore a white canvas or sailcloth peasant tunic, having on his head a black, knitted cap; for the prayer rule in his cell he used a short mantia; for letter writing and reading he wore glasses with old-fashioned steel frames. When leaving his cell, he wore in summer an old, black cotton ryassa and peasant shoes; in winter he walked about in a threadbare coat, covered with green "drape-de-dame," with a crutch in one hand and a prayer rope in the other. His face at first glance was neither striking nor handsome, but even somewhat irregular (due to a defect of the eyes). He gave the impression of constant immersion within himself, and therefore his appearance was more severe than kind. But such is the power of grace that this face, serving as a mirror of a pure, loving soul, shone with a kind of unearthly beauty, reflecting the characteristics of the inner man.

From this essay on the spiritual movement in Russian monasticism at the end of the eighteenth and the beginning of the nineteenth centuries, the reader can clearly imagine the spiritual atmosphere that must have enveloped Alexander Michailovich at his arrival at Optina. It becomes understandable why Fr. Hilarion of Troekurovo directed him to no other place, but to precisely this Monastery: "Go to Optina and you will gain experience." Precisely here were all the necessary conditions for the comprehensive spiritual perfecting of the young ascetic.

Abbot Moses, the solicitous preserver of true monastic precepts, governed the Monastery, being full of both spiritual and practical wisdom. His co-workers in the task of the spiritual guidance of the brothers and pilgrims were such pillars of spirit as Frs. Leonid and Macarius. At that same time many others were living in the Monastery—not as brilliant, but still quite prominent lamps of faith and piety. These were: Hieromonk Anthony (the brother of Fr. Moses) who, soon after the arrival of Alexander Michailovich, was transferred to be Superior of the Maloyaroslavets Monastery; Archimandrite Melchizedek, who had seen St. Tikhon of Zadonsk with his own eyes and had been deemed worthy of his instruction; the Valaam Abbot Barlaam, a hermit and man of prayer who possessed the gift of tears;

Hieroschemamonk John, who had converted from the Schism [of the Old-Believers] and who had himself written several books concerning it; Hieroschemamonk Job, a great lover of stillness and the confessor of Fr. Macarius; and others.

Under the influence of all these Elders, the monks acquired a special kind of bright, compunctionate, inspired frame of mind, which shone with true Christian spiritual enlightenment, as they constantly cleansed their conscience with pure-hearted confession of their thoughts to the Elders.

Into such a grace-filled environment, as if into a cozy spiritual cradle, the Providence of God placed His newly chosen one, Alexander Michailovich, thirsting for spiritual growth and education.

Here there lay ahead for him, under the able guidance of the Optina Elders, the unfoldment of his rich spiritual gifts, the reception of the wisdom of the science of spiritual life, his development into a great spiritual instructor, and his radiance as a brilliant star over the horizon not only of Optina but of the whole of believing Orthodox Russia and even the whole Orthodox East.

Observing this marvelous operation of the Providence of God in the destiny of Russian monasticism, in the life of Elder Ambrose, and in the history of the spiritual enlightenment of the Russian nation, how can we not cry out: *How magnified are Thy works, O Lord! in wisdom hast Thou made them all* (Ps. 103:26).

The entrance to Optina Skete.
Winter, 1996.

# 7

# *The Spiritual Growth of Elder Ambrose*

## UNDER THE GUIDANCE OF ELDERS LEONID AND MACARIUS

> *With patience I waited patiently for the Lord, and He was attentive unto me, and He hearkened unto my supplication. And He brought me up out of the pit of misery, and from the mire of clay. And He set my feet upon a rock, and He ordered my steps aright.*
> Psalm 39:1-4
>
> *They that sow with tears shall reap with rejoicing.*
> Psalm 125:6

HAVING FINISHED our necessary digression, let us return again to our long-abandoned wanderer.

Alexander Michailovich slowly labored along the sandy, arduous Belev road towards Optina, rejoicing at his release from the bonds of the world and entreating God's blessing on the beginning of a new life.

Suddenly, the white walls, the blue domes with stars, and

the gold crosses of the Monastery appeared through the dark green of the dense pine forest. It was Sunday, October 8, 1839, and the late Liturgy was being served in Optina.

Leaving his coachman at the courtyard of the guest house, Alexander Michailovich entered the church; and at the end of the service he set off together with the other worshipers to Elder Leonid, who was then living in the Monastery. His first impression of the Elder was unpleasant.

"I arrived at the Elder's cell," he later related, "and I saw him sitting on his bed. He was fat and was joking and laughing with the people around him. I did not like this the first time."

Alexander Michailovich headed from the Elder to the Abbot, Fr. Moses. He asked him whether or not he had liked the Elder. Alexander Michailovich replied that many people had been at the Elder's, but he kept silent about not liking him.

Soon however, his attitude towards Fr. Leonid changed. On that very day, or on the following day, he chanced to see Hieroschemamonk John from the Skete walking to Fr. Leonid's. He had just been tonsured into the schema, and his countenance was bright and angelic. Alexander Michailovich liked him very much and set off after the schemamonk to see the Elder. When he entered Fr. Leonid's cell, the schemamonk bowed down before him and said: "Batiushka, I've sewn a new podrasnik for myself—do you bless me to wear it?" The Elder answered, "Is this how they do it now? First get a blessing to sew it, then to wear it. Well, now that you've already sewn it, you'd better wear it—you can't tear it up!" Having witnessed this scene, Alexander Michailovich now understood the spiritual height of Fr. Leonid and the humility of the schemamonk, and from this moment he began to love the Elder and desired to entrust his spiritual upbringing to him. He was convinced that the path revealed by the Elder would lead him to true eternal blessedness.

## THE SPIRITUAL GROWTH OF ELDER AMBROSE

He bared his soul to Fr. Leonid, disclosed to him all the conditions of his life and asked for guidance, awaiting the Elder's decision on his fate with trepidation. The Elder heard him out with attention and concern. He told him to dismiss his coachman and to remain in the Monastery. Alexander Michailovich did just that. In the courtyard, where the new guest house is now located, there was a two-story annex to the left of the gate. A small room on the second floor was assigned to Alexander Michailovich. Once he had settled into his assigned quarters, he went daily to the church services and to the Elder. He closely observed Fr. Leonid's interactions with people, listened to his instructions and, in general, studied monastery life. During his free time in his cell he occupied himself with an assignment from the Elder—the copying of a manuscript named "Salvation of Sinners."* Thus, day after day passed unnoticed. Meanwhile, the overseer of the Lipetsk Theological School learned where Alexander Michailovich was living, and he appealed to Abbot Moses, inquiring whether the instructor of the school, Alexander Grenkov, was staying with him in the Monastery. As a result of this inquiry, Alexander Michailovich, at the advice of Elders Leonid and Macarius, wrote an apologetic letter to the overseer for his self-willed departure from the school and then sent a petition to Bishop Arsenius of Tambov for permission to become a monk in Optina Monastery.

Recalling this period, the Elder later said,** "I came to Optina and thought I would continue living there for a while, not [officially] joining the Monastery, and sent a request to

---

*Translation from modern Greek. Its general contents concern the warfare with the passions. Alexander Michailovich's assignment to copy this manuscript acquainted him with the lofty science of interior spiritual life.

**This account is perhaps not entirely precise in its details, but it is interesting as the Elder's personal recollection concerning his life in the Monastery.

Bishop Arsenius of Tambov for my discharge. He inquired of Archimandrite Moses—would they accept me? The Archimandrite came up to me and asked—'Do you want to be received officially into the Monastery?' I said, 'No, I would rather keep living this way for a while.' 'You cannot do it that way,' he said. Bishop Arsenius did not want to give me a release, not knowing beforehand whether I was going to stay in the Monastery. And so they received me still dressed as a layman. I lived for a year in the monastery kitchen. Five times I changed cells. I also lived in Fr. Ignatius' cell and in the tower. The year in the kitchen I kept my mouth shut—in other words, only if they asked me something would I tell them.... At first I was Fr. Genadius' helper, and Fr. Genadius was the cook. Later he left, and they made me the cook. He came back, and they gave him to me as a helper. I saw that he looked downcast. 'What's with you, Fr. Genadius?' I asked, 'Why are you looking at me sideways?' 'I am not at peace with you,' he said. We began to wash the dishes and he said, 'Since the water is too hot, let's sit and have a talk.' We talked until the water cooled down."

Those who were there asked, "Did you go to see the Elder?" "I went there every day, first to get a blessing for the food, then to ring the bell for trapeza. At the same time I was his reader. But after a year he made me his cell attendant." "How did this happen?" they asked. "It was like this: the Elder (Fr. Leonid) called Batiushka (Fr. Macarius) and said: 'Here comes a man to take shelter with us, but I'm already weak, so I'm giving him to you, from one field to another'—like they transfer horses," Fr. Ambrose added jokingly. "He (Fr. Leonid) called me a chimera." A nun asked, "What does chimera mean, Batiushka?" "When cucumbers blossom, some flowers bear fruit, but others are just empty flowers...."

"Once," continued Batiushka, "a nun from Sevsk was there, but I don't remember who—after all, just about everybody was

The interior view of the Skete.

there at the same time—men and women, monks and lay people. The Elder took the cap off her head and put it on mine...." "But how did you become cell attendant?" they asked. "Were you happy when they made you cell attendant?" Batiushka did not answer. "You could be closer to the Elder," the questioner explained. "Yes, closer," Batiushka said. "But you still peeled potatoes and cooked?" "How could it be otherwise?" said Batiushka, taking on a dissatisfied tone: "Of course I cooked—what do you think I am? I even learned to bake bread and prosphora. I knew how to figure out if the prosphora were ready, or if they were still underdone: you poke a splinter in them—if nothing stays on it, that means they are ready; but if they're not, then the dough will always stick to the splinter."

Alexander Michailovich did not remain long in the Monastery. Transferred to the Skete, he remained there about fifty years, until his final departure to Shamordino in the summer of 1890.

It is clear that Elder Leonid singled him out from amongst the other novices and, foreseeing his own approaching death, entrusted him to the special care of Elder Macarius. According to some, he occasionally pointed openly to Alexander Michailovich as to a future "great man." Even in his jokes, by which Fr. Leonid would often cover his clairvoyance—as, for example, when he took the cap off the nun's head and put it on Alexander Michailovich's head—it is impossible not to see an indication of Elder Ambrose's future care for the building of a women's monastery.

In July of 1841, Alexander Michailovich was visited by his old friend and colleague, Paul Stepanovich Pokrovsky. He was also inclined towards monasticism and was later tonsured in Optina with the name Platon. By this time Alexander Michailovich was already tonsured into the ryassa. When he entered his friend's cell, Paul Stepanovich was astonished at his

# THE SPIRITUAL GROWTH OF ELDER AMBROSE

extreme poverty. In the holy corner was a small icon—the Tambov Mother of God, the blessing of Alexander Michailovich's parents. On the bed was some kind of worn-out, ancient sheepskin coat, which served as a bed and pillow. On the wall there hung an old ryassa and klobuk. He did not notice anything else in his cell. Recalling his friend's former life in the school, Pokrovsky could barely refrain from tears at the sight of this poverty. But Alexander Michailovich was not embarrassed by his simplicity and the meagerness of his material belongings—on the contrary, he was comforted by it, recognizing that outward poverty brings the spirit closer to God.

On October 11, 1841 Alexander Michailovich bore a painful loss—his first spiritual director, Elder Leonid, reposed.

After this event, Alexander Michailovich became completely bound in heart to Fr. Macarius. In fulfilling his duty as cell attendant, Fr. Ambrose, together with a few other individuals, helped Fr. Macarius in his extensive correspondence. According to the Elder's directions he answered certain of his letters which were of less important content, since Fr. Macarius always answered the more important ones himself. He continued as Fr. Macarius' cell attendant for almost four years.

For Alexander Michailovich, these years were a kind of higher schooling, during which he learned the science of the monastic life. He was placed in constant and close contact with Elder Macarius and given the opportunity to closely observe his life: to listen to his talks and instructions, to act as mediator between the Elder and his visitors, and to learn wisdom in dealing with people.

After he had already become an Elder, Fr. Ambrose often used such expressions in conversation: "Batiushka Macarius said this," or, "with Batiushka Macarius it was like this," or, "Batiushka Macarius in such cases would act this way."

Along with the practical schooling of being in constant

contact with Fr. Macarius, Alexander Michailovich passed through another school—of course, under the direction and guidance of Fr. Macarius—that of cell prayers and the daily reading of the Word of God, Lives of Saints and the works of the Holy Fathers, in particular the ascetic ones. He found, in the person of Fr. Macarius, an experienced interpreter for every unclear word and every expression that required explanation. If we add to this the daily attentive examination of his conscience, which was often accompanied by tears of sincere grief over his sins, and the frank revelation of his thoughts to the Elder—then we will have the cycle of spiritual activity and experiences in which the soul of Alexander Michailovich grew and gained strength.

Alexander moved forward in his spiritual growth so quickly that three years after his arrival in Optina—on November 29, 1842—he was tonsured into the mantia and received a new name: Ambrose, in honor of St. Ambrose, bishop of Milan, whose memory is commemorated on December 7. Alexander Michailovich was exactly thirty years old at this time. Two months after being tonsured, Fr. Ambrose was ordained hierodeacon.

When some people later expressed surprise at how quickly he was tonsured into the mantia, Fr. Ambrose would answer, "Not really! It would happen that some would live there for twelve years [before the tonsure], but with me it happened this way! (Saying this, he would dismiss it with a wave of his hand). A resolution would always come before the Fast from the Synod, but it got to us in October. What happened was, a friend of mine served at the Synod, and he was very interested in me but did not know where I was. But as soon as he found out, he immediately went to work on the resolution. The next year I was made hierodeacon. They appointed us for ordination: myself and another one. He and I were talking, saying that

## THE SPIRITUAL GROWTH OF ELDER AMBROSE

we would not dare accept ordination, that we were unworthy; and we went to talk about this with the Elder (Fr. Macarius). We went in. Batiushka himself began, 'Well, they have appointed you; they've appointed you, that's good!' But we had our doubts. My friend began first. He said: 'That is just what I came to talk to you about Batiushka, I am really unworthy.' 'Think like that, always think like that, that you are unworthy,' the Elder interrupted. After that I did not even dare open my mouth," he added, laughing cheerfully.

Fr. Ambrose spent almost three years as a hierodeacon. Abbot Theodosius, who entered Optina in 1844, recalled that Fr. Ambrose always served with great reverence as a hierodeacon. When he was already an Elder, Fr. Ambrose once said to a feeble hierodeacon, who was burdened by carrying out his schedule of serving: "Brother! You do not understand the matter. After all, you are communing *life!*" In these words of the Elder one can see a reflection of the feeling with which he himself, being a hierodeacon, approached Christ's Holy Mysteries. But Fr. Ambrose did not conceal from us his own weaknesses of that time. Once when he was serving a late Liturgy in the Monastery, Abbot Anthony of Maloyaroslavets, the former Skete Superior, arrived at Optina. He was well known to the young hierodeacon who was serving. "While they were reading the Hours," Fr. Ambrose later related, "he came into the altar. According to custom, I bowed to him and went to get a blessing. 'Well, are you getting used to it?' the humble Abbot said to me. 'By your holy prayers, Batiushka, glory be to God, I am getting used to things,' I answered rather boldly. Suddenly, the Abbot changed his tone: 'To humility?'—I did not even know what to say." Thus did the spiritual Elders of Optina know how to direct the young monks, regardless of place or time.

In December of 1845 Fr. Ambrose was ordained hieromonk. For the ordination he had to go to Kaluga by horse. It was bitterly cold. When he arrived at the first station, he felt a strong pain in his stomach, and this was the beginning of all his later illnesses. After his return to Optina, Fr. Ambrose felt constantly ill, but he nevertheless did not cease to serve in his turn. But after a while he became so weak that, as he himself recalled, he could not hold the chalice in one hand for a long time. "Once, there were many communicants," he recollected; "I was serving the Most Pure Mysteries with one hand, and holding the chalice with the other. And suddenly I felt that my hand was becoming weak and growing numb. I went into the altar to put the chalice on the Holy Table so I could rest my hand for a little while; behind me, I heard the voice of a woman who was just approaching the Chalice: 'That means I, a sinner, am unworthy.' Ach, my God, I thought, I am crowded in from all sides!"

In the beginning of September 1846, Fr. Ambrose again left Optina and travelled eleven miles along the Belev road to meet Archbishop Iliodore of Kursk, whom he was to invite to visit the Monastery. Then on September 17 he fell so seriously ill and reached such a state of utter exhaustion that on October 26, during Matins, he was given Unction and Communion of the Holy Mysteries of Christ. At this time he was tonsured into the schema in his cell, retaining the name of Ambrose. This serious illness lasted for more than a year and had a very great significance for the inner spiritual life of Fr. Ambrose. Feeling extreme weakness and having lost hope in the recovery of his health, Fr. Ambrose handed in a request in December of 1847 that he be allowed to remain in the Monastery in retirement. Dr. Subotin of Kozelsk who, by assignment of the Theological Consistory looked after his health, gave this diagnosis about his illness: "Hieromonk Ambrose has a sickly yellow color to his face, with glassy eyes and a generally thin body. He is tall, with a narrow chest, and has a strong, mostly dry cough with pain in his chest under his rib cage, primarily on the right side; he has pain under his solar plexus and in the region of his stomach. He has constant indigestion, persistent constipation and frequent vomiting—not only of mucus and bile, but also of the food he has eaten. He has insomnia and, finally, occasional chills toward evening, which give way to a mild fever. These attacks denote a slow, debilitating fever, which is the result of the hardening of the abdominal organs, primarily the stomach."

On the basis of the district doctor's diagnosis, the Kaluga diocesan authorities considered Hieromonk Ambrose to be incapable of any monastery obediences and resolved to exclude him, as disabled, from the register of the brothers of Optina, leaving him to be fed and cared for by the Monastery. Fr. Ambrose was only thirty-six years old at this time.

Thus, despite the fact that Fr. Ambrose was so young according to normal human reasoning, his earthly activity appeared to have come to an end. Shattered by grievous illness and considered to be incapable of any useful work, he should have lived out his days as an invalid, in dependence on his monastery. But obviously, our thoughts are not God's thoughts, and our ways are not God's ways. That which according to human reasoning appears to be the end of life and activity was perhaps actually the beginning, origin and foundation of a new, true, exalted life. In this Fr. Ambrose fulfilled the words of our Lord: *Verily, verily, I say unto you, except a grain of wheat fall into the ground and die, it abideth alone: but if it die, it bringeth forth much fruit* (John 12:24).

This severe and prolonged illness was in reality only a new action of God's Providence, which had so clearly revealed itself in Fr. Ambrose's life. The similar serious illness which he endured in his seminary years had compelled him to consider monasticism seriously for the first time. God's Providence had brought him to Elder Hilarion of Troekurovo, aroused in him the desire to visit the holy relics of St. Sergius, directed his path to Optina, and left him here under the spiritual guidance of the great luminaries of true monasticism, Fathers Leonid and Macarius. And when the seed of the spiritual life sown by these Elders fell deeply into the soul of Fr. Ambrose, God's Providence found it necessary, as it were, to separate him from every kind of social activity, bind him to his sick bed, remove all external impressions from him, and stand him face to face with his sufferings and with God.... Why? So that the seed of new life which he had received into his soul would open, become refined, and enter, so to speak, into his flesh and blood, and would leave sprouts and roots there, becoming the living inheritance of his whole moral being.

This process of the reception of divine life demands from man above all a recognition of his powerlessness, his helplessness and his nothingness, and complete hope in God's mercy alone. The Savior says, *If any man will come after me, let him deny himself, and take up his cross, and follow me* (Matt. 16:24). To draw near to Christ, Who experienced all the bitterness of the sufferings of the Cross, is possible only through the path of suffering. A man who has not drunk this bitter cup can never grasp the true depth of Christianity and can never know how to understand and relieve the sufferings of others.

It was necessary for Fr. Ambrose, the future healer of ailing human souls, to pass through the crucible of sickness and sufferings himself, so that, being tempted himself, he could help those who were tempted—for according to the tradition of eldership, the untempted man is untested. One must add that had he been healthy, Fr. Ambrose—an educated, intelligent, active man—would have been threatened by the danger of following the normal path of monastic service, i.e. to occupy one or another of the outward monastic positions, thus gradually ascending the ladder. But this might have hindered him from developing as an elder to the fullest measure.... His grave illness and exclusion from the monastery roster blocked off the path of external advancement for him and completely directed his life to the path of interior spiritual development. Who could not perceive in this the wise and loving action of Divine Providence?!

It is clear that after his severe illness Fr. Ambrose was truly prepared for the service of eldership, since at this time Fr. Macarius began to direct many to him for spiritual guidance, despite his relative youth.

After spending almost 1½ years on his sickbed, Fr. Ambrose began to recover, to the surprise of all. In the summer of 1848 he went outdoors for the first time. "I remember," he recounted, "I went out of my cell for the first time on a clear, quiet, summer day and wandered, leaning on a staff, barely moving my feet, along the path behind the fish pond. (This very secluded path inside the Skete, runs along the eastern wall.) The first person who met me was Abbot Barlaam (the former Superior of Valaam). 'Well, are you better?' he asked. I answered, 'Yes, glory to the merciful God; I have been left here to repent.' The Abbot stopped and, gazing at me, humbly said: 'And what do you think, will you get better? No, you won't get better: you will get much, much worse....'" Recalling these words, Fr. Ambrose repeated: "Now I can see myself that I have gotten worse."

After his illness, Fr. Ambrose never fully recovered his health. For the rest of his life his ailments never left him. Either the inflammation of the stomach and intestines which made him vomit would grow stronger, or he would feel neural pain, or he would come down with a cold and feverish chills. He also began to suffer from vascular inflammation, which subsequently debilitated him so much that he lay in bed like a corpse.

Abbot Barlaam, of Valaam Monastery,
before his retirement to Optina.

Fr. Ambrose always reacted with extreme good-nature towards all these ailments despite the agony they caused him, recognizing that they were sent by God. In one of his letters he defined the significance of illnesses for a monk: "The Lord is merciful! In a monastery sick people do not die quickly, but drag on and on until the illness brings them real benefit. In a monastery it is helpful to be a little sick, especially for the young; the flesh becomes less rebellious, and less nonsense enters one's head. But when one is in full health, particularly if he is young, how much frivolity will enter his head...."

After Fr. Ambrose's deliverance from his life-threatening illness, he could no longer lead church services due to his weak health. But he continued to go to the temple of God, where he communed the Most Pure Mysteries of Christ—probably once

# THE SPIRITUAL GROWTH OF ELDER AMBROSE

a month, as is customary for schemamonks and as his Elder, Fr. Macarius, had done. As a result of his sickness, Fr. Ambrose wore a flannel shirt and wool socks both summer and winter, and he often had to change them, due to perspiration. His cell rule was read for him daily by a brother who was assigned to this obedience and who lived in a separate cell adjacent to his.

Even before his illness, Fr. Ambrose had been freed from his duty as Elder Macarius' cell attendant and was settled in a building located on the north side of the Skete church. Here his sickness caught him unawares, and here he remained to live after his recovery. Even then the conditions of his life were extremely simple. In the front corner there were a few icons. Near the door hung his ryassa, podrasnik and mantia. Next was a bed stuffed with straw with a linen covering on it, a straw mattress and the same kind of pillow. These were all of the furnishings in his cell.

One of the novices who was assigned to Fr. Ambrose also noticed that he had a wicker basket under his cot, which probably served him as a dresser or a chest, in which he kept his wool socks and flannel shirts (for which he now had extreme need). He asked: "What's this wicker basket for, Batiushka?" Wishing to conceal from him his extreme non-acquisitiveness, the humble Fr. Ambrose answered him in a joking tone: "I want a goose to sit on eggs in there." After such an answer both guest and host only laughed.

As before, Fr. Ambrose observed strict abstinence in the use of food. Despite his stomach ailment he continued, from time to time, to eat food from the trapeza. It must be noted that although the food cooked in the Optina Skete was rather tasty, the food year-round (excluding the six fast-free weeks) was prepared with vegetable oil, as we have already stated, and during the Fasts and on days prescribed by the holy Church, entirely without oil. Even for people with healthy stomachs there was sometimes a noticeable insufficiency of nourishment, and more so for Fr. Ambrose with his damaged, ailing stomach. However, he did not cease, when he had the chance, to go to trapeza with the brothers.

After his recovery, Fr. Ambrose continued to help his Elder, Fr. Macarius, with his correspondence. Along with this, he duly participated in yet another matter which had been undertaken by Fr. Macarius—the review and prepararation for printing of Fr. Paisius Velichkovsky's translations of the ascetical works of the Holy Fathers, which up to then were still not published in full.

By the special arrangement of God's Providence, the most faithful copies of the literary works of Elder Paisius were then located in Optina. Among them were several manuscripts which had belonged to Elder Paisius himself, which were copied with his blessing from the rough drafts in his notebooks by his closest disciples and corrected and signed by his own hand. Such, for example, was the manuscript of the Homilies of the great teacher of interior life, St. Isaac the Syrian.* In addition to

---

*The fate of this manuscript is particularly remarkable. It had been sent by Elder Paisius to Metropolitan Gabriel of St. Petersburg with an inscription in his own hand. It was written in semi-uncial script on sheets of white glossy paper. More than half was by the hand of the Elder's close disciple, Schemamonk Theodore, and it was finished by the latter's disciple, Schemamonk Nicholas. After the Metropolitan's repose, this manuscript passed, in some unknown way, into private hands and was brought for sale by a profiteer to Valaam Monastery, where it was obtained by Schemamonk Theodore, then living at Valaam, who greatly rejoiced over the lost and newly recovered treasure. After the blessed repose of Fr. Theodore, it passed into the possession of his beloved disciple and lifetime companion, Hieroschemamonk Leonid. During his life he gave it as a gift to his disciple, Schemamonk Antiochus; after his repose, it passed to another disciple of Fr. Leonid, Fr. Ioanicius, who was then living in the St. Alexander Nevsky Lavra. He gave it as a gift to Fr. Leonid's spiritual daughter E.T.L., from

## THE SPIRITUAL GROWTH OF ELDER AMBROSE

this manuscript, Elder Macarius' cell library also contained faithful copies of the following books to be used for their publications: 1) Ancient Slavonic translations of the writings of St. Macarius the Great, St. John Climacus, and Sts. Barsanuphius and John, with corrections by Elder Paisius; 2) St. Maximus the Confessor's homily consisting of questions and answers, [the writings of] St. Theodore the Studite (from modern Greek), the Life of St. Gregory of Sinai, a Homily of St. Gregory Palamas, and a few other ascetical works of the Holy Fathers translated by St. Paisius himself. The Elder himself benefitted from all these treasures and shared them with all who were thirsting for spiritual edification and salvation. He did not dare, by his own admission, to think about publishing them, being satisfied and giving thanks to God that He had vouchsafed him to have such treasures.

Meanwhile, developments made it possible to publish these precious manuscripts.

Not far from the city of Belev, which is about eighteen miles from Optina, is the village of Dolbino, the old estate of the Kireyevsky family. In 1805 the Dolbino landowner Basil Ivanovich Kireyevsky married the niece of V. A. Zhukovsky, Evdokia Petrovna Yushkova. From this marriage, on March 22, 1806, Ivan Vasilievich Kireyevsky was born in Moscow. He was later known as a man of letters and was a founder of the so-called Slavophile movement or, to put it simply, a Russian, popular, Orthodox trend of thought within educated society. He grew up within a circle of highly educated people and,

---

whom the book passed in 1849 to Hieromonk Ephraim who, in turn, gave it to his spiritual son, the monk Abramius. The latter, when he left for Mt. Athos in 1858, brought this manuscript as a present to Hieroschemamonk Macarius, who gave it as a blessing before his repose to Hieromonk Leonid (Kavelin), who was subsequently the Superior of the Holy Trinity-St. Sergius Lavra.

thanks to his virtuous heart, Ivan Vasilievich picked up their best traits. During his early childhood, V. A. Zhukovsky made an indelible impression on him. Under the guidance of his mother and stepfather, the highly educated A. A. Elagin, Ivan Vasilievich learned mathematics, French and German, and read a multitude of library books gathered by his father on literature and the history of philosophy. In Moscow he took lessons from the professors of the University: Merzlyakov, Snegirev and others, and listened to public lectures about nature by Professor M. G. Pavlov, a follower of the German philosopher, Schelling. At the same time he studied English, Latin and Greek. After the completion of his studies, Ivan Vasilievich joined the civil service in Moscow, where a group of serious youths who thirsted for enlightenment soon formed around him. A. I. Koshelev, the Venevitinov brothers, Sobolevsky, Shevirev and others entered into this group. They were later joined by M. P. Pogodin, M. A. Maximovich, the poet Baratinsky, and Alexei S. Khomiakov. Being in such an environment, Kireyevsky devoted himself at the beginning to the study of political economics, but from the year 1824 he became entirely engrossed in German philosophy.

In 1829 Ivan Vasilievich Kireyevsky appeared for the first time in the field of literature with an article about Pushkin, which revealed a remarkably clear understanding of the works of this poet. In this article he already expressed doubt in the absolute truth of German philosophy and pointed out the pressing need for the development of a school of original Russian scientific thought. "German philosophy can not take root in us. Our philosophy must be developed from our life, and must arise from current questions, from the prevailing interest of *our* people and their individual ways of life." But at the same time we must not reject the experience of Western European thought. "The crown of European enlightenment served as the cradle for our education. It was born when the other states had already completed the cycle of their intellectual development; and where they finished, there we began. Like a young sister in a large harmonious family, Russia was enriched by the experience of her older brothers and sisters prior to her entry into the world."

In 1834 Ivan Vasilievich married Natalia Petrovna Arbeneva, a deeply believing young Orthodox woman, whose spiritual father was Elder Philaret of the Moscow Novospassky Monastery, one of the disciples of Elder Paisius. Natalia Petrovna introduced her spiritual father to her husband, Ivan Vasilievich, who also became his spiritual son. Under the influence of Fr. Philaret, Ivan Vasilievich began to delve more closely and deeply into Orthodoxy, studying it in the works of the Fathers and teachers of the Church.

After his marriage, Ivan Vasilievich spent the winter in Moscow, but in the summer he left for his estate in Dolbino which, as we have said, is not far from Optina.

Living on the estate, he and his wife visited Optina and its Elders and then became acquainted with Fr. Macarius, who became the spiritual father of both Kireyevskys after the death of Fr. Philaret in 1842. At their request he often visited Dolbino, where a cell was built for him in the orchard by his thoughtful hosts and friends.*

In 1845 I. V. Kireyevsky published the journal *The Muscovite* and suggested to Fr. Macarius that he publish an article of spiritual content in this journal. The Elder accepted this suggestion with gratitude and answered that if it would be possible and convenient, he wished to submit the biography of Elder Paisius. Since Ivan Vasilievich shared Fr. Macarius's opinion about the services rendered by the Blessed Elder Paisius to all

---

*V. Lyaskovsky, *The Kireyevsky Brothers—Their Life and Works*, p. 48.

Orthodox monastics and to Slavonic literature in general (by confirming its use of ascetical terminology), he agreed with pleasure to the proposal to enhance the pages of the journal with this article. It was published in the twelfth issue of *The Muscovite* for 1845 and was adorned with a portrait of Elder Paisius. Thus began the printed presentation of the spiritual treasures of Optina.

In the following year, 1846, while the Elder was visiting the Kireyevskys at their estate, he touched upon the question of the lack of spiritual books which guide one towards the active Christian life. He mentioned that he had a fair number of manuscripts of Elder Paisius' translations of the works of the ascetic Holy Fathers, filled with spiritual understanding and power. It turned out that Natalia Petrovna Kireyevsky had preserved a few similar manuscripts as well, having received them as an inheritance from her former spiritual father, Elder Philaret of Novospassky. Then she herself raised the question—why not reveal these spiritual treasures to the world? The Elder, with his characteristic humility, remarked that he considered himself incapable of taking on such an important matter, that he had never done anything like this, that this was clearly not the will of God, etc. The Kireyevskys said that they would give a report about the matter to Metropolitan Philaret of Moscow and, if he blessed it, it would be necessary to begin printing the manuscripts. Then the Kireyevskys began to implore Fr. Macarius to immediately write an introduction to the planned publication.

Having prayed to God, the Elder wrote the first page. On that very day the Kireyevskys sent a letter to Moscow, to the professor of Moscow University, S. P. Shevirev, asking him, in their own name, to obtain a blessing from the Metropolitan for the publication of the manuscripts of Elder Paisius. The Metropolitan was so kind that, not only did he give his blessing to this project, he even promised to provide them with his own personal support.

In Optina, work got underway. The manuscripts were copied in final form and sent off to the censor, the Professor of the Moscow Theological Academy, Protopresbyter T. A. Golubinsky. Before the arrival of the Kireyevskys in Moscow in September of 1846, eight pages of *The Life and Writings of Elder Paisius* were printed by S. P. Shevirev, and in the beginning of 1847 the entire book was published under the following title: *The Life and Writings of the Moldavian Elder Paisius Velichkovsky* (with a portrait of the Elder).

Such was the beginning of this holy activity, which continued for fifteen years until Fr. Macarius' repose, with the ardent assistance of the Kireyevskys and under the lofty patronage of Metropolitan Philaret of Moscow. In becoming familiar with Elder Paisius' translations of the works of the Holy Fathers, these works made a profound impression on the thought process of Ivan Vasilievich Kireyevsky and led him to a final clarification of the spirit of true Orthodox Christian enlightenment, in contrast to Western European enlightenment. This was revealed by him in detail in his later philosophical works.

His soul always strove zealously toward the knowledge of truth, and he finally attained to a profound moral satisfaction and tranquility. United by strong bonds of love and gratitude to Optina and its Elders, he even willed to be buried within the walls of the Monastery, where his grave—along with the graves of his brother, Peter Vasilievich, and his wife, Natalia Petrovna—is situated at the feet of the graves of Elders Leonid and Macarius.

All work was directly guided by the Elder himself—both the preparation for the printing of the Slavonic translations of Elder Paisius (with explanatory footnotes of the unclear words and expressions) and the translation of some of these into the

Elder Macarius.

## THE SPIRITUAL GROWTH OF ELDER AMBROSE

Russian language. He was helped by his disciples from the Skete brotherhood: Hieromonk Ambrose, Monk Juvenal (Polovtsev),* Fr. Leonid (Kavelin)** and Fr. Platon (Pokrovsky).***

For their work, the aforementioned people gathered daily in Elder Macarius' reception cell. Though he did not cease his usual work with the brothers and guests, visiting them at a set time at the guest house, he nevertheless played the most active part in the labors of these disciples. One may positively state that not one expression, not one word was written in a manuscript that was sent to the censor without his personal approval. His activity in this connection was truly amazing—the Elder, naturally gifted with a lively, energetic character, truly oblivious of himself in his work, often sacrificed even the brief rest which was obviously necessary for his weary and worn out body. Although no one participating in these labors was lacking in zeal, it must be admitted that if anyone felt occasional exhaustion from the strenuous work it was by no means the Elder—he was tireless! Nevertheless, how generously he rewarded his co-laborers! Who, being attentive to himself, would not have given a few years of his life to hear what their ears heard—the Elder's explanations of passages in the writings of the Fathers, about which none of his disciples would have dared to ask him had it not been for the work they were engaged in. And had they dared, they would have undoubtedly received the humble answer: "I don't know about this, it's beyond my abilities; perhaps you've attained to it, but I know only: 'Grant me, O Lord, to see my sins! Cleanse my heart,' then you'll understand it!"

Who of his co-workers could forget how condescendingly the Elder heard out their childish remarks and made conces-

---

*Later Archbishop of Lithuania and Vilnius.
** Later the Superior of the Holy Trinity-St. Sergius Lavra.
*** The confessor of Elder Ambrose and of the pilgrims to Optina.

sions, in the hope of expressing a thought more gracefully or clearly, as long as he did not see a violation of the spiritual meaning. He would accompany his concessions with a good-natured joke: "Let it be that way—I'm not familiar with the latest literature; but after all, you're learned people!" If a disagreement arose in understanding, the Elder immediately eliminated it, or offered his own opinion, or left such a spot completely without explanation, saying: "This is beyond us—whoever does this will understand it; but what if we put our own rotten opinion in place of his (i.e., Elder Paisius') lofty spiritual understanding?"

Thanks to such constant joint labors, the second edition of the life and writings of Blessed Paisius was printed in 1847; at the end of 1848 *Four Catechetical Homilies to Nuns* by Nicephorus Theotokis was published, with a second edition in 1849. In that same year there was a separate printing of the writings of Elder Paisius on mental prayer and the *Commentary on the Prayer, Lord Have Mercy*. In addition to these, the following book was also printed in 1849: *The Written Tradition Concerning Skete Life of Our Holy Father Nilus of Sora*, with footnotes; and a collection from the writings of the Fathers entitled *Selected Ears of Grain as Food for the Soul*, translated by Elder Paisius Velichkovsky, with explanatory footnotes for the difficult passages.

In the year 1852 the book of Sts. Barsanuphius and John, *Guidance Towards Spiritual Life—Answers to the Questions of Disciples* was printed. This was an ancient Slavonic translation corrected by Elder Paisius, newly compared with the Greek original, published in Slavonic in Russian type, and provided with footnotes for the clarification of obscure passages in the text. It contained a special alphabetical index and was adorned with a lithographic picture of Sts. Barsanuphius and John.

On October 21, 1852 they began to work at compiling

explanatory footnotes for Elder Paisius' Slavonic translation of the book of St. Isaac the Syrian and compared it with the Greek text. On November 29 this labor was completed, the book recopied with the footnotes, and the manuscript sent to the censor. That year they also began the translation of the book of Sts. Barsanuphius and John into the Russian language, which was finished in April of the following year.

During the beginning of that year Elder Paisius' Slavonic translation of the *Catechetical Homilies* of St. Theodore the Studite was published; and at the end of the year the Commentary on the prayer "Our Father," by our holy Father Maximus the Confessor, and his homily on fasting, consisting of questions and answers, was printed.

In March of 1854 the most precious of all of Optina's publications was printed—the *Ascetical Homilies* of St. Isaac the Syrian, Bishop of Nineveh, translated from the Greek by Elder Paisius Velichkovsky. The book was printed in Slavonic in Russian type, and furnished with explanatory footnotes and an alphabetical index at the end of the book, on which Elder Macarius worked diligently. The first printed copy of this book was sent by the publishers to the Monastery on Pascha, April 13, and was received by the Elder as the most precious gift of that great day. However, not only Elder Macarius, but all lovers of spiritual literature were extremely pleased by the printing of this remarkable book.*

In 1855 the Russian translation of the book of Sts. Barsanuphius and John was printed; and in that same year the

---

*There was a time when zealots of monastic life and Christian love of wisdom would pay a sum of one hundred or more rubles for a manuscript copy of this book, but it was difficult to obtain—even more so since the Paisian translation of this book, published in Niamts Monastery in 1812, would only find its way to Russia accidently, owing to the prohibition against importing books printed in Slavonic regardless of their content.

chapters of our holy father Abba Thalassius on love, abstinence and spiritual life were translated from the Slavonic translation of Elder Paisius into Russian. Both the Russian and Slavonic texts were printed in Russian type. In 1856 the teachings and epistles of spiritual edification of our holy father Abba Dorotheos, with the addition of his questions and the answers given to them by Elders Barsanuphius the Great and John, were published in a Russian translation.

In that same year the life of our holy father Symeon the New Theologian was printed in Slavonic. In 1858 the moral-ascetical homilies of our holy and God-bearing father Mark the Ascetic were printed in a Russian translation. In 1859 a translation from Latin by Clement K. Sederholm of the book of the teaching of our holy father Abba Orsisius of Tabennisi on the order of monastic life was printed. Finally, in 1860, the Russian translation of the spiritual-moral homilies of our holy father Abba Isaiah the Solitary of Egypt was published.

Under the guidance of Fr. Macarius, the semi-Slavonic translation of *The Ladder* of St. John Climacus was compiled, on which Fr. Ambrose labored exclusively. The foundation of this work was the translation of Elder Paisius, a man filled with spiritual understanding and who passed, by way of experience, through the spiritual counsels of this Holy Father, which are incomprehensible through book learning alone. In addition, they began attentively to study and compare among themselves other known printings and translations of *The Ladder*—for example, the translation of the former missionary to the Altai, Archimandrite Macarius, as well as the original Greek text of the book. In so doing, they had the intention of making a translation which would facilitate, as much as possible, the fulfillment of the spiritual instructions contained in this book. And that is how it turned out—the translation of *The Ladder* by Fr. Ambrose, even up to this time, has no equal in terms of

## THE SPIRITUAL GROWTH OF ELDER AMBROSE

clarity, accuracy and a vital, easily applicable presentation of the moral truths that are contained in it.

Fr. Macarius himself compiled an alphabetical index of the subjects mentioned in the book for Fr. Ambrose's translation and copied it in his own hand. Subsequently, a Russian translation was made from this semi-Slavonic translation of *The Ladder* by Hieromonk Juvenal (Polovtsev). *The Ladder* was not among Optina's own publications, but was sent to be published by the Holy Synod.

His participation in fifteen years of the literary labors of Fr. Macarius, combined with constant, attentive reading and re-reading of the works of the ascetical Holy Fathers under the guidance of the wise Elder, made for the complete spiritual preparation of Fr. Ambrose for the independent podvig of eldership, into which he entered at the death of Fr. Macarius, which occurred September 7, 1860.

And thus, here are the steps by which the spiritual ascent of Fr. Ambrose was accomplished in Optina: his two years under the guidance of Fr. Leonid; a prolonged time as Fr. Macarius' cell attendant, as well as the trial of a long and agonizing illness; participation in the translation of the works of the Holy Fathers; long years of observation of the activity of the eldership of Fr. Macarius and assisting him in his spiritual labors; and, finally, the continual personal podvig of prayer and constant heedfulness to himself. By these steps—slowly, but noticeably to others—Fr. Ambrose ascended to his future service: independent eldership.

Elder Ambrose at the beginning of his ministry as the Monastery's principal elder.

# 8

# *The Eldership of Hieroschemamonk Ambrose*

> *Besides those things that are without, that which cometh upon me daily, the care of all the churches. Who is weak, and I am not weak? who is offended, and I burn not? If I must needs glory, I will glory of the things which concern mine infirmities.*
>
> II Corinthians 11:28-30
>
> *My little children, of whom I travail in birth again until Christ be formed in you....*
>
> Galatians 4:19

## 1. EARLY YEARS OF ELDERSHIP

FATHER AMBROSE had already begun to function as an elder while Fr. Macarius was still alive; of course his eldership proceeded under Fr. Macarius' blessing and guidance. Here we consider it necessary to differentiate the part of an elder from that of a father-confessor or simple priest. A father-confessor hears the confessions of a penitent Christian and absolves his sins according to the authority given to pastors of the Church by the Lord Jesus Christ. Eldership is not bound up with the

Sacrament of Confession, rather it consists in revealing the condition of one's soul to another more experienced in spiritual life, and the receiving of profitable counsel and guidance not at all connected to the remission of his sins. The father-confessor may only be a priest, while an elder may even be a layman of no priestly rank. A woman can also be an eldress. Of course, eldership can be a part of the father-confessor's part, but it is not essential.

In monasteries, father-confessors are appointed by the higher authorities from among those individuals who have earned such an appointment by their experience, and, finally, by their age. Elders are not appointed. The choice of an elder is a voluntary matter. The elder is such unofficially. There have been sad instances where those whom the brothers of a monastery as well as the lay pilgrims all unanimously accepted as elders were not accepted by the monastery leadership or by the diocesan authorities, and these authorities subjected the elders to persecutions. Thus it was with Elders Theodore and Leonid on Valaam, Elder Leonid in Optina, and Eldress Anthia in the Belev Convent.

Not long before Elder Leonid's death, in one of his letters to nuns he spoke of the difference between eldership and the role of a father-confessor, and of the path of "eldership" in general. "Is it possible that the numerous experiences cited in the teachings of the Divine Scriptures and Holy and God-bearing Fathers," wrote the Elder, "could not convince you of the truly salvific path on which the Holy Fathers travelled, which Fathers we diligently strive to emulate according to the measure of our strength? Although we are unworthy and barren of virtue, we still desire that you who wish to be saved would tread the path they have shown to you. Therefore we are not a little disturbed at your faintheartedness.... Having observed the albeit subtle action of the enemy of mankind, we see how he diligently strives, under the guise of truth, to turn you away from the chosen path of virtue. We ask you: is it possible for one who does not know a certain foreign language to teach that language to another? There is a great difference between one who knows from experience and one who knows only from hearsay. Let him who is called to a certain station abide in that station (cf. I Cor. 7:20). Experience is the best teacher. It is written: *Be in peace with many: nevertheless have but one counsellor of a thousand* (Sirach 6:6). But if you doubt our advice and counsel, then why do you run to us? We do not try to draw anyone to ourselves—you know that. In accordance with the rules of monastic tradition, a nun at tonsure is entrusted to an eldress at the reading of the Gospel and not to a priest. The newly tonsured one is to reveal her conscience to the eldress and receive advice and instruction as to how to withstand the enemy's temptations. However, this is *not a confession*, but a revelation; in this is fulfilled the apostolic tradition: *Confess your faults one to another* (James 5:16). The Sacrament of Confession is entirely another matter and has no relationship to revelation [of thoughts]; the father-confessor's duties are completely different from those of an eldress....

"As for the notion that it is not possible to pray in your cell without a priest—it is worthy more of amazement than belief. How many holy women do we know of who abided in deserts and shone in fasting? What were they occupied with if not prayer in solitude? St. Mary of Egypt brought forth her prayer in the desert without a priest, and only in the last year of her life was she vouchsafed to behold St. Zosima and receive from him the Holy Mysteries of Christ. As for not doing anything without the eldress' blessing, this is not only beneficial but also salvific. Of the many examples taken from the Patericon and the writings of the Holy Fathers, we recall the story of the disciple who, having been sent on an obedience by the elder to the city, nearly fell into adultery. But remembering the elder, he was carried away by an unseen power and found himself in his cell. All of this concerning elders would also apply in a convent to eldresses. Not all elders were priests. This is apparent in the Life of St. Paphnutius the Wonderworker of Borov (commemorated May 1); in his monastery of seven-hundred brothers there was not one priest, but all were subject to guidance by elders. Thus, it is better to conform with the rules of monastic life and be at peace. In *The Philokalia*, in the epistle of St. Cassian to Abbot Leontius there is written: 'Abba Moses said, "... True discrimination comes to us only as a result of true humility, and this in turn is shown by our revealing to our spiritual fathers not only what we do but also what we think, by never trusting our own thoughts, and by following in all things the words of our elders, regarding as good what they have judged to be so. In this way not only does the monk remain unharmed through true discrimination and by following the correct path, but he is also kept safe from all the snares of the devil."'*

An elder advances by his experience in spiritual life, or by the power of God's grace which is active in him. This experience, this power of grace, is felt by believers. The elder's every word, his counsel, his instructions, are accompanied by obvious good results. At times the elder's words betray obvious clairvoyance; at times they are endowed with the gift of miracle-working—all of this attracts people to him. And no obstacles, no bans or threats can stop this flow of people to the one from whom they receive obvious spiritual benefit, the one who makes their souls experience new, heretofore unknown feelings of moral renewal and living faith in God.

---

*St. John Cassian, "On the Holy Fathers of Sketis and on Discrimination," in *The Philokalia*, Vol. I (London: Faber and Faber, 1979), p. 103.

## ELDERSHIP

Such an elder was Fr. Ambrose, who had been prepared as heir to this great service by Elders Leonid and Macarius.

Fr. Ambrose was not the designated father-confessor of the Monastery; the father-confessors during his time were Fr. Paphnutius, Fr. Hilarion and Fr. Anatole. He was only an elder, although, possessing the priestly rank, he also received people for confession. It is generally considered that Fr. Ambrose was first directed to begin eldership in 1846, but that opinion begs contradiction. It is true that in the skete chronicles for the year 1846 it is written that on August 23 of that year Bishop Nicholas of Kaluga visited the Skete, attended Vigil there and, as he was departing, stopped near the skete gates, surrounded by the brethren. Addressing them, he said: "Save yourselves, fathers and brothers. Have peace and love amongst yourselves. Submit to your leaders." Then, turning to Fr. Ambrose who stood amongst them, he added: "And you, Ambrose, help Fr. Macarius in his duties as father-confessor. He is getting old. This is also a science—not one you learn in the seminary, but a monastic one." It is clear from these words spoken, as it may be supposed at the request of Abbot Moses and Fr. Macarius, that Fr. Ambrose, who was at the time only thirty-four years old, was already prominent for his vast spiritual experience. However, these words should not be construed as a blessing for eldership, but rather a request that Fr. Ambrose help Fr. Macarius fulfill his duties as the father-confessor to the brethren. As we know, an elder and a father-confessor are two different things. Yet, if we allow that Bishop Nicholas used the word "father-confessor" not in the denotative sense, but in the sense of spiritual guidance, then those who attach the inception of Fr. Ambrose's eldership to this incident may be correct. Just the same, there is more likelihood in the opinion that Fr. Ambrose began his eldership only in 1848, that is, after he endured his serious illness. From that particular year began distinct and precise witness of his eldership. Thus Hieromonk Gerontius told how he joined the Monastery in 1848, and Fr. Macarius immediately blessed him to relate to Fr. Ambrose as to an elder, for spiritual counsel. Fr. Gerontius also related about the nature of Fr. Ambrose's eldership during these first years. "I would come to him and tell him what I needed, and he would open a book and have me read a passage that answered my perplexity. At that time I had conceived a zeal for lofty spiritual ascetic feats, but Fr. Ambrose made me understand that my zeal was not according to knowledge and had me read St. Isaac the Syrian in *The Philokalia*. Incidentally, I shall note that during that five-year period beginning with the year 1848, only a few of the monastery and skete brothers went to Fr. Ambrose for advice, and those only at the blessing of Elder Macarius."

Another monk, Schemamonk Gennadius, similarly told how he often went to see Fr. Ambrose to seek advice on some matter. He recalled that brothers from the Monastery and the Skete came to Fr. Ambrose for advice and the revelation of thoughts. That some brothers came to Fr. Ambrose is self-explanatory, for Fr. Macarius could not have committed many people to his guidance from the very start, but would have accustomed him gradually to the work of eldership.

Particularly explicit and interesting are the stories of Fr. Ambrose's eldership during the life of Fr. Macarius as told by Abbot Mark, who entered Optina Monastery in 1854 and also received Fr. Macarius' blessing to turn to Fr. Ambrose for spiritual guidance. He spoke of his relationship to Fr. Ambrose in the following manner: "As far as I could tell at the time, Fr. Ambrose lived in complete silence. I went to him nearly every day to reveal my thoughts, and I always found him reading patristic texts. If I did not find him in his cell it meant that he was with Fr. Macarius—whom he assisted with the correspondence of those who turned to him for spiritual advice—or he labored in the translation of the Holy Fathers. Sometimes I found him lying on the bed in tears, which were always controlled and barely noticeable. It seemed to me that Elder Ambrose always walked in the presence of God, or as if he always sensed God's presence, according to the Psalmist: *I beheld the Lord ever before me* (Ps. 15:8); and therefore everything he did he strove to do for the Lord's sake and to please Him. Because of this he was in continual fear and trembling that he might offend the Lord, and this was reflected even in his facial expression. Beholding such concentration in my Elder, I always trembled with reverence in his presence. I could not have been any other way. As I knelt before him receiving his blessing, he would sometimes very quietly ask me: 'What good thing do you have to say, brother?' Perplexed by his concentration and spiritual feeling, I would say: 'Forgive me for the Lord's sake, Batiushka, perhaps I have arrived at the wrong time?' 'No,' the Elder would say, 'tell me what you need, but briefly.' Having heard me out attentively, he would give me some profitable instruction with his blessing and dismiss me lovingly. His instructions would come not from his wisdom or reason, although he was rich in spiritual wisdom. If he taught those who came to him for spiritual counsel, then he taught in the capacity of a student and offered not his own advice, but always the practical teachings of the Holy Fathers. For this he would open a book of one or another Holy Father, find some chapter appropriate to the state of the brother who came to him, and have him read it, afterwards asking the brother how he understood its meaning. If someone did not understand the reading, then the Elder would interpret the content of the patristic teaching in an entirely understandable way. All this was done with boundless fatherly love and desire to help. Sometimes it would happen that, enraged at my neighbor over some personal offense to my self-love, I would come to the Elder to disclose my thoughts without yet having calmed down. I would begin to tell him of my unreasonable sorrow and anger without any self-condemnation, against all teachings of the holy ascetic fathers, but, to the contrary, accusing my neighbor. By reason of the antagonism sown in my soul, I desired that the Elder immediately and sternly correct the offending brother. Having listened to all of this with his characteristic undisturbed calm and with compassion for my sorrow, the sickly Elder would say in a crying voice: 'Brother, brother! I am a dying man!' or 'I could die today or tomorrow. What can I do with this brother? After all, I am not the Abbot. You must reproach yourself, humble yourself before your brother—and you will calm down.' Having heard such a plaintively pronounced answer, I was dumbfounded. Deeply acknowledging my own guilt, I would humbly fall at the Elder's feet, asking forgiveness. Having received forgiveness and his blessing, I would depart calmed and consoled, flying away as though on wings.

"It sometimes happened that I would come to the Elder quite early, at five in the morning. After saying the usual prayer and being permitted to enter the cell, I always found him sober and vigorous, as though he had not been sleeping at all, and paternally affectionate above and beyond even my expectations. There was little or no indication of any displeasure at my early visitation. Fr. Ambrose would be quite pleased with whoever would heed his words of instruction or those of Elder Macarius; he would show him attention and even become more intimate with him. To the sinners who wholeheartedly repented and corrected themselves he was condescending and merciful beyond measure. He never discriminated between the rich and the poor, the worthy and the unworthy, according to the example of the Lord, Who ate and drank with publicans and harlots, if only He might bring them back to the true path and fear of God. He never reproached the sins of others and would not endure slander of a neighbor. He dealt harshly with slanderers without respect of person."

The foregoing story of Abbot Mark about his relationship to Fr. Ambrose is remarkable not only for its undoubting proof of Fr. Ambrose's practice of eldership long before Elder Macarius' repose, but also because it gives us a living and clear image of Fr. Ambrose as an elder. From the words of Fr. Mark can be seen what an introspective and concentrated life Fr. Ambrose already led at that time; how deeply he was immersed in prayer and divine contemplation; how he often wept; how all of his advice and instruction was founded not on his own reasoning, but on the clear witness of the Holy Fathers; with what love and attention he received those who came to him; how thoroughly he answered their perplexities, and with what degree of moral satisfaction and consolation they left him. In these spiritual features of the forty-two-year-old Hieromonk Ambrose we find all the fundamental features of his later spiritual countenance.

Sending to Fr. Ambrose a few of the brothers for spiritual guidance, Fr. Macarius also sent to him for discussion secular visitors, who had gathered in the cottage that adjoined Fr. Macarius' cell from outside the skete enclosure. Fr. Ambrose performed this obedience zealously and lovingly, turning to Fr. Macarius with any puzzling cases for advice and direction. Seeing Fr. Ambrose surrounded by a crowd of people wishing to talk, Fr. Macarius would say jokingly: "Look at that! Ambrose is stealing my bread and butter." To Fr. Ambrose himself he would note: "See that you remember these times."

At Elder Macarius' behest, Fr. Ambrose, like Fr. Macarius himself, went to talk to visitors also at the guest house. A bag with shirts and socks was his usual unnoticed travelling companion. As soon as he had to go to the guest house, he would pile it onto his shoulders and go.

They say that one day Fr. Macarius sent Fr. Ambrose to the guest house to see a wealthy lady visitor who was preparing to receive the Holy Mysteries. Having heard much positive talk about Fr. Ambrose, she began to tell him about some bad luck she had had, which had brought her to distress. She was expecting to hear some words of sympathy from Fr. Ambrose. But after listening to her speech, he calmly replied: "The thief receives torment according to his works." The lady did not like these words and so she cut off the conversation. Fr. Ambrose quickly retreated to his cell. The next day after Liturgy Fr. Macarius went to the guest house to congratulate this lady with receiving the Holy Mysteries, taking Fr. Ambrose along with him. When the lady saw Fr. Ambrose, she said "Well, Batiushka, I carried your little word around and nearly put off receiving Communion. I thought about it throughout Vespers and Matins. I came to the Liturgy and still simply could not be at peace. It was only during the Cherubic Hymn that I had to admit that you had spoken the truth."

In the 1850's a wealthy family, the Klyucharevs, came to Optina Monastery. The elderly father and mother intended to become monastics. This family stayed in the guest house, in small, separate quarters. Fr. Macarius had given Fr. Ambrose the obedience of caring for them, and so he visited them almost daily. "One day," Fr. Ambrose told us, "there happened the following: Mrs. Klyuchareva often sent a horse for me. Archimandrite Moses did not like this, it seems. He came out to meet me and stood leaning on a walking stick at the intersection over which I was to cross. There was nothing else to do—I took off my cap and bowed to him. From that time on I never rode, but only walked."

At that time Fr. Ambrose was given the task of spiritually nourishing the nuns of the Borisov Convent in Kursk Province, who came to the Optina Elders for guidance. Therefore, whenever they arrived at the Monastery, he quickly went to the guest house to see them, according to his obligation.

Thus, gradually widened the circle of individuals from among the brethren, monastics and lay people visiting Optina who enjoyed Fr. Ambrose's spiritual counsel and guidance. Fr. Macarius was apparently preparing him to become his successor. It is remarkable that not long before his repose, Fr. Macarius foretold to Fr. Ambrose his future activity, saying: "You will live in the cell on that side of the gate, and see to it—this is my commandment to you—do not let anyone who comes here leave without consolation."

Just the same, Fr. Ambrose was not generally and undeniably accepted as Fr. Macarius' successor after the latter's repose, as Fr. Macarius had been to Elder Leonid. When Fr. Macarius was dying, he did not point directly to Fr. Ambrose as his successor. At the brothers' question, "How shall we live without you, Batiushka?" he asked them to give him the *Alphabetical Patericon* and read there Abba Isaac of Sketis' answer to the same question asked him by his disciples. Abba Isaac answered them: "You have seen the way I have acted in your presence. If you desire to imitate me, follow God's commandments, and God will send you His grace and will preserve this place. If you do not fulfill His commandment, you will not stay in this place. We also grieved when our fathers were leaving us and departing to the Lord; but observing the Lord's commandments and the teachings of the Elders, we lived as though they were still with us. Do likewise and you will be saved!"

The holy Hierarch Philaret of Moscow, well acquainted with Optina affairs, wrote concerning Fr. Macarius' repose: "Optina has lost Fr. Macarius. I think that he has left good spiritual successors; but will anyone come forth who could support them in oneness of soul and lead them?"

By this illustration we see that Fr. Macarius did not have a particular successor to his eldership after his repose. Those who turned to Fr. Macarius during his lifetime for spiritual instruction and guidance chose different guides. Fr. Archimandrite Moses chose his brother, Abbot Anthony, as his elder and confessor; others went to the new Skete Superior, Fr. Paphnutius, who had also become the new father-confessor to the Monastery. Others chose Hieromonk Hilarion, who had been Fr. Macarius' cell attendant during his final years, while, finally, others became disciples of Fr. Ambrose. The extent to which many thought highly of Fr. Ambrose can be seen from the following remarks about him.

One of Fr. Macarius' spiritual sons, Clement Sederholm, about whom we will speak more particularly later, wrote on November 17, 1860 to his brother: "You and I have become orphans (after Fr. Macarius' death). It still seems to me that along with Fr. Macarius died all of my consolation. I am turning to Fr. Ambrose, Batiushka's true disciple, who is penetrated with his spirit." In 1861, the inspector of the Tomsk Seminary, Hieromonk Vladimir, expressed in a letter to Archimandrite Moses his joy that his brother who had joined Optina Monastery "was worthy to receive such an Elder as Fr. Ambrose as his spiritual guide!" About the same time, Hieromonk Anthony (Bochkov) wrote of Fr. Ambrose that Optina Monastery "is strengthened and edified by him. The reason is his meekness, kindness and simplicity. His beneficial example and counsel can work miracles.... It is useless to praise him. His works speak louder than words.... Apparently it is appointed to him to be saved through illness; his rare guilelessness and child-like Christian demeanor endure everything equally—divine chastisement as well as human unrighteousness." Bishop Benjamin of Voronezh, who came to Optina during Fr. Macarius' life, spoke long with him and afterwards always regarded him with deep respect.

Archimandrite Isaac.

As time went by, word of Fr. Ambrose's experience and wisdom in spiritual matters spread further and further, and the number of people who came to him grew. Those who at first out of ignorance did not trust him began to change their opinion of him.

There was one noblewoman who was deeply disturbed over the repose of Fr. Macarius, and when she heard that Optina had a new Elder, Fr. Ambrose, she exclaimed: "How could I, after knowing Fr. Macarius, go to that monk who used to fuss around Fr. Macarius' cell and walk about with a sack? It's impossible!" But after some time passed, having happened to talk with Fr. Ambrose, she came away from him very touched, and said later: "I knew them both, but I feel that Fr. Ambrose was even higher than Fr. Macarius."

In 1862 the Superior of the Monastery, Archimandrite Moses, reposed. The majority of the elder brethren chose the Skete Superior Fr. Paphnutius to be his successor. However, Bishop Gregory did not uphold this election because he had been informed by Fr. Ambrose that according to Fr. Macarius' directions, Fr. Moses should be succeeded by Fr. Isaac. Bishop Gregory therefore appointed Fr. Isaac as Superior of the Monastery, promising Fr. Paphnutius that he would not abandon him. This was soon fulfilled when the Bishop appointed Fr. Paphnutius Superior of Maloyaroslavets Monastery.

With the transfer of Fr. Paphnutius to Maloyaroslavets, many of his spiritual children began to turn to Fr. Ambrose. In 1865, Fr. Moses' brother, Abbot Anthony, reposed—the last of the great founding Elders of the Skete. A significant number of his disciples also turned to Fr. Ambrose. Now in Optina there were two main spiritual leaders: Fr. Ambrose and Fr. Hilarion, the brotherhood's father-confessor. By that time Fr. Ambrose had also become known to the holy Hierarch of Moscow, Philaret, who in that same year of 1865 sent to the Elder with his blessings an icon of the Savior "Made Without Hands" through an Optina monk who was currently living in Moscow.

When Fr. Ambrose began his eldership, he continued to carry his heavy cross of sickness, which became his inseparable companion until the end of his days.

In the winter of 1862, Fr. Ambrose was riding from the Skete to the Monastery to greet the newly tonsured monks whom he had received as spiritual children at the reading of the Gospel. By some twist of fate he fell from the sledge and broke his arm. As a consequence of unsuccessful treatment, he suffered badly for a long time. His health, already weak, became even more so, and from that time on he could no longer go to church for services; he even had to receive Holy Communion in his cell, either once a week, every other week or every third week. He never went outside in wintertime for the rest of his life.

As if to strengthen the physically infirm Elder, the Lord sent him right at that time several active and devoted assistants. In 1863 Constantine Karlovich Sederholm became numbered among the skete brethren. He was the son of the senior pastor of a Protestant [Lutheran] church in Moscow, a man with a university education and a friend of T. I. Philipov and the poet B. N. Almazov, a master of the Greek language and literature, who had at one time been an attaché for the Over-Procurator of the Holy Synod, Count Alexei P. Tolstoy. He had travelled to the East and was well acquainted with the condition of the churches in the Middle East, and had been converted from Protestantism to Orthodoxy ten years before in that very Skete by Elder Macarius. He was a deeply religious man and devoted to Orthodoxy, which he had felt drawn to from his very childhood.

When he joined the Skete, Sederholm became one of Elder

Ambrose's closest disciples. He helped him with his voluminous correspondence, as well as the publication of books that continued during Fr. Ambrose's time as it had been in Fr. Macarius' time.

In monasticism Sederholm received the name Clement, and, having lived for fifteen years in the Skete, he died of pneumonia in 1878.* Having entered the Skete at the same time as Fr. Clement were two whom Fr. Ambrose took as cell attendants—Maxim from Moscow, later Hieromonk Michael, who served as his cell attendant for twenty years; and John from Kharkov Province, in monasticism Joseph, who stayed with the Elder until his arrival in Shamordino and who himself practiced eldership in Optina until his repose in 1911. These two individuals and their helpers had the difficult task of informing the Elder about visitors, fulfilling various obediences of the Elder and caring for him. With the aide of Fr. Clement, Fr. Leonid (Kavelin), Fr. Anatole (Zertsalov), Fr. Agapitus and certain others, Fr. Ambrose continued the publication work begun by Fr. Macarius. Under Fr. Ambrose's supervision the following books were published by Optina Monastery during the sixties and seventies: 1) *The Life and Ascetical labors of the Elder of Optina Monastery, Hieroschemamonk Macarius* (compiled by Archimandrite Leonid Kavelin);** 2) A collection of Fr. Macarius' letters in six volumes; 3) A new edition of *Abba Dorotheos*, prepared for publication by Frs. Clement and Anatole; 4) *St. Symeon the New Theologian, Twelve Homilies,* translated by Frs. Clement and Anatole; 5) *The Life of Abbot Anthony* (compiled by Fr.

---

\* His biography was written by Constantine N. Leontiev and entitled: *Fr. Clement Sederholm, a Hieromonk of Optina Monastery* (Moscow, 1882), and published by the Kazan-Ambrose Shamordino Convent.

\*\* See *Elder Macarius of Optina*, by Leonid Kavelin (St. Herman of Alaska Brotherhood, 1995).

## ELDERSHIP

Clement);* 6) *Catechetical Homilies of Our Holy Father Theodore the Studite* in Russian translation—the work of Frs. Clement, Anatole and Agapitus; 7) *Instructions of St. Peter Damascene,* translated by Fr. Juvenal; 8) *The Life of Elder Leonid* (compiled by Fr. Clement);** 9) *Description of the Kozelsk Optina Monastery* (compiled by Fr. Leonid Kavelin); 10) *The Royal Path of the Cross of the Lord,* translated [edited] by Fr. Clement; 11) *The Life of Archimandrite Moses* (compiled by Archimandrite Juvenal); and others. Besides these books, Optina Monastery also published various brochures and printed new editions of previously published books.

In August of 1868, Fr. Ambrose was again attacked by his cruel, chronic illness: inflamation of the blood vessels. The bleeding continued daily for an entire five weeks. Due to the Kozelsk provincial doctor's absence, he was without medical assistance for nine days. Only on the 6th of September did the doctor arrive from Belev to give some relief to the sufferer. Seeing that the illness still had not abated, Fr. Ambrose's admirer and spiritual son who was visiting Optina at the time, Count Alexei P. Tolstoy, as well as others of the Elder's spiritual children, began to ask Fr. Isaac to send a monk to the village of Kaluzhenka (forty-seven miles from Optina) to the local priest with a request that the miracle-working Kaluga Mother of God icon be brought, so that all of the Elder's spiritual children could pray together before it for his healing. The holy icon was brought, and a Moleben with an Akathist to the Mother of God was served in the Elder's cell, followed by a cell Vigil. Although the illness lasted for a little while after this, everyone's hope in his recovery was revived. He actually did recover towards the

---

* See *Elder Anthony of Optina,* by Fr. Clement Sederholm (St. Herman of Alaska Brotherhood, 1995).

** See *Elder Leonid of Optina,* by Fr. Clement Sederholm, (St. Herman of Alaska Brotherhood, 1990).

end of September. But he had barely begun to feel better when, on November 1, Fr. Ambrose again caught a cold and fell ill. A cold and inflamation of the blood vessels attacked his right eye, so that he was unable to read for two months.

T<small>REASURING PRAYERFUL SOLITUDE</small> and needing a rest from time to time from the ceaseless flood of visitors and from his burdensome illnesses, Fr. Ambrose had the custom of spending a little time each summer in one of the monastery dachas\* deep in the woods.

In 1869 his admirers had the idea of building him a comfortable house in one of these solitary places. The matter was initiated in the following way. Fr. Ambrose arrived at the spot designated for the cell together with his secretary, Fr. Clement, the monastery correspondent, Fr. Michael (Strukov) and his little son, Eugene. Addressing his companions, the Elder said: "Bless to build a cell here, brothers." All were silent. Then the Elder, taking the little boy's hand, made the sign of the cross over the spot with it and made him repeat these words after him: "In the name of the Father, of the Son, and of the Holy Spirit. Amen. May God bless me to live here so that good shall come forth."

By the following summer Fr. Ambrose's cell was built. In the evening of June 13, Father moved into the new quarters. The first thing the Elder did was to bless the place with prayer. They served an All-Night Vigil to the Mother of God, St. John the Forerunner and St. Ambrose of Milan. The next morning a Moleben was served to the Savior, St. Nicholas the Wonderworker, St. Macarius the Great and holy Righteous Prince Alexander Nevsky. The prayer was read for the blessing of a house, and the whole house was sprinkled with holy water.

---

\*A dacha is a vacation house, or area, of any size.—T<small>RANS</small>.

# ELDERSHIP

Elder Ambrose came to this solitary place from the Skete several years in a row, usually trying to come on weekdays for five or six days at a time.

One of Fr. Ambrose's spiritual sons, the writer Constantine N. Leontiev, described this summertime retreat:

"Five miles from Optina, in the forest wilderness there is a dacha where the Elder Fr. Ambrose comes to rest, exhausted from crowds of people. There on a small, green meadow is a simple, clean and spacious cottage in which Fr. Ambrose comes from time to time for a few days. People find him there anyway. When I visited Optina for the first time, I was supposed to go to that dacha to deliver letters from Mt. Athos to the Elder.\* There were many people gathered around the cottage on the meadow: monks, peasant men and women, nuns and ladies. Long poles were placed along stumps on all sides, so that everyone would not push at once to see the Elder and did not disturb his conversation with those whom he had called in. Everyone waited patiently. Some sat on the grass, others stood leaning against the poles in hopes that the Elder might bless them or say a word to them as he passed by. Many simply wanted to begin some work; they hoped that he would even silently make the sign of the cross over them and nothing more. Many came from very far away for this. It was very hot. The sickly Elder walked quietly through the meadow under a large, striped umbrella and conversed with some peasant man. They talked for a long time. When it came to my turn the Elder was already exhausted from walking and called me to his room....

"The Elder welcomed to his summer retreat with special warmth those monks who were close to him. They would come in the evening by twos and would be invited to a modest dinner. When the weary travellers would fall asleep, the Elder would

---

\* Leontiev came from Thessalonica, where he was the Russian Counselor.

not allow them to be awakened early, even for the morning rule. When the guests would get up after having listened to the Hours with the Elder, they would go to him for a blessing, ask forgiveness for having slept through Matins, and he would say to them with paternal condescension: 'Well, we don't disturb guests.' Another time, when some monks came to the Elder's dacha from Optina, the head cell attendant went to wake them up but the Elder said to him: 'Silly! Did they come here to hear you pray? They will pray enough in the Monastery—now they need to rest.' Such was the Elder's love!"

One of Fr. Ambrose's favorite guests at his summer cell was the novice Elisha, who had lived for fifty-two years in the Monastery and always refused any monastic promotions or distinctions. He lived about a half mile from the Elder's dacha, in a tiny watch-house, and guarded the forest. Fr. Abbot Isaac once offered to tonsure him into the mantia, or at least into the ryassa, and even threatened him: "If you don't, I'll send you to the kitchen!" "And that," replied Elisha, "will be my ryassa!" "I will give you prostrations!" the Abbot insisted. "And that will be my mantia!" Having lived a long time in the forest solitude, Elisha became as it were a child of nature. In winter he fed the forest birds from his hand. He would come out of his cell, sprinkle flax seeds on his head, his beard and in his hand and no sooner had he called: "Birdies, birdies, birdies!" then they would come flying to him from all directions. Some would light on his head or beard, others on his hands, and they would completely cover him. He died in deep old age in the monastery hospital. Before his repose, when the brothers came to give him words of consolation and encouragement, he answered: "Glory be to God! Even here He has consoled me—He granted me to love, praise and glorify Him! With God it is well here and there—everywhere. God is with us, understand ye nations, for God is with us!"

In February 1871, the Elder again began to have attacks of vascular inflammation. But on February 24 he was sent from Mt. Athos a large icon of the Great Martyr and Healer St. Panteleimon, ordered by the Elder's spiritual daughters, the nuns of Belev Convent. That very day a Vigil service was conducted in the Elder's cell to the God-pleaser, and the next day a Moleben was served. From that day the illness, that had bothered him for nearly a week and had not responded to any medical treatment, ceased.

However, on August 8 of the same year the illness returned in even greater intensity and did not leave the Elder until September 10. At the Elder's wish a Moleben with an Akathist before the Kaluga Mother of God icon was served in his cell, and on the eighteenth another was served before the Akhtyrsk Mother of God icon brought from Kozelsk. Finally, on August 30 the miracle-working icon of the Mother of God "Joy of All Who Sorrow" was brought from the Meschevsk St. George Monastery, and before it everyone surrounded the sufferer and prayed fervently with him for his recovery. The Elder wrote to his spiritual son, Bishop Peter of Tomsk, about this illness: "My health is currently even worse than before. This summer, as in previous years, I went several times to my cell in the woods. And there, although I was free during Morning and Evening Prayers, the rest of the time the visitors burdened me so that by summer's end I was completely exhausted, and in August I fell ill. I had vascular bleeding that continued all month. Then, thanks be to the Lord, I began little by little to recover; but after this illness I became noticeably weaker."

In December the vascular bleeding was repeated, although to a lesser degree than before. The Elder completely lost his strength. On his nameday, the seventh of December, he was so weak that he could not even receive any congratulations. His cell attendants carried him from cell to cell. However, the

A rare portrait of Elder Ambrose.

prayers of his spiritual children once again lifted the Elder up from his bed of pain, and again he began his usual much-caring labors with determination. He continued to suffer periodic attacks of this same illness until the end of his life.

## 2. FR. AMBROSE'S CORRESPONDENCE WITH LAY PEOPLE AND MONASTICS

With the increase in the number of his spiritual children, Fr. Ambrose's correspondence with those seeking his spiritual guidance also increased. Not only monastics turned to him, but also lay people from every walk of life, station and even nationality and religion, with the most multiform questions concerning faith and Christian life. Fr. Ambrose considered it his duty to provide answers to the questions they directed to him, and these answers vividly reveal Fr. Ambrose's personality, his views on various questions of faith and life, and his relationship to people. In this light we consider it necessary to acquaint the reader with the most important content of the Elder's correspondence.

Fr. Ambrose persuaded those who sought his advice that they must never, under any circumstances of life or unpleasantness, be depressed, but they must always hope in God's Providence. "People of olden times decided," writes Fr. Ambrose, "that you will never live your life through without a lesson," and added that "if a pot clashes with a pot, how much more impossible is it for people to live together without clashing. This particularly occurs from differing views on things—one thinks one way about a matter, and another another way. One is convinced in his own concept which seems firm and well-founded, while the other believes in his own reasoning. In the first rule of arithmetic one plus one equals two; in the third rule two times two equals four; if we come to fractions, then we have a number above and a number below, and between them a bar—thus it is in human affairs. If you divide people up, you end with displeasure above and below, with some kind of barrier in between. As I said and wrote to you earlier, so will I tell you now: if you trust in God's Providence and hope in God's omnipotent assistance, then you will not meet with such problems as you suppose. Furthermore, peace of soul will always be within your reach."

In another letter Fr. Ambrose writes:

"I received two despairing little letters from you. You write to me: 'I have perished, for my horses have been stolen from my homestead.' Come to your senses—what are you saying? That your horses have been stolen is not some sort of mortal sin for which you must perish. Furthermore, you would not be able to take those horses with you to the other world. We take there only our deeds—good or evil. If we do not possess any virtues, then we will try at any rate to be delivered from our sins through repentance and endurance of the sorrows that God's Providence has sent us to cleanse our souls from sins and vices and all impure dross. I know that you have many sorrows and much domestic unpleasantness. But tell and enlighten yourself with the remembrance that in hell it is much worse, more wearying and doleful, and there is no hope of deliverance from it. If a person endures sorrows with submission to God's will, confessing his sins, then he will through this be delivered from eternal torments. Therefore we had better endure unpleasantries here, no matter how difficult they are, turning our grief over to God and praying to Him with humility that He deliver us from faintheartedness and despair, which are the worst of all sins."

To a mother who grieved over her son's atheism and rebelliousness, Fr. Ambrose wrote: "You wrote that you were disturbed when the beggar to whom you gave alms, asking him to pray for your son, prayed for the repose of his soul. Do not be disturbed at this. Nothing could have happened or is happening to your son because of a beggar's mistake and misunderstanding. And there is nothing greater or better to wish for someone than that they be made worthy in their time of the heavenly kingdom. If in your sorrow over your son you have sometimes thought that it would be better that he were dead than living as he does, then you should reproach yourself for it and give yourself and your son over in complete faith to the will of the all-good and all-wise God. If the Lord extends one's days, then He is bestowing benefactions; if He should cut short one's days, then He bestows just the same. In general, according to the sayings of the holy Church, the Lord in the depths of His wisdom dost provide all things out of love for mankind, and grantest unto all that which is profitable.* Therefore there is nothing better or more profitable for mankind than devotion to God's will, and the ways of God are unfathomable. You know that we ourselves are in many ways guilty in that we did not know how to raise our son as we should have. Self-reproach is profitable, but with it you must be aware of your guilt, humble yourself and repent, and not be distressed and in despair. Neither should you be over-troubled by the thought that you exclusively are the involuntary cause of your son's present condition. This is not altogether true—every person is endowed with free will and must answer for himself before God.

"You ask if you should not write to your son in Moscow, and how you should write to him in order to touch his heart. Write briefly to him at first just to find out where he is. When you find him you can write him in more detail. Then you can tell him that now he has learned through his own experience

---

*From the Pannikhida, or Requiem service.—ED.

what atheism and rebellion leads to; that, in craving unbridled freedom he forgot that from sin, especially defying one's parents, came slavery itself, which had not existed before on earth, etc. Having prayed to God, write as the Lord puts it in your heart to do.... In general you should not be concerned now so much with enlightening him as with praying for him, so that the Lord Himself through ways known only to Him would enlighten him. Great is the power of a mother's prayer. Remember how Blessed Augustine's pious mother's prayers drew her son out of such a depth of evil. And as you pray for your son pray also for yourself, that the Lord would forgive you for whatever sins you may have unknowingly committed."

To another mother who grieved over her daughter's illness, the Elder wrote: "I have heard that you are grieving beyond measure, seeing your sick daughter's suffering. Truly, it is humanly impossible for a mother not to grieve when she sees her little one in such pain and suffering day and night. In spite of that, you should remember that you are a Christian who believes in the future life and the future blessed reward not only for labors, but for voluntary and involuntary suffering. Therefore you must not become unreasonably fainthearted and sorrowful beyond measure, like unto pagans or unbelievers who believe neither in eternal blessedness nor eternal punishment. No matter how great are the involuntary sufferings of your little child S., they cannot after all be compared to the voluntary sufferings of the martyrs; and if they do compare, then she is equal to them and will receive a blessed state in the paradisal abodes. By the way, you must not forget also our twisted times, in which even little children's souls are damaged by what they see and hear and therefore require cleansing, which cannot occur without suffering. The cleansing of the soul happens most often through physical suffering.

Let us suppose that there was no damage to the soul. Even so, you must know that paradisal blessedness is not given to anyone who has not first suffered. Do even the tiniest infants pass into the future life without sickness or suffering? By the way, I do not write this way because I wish that the suffering child S. would die, but I write particularly for your consolation, enlightenment, and true persuasion not to grieve unreasonably and beyond measure. No matter how much you love your daughter, you must know that our all-good God, Who uses any means for our salvation, loves her more than you do. He Himself bears witness in the Holy Scripture as to His love for every believer, saying: *Can a woman forget her suckling child, that she should not have compassion on the son of her womb? Yea, they may forget, yet will I not forget thee* (Is. 49:15). Therefore try to calm your sorrowing over your sick daughter, turning this sorrow over to God: *Having made known unto us the mystery of his will, according to his good pleasure which he hath purposed in himself* (Eph. 1:9). I advise you to commune your daughter following a confession. Ask the confessor to question her wisely and carefully during the confession."

Fr. Ambrose gave the following advice to a couple about to be married and begin family life: "You must always remember that our lives will only pass peacefully and happily if we do not forget ourselves or God, our Creator and Redeemer, the Giver of everything good—temporal and eternal. Not forgetting Him means trying to live according to His divine and life-giving commandments; and when we break them because of our infirmity, to sincerely repent and to set about straightway to correct our mistakes and departures from those commandments."

"If spouses always shared equally in a Christian manner the burden of their lives," the Elder wrote in another letter, "then life would be good for people even on earth. But since spouses are often slack, one or both of them, our earthly happiness is not enduring."

The following incident reveals what love Fr. Ambrose had for his spiritual children. To one of his disciples who expressed the fear that he might abandon her, Fr. Ambrose wrote: "I wanted to put you at ease long ago, much-worrying N., concerning your fear that I might abandon you and stop writing to you. If due to my weak character I did not abandon you when I hardly knew you, but rather agreed to your request, for I did not wish to grieve you in your time of extreme spiritual need—could I abandon you now that I, because of my lack of any real sense, have neglected my own soul and left its salvation to its own fate, thinking to care for the profit of my neighbors' souls? I don't know—could there be anyone more foolish than I?!"

Why do people experience depression? "Depression, according to Mark the Ascetic, is a spiritual cross sent to us in order to cleanse our former sins. Depression comes also for other reasons: from offended self-love, because we are not getting our own way; also from vainglory when one sees that his equals enjoy greater privileges; from stressful situations during which our faith in God's Providence and hope in His mercy and omnipotent help is put to test. We often lack faith and hope, and that is why we are tormented."

It is not personality but the direction of the will that is significant in God's judgment, Fr. Ambrose would say. "You know, personalities are only significant in human judgment, and that is why they are praised or scorned. But in God's judgment, personalities, like natural tendencies, are not approved or disapproved. The Lord looks at good intentions and struggle for the good, and values opposition to the passions...."

How should we confess? "We should confess how we sinned and what sin we committed—that is all. It is good to write a confession ahead of time, not according to the books,* and read it yourself to the confessor. It will be understandable and less burdensome for the confessor, as well as easy and consoling for the penitent."

When asked what children should be given to read, Fr. Ambrose wrote: "It is my opinion that a young mind should first of all be occupied with sacred history and readings of the Lives of saints of your choice, which will unnoticeably sow the seeds of the fear of God and Christian life. You especially need to make them understand, with God's help, how important it is to keep God's commandments and what disastrous consequences follow breaking them. All of this will lead them away from the example set by our first parents, who ate the forbidden fruit and were therefore exiled from Paradise. You can put Krylov's fables away until later, for now teaching your child some prayers by heart, like the Symbol of Faith and certain Psalms, for example: *He that dwelleth in the help of the Most High* (Ps. 90), *The Lord is my light* (Ps. 26), and the like. The main thing is that the child himself be occupied, according to his strength, and directed toward fear of God. Everything good and kind comes from this, while, to the contrary, idleness and not being instilled with the fear of God are often the cause of all evil and misfortune.

"When the fear of God is not instilled, children will not bring forth the desired fruits of good morals and a well-ordered life, no matter what you occupy them with. When the fear of God is instilled, all occupations are good and profitable."

In another letter, Fr. Ambrose wrote about the upbringing of children: "You write that you have noticed a dryness, insensitivity and other inadequacies in your son. But there are not

---

*That is, not just according to the published guidelines on confession.—Ed.

many children who have real and true feelings; they usually come forth at a riper age, when a person begins to understand and to experience life. Besides, an abundance of inner feelings inadvertently becomes a reason for secret self-exaltation and judging others; while a dearth of feelings and dryness involuntarily humbles one when one begins to understand this. Therefore do not be overly concerned that you notice this inadequacy in your son; in time inescapable trials in life will inevitably awaken necessary feelings in him. But just try as much as you can to impart to him a healthy understanding that is in accordance with the teachings of the Orthodox Church.

"You write that up till now you have studied with him yourself and have gone over the sacred history of the Old Testament; and you ask, how and what should you teach, and whom should you choose to teach him? Having gone through the Old Testament with him, you yourself should finish this with him, that is, you should proceed to the New Testament. Then you should begin the catechism. You are afraid that the dryness of the catechism will not make him any warmer. The catechism does not make anyone warmer—it is sufficient that children should have a correct understanding of the dogmas and other subjects of the Orthodox Church. If you wish that the Orthodox teaching would also influence your son's heart, then read the *Orthodox Confession* and the *School of Piety* with him. Then let the teacher of religion instruct him in the catechism as is acceptable in learning institutions. Concerning your choice of teachers—as I do not know any of the Moscow clergy, I cannot indicate anyone to you. But I seem to recall that Fr. Macarius advised someone to choose a deacon rather than a priest as a Law of God teacher for a young child. That is simpler and therefore is often more successful. Moscow deacons are all seminary graduates and know the catechisms well.... You should put more care into finding him a confessor. So as not to upset your own confessor, you should explain to him beforehand that you are seeking what is necessary and profitable for your son. Ask him in addition for permission to arrange this, for in your understanding a holy atmosphere is needed for a child during confession, although for one who has an understanding of confession this does not have any special significance. Before confession you yourself must work with your son to prepare him for this Mystery as well as you are able. Have him read the commandments before confession and explain them to him. Concerning the correction of his shortcomings in general, you can talk to him in a half-joking tone: 'You are a young prince after all, don't muddy your face with a fall.' You write that you are deeply convinced that there is no other source of goodness on earth nor of blessedness in Heaven than the Church of Christ, and that anything outside of this is worthless; and you wish to transmit this conviction to your children, so that it would become as it were the treasure of their life. But it seems to you that you are not endowed with a teaching vocation and cannot speak with the strength of conviction required for this great subject. As a loving mother, you yourself must witness to these subjects to your children as best you can. No one can take your place in this because to another you would first have to explain your own understanding and desires. Besides, no one else can know your children's souls, emotional structures and needs. Futhermore, a mother's words will have a greater effect on them than those of an outsider. An outsider's words affect the mind, while a mother's words affect the heart. If it seems to you that your son knows a great deal, understands a great deal, but feels little, then I repeat: do not be distressed over this. But pray to God about it, that He would arrange what is profitable for him as He knows best. You write that he has an excellent memory—use this as well. Besides your instructions, tell him soul-profiting stories, asking him at times to repeat them to you as he heard and understood them. Everything he hears from you will be preserved in his memory and mind, and then, with God's help, when he experiences life these things will pass from mind to feeling."

The Elder wrote about this same subject to one of his spiritual daughters: "The experience of the ages shows that the sign of the cross has great power over all a person's actions during the entire course of his life. Therefore it is necessary to strive to root in children the habit of protecting themselves with the sign of the cross often, especially when receiving food and drink, going to bed and waking up, before departing somewhere in a vehicle, before leaving and entering any place; and they should not make the sign carelessly or according to fashion, but precisely, beginning with the forehead to the solar plexus, then to both shoulders, so that a proper cross is produced.... The sign of the cross has saved many from great dangers and afflictions.

"You write—'I would like that my husband and I could escape the destructive disagreement in matters of upbringing that I seem to observe in almost all marriages.' Yes, this is truly a subtle thing! But it is not good to argue about this in front of the children, as you yourself noticed. Therefore, in cases of dispute, either turn away from it and leave, or pretend not to have heard it—but never argue about your differing views in front of the children. Counsel and discussion about this should be in private and as dispassionate as possible, so that it will be more real. Incidentally, if you succeed in implanting the fear of God into your children's hearts, then various human foibles can not have such a corruptive effect on them."

The Elder wrote to one of his daughters the following about the impermissibility of divorce: "You write that your mother tries in any way she can to get you to persuade your sister-in-law to divorce her husband, but you are not in sympathy with this.

You are right not to support them in this. Divorce is hateful to God. If it is allowed, it is only because of human weakness. Defend your sister-in-law as much as you can. You should not allow your mother to do this, even though this might cause you to bear unpleasantness from her. You should not only save yourself but your mother from sin…. Calling for peace and God's blessing upon you, your husband, your sorrowing sister-in-law and her children, I remain, with sincere best wishes, the much-sinful Hieromonk Ambrose."

Being himself a strict ascetic and precise keeper of the rules of the Church, Fr. Ambrose was at the same time very condescending to the actual infirmities of other people, placing humility and self-reproach above all bodily ascetic labors.

"During the present fast," he wrote to one of his spiritual daughters, "try to keep it wisely, in accordance with your physical strength. In cases of illness the sixty-ninth apostolic canon allows oil on Wednesdays and Fridays, and to some even during Holy Week if it is done with repentance and self-reproach, remembering the wise saying of the Holy Fathers, that we are not killers of the body, but killers of the passions. St. Isaac the Syrian writes of one elder who only ate every third day. If he had to speak with visitors for an hour or two, then he could not take food according to the usual schedule, but had to shorten the time between meals and eat more than the usual portion. You should remember that you are the mistress of the house and surrounded by children, besides which you tend to have health problems. All this shows that you need to concern yourself more with the virtues of the soul. As far as the taking of food and other physical ascetic labors go, good reason and humility should be your first concern. If in the case of psychological shortcomings one offers repentance joined with humility, then in the matter of physical infirmities self-reproach and repentance have an even greater place. St. John Climacus has this to say about it: 'David did not say, "I have fasted," "I have kept vigil," or "I have lain on the bare eath," but "I humbled myself, and straightway the Lord saved me."'* After praying to God, begin by taking oil with your food during the fast. You can take medicines or more if necessary for your illness. Present your infirmities with humility before your Lord, and He is powerful to provide all good things. When preparing to receive the Holy Mysteries you should go for a few days without oil, but I advise you to take at that time more nutritious foods—dried fruit and such as your stomach can take, so that you will be able to attend services (if possible) and look after the children at home."

Although he would ease the fast for the infirm, Fr. Ambrose sternly judged the anti-fasting tendencies current in many and advised against heeding the opinion of doctors who are against fasting.

"You do not like that N. urges his wife to eat dairy products on fast days. Of course, it is impossible for a well-intentioned person to like it; only modern and fashionable people could. You could tell him in private not to force his wife to do this; otherwise there could be harmful consequences and unpleasantness even for him. When a wife first involuntarily burdens her conscience with contempt for the holy fasts out of desire to please her husband, then she herself will have contempt for the fast and other things. Evil does not stand still but usually grows and multiplies."

"You write that the doctor advises you to use dairy products even on fast days.... It seems to me that if you could pass through the entire Great Lent without dairy products, then why shouldn't you fast two days per week? One should not put too

---

* *The Ladder of Divine Ascent* by St. John Climacus (Holy Transfiguation Monastery, 1978), p. 153.

much trust in the words of doctors, because doctors are usually against Lenten foods. I heard that in Moscow there is only one doctor who is dispassionate on this account. Although he is a Lutheran, it seems he himself does not eat meat products and does not force the eating of meat on fast days. If you like, you can talk to him."

Reproaching breakers of the holy fasts, Fr. Ambrose also stood firm in defense of the truth and purity of Orthodoxy against all manner of delusion. This is what he wrote about spiritism: "Spiritism is nothing more than a new delusion and prelest of the enemy. This teaching is an alliance between people and spirits, but clearly not spirits of light, but of darkness. The Apostle Paul writes: *But though we, or an angel from Heaven, preach any other gospel unto you than that which we have preached unto you, let him be accursed* (Gal. 1:8). The Apostle is saying this not in reference to good angels, because good angels will not preach anything contrary to the evangelical and apostolic teaching; he is obviously speaking of the angels of darkness who were cast out of Heaven, who take on the appearance of angels of light in order to delude the indiscriminate.... Through spiritism atheists seemingly become quite religious. But if you penetrate thoroughly into the emotional state of these false prophets, then you will discover that they have become even more dangerous to those who come into contact with them than when they were simply atheists. People are repulsed by the openly atheistic; but those who hide behind a false religious appearance, who are permeated in soul with some old or new demonic delusion, are not immediately detected even by those who understand the matter. The Apostle says: *Jesus Christ, the same yesterday, and today, and for ever* (Heb. 13:8). This means that the teaching of the Orthodox Church implanted by the Holy Spirit through the Apostles and the Fathers of the Ecumenical Councils shall continue until the end of time. All new teachings are nothing other than new errors, sown in one way or another by the ancient enemy, hater and slanderer of mankind, who, in the words of the holy Apostle Peter: *as a roaring lion walketh about, seeking whom he may devour* (I Peter 5:8). This enemy conceals himself within the teaching of spiritism in the guise of dead souls called forth, which pretend more clearly to illuminate the Gospels. But this is an obvious demonic delusion and clearly leads into error those people who choose to believe these dark spirits who appear in the form of dead people. The verification that a soul has attained sanctity in the Orthodox Church is entirely different. Such souls are proven holy by an obvious incorruption of their relics. Sinful souls, according to the teaching of the Orthodox Church, are imprisoned in hell and not only have no authority to teach others, but cannot even leave there, waiting in fearful groaning for the Last Judgment of God. It follows that what is being invoked are not the souls of the dead, but spirits of darkness, the sinful deluders of mankind."

Concerning one man who was proposing a duel, the Elder wrote: "You want to end your enmity in a pagan way, that is, after the manner of unbelievers who believe neither in the future life nor eternal blessedness, nor future eternal torment—to end it by a duel, that hellish bond of dual murder, or more precisely, the joining of murder to a suicide. For although one dueler sometimes remains alive, each thought to murder the other, and each to give himself over to death, having first died in soul. Is this something a decent Christian would do? Look at the Initiator of the Faith and Perfecter of our salvation, the Son of God, King of the angels and archangels—how He did not turn His face away from spitting and blows, humbly bearing all manner of mockery and humiliation! We, however, while calling ourselves His followers, do not want to humble ourselves in a Christian way!... I beg you in the name of our Lord Jesus

Christ—for the sake of your salvation, wisely bear the offense given you, without involving yourself unduly with anyone, for anyone, or for any reason. It is good to sacrifice your soul for the Lord, for the profit of your neighbor and for your own salvation. But it is not only not good—it is unreasonable and worthy of all regret to sacrifice yourself for the destruction of another and of your own eternal, never-ending, unreturnable soul. Emulate our Redeemer, Who prayed to our Father for those who crucified Him: *Forgive them, for they know not what they do* (Lk. 23:34)."

As a deeply religious Orthodox Christian, Fr. Ambrose had no doubt in the ultimate victory of good over evil in the world, but he denied the moral progress of mankind.

One day Fr. Ambrose was sent the following question to resolve: The duty of a Christian is to do good and strive for the triumph of good over evil. At the end of the world, the Gospels say, evil will triumph over good. How can we strive for the triumph of good over evil when we know our efforts will not be crowned with success, and that evil will eventually triumph over good? According to the Gospels, human society at the end of the world will take on a most horrible appearance. This refutes any possibility of man's continual perfecting. Is it possible then to labor for the good of mankind, being convinced that there are no means by which we are able to achieve an ultimate result of morally perfecting mankind before the end of the world?

The Elder answered: "Evil is already overcome—overcome not by human strivings and powers, but by our Lord and Savior Himself, the Son of God, Jesus Christ, Who descended from Heaven to earth, became incarnate, suffered at the hands of men, and by His sufferings on the Cross and resurrection destroyed the power of evil and its chief, the devil, who had reigned over the human race. Christ freed us from slavery to sin and the devil, as He Himself has said: *Behold, I give unto you power to tread on serpents and scorpions, and over all the power of the enemy* (Lk. 10:19). Now every Christian is given through the Sacrament of Baptism the power to destroy evil and do good by keeping the evangelical commandments, and no one is ever forcibly possessed by evil other than those who are careless about keeping the divine commandments—mainly those who voluntarily give themselves to sin. The desire by one's own strength to triumph over evil—which was already overcome by the coming of the Savior—betrays a lack of understanding of the Christian Mysteries of the Orthodox Church and reveals the signs of proud human self-reliance, which wants to do everything by its own power without turning to God for help. The Lord Himself clearly said: *Without Me ye can do nothing* (John 15:5). You write: it is written in the Gospels that at the end of the world evil will triumph over good. This is written nowhere in the Gospels; it is only said that in the last times faith will depart (cf. Lk. 18:8), and: *Because iniquity will abound, the love of many will wax cold* (Matt. 24:12). And the holy Apostle Paul says that before the Second Coming of the Savior *the man of sin (will) be revealed, the son of perdition; Who opposeth and exalteth himself above all that is called God* (II Thess. 2:3-4), that is, antichrist. But it is written in that same place, that the *Lord shall consume with the spirit of His mouth, and shall destroy* him *with the brightness of His coming*. Where do you get the triumph of evil over good? Any triumph of evil over good is altogether illusory and temporary.

"On the other hand, it is also not right to say that man continually perfects himself on earth. Progress or betterment can only be in external human affairs, in the comforts of life. For example, we use the railroad system and telegraphs that did not exist before; coal is dug from the bowels of earth where it was previously hidden, etc. In the Christian-moral realm there is no collective progress. Throughout all times there were people who have attained a very elevated moral state of Christian perfection, directed by a true faith in Christ and following the true Christian teaching in accordance with divine revelation as God has revealed in His Church through divinely inspired prophets and apostles.

"There will even be such people during the time of antichrist, for whose sake the time will be cut short, as it is written: *but for the elect's sake those days shall be shortened* (Matt. 24:22). And again: there have always been people who were given to various vices and iniquities, or fell into various heresies and errors, caught up in so-called science (cf. I Tim. 6:20). They philosophized according to earthly principles, ignoring the warnings of the holy Apostle Paul who said: *Beware lest any man spoil you through philosophy and vain deceit, after the tradition of men, after the rudiments of the world, and not after Christ* (Col. 2:8).... Moral perfection on the earth (which is not perfect) cannot be attained by all of mankind collectively, but by each believer in part, according to his keeping of the commandments and the measure of his humility.

"Ultimate and perfect perfection is attained in Heaven, in the future everlasting life, for which our brief earthly human life serves as but a preparation, just as a man's youthful years serve as preparation for future practical activity. If man's lot were limited to his earthly existence, if everything was concluded for man on earth, then why would *the earth and also the works therein be burned up* (II Peter 3:10)? The same Apostle then adds: *We look for new heavens and a new earth, wherein dwelleth righteousness* (II Peter 3:13). Without the future blessed, eternal life our earthly pilgrimage would be useless and incomprehensible. The desire to labor for the good of mankind is altogether well-seeming, but given the wrong priority. The royal Prophet David said first to *turn away from evil* and then to *do good* (Ps. 33). Nowadays people go about this in the other direction.

Everyone wants to labor in word, as opposed to in deed, for his neighbor's good, but he takes little or no concern for the fact that he must first turn away from evil and only then worry about his neighbor's profit. The broad schemes of the young generation for great activities for all of mankind's profit resemble a man dreaming he could be a professor and great university instructor without having finished high school. On the other hand, to think that if we cannot advance all of mankind it is futile to labor at all is another extreme. Every Christian is obligated according to his strength and station to labor for the good of others, but with the condition that it all be timely and orderly, as stated above, and that the success of our labors represents God and His holy will."

In one of his later letters (1875) Fr. Ambrose refutes the slew of accusations that are often directed against the Orthodox Church in our times. He brings out these accusations pronounced by a brother of one of his spiritual daughters and takes them apart one by one. "Your brother writes to you that there are very few dogmas belonging to the Evangelists. There are two main dogmas of the Orthodox Church: the dogma of the Holy Trinity and the dogma of the incarnation of the Son of God. The entire Gospel speaks of these two dogmas. This is briefly and concisely set forth at the beginning of every Psalter.... Read it yourself and show your brother.

"Your brother writes: 'The dogmas are clearly formulated postulates. The dogmas were contrived by the Ecumenical Councils.' Dogmas are not human postulates, clearly formulated, but the divine truth about God—a truth which people themselves could not possibly arrive at had it not been revealed to them by God. Truth can be investigated, truth can be known, truth can be proven, but truth cannot be contrived. Your brother asserts: 'Dogmas are as far from the Christian spirit as the stars from the earth.' This is not true. When the incarnate Son of God revealed the dogma of the Holy Trinity to His disciples the Apostles, saying: *Go ye therefore and teach all nations, baptizing them in the name of the Father, and of the Son and of the Holy Spirit,* He inextricably united the dogma with the teaching about the spirit of Christianity, saying: *teaching them to observe all things whatsoever I have commanded you* (Matt. 28:19-20)....

"Your brother writes: 'Heresy is a departure from the majority opinion.' This is not true. Heresy is a departure from the divine truth and not from the opinion of the majority. It is not to the majority that the Lord entrusted the truth when he said: *Fear not, little flock, for it is your Father's good pleasure to give you the kingdom* (Luke 12:32). The Roman Catholic Church's members number several times larger than the Orthodox Church's, but in departing from the truth it has entered into heresy.

"Your brother writes: 'I consider it entirely possible that a man may decisively accept all the dogmas of the Faith and yet be far from the spirit of Christianity.' It is true that, unfortunately, this happens. But such people can easily find the way to salvation if they want to correct their lives. But he who possesses an incorrect, contradictory and false understanding of the Faith and Christian Truth has difficulty finding salvation, even when he wants it. Even more difficult is it for him to possess a Christian spirit and the spirit of Christ.... You write that your brother graduated from a Petersburg university. If someone were to tell your brother that in order to obtain a good position as a district attorney or even a judge one does not need any high school or university education, but only love for his fellow man, would he believe it? It is just as impossible for a man who does not have a correct and true knowledge of the dogmas of the Christian Faith to possess a Christian spirit. Due to lack of time and poor health I am unable to write more. But I will tell you briefly: if your brother is a sincere and conscientious person, as you write, then let him pray to our Lord Jesus Christ with faith, so that He would enlighten him with the Truth; and then let him read also with faith *Orthodox Confession* by Peter Moghila. (This book is in the Zadonsk bookstore, but if you cannot find it I can send it to you.) As the all-good Lord arranges for your brother, may it be so. The Lord *will have all men to be saved and come to the knowledge of the truth* (I Tim. 2:4)."

To one student, a linguist, who had turned to Fr. Ambrose with his perplexities, the Elder wrote (1871): "You write that, consciously believing in the existence of God, you have almost come to the conclusion that His representation in three Persons and the division of the heavenly powers is nothing other than the ideal of a government.

"This understanding of yours is entirely unreliable and far from the truth, especially because of some mixture of the Divinity with the creatures He created. The One God in three Persons is one thing, the nine angelical hierarchies that He created is another, and, finally, another thing is earthly and human government. The Triune God is invisible and inaccessible to the creation, even to the angels, much less to men. He was in part made known through revelation, first to the prophets by the Holy Spirit, and then through the Only-Begotten Son of God, Who was incarnate, as the holy evangelist John the Theologian said: *No man hath seen God at any time; the only-begotten Son, which is in the bosom of the Father, he hath declared him* (John 1:18). As the One God is in three Persons, we can see some resemblance in the three lights of the sun. One is the sun itself, another is the light it radiates, and another are the rays that come from it. All of this is one essence and undivided, but at the same time triune. A second similarity can be seen in the human soul. The mind of a man is one thing, while another thing is the internal word born in the mind and which is given to another person yet remains within us. Another thing is the spirit that enlivens man and sees his secrets, as it has been said: *For what man knoweth the things of a man, save the spirit of man which is in him? Even so the things of God knoweth no man, but the Spirit of God* (I Cor. 2:11). All of this comprises one reason-endowed human existence, and at the same time there is a three-fold existence. Created beings, especially people, can only come to one conclusion about the God Who is One and Triune. All that is visible is from the Invisible. All that has matter is from That which is without matter. All that has a beginning is from the Beginningless. All that has end is from the Endless. All that is temporary is from the Eternal. All that is limited is from the Limitless. All that can be measured is from the Measureless. All that can be attained is from the Unattainable. Some of the Holy Fathers suppose that first were created the ten angelic hierarchies.... But the tenth order fell; there remained only nine ranks of angels, in emulation of which there exists on earth not some sort of ideal human government, but the one true universal Church, founded by the Son of God, our Lord Jesus Christ, and it is redeemed by His most precious divine blood.... As far as human governments go—they have no relationship to the heavenly hierarchy or even to the earthly, because the one, true Church is not confined to any government, but exists throughout the universe; and its members are the truly faithful and truly pious Christians. To God it matters not what nation a man is from, only whether he is a truly faithful and pious Christian. 'One man who has pleased God is worth more than a thousand of the impious,' as St. John Chrysostom says. It is true and indisputable that it is pleasing not only to God but to all the pious that an entire nation should flourish with piety and a true understanding of the Faith. But what can we do, now that the time has come when many only concern themselves with the vain things of the world, neglecting the one thing needful."

Fr. Ambrose spoke once about the theater: "Your friend N. considers the theater to be the one and only true school of morals. Then why does he himself go to church and receive the holy Mysteries of Christ? It would imply that the theater is not the only school of morals.... And it is wrong to attach any particular importance to the theater as a moral teacher. Take, for example, two scenes—one of spiritual content, such as the crucifixion of our Lord Jesus Christ, Who endured the most horrible sufferings and the most shameful death in order to save the fallen human race; the other scene, a worldly one from people's lives, such as a husband and wife who have fought and separated. Let N. tell you according to his conscience which of these scenes will have the most beneficial effect on a person's moral character. If his taste in moral objects is not completely corrupted, then without a doubt he should place more importance on the scene depicting our Lord's crucifixion for our sins. However, in the theaters scenes from people's lives are presented to the audience. I must add that sometimes these scenes are quite dirty. Besides, what kind of atmosphere is there usually in a theater? Worldly music that does not allow even one spiritual thought or one spiritual feeling. And the spectators' absent-minded expressions: glancing to-and-fro, laughing, sometimes out-laughing one another. At certain cynical representations they are brought to displeasure that is expressed in tempestuous shouts, or when entertained by pleasurable feelings, they are accompanied by ceaseless laughter and heated applause, etc. This is a school of morality? On the contrary, this is a school of immorality, capable of smothering the last traces of morality in a man's soul, if there were any traces there at all. This is why such people as your N. now appear—quarrelsome, stubborn, irascible—because they study morality in theaters. I have even had to hear that some call the theater the threshold of the Church. I might agree with the statement that the theater is the threshold of the Church, only it is the rear exit."*

The Elder was asked, is it right to pray for convicted state criminals? Fr. Ambrose answered the following about the death of Karakozov: "If he has sincerely repented and brought before the Lord and his confessor sincere awareness and confession of all his sins, then G.A.P.'s words are just, and he can be commemorated without a doubt no matter how they buried him. It is not so important how a man is buried, but in what state his soul departed this life. If he only repented superficially, for human appearance's sake, then what good will any church commemoration do him? But we have no idea whether or not his repentance was sincere, or even if he received Communion; let those who are interested in this find out and then act accordingly. That he was deprived of a burial and that he ended in such a shameful death, etc.—all of this, in the presence of sincere repentance, may serve to dispel some of the onerous guilt of his crime. It will serve as a lesson to others, so that they would not forget themselves to such an extent and be so audacious. May the all-good Lord enlighten us all, whether we will or not, and have mercy on us as only He knows how."

About the authority of evil spirits over people, Fr. Ambrose wrote: "Demons have the quality of first darkening the mind, and then of touching the heart; and then only do they take possession of the whole body, like wild beasts, first sucking the blood out of the head, and then devouring the entire body."

Fr. Ambrose wrote more particularly concerning the power of evil spirits over people in the following letter:

"Forgive me that I was not able due to lack of time to answer your letter of June 3. "You ask: 'Could it really be possible that

---

*This whole letter is very interesting [auth.].

a demon can enter into a person simply at the behest of some old woman,* and into whomever she wants?' From the example that you yourself set forward about the swine (cf. Luke 8:32), it is clear that it is entirely incorrect to suppose that someone can be subjected to the enemy's actions according to an evil person's desire alone. This occurs only with those to whom God allows it, and God does not allow it without reason, but for various sins—for pride, for malice and enmity, or for an unclean life, as is written in one letter by the blessed Elder Macarius. Just as the Lord allowed the demons to enter the swine, so does He sometimes allow demonic powers to invade those who conduct a swinish life, or who are enslaved to other passions. But he who leads a proper Christian life according to the divine Gospel commandments is subject to the influence neither of malicious old women nor even the demons themselves, as it is written: *Upon the asp and basilisk shalt thou tread and thou shalt trample upon the lion and dragon* (Ps. 90:13); and *if they drink any deadly thing it shall not hurt them* (Mark 16:18). Further on you write: 'Is it possible that baptism, the receiving of the Holy Mysteries and in general all the sanctification that we receive from the different Sacraments are powerless to protect us from such activities?' These Sacraments not only do not protect us if we receive them unworthily, but even give the demonic powers greater access to us, as we can see in the example of Judas who, having the evil thought of betrayal, unworthily received the Last Supper. That is why it is written in the Gospels: *then entered satan into Judas* (Luke 22:3). You also write: 'It seems that the Church forbids us, and not only forbids but teaches, not to believe in any form of fortune-telling, sorcery, and the like.' The Church forbids us to have recourse to these activities, but this very forbidding indicates an acceptance of their existence

---

*That is, an old woman who practices witchcraft.—ED.

and actuality. The Church simply commands not to believe in various superstitions, for example, omens, signs, differentiation of days,* etc. You ask, 'Why aren't these secrets known to the educated? After all, they could work even more evil with them.' They are quite known. What is this current spreading of spiritism and the like amongst the educated if not the same demonic delusion? Half of America is now practicing this. How many pastors in Holland have gone mad over it? How many people in Petersburg has the magician Yum drawn into it? And is it not from demonic suggestion that educated people have shaken the faith and good morals of whole generations? Through ignorant people the devil works by ignorance and superstition, but through the educated, by sophisticated means. Did not Voltaire work not a little evil by propagating the poison of unbelief and atheism at the suggestion of the devil?

"What is this free thinking that leads people away from God and His Church, if not the invention and suggestion of the demons? So also are the tricks of some of them, the so-called magicians, and there are a number of them. They cannot be explained as mere agility or deception, to which they themselves attribute their magic. This is the same thing as sorcery among the simple folk, except that among the simple folk it is based on superstition and crude maliciousness, while this is based on money-making and subtle maliciousness. You write: 'If it pleases God to punish the impious, then why does He need to use such instruments as sorcerers, as if He were not able to do it without them?' The Lord does not encroach upon people's free will, and He sometimes allows evil people to do evil with the aid of demonic powers when He wants to punish others. And why should He use some other means when there are already willing instruments? This is apparent in the words of the

---

*He is probably referring to such practices as astrology.—ED.

Apostle Paul: *But if our unrighteousness commend the righteousness of God, what shall we say? Is God unrighteous who taketh vengeance?* (Rom. 3:5). You also write: 'The laws of Peter the First do not address damage done by sorcerers. Probably they were approved by the Holy Synod.' Probably they were *not* approved, or this would not be so. Furthermore you are surprised that a priest was unable to exorcise a demon from one of his daughters, although he was able to exorcise the demons from almost all of the possessed people brought to him. Almost all—that means not all, which would mean that the reason lies in the people he was not able to exorcise. Finally you ask: 'Why do not all priests exorcise the demonized?' The authority is given to all priests, but in order to use it one must have firm faith, a pious life and a particular calling.

"I desire that you have an evangelical-Orthodox understanding."

Being a zealous defender of Orthodoxy, Fr. Ambrose wrote several articles and letters containing detailed and concise rebuttals of the Lutheran and Papist heresies, even during Elder Macarius' lifetime.

When people of heterodox denominations turned to him for advice, something that happened not rarely, the Elder resolved their problems with love, always pointed out to them the mistakeness of their confession and had the joy of bringing them to the Orthodox Church.

One French Catholic woman wrote to Fr. Ambrose the following: "Much respected and good Father! Forgive me that I have made bold to write you a few lines. I heard that you are a true man of God, and therefore I have allowed myself to ask through this letter your wise advice, of which I am in great need. The demon of pride rules me to such an extent that it does not allow me to fulfill my obligations as necessary. What should I do to escape this? Several years ago, I was dangerously ill, and I promised God then that if He would save my life and restore me to health, I would behave in such a manner that the Lord might forget my previous sins. But alas! This promise that I made then on my death bed I have not kept. The Lord preserved my life, but I, instead of keeping my promise, have only become worse than before; therefore, God is punishing me by devastating me with what I hold dearest. I had a friend that lived with me, who was very dear to me. He was a Catholic priest. God who had granted me this friend, took him away—he died of tuberculosis in Naples—and pangs of conscience do not leave me alone. I do not know what the reason was for his illness, because he never told me about it. Perhaps my letters were intercepted? Or maybe he was angry with me? Why did he not tell me about his illness? These are the questions that I constantly ask myself and which ceaselessly torment me. Sometimes I am afraid that I will lose my mind, because some kind of voice tells me that he wrote me. But where is his letter? Of whom should I demand it? Then another thought comes: perhaps I am the cause of his death? Perhaps he bore punishment for his own guilt? Why did I torment him with my letters? Why did the demon choose me to tempt him? And why did I suffer so—and still suffer for him—why do I stubbornly refuse to forget him? My father, help me, give me advice. What should I do? I want to die just to be able to see him. Life holds no attraction for me. I am guilty, I am very stupid and am not able to appear before God, for I would be judged and am, as I am afraid, already cursed. The torments that I am experiencing have their cause. Why does God send them to me? So that I would bring forth repentance—but in my present condition, that is very difficult. My responsibilities require that I be healthy and cheerful. What should I do? Tell me. Forgive me that I am asking you to answer me at the stated address. If you do not count me unworthy of your answer, then I beg you to answer me. If I do not receive a letter from you, then I will think that you also condemn me."

Fr. Ambrose answered tactfully this howl of a sick, sinful and tormented soul in the following letter, full of Christian love: "I received a letter from you in December of last year, and I am not a little amazed that you, without even knowing me, have written to me with such trust. If you have for God's sake approached me, an unworthy one, so trustingly, then I could not possibly leave your letter unanswered. Only I will first answer your second question, and then I will answer the first one, that is, about pride.

"You write that you had a friend that died of tuberculosis. Now you are tormented by various thoughts, doubts and perplexities, that perhaps you were the cause of his death because you tormented him with your letters, which he did not answer.

"To this I will tell you that you cannot kill a man with letters. The reason he did not answer you could be very simple—either he did not want to distress you with news about his illness, or he hoped to recover soon; and then he would have written to you, as all tuberculosis victims think and cherish such hopes. You further write: Perhaps he has been punished for his own guilt? If you both bear the same guilt, then you must bring forth repentance and pray to the merciful Lord, that He would forgive you and your friend your guilt. For the Son of God came into the world in the flesh in order to call not the righteous but sinners to repentance. You also write that although you are suffering, you cannot forget your friend. That is how it is with all who love someone not with Godly love, but with human love. Incidentally, if you will remember your friend as I said above, that is, with the thought of repentance before God, then such remembrance will be profitable for him and for you. You are also obligated to have such a thought by your former promise to correct your life and live it in a way that will please

God. But you write that your present responsibilities prevent such a disposition of spirit, as it requires health and cheerfulness. Neither external cheerfulness nor physical health can hinder thoughts of repentance, for although repentance requires some degree of inward sorrow, this sorrow can be mingled with a certain joy, as the Apostle Paul writes: *Rejoice evermore. Pray without ceasing. In every thing give thanks: for this is the will of God* (I Thess. 5:16-18). The words of the Apostle show that not only the righteous but even sinners can rejoice to some degree at the thought that the merciful Lord has granted them the means to receive God's eternal mercy; and this means sincere repentance and strenuous correction of one's life.

"Now I will speak about your first question. You write: 'The demon of pride rules me to such an extent that it does not allow me to fulfill my obligations as I should. What should I do to escape from it?' To this I will have to make a reply that is not easy to accept for everyone, only for those of good will who are sincerely searching for the truth and the ways of truth. And I will speak not from myself, but as the ancient Holy Father, St. John of the Ladder writes: pride is conquered by humility, and the virtue of humility does not belong to all people of different religions, but only to the right-believing. There is only one right and true Faith, and not many, as the Apostle Paul bears witness: one Lord, one faith (cf. Eph. 4:5). The words of the Apostle show that there is one true God, just as there is one true Faith, and not many faiths into which human opinions were brought in place of divine truth. For instance, in the Gospels the Lord Himself says of the Holy Spirit that He proceeds from the Father. But in your Roman Church the words 'and from the Son' are added out of human deduction. Also, the Lord says of the holy Mystery of Communion of His holy Blood: *drink ye all of it* (Matt. 26:27). But in your Roman Church only the clergy have assumed the privilege of drinking the Blood of

Christ, while the lay people only take the Body of Christ, and the clergy justify themselves by saying that where the Body is, there is the Blood. Here I have pointed out two mistakes of the Roman Church, the chief hierarch of which allowed a third incorrectness because of his vainglory, assuming primacy before the other patriarchs of the Church of Christ. Having allowed vainglory which is contrived and inappropriate, it is not even possible to war with the passion of pride. For this reason I invite you to study the teaching, rules and customs of the Orthodox Church, which has preserved unchanged the original Christian teachings, having begun in Jerusalem, where the Lord was crucified, and from which the Apostles began their preaching. What do you say to my proposal? Reply sincerely."

To another Catholic, a senator, Fr. Ambrose wrote: "Forgive me magnanimously that having received from you through Fr. Abbot ten rubles for the poor, I did not inform you or thank you in a timely manner. Having received also from you twenty-five rubles (ten rubles from your brother for the poor, fifteen from you to use at my sinful discretion), I send to both of you my sincerest gratitude for your zeal and include the words of the Psalmist: *"Blessed is the man that hath understanding for the poor man and the pauper; in an evil day the Lord will deliver him* (Ps. 40). I also thank you for the package, the Bible with the beautiful binding and small format, that you sent to me, a sinner. When I received these books the thought came to me: There is only one Bible, but its meaning is interpreted differently by different Christian denominations. Where did this difference come from? This is the reason: The Eastern Orthodox Church accepts the Bible in all its fullness—the Old Testament and the Christian teaching, following the words of the Lord Himself spoken to the Apostles: *Go ye therefore and teach all nations, baptizing them in the name of the Father, and of the Son and of the Holy Spirit: teaching them to observe all things whatsoever I have commanded you* (Matt. 28:19-20). Other denominations do not consider it necessary to fulfill all things, but have compiled a religious teaching according to their choice—what they like they accept, and what they do not like, they reject. From such choosing has come various heresies. The word 'heresy' comes from the Greek word 'aireo', meaning 'I choose.'

"The Western Roman Catholic Church gave the various European denominations the first cause [for heresy] when, out of human logic, to the words of the Lord Himself it added that the Holy Spirit proceeds also from the Son. After this addition followed omissions according to choice against the words of the Lord Himself, Who said: *Till Heaven and earth pass, one jot or one tittle shall in no wise pass from the law, till all be fulfilled* (Matt. 5:18). Well, this is what occurred to me when I received the Bible from you, and this is what I have written. Forgive me if I have written out of place or without need. St. John Climacus writes: 'Do not act wise in the presence of the wise.'"

W E SHALL TURN from Fr. Ambrose's correspondence with lay people to his correspondence with monastics. In light of its more specific character, we will touch on it only briefly.

Fr. Ambrose had a custom on the great Feasts of the Nativity of Christ and the bright Resurrection of Christ to send to his spiritual children, mainly to the nuns, short greetings with the coming Feast. As the number of his spiritual children grew significantly while the Elder's sickliness and weakness increased, he had to exchange these separate, personal greetings for general greeting letters, which were sent to all the convents with which Fr. Ambrose was involved. These general greetings began in 1870 and continued until the Elder's repose. Furthermore, they took on the character of a deeply comprehensive discussion about the meaning of the coming Feast, or contained explanations of one or another less-understood church hymn or passage in the Holy Scriptures, and sometimes they were moral instructions concerned mainly with monastic virtues—humility, obedience and others.

Thus, for Christmas of 1870 the Elder wrote to his spiritual children about the lofty meaning of the Incarnation: "Wisdom seekers in the Lord! By the mercy and long-suffering of God we are once again reaching the yearly time of the Feast of Christ's Nativity.

"Instead of the usual simple greetings with the Feast, I want to say a few words to you about the great Mystery of this glorious Feast. The Church in its hymns already calls the faithful to contemplate with lofty mind: 'the Sovereign's pilgrimage, and with cleansed hearts to mystically delight in an immortal feast within the lowly cave': As the Omnipresent has bent the heavens and descended to earth without leaving the bosom of the Father; as the Invisible has become visible; as the Co-unoriginate Word and Co-eternal Son of God has become the Son of the Virgin; as the Pre-eternal and Incomprehensible One is now born of the Virgin as a babe; as the One unapproachable to all is now as a babe embraced by maternal, virginal arms; how He Who covers the heavens with the clouds is now as a babe wrapped in swaddling clothes; how He Who hast created all things in wisdom, now as a swaddled babe, is laid in a manger of irrational beasts to save men from irrationality; how He Who nourishes all things now as a babe drinks His mother's milk. O awesome Mystery! O things incomprehensible! How God without undergoing change has become a man, and makes man as a god, as the prophet foretold: *'I said: Ye are gods, and all of you the sons of the Most High!'* (Ps. 81:6). But, O our sinfulness! We as humans are dying. O, our vanity and carelessness for divine sonship! We love our slavery to the passions and evil will, willingly and unwillingly bending our necks to the yoke of the enemy. O, our blindness and obscurity! The blessed ears of the shepherds, when they heard the Angels singing in the air: *Glory to God in the highest!* (Luke 2:14), brought the good news of peace on earth and good will to men. Their blessed eyes were in awe when they saw the spotless Lamb which had come from Mary's womb. Blessed are all they who keep God's will and peace, which transcends human minds. The blessed and wise Magi came from distant lands to bow down before the One born of the Virgin, bringing Him worthy gifts: gold for He is King, frankincense for He is God, and myrrh for He is the One that dies and yet is immortal. Blessed are all they that worthily bow down before Him in spirit and in truth, bringing Him gifts according to their strength: as gold, righteous mites of compassion; as frankincense and sweet-smelling incense, praises and pure prayers of repentance and confession; as fragrant myrrh, grateful remembrance of His suffering and reverent worship of the life-creating wounds of Him Who became incarnate and crucified in the flesh for our salvation. But we, the slothful and insensitive, of whom I am the first, are unable to raise our minds above the earth and with purified hearts to delight in the immortal feast in the lowly cave. Humbling and reproaching ourselves, may we fervently and reverently be attentive to the readings and hymns in the Church and, as from the source of life and immortality, drink in consolation and enlightenment and salvation, through the mercy and unspeakable lovingkindness of the One Who was incarnate for our sakes, the Son of God, to Whom be glory, honor and worship, together with His unoriginate Father and His most holy and good and life-creating Spirit, now and ever and to the ages of ages. Amen.

"Thou Who wast unutterably born of the Virgin, have mercy on us who have grown cold, through the prayers of Thy Most Pure Mother and all who have pleased Thee!"

For Pascha of the following year, 1871, the Elder sent an epistle to his spiritual children which elucidated the spiritual meaning of the Paschal services:

"O ones wise in the Lord! For the Feast of the Nativity of Christ, in place of the usual greetings I wrote to you about the great Mystery of this glorious Feast. And now I would like to say something to you about the mystical meaning of the Triumph of Christian triumphs, that is, the Resurrection of Christ. But because of my weakness and sickness I have neither the strength nor the opportunity. I can only tell you briefly that the yearly triumphant and bright Feast of the Resurrection of Christ, besides having its own meaning, serves also for us as a reminder of the general resurrection of the whole world, which is particularly apparent in the remarkable Paschal Matins.

"First: During the radiant night, after the reading of the Midnight Office, there is the triumphal procession around the church by the clergy and all the faithful with lighted candles, together with the cross, the icons, and the ringing of the bells. This is clearly reminiscent of the Gospel parable of the ten virgins woken at midnight with the cry: *Behold, the bridegroom cometh! Go ye out to meet Him. Then all those virgins arose, and trimmed their lamps* (cf. Matt. 25: 6-7). These virgins are the souls of the faithful, and the Bridegroom is Christ. The night is our temporary life. The lamps are our faith and good works. Do not the Gospel parable as well as the triumphant procession around the church by the faithful accompanied by the ringing of bells represent the general resurrection at the end of the world, when the voice of the archangels' trumpets will awaken all the dead, and the faithful in the Lord, like the Gospel virgins, will go forth to meet Him with their lamps, each according to her own worthiness?

"Second: While this triumphant procession around the church is being performed, the church doors are closed. The faithful that walk see the light in the church, but on the path before them they see only impenetrable darkness, and thus they come to stand before the closed doors of the church. Does this not mean that all who are resurrected at the universal resurrection will see the heavenly bridal chamber of glory, but not all will enter therein—only those who are worthy—whose lamps, like those of the wise virgins, do not go out at the meeting of the Bridegroom Christ? All the rest, who like the foolish virgins have let their lamps go out, will pitifully repeat the beginning of the hymn: *I see Thy bridal chamber, adorned O my Savior, but I have no wedding garment, that I may enter there* (Exapostilarion, Matins of Holy Week).

"Third: Before the closed doors of the church, the presiding clergyman gives the usual initial Paschal glorification of the Holy Trinity and the singing of 'Christ is Risen.' Then, with the cross in hand, he opens the doors and enters the church first, and after him enter all the other Christians, singing the joyous hymn: *Christ is risen from the dead, trampling down death by death, and upon those in the tombs bestowing life*. Repeating this many times, to it is added yet more joyful singing: *It is the day of Resurrection! Let us be radiant, O people! It is the Pascha, the Pascha of the Lord! From death to life and from earth to Heaven, Christ our God has passed us, who sing the hymn of victory!* (Irmos, Canon of Paschal Matins). No longer is heard the usual singing that arouses us to compunction, only the ceaseless sweet singing awakening joy in all. The clergy continually come forth from the altar in brilliant vestments; ceaselessly we look upon the Cross of Christ and venerate this symbol of our salvation; ceaselessly we are surrounded by clouds of holy incense. All hold lighted candles in their hands; on the lips of all—those who serve and those present who stand and sing—is heard only the joyful: Christ is Risen!

"Thus is celebrated the temporal Pascha of Christ on earth,

and all Christians are allowed to celebrate—the worthy and the unworthy, because the present life is subject to change. Often the worthy become unworthy and the unworthy become worthy, which is clearly portrayed by Judas and the thief. At first Judas was among the chosen twelve Apostles of Christ, following Christ for three years, listening continually to His teaching, having the power to cast out demons and heal many different diseases. But at the end he went mad from carelessness and love of money, betrayed Christ, then perished eternally. The thief had been part of a band of hard-core robbers for three years, but, being enlightened upon the cross, he confessed willingly the Crucified Son of God, Lord and King, and was the first to enter Paradise. May we always hold these examples in our remembrance, so that we might always refrain from the sin of judging, even though we might see someone sinning at the very end of his life, as St. John of the Ladder assures us.

"But it will be different at the heavenly Feast of the eternal Pascha, after the general resurrection and judgment. To that Feast will be allowed only the elect, the worthy. And whoever will once be allowed into the heavenly bridal chamber, to the Feast of the eternal Pascha, will remain eternally among the ranks of celebrants, giving voice to their joy. Whoever is shown to be unworthy to participate in the celebration will be deprived and estranged eternally.

"However, now is not the time to speak particularly of the bitter fate of these last, for it is the all-joyous Feast. We will only say that all of us Christians, while we are still alive, should be careful and attentive to our salvation. And those who think they stand, in the words of the Apostle, should take care lest they fall, remembering always the terrible example of Judas who perished. In those of us who are infirm and falling, may the hope of correction be awakened, seeing the comforting example of the wise thief who inherited Paradise.

# ELDERSHIP

*"O, great and holiest Pascha, Christ! O, Wisdom, Word and power of God! Grant that we may more perfectly partake of Thee in the unending day of Thy Kingdom!"* (Canon of Paschal Matins).

The Elder sent another sort of Paschal greeting in 1881:

"Sisters in the Lord and mothers! Christ is Risen! Christ is Risen! Christ is Risen! I congratulate you all with the bright Feast of the Resurrection of Christ and fervently wish that you all may greet and pass this all-joyous Christian triumph in peace, rejoicing, and spiritual consolation, whoever is not hindered by the inimical infirmity. You ask, what kind of infirmity is this? Perhaps you think that by this I mean not keeping the Great Lenten fast. But St. John Chrysostom condescends to us and says: 'Those who fasted and those who have not fasted rejoice today, the continent and the lazy, revere the day!' (Paschal Homily of St. John Chrysostom). Perhaps you also think that this relates to the memory of previous sins, which hinders rejoicing. But he says also about this: 'Let no one weep over his sins, for forgiveness has shown forth from the grave.' Then what, you ask, is this infirmity? That inimical infirmity that inspired Cain to kill the guileless Abel and that inspired the Jews to crucify Christ the Savior and Redeemer of the world.

"You yourselves can understand that I am speaking of the passion of envy, which according to the Scriptures prefers not that which is profitable. The passion of envy does not allow anyone who is possessed by it to rejoice completely at any joyous feast or in any joyous circumstances. Like a worm, it always gnaws at the soul and heart with its turbid sorrow, because the envious considers his neighbor's happiness and success to be his own unhappiness, and the preference given to others he considers his own unmerited offense.

"One Greek emperor desired to know who is worse, the miser or the envious, for they both desire misfortune for the other. With this goal in mind he called two men in, a miser and an envier, and said to them: each of you ask of me whatever you wish; only know that the second one will receive twice as much as the first. The envious man and the miser argued a long time, each one not wanting to ask first, so that he might receive twofold. Finally the emperor asked the envious man to ask first. The envious man, full of ill-will toward his neighbor, instead of receiving something resorted to evil plotting and said to the emperor: 'Your Highness! Order me to pluck out my eye!' The amazed emperor asked him why he expressed such a desire. The envier replied: 'So that you, your Highness, would then order my comrade to pluck out both his eyes.'

"Behold, how harmful and soul-destroying is envy, ever wishing harm to others. The envious is ready to harm himself, if only his neighbor might be harmed twice as much. We have presented an advanced degree of envy. But it, too, like other passions, has varying degrees and sizes; and therefore we should strive to squash and expel it at the first sensation, praying to God, the all-powerful Seer of Hearts, with the Psalmist's words: *from my secret sins cleanse me, and from those of others spare Thy servant* (Ps. 18:12). Also, with humility we must confess this infirmity to our spiritual father. The third means [to overcome envy] is to try in every way never to say anything bad about any person that we envy. Using these means we can, with God's help, be healed of the infirmity of envy, though it may not be right away.

"Envy comes from pride and also from carelessness in fulfilling what we should. Cain was careless in bringing a chosen sacrifice to God. When God disdained his sacrifice because of this carelessness, but accepted the fervent and chosen sacrifice of Abel, then Cain, possessed by envy, decided to kill and actually did kill righteous Abel. It is always better, as I have said above, to strive to expel envy from the very start through humble prayer, humble confession and reasonable silence. Whoever with God's help is able to expel the passion of envy from within himself can hope to triumph over other passions as well, and then he can rejoice with unutterable rejoicing not only on the bright Feast of the Resurrection of Christ and all other Christian feasts, but even on simple days will he always be in a good spiritual state and disposition. Amen.

"But forgive me for this unfestive greeting. I wanted to say something to you that was somewhat profitable, and the profitable rarely corresponds to the pleasant. Whoever does not like this greeting may read it on Thomas Sunday and notice that envy is at first revealed in irrational jealousy and rivalry, then in zealous attacking and criticizing the one whom we envy. So let us be wise and careful at the first signs of envious feelings, striving to reject them, asking for the all-powerful help for the sake of Christ the Lord, Crucified and Risen on the third day. Amen! Amen!!!"

Other festal epistles not presented here mostly contained the Elder's explanations of parts of the Psalms or other hymns, for example: *My mouth shall speak wisdom ...* (Ps. 48:4), or *With chastisement hath the Lorth chastened me ...* (Ps. 117:18), or *Will the Lord forget to be merciful ...* (Ps. 76:9), or *Thy virtue hast covered the heavens, O Lord ...\** or *Rod of the root of Jesse ... \*\** or *A strange mystery ...\*\*\** etc. *We will only say that by these letters Fr. Ambrose created one collective festive mood, and in this manner united his spiritual children into one spiritual family.*

General letters comprise only a small part of those letters to monastics that Fr. Ambrose wrote during his thirty years of

---

\* Irmos for the Feast of the Meeting of the Lord.
\*\* From the Canon for the Feast of the Nativity.
\*\*\* Also from the Nativity Canon.

eldership.* These letters are not so varied in content as the letters to lay people. He teaches all of them the same thing—how to have the fear of God, how to uproot the passions, how to progress in prayer, how generally to live as a monk or nun, escaping prelest and delusion. Nevertheless, they are deeply instructive and can be useful not only to monastics, but also to lay people. This is the main message of some of them: Christian wisdom is in preserving faith in the Lord during times of temptation; vigor comes from solitude with the Lord; depression is from ambition; consciousness of one's weaknesses, self-reproach and patience are the three steps to humility; the shortest path to Christ is to bear one another's burdens; the main hindrance to the acquisition of holiness is the lust of the flesh, lust of the eyes and vain pride (cf. I John 2:16); serious illnesses cause us to turn more seriously to God; spiritual rebirth begins with freedom from the passions and is perfected by attaining the virtues; it is more profitable for the sinner to remember hell than Paradise; a proud disciple should seek a tough elder; finding perfection without repentance is self-deception; prayer rules and fasting without keeping the commandments will not save us; we must go by the middle way; we must not insinuate ourselves into others' business, but attend to ourselves; works done with temperance are priceless, but extremes are from the devil; about temptations during prayer; etc.

## 3. THE CELL OF FR. AMBROSE. WEEKDAYS AND FEAST DAYS. EXCEPTIONAL DAYS.

Elder Ambrose's exterior life was very modest. As mentioned earlier, he occupied a small building to the right of the

---

*Fr. Ambrose's letters to monastics were published by Optina Monastery in two editions, compiled by the author.

skete gates. A small stairway from outside the Skete led to the porch, and from there to a low, dark corridor, on either side of which were benches where monks and male visitors waited. From the corridor, the first door to the left led to a small waiting room, where the Elder also came out to give general blessings. The front corner of the hall was filled with icons. The walls were hung all around with spiritual pictures and portraits, amongst which could be seen portraits of the Tsar; Metropolitans Philaret and Innocent of Moscow, and Philaret, Arsenius and Ioannicius of Kiev; Bishops Gregory II, Vladimir and Anastasius of Kaluga; the Moldavian Elder Paisius Velichkovsky and other spiritual elders from Optina and elsewhere. In the hall were a couch, chairs, tables and a bookcase with spiritual books, so that visitors could read while waiting for the Elder. Next to the waiting room was a small cell where the cell attendant, Fr. Michael, lived. Across from the waiting-room door was Elder Ambrose's cell, which was always hooked shut; it was opened only during cell Vigils and on certain other occasions. The Elder's cell had an anteroom where hung his simple, even patched clothing—two quilted cassocks and two lightweight ones, a simple peasant tunic, a light fur ryassa made from Little Russian white astrakhan. His woolen mantia, ryassa and klobuk were also kept there. The Elder's cell itself was hung with icons and portraits of spiritual people, mostly brought to the Elder as presents from his admirers. Amongst the icons that drew the most attention were: a) a small icon (about seven inches high) of the Tambov Mother of God, a blessing from Elder Ambrose's parents and before which a perpetual flame burned; b) a "Quick to Hear" icon of the Mother of God (about fourteen inches high), sent to the Elder as a gift from the Mt. Athos Chapel in Moscow; c) a large icon of the Great Martyr and Healer Panteleimon, before which a lampada also burned perpetually; d) a large image of the Kiev-Caves Mother of God

Exterior view of Elder Ambrose's cell.

with Sts. Anthony and Theodosius kneeling before Her, (this icon stood in front of Fr. Ambrose's cot, on his corner-shelf); and e) an artistic icon of the Savior "Made Without Hands."

Among the portraits of spiritual persons were the Troekurovo recluse Hilarion; the Vysha recluse, Bishop Theophan [now St. Theophan]; Archpriest Theodore Alexandrovich Golubinsky; the Kronstadt Archpriest Fr. John Ilyich Sergiev [now known as St. John of Kronstadt]; and others.

Along the east wall of the cell was a small writing desk, where the secretary wrote letters at the Elder's dictation. In the holy corner was an analogion with a little compartment containing a Psalter, an Horologion and other books necessary for reading the prayer rule. Along the southern wall was another table on which were various icons, candlestands with candles and a few spiritual books. Along the west wall was the Elder's cot, and near it was a brick wood-burning stove, which was covered during the wintertime with socks and flannel shirts. By the northern wall stood a bookcase which was filled with patristic and other spiritual texts. Between the bookcase and stove was the door. Next to it were three or four benches and two antique armchairs for honored guests. Next to the Elder's cell was the cell of another cell attendant, Fr. Joseph, also filled with icons and portraits.

Across from the entrance, at the end of the corridor, was the door to the hut, the rather large annex built for visiting women consisting of several rooms and a corridor that led to another log cabin behind, from which there was an exit to the outside of the Skete. Here there were a multitude of icons, amongst which was a large Athonite icon of the Mother of God named "It is Truly Meet." Such was the external atmosphere of Elder Ambrose's life.

The Elder usually began his weekdays with prayer. The cell attendants read the rule in turn while the Elder listened either standing near his bed or, as was usually the case because of his weakness, sitting on the seat placed there for him.... When he was sick he lay there during the reading, but he never skipped the rule. In order to hear the entire rule he would first awake at four in the morning, ring, and his cell attendants would appear and read the Morning Prayers, the Rule of the Twelve Psalms and the First Hour. Then after a brief rest, the Elder would hear the Third and Sixth Hours with Typica and, depending on the day of the week, a Canon with an Akathist to the Savior or the Mother of God; he always heard Akathists standing. The described rule was always carried out by the Elder with more or less extended pauses. For example, having listened to half of the morning prayer rule and feeling weak, he would dismiss his cell attendants; then having rested a little, he would call them back in to finish the rule. It was the same during the Hours. It could be that there were more important reasons for the Elder's pauses, namely, practicing mental prayer, which is highly probable. Having listened to the appointed prayers, the Elder began to wash up. One of the cell attendants would place a copper basin on a stool near his bed and pour a little warm water onto his hands from a large teapot, and the Elder would kneel over the basin and wash up. During this activity questions would begin to come from the cell attendants: "Batiushka! So-and-so is in such-and-such a situation. What should he do?" or "So-and-so asks a blessing for such-and-such a matter. Do you bless her to do it?" and so on. The Elder would do his business and answer questions at the same time. After washing the Elder would strengthen himself with some tea, during which he would dictate letters, and afterward he would go out to see the visitors.... Incidentally, this is how it was before the 1870's, when the Elder was stronger. After that, with the increase in the number of visitors resulting in his extreme exhaustion, he would arise for the morning rule later, at around 5:00; and, having heard the Hours with the Canon and Akathist, he would often lie down on the bed for a little rest. When arising, he would at times utter: "Oh! Everything hurts...." During the wintertime he often caught colds. He would wake up with his face swollen, with feverish chills or rheumatic pains throughout his body. He would wash up, then rub himself with alcohol or some other lotion. The cell attendants would nevertheless ask questions, and the Elder would answer in a barely audible voice. At that time the Elder would change his clothes and shoes; this would be repeated many times throughout the day. He often wrote about his bad health in letters to his close ones: "Weakness and sickliness increase, and the changing of shoes and shirts have tripled; I cannot bear heat or cold. I can bear only a sixty-three-degree temperature; anything higher or lower than that affects me poorly. Just try to keep one constant temperature when you have only natural wood heating, which is always raising the temperature."

While the Elder was dictating his letters at morning tea, visitors would approach his living quarters one by one—men from the inside and women from the outside. He would not even be able to finish a needed letter before people would already be knocking at his door and ringing the little bell. The cell attendant would go out. They would ask him to tell the Elder something. The cell attendant would usually say: "The Elder is busy." Soon another knock and ring would come from the impatient visitors, again the request, and again the same answer. But the longer this would continue, the greater the visitors' impatience would grow, even to the point of murmuring. The knocking and ringing would become more repeated. This time they would more unceremoniously ask the cell attendant, "Why don't you tell him?" or "You don't want to tell him," and so on. Nuns from various convents would crowd into the cabin together with lay women. Someone would say: "I have been living here and coming to see the Elder for over a week now, and I still can't reach him." Another would say: "I have been here for two weeks." No sooner would the cell attendant come out than a hundred voices would cry out to him, "Tell him, tell him." Wishing to calm the visitors if only a little bit, he would ask: "What shall I tell him?" Each one, of course, would tell him where she had come from. But how would he remember each one out of that pandemonium? Fr. Michael had a particular way of announcing them. He would come to the Elder and say: "They are waiting for you in the hut, Batiushka." "Who is there?" the Elder would ask. "People from Moscow, Viazma, Tula, Belev, Kashira, and other towns." "Tell them to wait." He would come out again. "Well," they would ask, "did you tell him?" "Yes." "So what did he say?" "He tells you to wait." "Yeah—you didn't even tell him."

Meanwhile, the sickly Elder would prepare himself to go out to the visitors, having changed his shoes and clothes and having been busy with one or with several of the brothers all at once, carrying on some group discussion. While listening to the Elder's words of instruction, those present would help him change his clothes and shoes. They would take off his boots and damp socks, give him dry ones, and so on. It was always like that. Finally, perhaps at around 9:00 in the morning, if not later, the Elder would come out to the long-expectant visitors. He would pass along the corridor where the men would wait, blessing some along the way, saying a few words to others. Those who were in particular need he would take into the little hallway and spend a little time with them. Then he would enter the hut, and there he would stay for a long time. It was impossible not to notice that not everyone came to the sickly Elder with a need, but some only took up his time, thereby especially burdening him.

He complained about such visitors in his letters: "Old age,

weakness, loss of energy, much-caring and much drowsiness—and all of their futile talk doesn't allow me to catch my breath. One explains that his head and feet are weak, another complains that he has many sorrows, yet another tells me how he is in a state of constant anxiety. Just try to listen to it all and then give an answer—and you cannot just be silent to some, for they will take offense and grieve. It is not for nothing that they often say: 'Talk to a sick person with medical treatment.' A sick person wants to describe his condition, and the doctor gets bored hearing it. But there is nothing else he can do—he listens, not wanting to further irritate or worry the loquacious sufferer."

To some impatient visitors the Elder would present the great God-pleasers as examples and, counselling them to endure, would say to them in his usual good-natured way: "Moses endured, Elisha endured, Elias endured, and so will I."

Midday approaches—it is time to have lunch. Without dismissing the visitors, the Elder would go to the cell adjoining his own, the cell of his cell attendant Fr. Joseph. There, half lying near the table from exhaustion, he would eat his two-course meal—fresh fish soup, not very oily, and cranberry kisel (juice thickened with cornstarch). On fast days they made him a stew or potato soup with vegetable oil instead of fish soup. Once the thought came to him to go without oil and, so that the lenten food would not be too austere, he asked that crushed walnuts be sprinkled in. It happened that he decided to honor an abbess acquaintance of his with this repast. "What is this you are eating, Batiushka?" she asked him. "This is nauseating."

The Elder ate no more than would a three-year-old child. His lunch lasted ten or fifteen minutes, during which his cell attendants would again ask him questions about various individuals and get his answers. But sometimes, in order to give his head a little rest, he would ask one of his close ones to read him something light. He sometimes loved to listen to one of

Krylov's fables. That book almost always lay near him on the table in this cell. One day they brought him a composition by some nobleman about Russian monasteries in which, unfortunately, the respected author noticed nothing but the dirt. The Elder listened to this book with a sad but serious countenance and never expressed his opinion on it.

When the Elder finished eating, if he was weak he would receive someone who was in greater need right there as he lay on his cot. Or sometimes he would receive everyone for a general blessing, beginning with the men, and then the women. The cell would fill up to the maximum. At these general receptions the Elder would enlighten those who needed it with some apt remark, often by some folk saying that would be understood by the one at whom it was directed. Or, he would tell a story that would serve as an answer to someone's secret thoughts. Sometimes he would have one of the visitors read some appropriate fable out of Krylov, then he would say some words of instruction in a humorous tone, and finally, having blessed everyone, head for his cell. Following him would be a hundred voices calling, "Batiushka! Batiushka! Give me a little word, just a couple of words." But the weary, sickly Elder would somehow manage to push through the crowds with the aid of the cell attendants and enter his cell, then latch the door from the inside with the hook, so that the crowd would not surge in there as well.

If the Elder had enough energy after lunch he would go out to bestow a general blessing in the hut. The cell attendant would arrive beforehand to close all the windows, so that there would be no drafts. Everyone who sat there would arise and stand along both sides, leaving a small passageway for the Elder. Finally, the door would open and the Elder would appear in a white tunic, over which he would wear, winter or summer, a light fur ryassa, with a quilted kamilavka on his head. Coming

Отецъ Небесный не судитъ никому же, а весь судъ предаде Сыну Своему; а ты кто такая?!!!
Носить, что судить другихъ значитъ осуждать свою душу по слову Спасителя,
 
The handwriting of Elder Ambrose.

through the door and stopping on the steps, he always prayed before the icon of the Mother of God "It is Truly Meet" and then proceeded further, attentively glancing at those people who sought his blessing and making the sign of the cross over them. Questions could be heard coming from the crowd, which he would answer simply but wisely. Sometimes the Elder would sit down, then all present would kneel around him and listen with deep attention to his talks, the meaning of which was always to be found in profitable moral teaching or a rebuke of someone's sins. Most often he would offer advice about patience, condescension to one's neighbors' weaknesses, and forcing oneself to do good, saying that the *Kingdom of Heaven suffereth violence* (Matt. 11:12), that *we must through much tribulation enter the Kingdom of God* (Acts 14:22), and *he that shall endure to the end, the same shall be saved* (Matt. 24:13). Sometimes these enlightening talks or general blessings encroached upon the Elder's rest period, and the cell attendant would remind him of this. Then he would remove his cap, bow to all and say in his usual humorous tone: "I am much obliged that you came to visit. Fr. Joseph says that it is time...." Another time the cell attendant would say: "Batiushka, it is already two o'clock." Batiushka would answer: "Turn the hands back and it will be one." In the summertime on warm days he would come outside to bless. His appearance would be a true joy to everyone that languished in expectation of him. From the porch to the hut were railings, on the one side of which stood the crowd, on the other side walked the Elder, bestowing his blessing along the rows of people, stopping here and there to answer questions. No one dared to cross the boundary without the Elder's blessing and invitation, and if someone should be so audacious, the Elder would give him several prostrations to make.

Although it was rare, there were some days when the Elder

did not rest at all after lunch, perhaps because he felt strong enough to do without it or just could not sleep. Then he would ring the secretary and dictate a letter to someone. Thus he had not an idle minute. No one disturbed the Elder when he rested. The crowd would go to the guest house. All around the doors were locked—in the hut and in the Skete at the main entranceway. After a brief midday rest, the Elder would again be on his feet; and if he felt sufficiently healthy, he would again go out to discuss things with the visitors. If he was feeling weak, he would receive visitors in Fr. Joseph's cell, lying on his bed. Here he would drink tea at about 5:00 in the evening, between visitors. Again and again he would receive and discuss, discuss and receive. Sometimes the Elder would unexpectedly interrupt his discussion with visitors and go to his cell for a little while—these were moments when he felt the need to be alone with God in prayful contemplation, so that he could again return to the people with a refreshed soul and continue his work. The Elder ate supper at 8:00 p.m., at which time the table was laid with the same meal as at lunch. During supper the cell attendants would again ask him about something, and the Elder would continue answering; or he would again ask them to read. Soon after supper, if the Elder's strength was entirely exhausted, he would limit himself to bestowing a general blessing. If his strength had not completely given out, then the usual receptions and discussion would begin again and last until as late as 11:00 at night.... In spite of the Elder's extreme exhaustion and sickliness, the day would always conclude with the evening prayer rule, consisting of Small Compline, a Canon to the Guardian Angel and the Prayers Before Sleep. From almost incessant day-long reports, plus all of the Elder's and his visitors' business, the cell attendants were barely able to stand on their feet; nevertheless they would take turns reading the appointed prayer rule.... At the end of the rule the Elder would usually ask forgiveness of all present, if he had sinned in any way in word, deed or thought. Finally the cell attendants would receive the Elder's blessing and head for the door. Sometimes the clock would strike. In a weak and barely audible voice the Elder would ask: "What time is it?" "Twelve," they would answer. "We are late," he would say.

The Elder always went to sleep in his clothing—in summer in a tunic, in winter in a quilted cassock, always belted with a leather belt. He always had a monastic cap on his head and a prayer rope in his hands. He only took off his boots, but left his socks on. God alone knows how the Elder spent his nighttime hours. Only when they came to him for the morning rule did the cell attendants notice that during the night he had changed his flannel shirts several times, from which it can be deduced that he did not sleep without interruption.

On the eve of every Sunday and feast day Fr. Ambrose always listened to the All-Night Vigil in his cell. At first, during the sixties, the Elder's devoted spiritual son, Hieroschemamonk Gabriel, always served. Near the doorway would stand two or three readers. The future Skete Superior, Fr. Anatole (Zertsalov), at the time a simple monk, sang bass. The cell attendants were the readers, and Fr. Clement was the canonarch. As time passed, things changed. Sick and infirm skete brethren asked the Elder's blessing to attend his cell Vigils rather than go to the Monastery. The Elder, of course, gave them his blessing. Thus the number of people present increased. Therefore, so that it would not get too hot and stuffy in the Elder's cell, the choir was asked to stand in the anteroom, and finally in the corridor, into which the Elder's cell doors were opened during the Vigil. In the cell itself only the serving hieromonk remained and perhaps someone close to the Elder. Later the Elder even blessed people to stand in the hut and listen to the Vigil through the doors. During the summertime Count

Alexei P. Tolstoy often came to Optina Monastery, and he always loved to attend the Elder's cell Vigils. The Elder himself rarely listened to his Vigils without attending to his usual business. During the reading of the Kathismata and Canons he would either be confessing someone in Fr. Joseph's cell or receiving visitors, whomever he had not managed to see during the day, or finally he would strengthen himself with an evening meal. He would always listen to the Six Psalms and the festal magnification and Gospel reading standing by his bed with noticeably deep concentration. He would sing along during the magnification. In spite of his old age, his voice was a bright and pleasant baritone. He always sang from the heart and, in the words of the Holy Scriptures, *with understanding*. If there were not any visitors or persons who had come for confession present during the Elder's cell Vigil, then he would listen to most of it sitting in deep contemplation; sometimes he would be lying down if over-tired. Tears were often seen on his face at these times. If the Elder had not finished his work before the Six Psalms were about to be read, the service would be momentarily interrupted while they waited for the Elder. At the end of the cell Vigil, which usually lasted about three hours and ended at about the same time as the Vigil served in the church, the tired cell attendants would read the prayers before sleep and, after receiving a blessing, would leave to rest.

In the morning, if the Skete had its own Liturgy, which usually started no earlier than six o'clock, the Elder arose with the cell attendants about a half hour or an hour before services, listened to the Hours and dismissed the cell attendants to go to church, while he himself remained with the One God. This short time was the only time he had to sit in silence.

How he spent this time no one knows. But the cell attendants who returned from the church with the secretary would almost always find him sitting on his cot with his legs drawn in, reading a book—either the Epistles, the Psalter, *The Philokalia,* St. Maximus the Confessor, or lastly, St. Isaac the Syrian.

He read all these books without fail in the Slavonic language, which he loved very much. He would sometimes make notations in his own hand in the books, for instance, under the Apostle's words, *There was given me a thorn in the flesh, the messenger of satan to buffet me* (II Cor. 12:7), the Elder wrote: "Alexander the blacksmith." In *The Philokalia* and in the book of Isaac the Syrian the Elder underscored many passages. Returning from church, the secretary and the cell attendants would enter the Elder's cell with the usual prayer and receive his blessing. The Elder, sitting at his book, would often immediately show someone a particularly edifying little passage and give it to him to read. Then he would dismiss them to go strengthen themselves with tea, and he would do likewise. Soon the secretary would return to the Elder and the usual dictation would commence, while visitors would gather, male and female. And thus it would continue until late evening, as on weekdays. Sometimes the flood of visitors would be even greater on feast days than on regular days.

The Elder greeted the great Feasts of the Nativity and of Pascha in a somewhat particular way. About two weeks before the Feast the Elder would dictate his customary "general greetings," which were then copied in no small number. The Elder had a remarkable memory. Over the course of twenty-one years he dictated these greetings, and in spite of the fact that no one managed to preserve these letters from year to year, he always wrote on different subjects each year. As the eve of the Feast arrived, the cell attendants would be busy cleaning the Elder's cells. The quantity of outside visitors would relatively decrease, as all would want to greet the Feast in their own homes. The Elder would be more occupied with confessions, including those of his brothers. Sometimes he would unhurriedly move around from one cell to another for various needs. His face would be so bright and exultant. It was obvious that grace-filled peace and undisturbed quietude filled his pure soul. His loving heart was open to all. His fatherly, affectionate word, glance or touch of the hand would bring tears of tender feeling to those around him.

The Elder would lie down for a short rest a little earlier than usual, and then at midnight he arose as the monastery bells rang for Matins. The serving priest and choir would be ready. Candles would be lighted before the holy icons, and Matins would begin, usually ending a little earlier than in the monastery church. Then the frail Elder would lie down for a rest—a brief one, for soon the monastery choir would come immediately after the service to congratulate the Elder with the Feast, and following them would be the skete brethren.

On the Feast of the Nativity of Christ they would sing Christmas hymns, and on Pascha they sang the ninth ode of the Paschal Canon with a litany for the Elder's health. Afterwards the Elder, sitting on his cot, would kiss each one there three times and pass out red eggs. Before the Liturgy the Elder would customarily listen to the Festal Hours, then dismiss all his cell attendants to the Monastery for the early service. There were no services in the Skete during the first days of these Feasts. After the Liturgy had ended, although there were hardly any of the usual visitors with their sorrows and needs, many would come to greet him with the Feast, so that even on the great feast days the Elder had to talk continually. On the following days of the Feasts of the Nativity of Christ and Pascha, the Superior of the Monastery, Fr. Archimandrite Isaac, would come to concelebrate the Liturgy in the Skete. After the Liturgy he would come together with the concelebrating priests and deacons to greet the Elder with the Feast. The Elder would receive these dear guests with love, and, sitting on his cot with his legs tucked under, he would have tea with them. Light conversation with his close ones, especially the older brothers, was a manner of entertainment for him. He loved to listen to the news, ecclesiastical and social, and he himself would at times tell a story. After they had finished their tea, the Archimandrite would have lunch in the skete refectory; the Elder would then receive more greetings and simple visitors.

One of the most solemn days in Fr. Ambrose's life was the day they brought the miracle-working icon of the Kaluga Mother of God into his cell:

Listening to a Vigil and Moleben before the icon, the Elder could hardly hold back the tears that involuntarily streamed down his face.... Something very touching and festive was felt at the time in the souls of all those around the Elder-intercessor—they felt a more living faith in the intercession before God of the Mother of God and the saints for the Orthodox people.

Elder Ambrose's nameday on the seventh of December, the Feast of St. Ambrose of Milan, was also a solemn occasion. The Elder deeply venerated his heavenly protector. In the evening a Vigil to the holy Hierarch Ambrose was served in the Monastery as well as in the Skete, and particularly in the Elder's cell. One of the monks of Optina Monastery in the 1870's compiled a special service with an Akathist, which they always sang in the Elder's cell on that day. On the feast day itself, Liturgies concelebrated by many priests were served in the Monastery and the Skete, with Molebens to St. Ambrose and a litany wishing many years to Elder Ambrose. After this the brothers would head for the Elder's cell and congratulate him with his nameday. He in turn would invite them to tea and treats. He always treated the outside visitors with the same generosity on that day.

Other special days in the Elder's life were those days on which the Kaluga bishops came to visit him, which usually occurred in the summertime in conjunction with their tour of the diocese. The Elder would dress in full monastic garb—a ryassa, mantia and klobuk—to meet his archpastor. He would go out to the porch and there bow to the hierarch's feet, receive his blessing, then lead him into the hallway. Here he and the archpastor would spend a little time in private mutual discussion. The Elder had particular reverence for Archbishop Gregory. The Elder's comment about him was always: "He is intelligent and holy." In 1887 the Metropolitan of Moscow, Ioannicius, visited Optina Monastery accompanied by Archpriest Vladimir from Kaluga. The Elder was told to meet the Metropolitan in the church together with the skete brethren. Not knowing about this, the Metropolitan said after looking over the church, "Well, now let's go to see the Elder." But no sooner did he turn around than he saw the Elder right in front of him. Surprised to see him there, his Eminence compassionately said to him: "Why did you take the trouble to come here? I myself will come to you directly," and he asked him to go to his cell. The Metropolitan actually did come to his cell, talked a long time with him in private, and coming out of the cell he reverently bade him farewell. "A grace-filled elder!" said His Eminence, walking away along the path.

Not only did archpastors of the Church visit Fr. Ambrose, but also a number of eminent lay people came seeking direction in their lives' paths and answers to questions about their lives that tormented them. In the 1870's Feodor M. Dostoevsky came to see him, seeking consolation after the death of his ardently beloved son. The Elder was well disposed to him and said of him, "This is a man who repents."

Together with Dostoevsky came Vladimir S. Soloviev, of whose views, as they say, the Elder did not approve. Constantine N. Leontiev lived several years near Elder Ambrose and was tonsured a monk in Optina with his blessing.

In 1887 His Imperial Highness the Grand Prince Constantine Constantinovich visited Fr. Ambrose and spent some time with him in a heart-to-heart talk, lovingly remembering him from that day.

Leo Tolstoy visited the Elder several times, and it must be said that he always related respectfully to Optina Monastery and to monasticism in general.

The first time Leo Tolstoy visited the Elder he was with N. N. Strakhov in 1874. The second time in 1881 or 1882, he came on foot in peasant garb with his clerk and village schoolteacher, and the third time he came in 1890 with his family.

## 4. AN IMAGE OF THE ELDER AND HIS PASTORAL CARE FOR PEOPLE

At the same time that our foremost authors of secular literature—Gogol, Turgenev, Dostoevsky and others—unsuccessfully strove to create a literary type of the ideal man, the Orthodox Church has from ages past nurtured, and nurtures still in its heart, not imaginary but living people who are penetrated with the spirit of truth and unhypocritical, active love for God and neighbor.

They say that Dostoevsky took his character, Elder Zosima, from Fr. Ambrose. But even if that be true, it must be said that the image by no means does justice to its prototype, and Dostoevsky did not completely present Elder Ambrose's fullness and greatness of spirit; he did not sufficiently portray either his determined love for people or especially his vibrant love of God.

Only an accurate picture of his life can give us a real image of the Elder, and that only to the extent that memories of him are preserved in those who knew him. We will try to portray this image, as much as we are able, based on fragmented sketches by eyewitnesses of the Elder's inward spiritual countenance.

The overwhelming feature of his relationship to his neighbor was a deep, compassionate love.

"To love his neighbor so that he wished him every happiness that God may bless, and to try to bring him that happiness—that was his life and breath," said one man who knew him personally. "And there was such power in this flood of love that poured on all who came to Fr. Ambrose that it could be felt without any words or actions. It was sufficient only to approach Fr. Ambrose in order to feel the strength of his love; and in response to this love one's heart opened up, and a complete trust and utter kinship was born.

"In a world of general coldness and indifference, people are often completely averse to seeing others or even to being aware of their own existence, and many find it hard to live. They need a man to whom they can bring everything that troubles their souls, to whom they can disclose all their thoughts, hopes, and every secret, without holding back in the least, so that their lot might be easier and happier. In order to maintain that trust, there must not be the least surprise perceptible in the sensitive answer to the sufferer's questions. This sympathy, one of the hardest things to find in life, must shine in every sound, every movement. One craves a compassionate look, an affectionate word; and the awareness that someone loves him and believes in him. One needs that which is the rarest and greatest treasure in the world—an attentive heart. Such a heart beat in the breast of Fr. Ambrose.

"The love that animated Fr. Ambrose was of the kind that Christ commanded his disciples to have. It differs greatly from the feeling that the world knows as love. It is no less poetic, but it is broader, purer and knows no bounds. Its main difference is that it gives everything and asks nothing in return."

"The love that Fr. Ambrose had flowed inextricably with his faith. He firmly and unwaveringly believed in man and in his divine soul. He knew that even in the greatest perversion of a man there lies a spark of divine good, and Fr. Ambrose honored that spark. No matter how sullied was the man with whom the Elder spoke, his skillful counsels made the sinner aware that the holy Elder looked at him as an equal, and therefore he had not utterly perished and could be reborn. He gave even the most fallen people hope, encouragement and faith that they could walk on the right path."

To sum up Fr. Ambrose's great effectiveness with people, it could be said simply that he had compassion for them.

Just the same, this all-encompassing Christian love that Fr. Ambrose possessed, his sympathy and compassion for people, though rooted in his spiritual nature, was strengthened and enlarged in him under the influence of his ascetic life. Christian love, as a gift of God's grace, is unceasingly and deeply linked with Christian faith and heartfelt prayer; but faith and prayer can perhaps only be obtained by true humility, which is fostered in a man by unceasing inner struggle, self-abasement, sorrows and all manner of trials. All the saints walked this long path, which is clearly indicated to us by the Church and her great ascetical fathers. Fr. Ambrose also travelled this path under the guidance of his spiritual instructors before he reached full spiritual maturity. He passed through the spiritual dangers and temptations spoken of by Fr. Macarius in one of his letters: "Respected A. came to the Monastery with an entirely good disposition and the desire to 'seek Jesus,' that is, to acquire His love. This is very good and noble, but it needs to have a firm foundation: for love is tested by opposition.

"Because of her fervency and purity of soul, she will soon

experience consoling and pleasing feelings. This will give her hope in acquiring Jesus and His love. But these feelings are very dangerous and close to prelest, for without her having first warred with the passions, without coming to know her weaknesses and humbling herself, they are not reliable nor consoling feelings. Let them come when they do, but she must not accept them or be deceived by them, but rather consider herself unworthy. St. Isaac the Syrian writes in his second homily: 'The activity of taking up the cross is twofold, in conformity with the duality of our nature, which is divided into two parts. The first is patient endurance of the tribulations of the flesh, which is accomplished by the activity of the soul's incensive part and this is called righteous activity. The second is to be found in the subtle workings of the intellect, in steady divine rumination, in unfailing constancy of prayer, and in other such practices.... Every man who, before training completely in the first part, proceeds to that second activity, though it be not out of sloth but out of passionate longing for its sweetness, has God's wrath come upon him, because he did not first mortify his members which are upon the earth, that is, he did not heal the infirmity of his thoughts by patient endurance of the labor which belongs to the shame of the cross. For he dared to imagine in his mind the cross's glory,'* (that is, consolations), which are given only after the soul is cleansed from the passions, and humility is settled in the heart; then it will not be dangerous. Therefore we propose that you take care to caution her should she begin to have feelings of delight, that she should not rely on them and not consider them to be anything great; they will soon leave her. If on the other hand she is deceived by them and accepts them out of time, she will

---

*Ascetical Homilies of St. Isaac the Syrian* (Boston: Holy Transfiguration Monastery, 1984), p. 13.

soon be deprived; and when it is time she will not receive them, like a careless and foolish husbandman who, when he sees a blossom growing plucks it as though it were fruit—he will never have any fruit. Many have suffered along this path and have gone astray. Instead of humility they had a high opinion of themselves, seeking exultation. In the words of the same St. Isaac: 'The prayer of one who does not consider himself sinful is not well-pleasing to God.' Remind her that divine love is tested by adversity: various passions will rise up with which she must struggle, and for him who possesses humble wisdom even the struggle can be uplifting. But against him who has a high opinion of himself and relies on his consoling feelings, a greater warfare is allowed, so that he would be humbled by an awareness of his weakness. Defeat is unbearable to such people and makes them fainthearted—and that is a sign of their pride. One must beware of prelest, which is multiform. Either by deceiving her with false sanctity it will blind the eyes of her soul, or, if after a burst of joyful and consoling movements she is deprived of them, she will fall into various kinds of passions. But if you work with her gradually and steadily lead her, working meticulously, then something good can come of her in time. Tell her to read the more active patristic teachings: Abba Dorotheos, St. John of the Ladder, and St. Symeon the New Theologian; and have her reveal all of her words, deeds, thoughts and actions to you. For what is revealed is light, and what is not revealed is darkness."

Having passed along this sorrowful way of the cross under the guidance of experienced elders, Fr. Ambrose acquired true humility, true faith, prayer, purity of heart and love, that is, the totality of those gospel perfections, thanks to which he became a good pastor, instructor, guide, helper and consoler to all who wandered in the darkness of the passions, still tempest-tossed by sinful temptations and lusts.

## ELDERSHIP

In the 1860's, Fr. Ambrose had a remarkable dream that revealed to him the inevitability of this sorrowful way of salvation. "It seemed to me," the Elder related later to his spiritual children, Fr. Clement and Fr. Anatole, "that I was in my cell. Suddenly a man came to me who appeared to be in authority and ordered me to follow him. I came out of my cell. I saw there a dark, stormy night. It was as if a sea or large lake swirled before me. By the shore was a boat with oars, but it was impossible to see the oars clearly in the darkness. At the behest of my guide I sat in the boat, and it rocked away from the shore. The angry waves began to toss the boat to-and-fro like a feather. I was in great terror of my life. But there in the distance, in the yawning abyss, out of the impenetrable darkness an extraordinary light appeared to me; and I saw some kind of city of such wondrous beauty as I had never seen in all my life. All my attention was riveted on it. The sea, the waves, the storm—all this was forgotten, and I was in a sort of sweet rapture until the boat rocked up to the shore. The thud of its side against the ground recalled me from my reverie. Stepping out after my guide onto the shore, I went into a house at his behest, where there were two men whom I knew. One, after having received a blessing from me, called himself Vsevolod, a Czech prince, while the other seemed to me to be the Russian prince Boris Vladimirovich [St. Boris]; then I quickly woke up."

In this dream of the Elder's there is a deep and consoling meaning to every ascetic who conducts inner warfare. The ascetic should always remember that trials are followed by reward. Without trials there in fact cannot be a reward.

Now we shall turn our attention to those great qualities of soul that Fr. Ambrose had acquired through the trials he experienced.

Humility was the basis for all of Fr. Ambrose's ascetic life.

He wrote about this spiritual trait to one of his spiritual daughters: "You always ask that the Lord would grant you humility. But you see, it is not given as a gift from the Lord. The Lord is always ready to help people to acquire humility, as well as all good things, but it is necessary that the person work on himself. As the Holy Fathers say, *give blood and receive spirit* (St. Peter Damascene). This means labor to the spilling of blood, and then you will receive spiritual gifts. You seek and request spiritual gifts, but you are stingy about spilling your blood; that is, you do not want anyone to touch you or disturb you. How can you obtain humility in an undisturbed life? For humility consists in seeing yourself as worse than all, not only worse than people, but even dumb beasts and even the evil spirits themselves. When people bother you and you see that you cannot endure it and get angry with them, then you will have to consider yourself bad. If at this you lament and reproach yourself for your badness and incorrigibility and sincerely repent about it before God and your spiritual father, then you are on the path of humility."

By these words Fr. Ambrose not only teaches what humility is, but also points out the very path to humility; and he does it precisely so that we can clearly see that he knows it by his own personal experience.

We shall present an example that confirms the justice of the words of the Elder written above:

One sister in Shamordino was subjected to a severe rebuke from the superior for an involuntary disobedience. The sister could not have acted in any other way and wanted to explain this, but the wrathful superior did not want to hear it and threatened her with public prostrations right then and there. It was painful and grievous to the sister, but seeing that she must not justify herself, she stifled her self-love and was silent, only asking forgiveness. When she returned to her cell, this sister noticed to her great amazement that although she had endured this undeserved accusation, her soul, rather than being embarrassed and disturbed, felt light, consoled and good, as if she had received something joyous. In the evening of the same day she told Fr. Ambrose about all that had happened. The Elder said: "This incident was providential. Remember it. The Lord wanted to show you how sweet the fruit of humility is, so that having perceived it, you would always force yourself to be humble—at first outwardly and then also inwardly. When a person forces himself to be humble, the Lord consoles him inwardly, and this is the grace that God grants to the humble (cf. James 4:6). Self-justification only seems to ease the pain, but it actually brings darkness and disturbance to the soul."

Giving wise advice to others, the Elder at the same time, because of his humility, also sought advice of others, not relying on his own reason even with his wealth of discernment. After the repose of Elder Macarius he did not have anyone to turn to for advice in his Monastery, so he turned to his Archbishop, Gregory. In time he learned from trustworthy people about one hidden, wandering spiritual elder and immediately tried to become close to him, later writing him secret letters in order that he might do everything with another's counsel. In this he saw an expression of God's will, for he was afraid to act according to his own will.\*

---

\* It is supposed that this mysterious pilgrim was none other than a bishop who had left his cathedra and chosen the path of a pilgrim. Could this have been the pilgrim who wrote the *Candid Narrative of a Pilgrim to His Spiritual Father about the Grace-filled Effects of the Jesus Prayer* [*The Way of a Pilgrim* in English], a manuscript which was found among Fr. Ambrose's papers after his repose and the compilation of which some attributed to Fr. Ambrose himself? [See the introduction to the book: *From the Stories of a Pilgrim about the Grace-filled Effects of the Jesus Prayer,* published by Optina Monastery, written by Bishop Nikon.] On this subject, we present here a very interesting

## ELDER AMBROSE OF OPTINA

Here is another example of the Elder's humility: one day they were looking at a portrait of the ascetic Elder Basilisk that was printed in his Life. Someone said: "His lips are somehow very bright. It is probably because he died with the Jesus Prayer on his lips." "Yes, that could very well be," said the Elder. "In Glinsk Hermitage one elder died—for three hours after his

---

story told by one of the Elder's spiritual daughters about one such mysterious pilgrim, perhaps related to that same pilgrim with whom the Elder corresponded. A court investigator of important matters, a good and pious man, related the following. Once on Pascha he and his wife and daughter sat down to take supper on the gallery that ran alongside their house. Suddenly from the yard came a pleasant, clear voice: "Give alms for Christ's sake; I haven't eaten for three days." The investigator looked out the window from the gallery (the gallery was on the second floor) and saw a pilgrim who did not resemble a pauper, wearing a cassock belted at the waist with a leather belt and having a knapsack on his shoulder. His face was remarkably pleasant. The investigator put his hand into his pocket, took out thirty kopecks, as much as reached his hand, thrust it into the servant's hand and told her to go quickly and give it to him. But then he suddenly realized that the man was asking for food and he was poking money at him.... He flung himself after the servant and said, "Come eat supper with us, we have only just sat down." "No," he answered, "I will not eat, but give me some of the kvass that you have on the stool." The investigator immediately fulfilled the pilgrim's request. The pilgrim poured some kvass from the bottle into his own cup and left. When he returned, the investigator began to make sense of it: "How did he, standing outside near the main gate, see what we had on our stool? He must not be an ordinary man!" He ran after him with all his might, but the pilgrim was neither in the courtyard nor on the street, and no one else saw him. When the Elder's spiritual daughter told him about this incident, he asked: "Did he describe his appearance at all? Tall, light-haired, hook-nosed?" The woman was amazed. "Batiushka, do you know him?" "Silly! Of course, I know that such a man walks about. He asks for kvass, pours it into his own container and leaves." "But why didn't anyone else see him, and where did he hide?" "Well, you understand, he is a man of elevated life, his flesh is subtle," said the Elder. The woman did not dare to ask anything else.—Ed.

death his hand did not stop counting the knots of his prayer rope. But I, a sinner, do not even know that I have counted them at all," the Elder added with a sigh, and sadly waved his arm. "I lived in the Monastery for only one year. From the time they took me to be Fr. Macarius' cell attendant I have lived in the market place."

"Well, Batiushka, your prayer is not in your hand, but there in your heart you pray unceasingly," someone said. "No—you cannot pray in the market place," the Elder answered and then changed the subject of conversation. Another time the Elder said: "I have lived in the Monastery for forty years and have not earned forty turnips. Truly I have roofed other people's houses but my own is still uncovered—and I am already approaching my sixty-seventh year." In his letters to different people Fr. Ambrose often asked them to pray for the one who "does not practice what he preaches." Fr. Ambrose's humility was revealed by his readiness to endure people around him who had the most difficult, unpleasant personalities. One exceedingly unpleasant nun often attacked him. People asked him how he could endure her. He answered: "If it is hard for her here, where I always try to pacify her, then how will it be for her there, where everyone will be against her! How can I not endure her?"

The Elder's deep humility was the foundation for his deeply prayerful state of being. As we said before, tears often poured from the Elder's eyes as he prayed. He wept during services and prayers that were read in his cell for some occasion, especially when a Moleben with an Akathist was served at the request of visitors before his revered cell-icon of the Mother of God "It is Truly Meet." While they sang the Akathist he stood by the door, not far from the holy icon, and looked tenderly at the grace-filled countenance of the Mother of God. Each and all could see how the tears streamed down his withered cheeks.

During prayer he was immersed in contemplation of unspeakable heavenly glory, and his entire face was transfigured.

Thus, one evening the Elder had set a time for a married couple with an important issue to come to him early in the morning when he would not yet have begun receiving. They entered his cell. The Elder sat on his bed in a white monastic tunic and cap. In his hand was a prayer rope. His face was transfigured. It was somehow especially illuminated, and everything in his cell had taken on a solemn appearance. The visitors trembled and were seized with an inexpressible happiness. They could not utter a word and stood for a long time in a reverie, pondering the Elder's countenance. All around was quiet. Batiushka was silent. They came up to receive his blessing. He wordlessly made the sign of the cross over them. They glanced once more at this scene, so that they might forever preserve it in their hearts. The Elder still sat with the same transfigured face, immersed in contemplation of the heavenly world.

Here is another incident. One day his secretary, Hieromonk Benedict, came to the Elder's cell at the end of the morning rule. The Elder, having finished the rule, sat on his bed. Fr. Benedict came up for a blessing and to his great amazement saw the Elder glowing. But no sooner had he finished blessing him than the light disappeared. After a while, Fr. Benedict again approached the Elder, who had gone into another cell and was talking with people. In his simplicity he asked the Elder: "Batiushka, have you seen some kind of vision?!" The Elder did not answer a word, only lightly tapped him on the head. This was a sign of the Elder's special favor.

The Elder's gift of prayer, his prayerful contemplation of the spiritual world, together with his ardent love for people can also be seen in the following story of one nun: "I knew a certain family in Moscow. The husband was an educated man and intelligent; he was entirely indifferent to the Faith and had not gone to confession for several years. He also had a passion for alcoholic beverages. His wife grieved over him and prayed, but she did not have the strength to influence him. Finally he lost his job in Moscow and moved to V. Province, where he found a position as a steward of property. Nevertheless, even here he continued to lead the same way of life, so that one day he was taken out of the city sick; and in a few days he died unexpectedly to all, without having made a confession or having communed of the Holy Mysteries. This grieved his wife greatly, and she never ceased to weep and pray about him, thinking only about what she needed to do to give his soul repose. Not long before his fortieth day she saw her husband in a dream, and he told her firstly that she had not accurately determined the fortieth day after his death and that was her particular mistake; and, secondly, only almsgiving could bring his soul repose." Soon after this the nun who told the story was visiting Fr. Ambrose and, at the request of the deceased man's wife, asked Fr. Ambrose to advise her how to pray for the deceased and what she should do in his memory. Fr. Ambrose was very distressed over the nun's story and asked how the man could be allowed to die without repentance. Then he said: "I cannot tell you anything now—I will tell you later." Several days passed. Then one day, after his general blessing, Fr. Ambrose unexpectedly sent his cell attendant for the nun. She came to the Elder and found him in such a state as she had never seen before: distress showed on his face, tears flowed from his eyes. Meticulously shutting the door so that no one would hear his words he said: "Save this unfortunate soul quickly from hell! In order to save him, let his wife sell all of his property and give the money to the poor!" Apparently, the Elder had prayed all those days about the unhappy man, and his lot was revealed to him along with the way to save him. The Elder's words fully corresponded to the words of the man in his wife's dream, although the nun had not told Fr. Ambrose about this dream.

The wife carried out the Elder's advice—she sold all her property and gave the money to the poor, and she herself became a teacher. We shall add to the foregoing that after some time had passed, the wife again saw her husband in a dream. He was carrying a sort of notebook in his hands and said merrily to her: "I have received a certificate." Then he turned the page and read: *Glory to God in the highest ... Praise ye the name of the Lord!* and with these words he disappeared.

The Elder never made any decisions, it can be surmised, without fervent prayer or a clear indication from God. One Shamordino nun related that Fr. Ambrose appointed her to a difficult obedience in the refectory as soon as she had entered the Monastery. Having little hope in her own strength, she went to the Elder several times to refuse, but the Elder did not excuse her. Finally, he told her in a serious and penetrating tone, "You see, it is not I who gave you this obedience—such is the will of the Heavenly Queen."

Fear fell upon the nun, and she, begging the Elder's forgiveness, stopped bothering him with her request, then spent 7½ years in that obedience absolutely peacefully and easily.

One nun wanted very much to change from another monastery to Shamordino and fervently asked the Elder to accept her. Living in the guest house in Shamordino, she went daily to the Elder for the general blessing, and daily she asked him to take her into his community. The Elder blessed her, but never answered a word to her request. Thus much time passed. Finally, tormented by the suspense and her indeterminate position, the nun said tearfully to the Elder: "Batiushka, say something to me—I have lived for three months in the guest house; I am ashamed to return to my mother-abbess...." The Elder answered: "What can I say to you if the Heavenly Queen doesn't announce anything to me?" A few days passed and suddenly the Elder himself sent for the nun at the guest house, and when she came out to him he merrily and joyfully said to her: "Well, stay, stay with us!" He had verily received knowledge about it from on high.

Another fruit of the Elder's humility was his deeply compunctionate heart, for his own sins as well as the sins of his neighbors. One hieromonk of Optina Monastery, Fr. Platon, told of his confession, having been at one time Fr. Ambrose's father-confessor. "How edifying were the Elder's confessions! What humility and compunction of heart he expressed over his sins! And what sins! He confessed such things as we wouldn't even consider sins. For example, because of the weakness of his stomach, he would out of dire necessity at times have to eat two or three pieces of herring on Wednesday or Friday contrary to the rule of the Holy Church. And this sin the Elder confessed with tears before the Lord. He knelt then before the holy icons like one condemned before the fearful and unrequiting Judge, hoping for mercy from Him Who grants mercy. It seemed that he was even wondering if He would grant mercy, if He would forgive him his sin. I would look and look at the weeping Elder, and I myself would begin to weep."

Having a compunctionate heart, the Elder desired to see the same compunction in the hearts of all who came to him. Therefore, if he saw absent-mindedness and inattentiveness to themselves in any of his spiritual children, then he would peer at them reproachfully and say: "Oh, no pain of heart!" He also loved to repeat the words of St. Ephraim the Syrian: "Persistently suffer hardships in order to avoid the hardship of vain sufferings."

Humility and constant purification of his heart by sincere repentance, self-condemnation and prayer created a bright, peaceful, joyful state in the Elder's soul, which did not abandon him even during moments of difficult physical sufferings. How many times he had to experience various kinds of sorrows, attacks and sicknesses, but nothing could greatly disturb him—he was always cheerful and calm. Lying on his bed of sickness, he would at times, according to his custom, joke with the monks around him. Although he himself would be in a state of extreme exhaustion, he consoled the fainthearted, either by a word brought forth in over-exertion, or by his paternally affectionate glance, or with the touch of his enfeebled hand. Usually, when the Elder was very sick—and that was not rare—almost all of the skete brethren would be depressed, especially the recently accepted novices. There was one monk in the Skete, already of advanced age and balding. When the Elder was seriously ill, the distressed monk came to him in his cell in the hope of receiving even a silent blessing from the Elder. His hope did not betray him. With anguish of heart he approached the bed of the reclining sufferer, bowed as was the custom to the Elder's feet, and stretched forth his hand to receive a blessing. Having given his blessing, the Elder lightly tapped him on the head, jokingly uttering in a barely audible voice: "Well, you, bald abbot!" "It was as if a mountain had fallen off my shoulders," the monk said afterwards, "my soul became so very light!" When he returned to his own cell, he could not sit still for the joy. He just walked around his cell affirming: "My God! What could this be? Batiushka, Batiushka—barely breathing, but still joking...."

The most remarkable of all Fr. Ambrose's spiritual gifts was the gift of discernment, which with the aid of God's grace became clairvoyance. We will speak now only of discernment, and of clairvoyance we will speak in another place.

The gift of discernment in Fr. Ambrose consisted in his ability to immediately determine, within just a few minutes, the spiritual condition of anyone who came to him, making sense of all his situations, as a spiritual father and in the material sense as well, explaining the person's condition to him and giving him advice that was profitable to him in his situation. This is the gift of discernment—at other times clairvoyance—and wisdom that drew to Fr. Ambrose thousands of people who had lost their way among the vicissitudes of spiritual and everyday life and who needed the guidance of an experienced instructor.

Fr. Ambrose possessed an all-encompassing experience and extraordinarily broad vision and could give advice to any question, not only within the realm of the spiritual, but even household and trade questions, appropriate to any given person or situation.

Here are a few examples. A rich Orel nobleman came to the Elder and told him that he would like to construct an irrigation system in his vast apple orchards. "People say," the Elder began in his usual way of beginning in such situations, "that it is best to do it this way." Then he described an irrigation system in detail. The nobleman returned to his property and began to read about the subject. It turned out that Fr. Ambrose had described the latest invention in the field. The nobleman came again to Optina. "Well, how is your irrigation system?" the Elder asked him. The irrigation system had been built according to the Elder's instructions and had already begun to bring great profit—the neighboring orchards had a poor apple harvest, but this man's harvest was rich and the apples excellent.

One young man, who came to the Elder often, once said that he wanted to build a shower in his home. Fr. Ambrose sympathized with him. "You need it to take up as little space as possible? That's possible—do it this way...." Several years passed. There followed an advertisement that new and improved showers were being built. They turned out to be built in just the way that the Elder had described long before to the young man.

Merchants also came to Fr. Ambrose asking advice and direction in areas of trade. The Elder recommended a steward to them or gave agricultural advice. He told people how to manage capital or real property most effectively, how to manage temporal affairs in monasteries, how to conduct court cases, etc.

When Shamordino was being built, the Elder knew every corner of Shamordino in detail without ever having left his cell. A monk came who was in charge of the construction project, and they began to discuss sand. "Well, Fr. Joel, your sand has been delivered—about ... (Father estimated the amount exactly in his mind) five square feet with a depth of about a foot—is that what you have or not?" "I don't know, Batiushka, I haven't had time to measure." Fr. Ambrose asked two more times about the sand, but they still had not measured it. When they finally did measure it, there was just as much as the Elder had said.

Particularly valuable and interesting were the Elder's counsels in the realm of inward, religious-moral life. We must note that the Elder usually gave advice in the form of separate ideas, aphorisms, or short, edifying stories. This is how it was during the general receptions of his visitors, or in answer to individual questions. At other times he would become the leader and builder of the entire life of those who came to him, often arranging things in direct opposition to their own desires and expectations; but the Elder found it necessary and, of course, for the better. The Elder at times gave separate instructions and advice related only to monastics, and at other times for both monastics and lay people.

First we present an example of the first category, written by his spiritual daughter, the reposed in the Lord Superior of Shamordino Convent, Abbess Euphrosyne (Rosova):

"When there is a Vigil, you should shorten your evening prayers to about eight minutes."

"After the Vigil when they come to your cell, you should

arise, light a candle and say: 'Well then, sister Barbara, read the evening prayers,' and thus each one in turn. This way you will teach them not to come to your cell."

"When you lie down to go to sleep, make the sign of the cross around your cell and over your bed with the prayer: 'Let God arise.'"

"When you wake up, first of all cross yourself. In whatever state you wake up, that is the state you will be in all day. This is written about by St. John of the Ladder."

"When you wake up in the morning, say: 'Glory to Thee, O God.' Fr. Macarius always talked about this. And you should not recall the dreams you had."

"It is a sin to spend time idly. It is also a sin to skip church services and prayer rule for work. See that you not be punished by the Lord for that."

"Always go to the beginning of the services—you will be more sober and concentrated."

"You should not talk in church. This is an evil habit. Afflictions are sent for that."

"Prayer ropes are given so that we would not forget to pray. During services we should listen to what is being said and at the same time say the prayer with the prayer rope, 'Lord, have mercy,' and when we cannot hear (the reading) then: 'Lord Jesus, Christ, Son of God, have mercy on me a sinner.'"

"Always say the prayer (of Jesus) with the lips, for it is not profitable to say it with the mind—you can be damaged."

"At least whisper the prayer (of Jesus). Many have been harmed by mental prayer."

"You doze off in church and don't hear the services because your thoughts wander from here to there."

"You should go to church services without fail, or you will get sick. The Lord punishes this with sicknesses. If you go you will be more healthy and concentrated. Fr. Macarius would get sick, but he still went to services. He would go out to the bishop's cell, but not be able to sit still there. Then he would go to Fr. Flavian's cell and stay there a while. When he saw that he no longer had the strength to stay in church, he would cross himself and leave. But he never trusted himself."

"Before all you should ask mercy from God and pray: *all ways are Thine*, have mercy on me, a sinner."

"Say the prayer 'Rejoice, O Virgin Theotokos' twelve or twenty-four times a day. She is our only Intercessor."

"When you pray fervently, watch, for there will be temptations. This happens to everyone."

"You should not pray for the sisters.* It is the devil in the form of goodness that suggests this. This is the work of the perfect. But you should just cross yourself and say: 'Lord have mercy on us.'"

"After receiving Communion you must ask the Lord to grant you to preserve it worthily, and ask the Lord to grant you help not to turn back, that is, to your former sins."

"When they ring at 'It is meet' [during Divine Liturgy] (and you are in your cell), you should arise and make three prostrations to the Holy Trinity: It is meet and right to worship Father, Son and Holy Spirit. Ask for the intercessions of the Heavenly Queen and say: 'It is truly meet....' But if someone is in your cell then only cross yourself."

"When they ring for the Hours, you should cross yourself and pray: Lord Jesus Christ, Son of God, have mercy on me a sinner. As St. Dimitry of Rostov wrote: 'Have mercy on me for an hour has passed, and I am nearer to death.' You do not have to cross yourself in front of everyone—as you see fit, with

---

*These words were spoken to Mother Euphrosyne when she was still a novice at the Belev Convent and were intended to warn her against self-opinion.

whom you can and with whom you cannot—but you should mentally say the prayer."

"If anything comes up, cross yourself."

"Do not believe in omens, and they will not come true."

"Light your lampada; but if you have no oil, do not worry—let it be unlit."

"Do not light candles in church—be a candle yourself."*

"You should read books in the morning for a quarter-hour before work; then all day chew on what you read, like a sheep chews its cud."

"Of course you may write things down from books; only integrate it. Understand what you read. You should read less, but understand it."

"You can read the Gospels sitting down, but never lying down."

"Before receiving Holy Communion read St. Ephraim the Syrian on repentance."

"On that day (when you receive Communion) you should read more, especially the New Testament, the Epistle to the Ephesians and Revelation [of St. John]."

"You do not like patristic texts because they reproach you."

"Give books to read. Even if they spill oil all over them, that's okay. Only use discrimination concerning who is reading."

"Do not work on Sundays. But if it is a feast—for St. John Chrysostom, for instance—you can work in the evening."

"A gluttonous mouth is a pig's sty."

"You should thank the Lord that He sends you everything. This is for three reasons: to bring you to your senses, to awareness and to thankfulness."

---

*Of course, the Elder was not refuting this Orthodox custom, but rather instructed what feelings one should have while doing it.

"When you judge someone, say to yourself: 'Hypocrite! Remove first the beam that is in your own eye' (cf. Matt. 7:5)."

"God heals the proud Himself. This means that inward afflictions (by which God cures pride) are sent by God, for the proud will not endure afflictions sent by people. But the humble will bear them from people and always say: 'I deserve this.'"

"When you feel that you are filling up with pride, then know that the praise people give you makes you arrogant."

"When pride attacks, tell yourself: 'There goes a kook.'"

"The house of the soul is patience, the food of the soul is humility. If there is no food in the house, the resident will go out looking for it."

"When you scold someone, reproach yourself—say: 'Sinner! Why did you go on like that? Who is afraid of you?'"

"Ambition and pride are one and the same. Ambition displays its works so that people will see how well you walk, how nimbly you do something. Then pride begins to have contempt for everyone. Just as the caterpillar first crawls and bends, so does ambition. But when it grows wings and flies upward, that is pride."

"If you touch vainglory with your finger, it screams: 'They are flaying me!'"

"Say to the one who praises you: 'Do not praise me, or we will argue afterwards.' *The Ladder* tells us to beware of such people. It is better to accept a malicious person."

"Praise is not profitable. Praise is terribly difficult. Because people glorified and venerated you here, the body rots after death and pustules form. Abba Barsanuphius says: 'Serida was such an Elder, but even his body decomposed after death.'"

"One must be respectful of everyone. Be friendly, but not catering (to people). Bow to people, but hurry on your way."

"You should look at the ground. Remember: earth thou art and unto earth shalt thou return (cf. Gen. 3:19)."

"Humility is when you yield to others and consider yourself the worst of all. This will be much more peaceful for you."

"Sister, repent, humble yourself. Yield to your sisters in whatever possible, and do not judge others—we all have our weaknesses!"

"Humble yourself, and everything you do will work."

"If anyone gets angry with you, ask him why."

"If your thoughts tell you: 'Why didn't you tell that person who offended you this or that?' then say to your thought: 'Now it's too late to say that—you missed the chance.'"

"Be condescending to others."

"Look at everything simply."

"Living simply means not judging. Do not judge anyone. For example, here comes Elikonida. She passed by, and that is all. This is what thinking simply means. Otherwise, at seeing Elikonida passing by, you could think about her bad side: she is such and such, her character is thus and so. That is not simple."

"Laughter casts out the fear of God."

"If blasphemous thoughts come to you for judging others, reproach yourself for your pride and do not pay any attention to the thoughts."

"When a day comes that you are living well, cheerfully and peacefully, then when suddenly you become unsettled and your thoughts begin to trouble you, say to yourself: 'Why are you troubled? Remember when it was so peaceful.'"

QUESTION: How can I acquire the fear of God? ANSWER: "Always have God before you. *I beheld the Lord ever before me* (Ps. 15:8)."

"The fear of God is also acquired by fulfilling God's commandments and doing everything according to your conscience."

QUESTION: How can I be attentive to myself? Where should

I start? ANSWER: "First you need to write down how you go to church, how you stand, how you look around, how you become proud, how you become vainglorious, how you get angry, and so on."

"Do not go to other people's cells and do not bring any guests to your own."

"If someone says: 'Come in (to my cell),' you say, 'I am in a sour mood right now—I can't.'"

"Confess your own sins and accuse yourself rather than other people."

"Do not speak of other people's business."

"You should reveal the thoughts that bother you. One thought might come up all day, and it is nothing. But another time it might snag you—then you need to reveal it."

"Depression means the same thing as laziness, only it is worse. Depression makes you weak in body and spirit. You do not feel like working or praying; you go to church with insensitivity, and your entire being weakens."

QUESTION: The thought came: why try to save ourselves? We will not save ourselves anyway, no matter how we live. Why is there no one who saves himself now, as it was written in the vision of the Athonite monk? ANSWER: "This was written to imply that there are not any perfect ones now, but there are people who labor for their salvation. Not everyone can be a general. One is a general while another is a colonel, another a major, a captain, a soldier, and a simple man, just as they are."

QUESTION: N. has been dying a long time but does not die, and she keeps imagining cats and such. ANSWER: "You need to write down every sin no matter how small, and then repent. That is why many people take a long time to die, because they are holding on to some unrepented sin, and as soon as they confess it they are relieved. In Optina we had a servant that worked in the barn who had tuberculosis. She had three forgotten sins. She imagined that cats were scratching her and that a girl was smothering her, but as soon as she repented she died. In the Skete there was a sick ryassaphore monk. He kept thinking that someone was lying next to him, and he just could not remember his sin. During the week he remembered his sin and died as soon as he repented of it. You must write down your sins without fail, as soon as you recall them. Otherwise, we put it off—either the sin is too small, or we are ashamed to say it, or we will say it later. Then when we come to confess we have nothing to say."

QUESTION: Why is it that after receiving Communion I sometimes feel consolation and sometimes coldness? ANSWER: "Coldness comes when one seeks consolation from Communion, but when one considers oneself unworthy, then the grace remains with him."

QUESTION: What does it mean to live according to one's heart? ANSWER: "Not to meddle in the business of others and to see only good in others."

QUESTION: When I am angry then I pray absent-mindedly. ANSWER: "When one gets angry, he is deprived of God's protection. One must pray without the remembrance of evil."

QUESTION: Batiushka, pray for me, that I would be able to bring peace to others. ANSWER: "First be at peace yourself, then you will be able to bring peace to others."

"You must have love, a love with wings—on one side, humility, and on the other side mercy and condescension toward your neighbor."

QUESTION: What does it mean to sincerely confess? ANSWER: "To hide nothing, speak plainly and not beat around the bush."

QUESTION: What does this mean: *Therefore if thine enemy hunger, feed him; if he thirst, give him drink: for in so doing thou shalt heap coals of fire on his head* (Rom. 12:20). ANSWER: "Coals of fire on the head means the mind. When you treat your enemy hospitably, then you warm his mind toward you with love."

QUESTION: They say that when you receive Holy Communion, you should eat only fasting foods that day. ANSWER: "Fr. Leonid said that you must honor the day and not eat milk products, but Fr. Macarius was condescending to our weakness and said that we could eat them."

QUESTION: In the book *[Questions and Answers of St. Barsanuphius the Great]* it is written: "Lay down your infirmities before God (Question 251)." How does one do this? ANSWER: "When thoughts attack and you haven't the strength to struggle with them, then say: 'Lord, Thou seest my infirmities. I haven't the strength to struggle—help me!'"

QUESTION: Batiushka, pray for me, that I might correct myself. ANSWER: "You need to work on it yourself. The prophet Nathan prayed for King David, and King David lay there drenching himself with tears. He prayed also for Saul, but Saul only *snored and slept.*"

Fr. Ambrose said: "Four virtues are: courage, discernment, chastity and truth. Chastity consists in watching over yourself in all actions: in words, deeds and thoughts; it means to preserve whole all the virtues. Demons can also be pure, but they are proud."

"You must always speak the truth and not be a man-pleaser. We had one priest; I always spoke the truth to him when he came to me. He did not like this. When he left us, he told me: 'If you had not told me the truth, I would not even have been able to live here.'"

Fr. Ambrose related that when people came to Elder Leonid and did not consider themselves to be sinners, then Fr. Leonid said: "If you are not sinful, then go—sinful people are waiting."

QUESTION: In a worldly house I was ashamed to cross

myself, not wanting them to see it. ANSWER: "P. B. S. was in a nice house and she wanted something to drink, and Fr. Macarius blessed her to cross herself first. She thought, she can't not cross herself, but she doesn't feel like it. So she did not drink. You too—if you don't want to cross yourself, then do not drink tea."

QUESTION: Sometimes stinginess attacks. ANSWER: "Give whatever you can, whatever your hand allows. One pilgrim begged alms. One woman was stingy and gave him a worn kerchief, while another was kind and gave the pilgrim whatever he asked for. As soon as he walked away from them they had a fire, and everything burned. The pilgrim turned back and returned to them all they had given him—to the one who had given him much, he gave much. But to the stingy one he said: 'Here's your kerchief.'"

QUESTION: What does the Gospel passage mean: those *that labor and are heavy laden* (Matt. 11:28)? ANSWER: "Those that labor are those who voluntarily labor; those who are heavy laden are those who for their sins endure afflictions with difficulty, but nevertheless endure them."

Fr. Ambrose related: "The cook once came to Fr. Macarius and said: 'There is no one to clean the fish.' Fr. Macarius put on an apron and went himself. The brothers saw him and all gathered 'round. Fr. Macarius said to the cook: 'And you said that there was no one to clean the fish.'"

"Thoughts of self-opinion must be revealed without fail. We had one brother who had such thoughts, but he never revealed them to Fr. Macarius for some reason; he did let it out to a brother, who also never told Batiushka. He left the Monastery and shot himself."

QUESTION: When I fall into crude temptations I get depressed and even despair. ANSWER: "When Fr. Abbot Anthony was sick, Fr. Clement and I came to him before his death. Fr.

Clement was in doubt about someone and Fr. Abbot said: 'Do not despair over anyone. Only the devil is despaired of, but everyone else can be saved.'"

"*A man shall draw nigh, and the heart is deep; And God shall be exalted. As an arrow of infants are their blows* (Ps. 63:7-8). The evil enemy approaches a man and sows tares in the Lord's field. *The heart is deep*—he who is attentive to himself and does not notice who does what and how, if he calls on God, his prayer will triumph and rout the attacking enemy; and then the enemy's arrow will be like the arrows of infants, like flies biting."

Fr. Ambrose also said: "*As for man, his days are as the grass* (Ps. 102:13). He who is proud wilts like grass, but he who fears God will receive mercy from the Lord."

QUESTION: What does this mean: *Cast thy care upon the Lord* (Ps. 54:25)? ANSWER: "This means living simply and placing all your hope in the Lord, not worrying about what someone else did, or about what will happen and how. When King David thought and reasoned in human terms, he came to a hopeless state, not finding any consolation: *my soul is troubled greatly* (Ps. 6:2). But when he placed all his hope in God he was comforted: *I remembered Thy judgments of old, O Lord, and was comforted* (Ps. 118:52)."

"The enemy attacks man with the passions, and man does everything that the enemy suggests to him; all of this leaves its mark on man."

"Be condescending to others. Symeon the New Theologian wrote: 'If you make peace with a hundred men but offend one, it all goes to waste.'"

QUESTION: What does this mean: *Thy rod and Thy staff, they have comforted me* (Ps. 22:4). ANSWER: "The rod is the cross, afflictions, and the staff is the Jesus Prayer. The rod is the active part of virtue, and the staff is the noetic part."

# ELDERSHIP

QUESTION: I have thoughts that you trust me. ANSWER: "I will tell you a parable. One desert dweller was chosen to be a bishop. He refused for a long time, but they insisted. Then he thought: 'I did not know that I was worthy; there must be something good about me.' Then an angel appeared to him and said: 'Simple monk, what are you so exalted about? People have been sinning and they need punishment; that is why they have chosen you—they could not find anyone worse.'"

Fr. Ambrose never blessed to rebuke or scold during a time of trouble. He told how Archimandrite Moses had a cell attendant, Fr. Niphon, who did something he shouldn't have and waited for a scolding, but the Archimandrite was as if he had not noticed anything. Fr. Niphon came to him and expected to be chewed out, but the Archimandrite just gave him various orders. Thus it happened several times. Once Fr. Niphon came very cheerfully to the Archimandrite, and the Archimandrite immediately shut the door and locked it, then began to scold him.

According to another nun's notes, Fr. Ambrose said: "Bad dreams come from three things: from judging, from vainglory and from gluttony."

"Someone asked a monk: 'Who taught you to pray?' He answered: 'Demons.' 'How did demons teach you?' 'This is how! They warred against me with various thoughts, and I beat them off with prayer.'"

"Without devotion to God's Providence, you will not acquire peace. You do not humble yourself, and that is why you have no peace."

"St. Chrysostom says: If you want to know the truth about yourself, seek it from your enemies. They will tell you."

"Three invalids hang on each other: hate on anger, anger on pride."

"When you speak with a humble man, you are at rest, and

it is easy to be with him. But when you speak with someone who justifies himself and blames others—oh, how exhausting."

"When you are insensate you especially need to practice oral prayer."

"When the heart clings to the earthly, then you must remember that the earthly will not go with us to the Kingdom of Heaven."

About afflictions that arose in the Monastery from gossip and judgment, Fr. Ambrose said the following in letters and personally: "Whoever joins the Monastery and straightway takes the path of humility and fear of God—preserving according to conscience his eyes, ears and tongue, and hurrying to reproach himself when mistakes are made—will see very few unpleasant incidents, and the word 'gossip' will not exist for him. If the Lord endured spitting, buffeting and all manner of humiliation for the sake of our salvation, he who wishes to be saved should know, if only he has a proper yearning for salvation, that he should bear the same, albeit to a lesser degree, for his sins and for the sake of his salvation. The foremost thought at the tonsure is expressed this way: 'He must endure being attacked, humiliated, persecuted, and bear all afflictions.' For whoever knows this and remembers it, the word 'gossip' can have no power. If someone should ask for whom it exists and has power—it is obviously for the infirm, who, although perhaps well-intentioned, are still strongly possessed by self-love, though it may be hidden under the attractive cover of some deceptively blessed pretext. For those who look at things with human eyes, at least in some instances, are not yet freed from the desire to receive attention, affection, greetings, and some respect, even preference, especially when it is based on that certain pretext—their previous good deeds. The holy Apostle Paul speaks of both states clearly with reproach: *having begun in the spirit, are ye now made perfect by the flesh?* (Gal. 3:3).

"How can we not be weak in such a case? It is very simple: admit our weakness, hurry to self-reproach and humility, in unpleasant circumstances blame yourself and not others, and first of all look at things simply. We are all human individuals and everyone sees things his own way, understands things his own way, judges and explains things his own way. We will be judged for this only by the Son of God, to Whom alone is given authority from God the Father. When we abandon simplicity and begin to wonder and explain how and what and why and for what, and who are they, and how are they, then it will not be simple but complicated and all the more impossible to understand. There will be perplexities and misunderstandings; complaints will be inescapable. And the sorrows, the sorrows—they will be unbearable. But—I do not remember where it is written—if you touch vainglory with your finger it will scream, 'They're flaying me.' Although it is not always this way, it does happen, and not in small part, but it is usually in various forms. Self-love is the root of all evil. It is the beginning of all the passions, the cause of all our misfortunes and sufferings—sometimes presently, sometimes as the result of our previous mistakes. By the way, self-love is not always the cause of our afflictions, for often the cause is the good determination to live piously, as the Apostle says: *All that will live godly in Christ Jesus shall suffer persecution* (II Tim. 3:12). And in another place it is written: *Many are the tribulations of the righteous,* only with the added encouragement: *and the Lord shall deliver them out of them all* (Ps. 33:19). Blessed are those who belong to this group and endure afflictions for the sake of the truth and a pious life. But what should those people do about whom it is said: *Many are the scourges of the sinner* (Ps. 31:10)? Even they should not despair, but without shame and with hope in God's mercy should stretch forth their hands to humility and repentance, imitating the publican who, seeing his own incorrigibility, cried out to the Lord: *God, be merciful to me, a sinner* (Luke 18:13). Striving to live piously, we should remember and never forget that everything we read or understand should be applied to ourselves and not to others. We must be prudently strict with ourselves, but condescending to others. Prudently strict means not getting upset without reason. We can see an example of this in children of different ages, to whom we condescend according to their level of understanding. There are also spiritual children, whose age is not reckoned by their years, beards or wrinkles, but it is appropriately said: *But wisdom is the gray hair unto men, and an unspotted life is old age* (Wis. 4:9). Will we soon reach such an old age? Not having reached it, we all require condescension from one another, according to the love of God: we must listen condescendingly, see condescendingly, and condescendingly judge what we see and hear. All this is said to let you know not to be unreasonably afraid. There is really much to feel and experience, because a person does not immediately attain passionlessness. And where there are passions, there are afflictions with many perplexities and misunderstandings."

F<small>R</small>. A<small>MBROSE</small>'<small>S INSTRUCTIONS</small> given in his hut to lay people as well as monastics had a slightly different character.

We must recall the impression this hut itself made! "How joyfully the heart begins to beat," related one regular visitor, "when walking along the dark fir forest you see the skete bell tower, and to the right the humble ascetic's lowly little cell! How light your soul becomes when you sit in this crowded and stuffy cabin, and how bright it seems in its mysterious low light! How many people have been here! They came pouring bitter, sorrowful tears, but they left with tears of joy. The despairing left consoled and encouraged; the unbelieving and doubtful left as true children of the Church.

"Here lived 'Batiushka,' the source of so much beneficence

Elder Ambrose.

and consolation. Neither a person's social status nor wealth meant a thing in his eyes. Only a person's soul was important to him, and he considered that soul to be so valuable that he forgot himself and gave all his strength to save it and set it on the true path. From morning till evening, worn out by illnesses, the Elder received visitors and gave them each what they needed. His words were accepted with faith and were law. His blessing or special attention was considered a great happiness; and having been vouchsafed it, people walked away from him crossing themselves and thanking God for such a consolation."

The grace-filled Elder's quiet speech in the hut flowed in a bright, beneficial and inexhaustible stream, and this stream also poured out upon attentive and tender hearts of listeners in the farthest corners of Russia, passed along by word of mouth, as precious lessons of holy, pure and Christian life.

"How should we live?" said the Elder, "Live and do not grieve, judge no one, attack no one, and to all—my respect."

"We must live unhypocritically, and behave ourselves well, then our works will be true; otherwise we'll be blue."

"We should live on the earth as a wheel turns—as one point touches the earth, all the rest reaches upward; but we lie on the earth and then cannot get up."

"In order to join the Monastery you need not one cartload of patience, but an entire barn."

"In order to be a nun, you need to be either made of iron or of gold. Iron means having great patience and gold means having great humility."

"Go where they lead you, look at what they show you and always say: 'May Thy will be done.'"

"What business is it of yours what people say about you?" the Elder once said. "If you listen to other peoples' sins, you have to carry the ass on your shoulders."

"A promise unfulfilled is like a tree without fruit."

## ELDERSHIP

The Elder also said: "Where it is simple, angels number a hundred and one; but where it is complicated there are none." Sometimes he would add, "Where there is no simplicity, there is only emptiness."

When someone would say to Fr. Ambrose, "I cannot do it," he would often tell the story of one merchant who would always say: "Can't do it, can't do it—I'm weak." Once he had to travel in Siberia. He rode wrapped in two fur coats in a sledge. One night he dozed off, and when he opened his eyes he saw something glowing before him, as if stars were twinkling. He looked, and it was the eyes of wolves.... He jumped out of the sledge right into a tree, forgetting the weight of his fur coats...."

"A requested cross is hard to carry. It is better to give yourself over to God's will in simplicity. *God is faithful, Who will not suffer you to be tempted above that ye are able; but will with the temptation also make a way to escape, that ye may be able to bear it* (I Cor. 10:13)."

About the fact that we cannot be saved without humility, Fr. Ambrose related: "One noblewoman saw in a dream the Lord Jesus Christ with a crowd of people before Him. At His beckoning a peasant girl came up to Him first, then a peasant man in bast shoes, and then all the people of peasant birth. The noblewoman thought that for her kindness and all her virtues surely the Lord would call her soon. What was her amazement when she saw that the Lord stopped calling anyone. She decided to remind the Lord herself, but He turned away from her completely. Then she fell to the earth and began to humbly acknowledge that she was truly the worst of all and not worthy of the Kingdom of Heaven." Then Batiushka added, "Well, those are the very ones who are fit; those are the ones they need there."

At the words of one woman standing near the Elder: "My pride ruins everything," he answered: "Wrap yourself in humility. Then even should the sky fall into the earth, it will be alright."

Man forgets himself in good fortune and attributes it all to himself—to his powerless power and his false authority. But as soon as some misfortune befalls him, he begs clemency even from his imagined enemy. Fr. Ambrose expressed this truth in this way: "Man is like a beetle. When it is a warm day and the sun is playing, he flies around, proud of himself and buzzes: 'All the forests are mine! All the meadows are mine! All the meadows are mine! All the forests are mine!' But when the sun hides itself, the cold freezes and the wind dances, the beetle forgets his vast expanse, clings to a leaf and only squeals: 'Don't blow me off!'"

The Elder also talked about how sometimes circumstances unexpectedly humble a man: "Once someone arranged a dinner and sent all his servants to invite the guests. One of the invitees asked the servant sent to him: 'Couldn't your lord find someone better to send to me than you?' At this the servant answered: 'He sent all the good ones to the good, and me to your benevolence.'"

Fr. Ambrose also spoke of humility: "One visitor came to the Superior, Fr. Archimandrite Moses, but, not finding him at home, went to his natural brother, Fr. Abbot Anthony. During the conversation the guest asked the Fr. Abbot: 'Tell me, Batiushka, what is your rule?' Fr. Anthony answered: 'I have had many rules—I lived in the desert and in monasteries, and there were different rules. But now I have only the rule of the publican: *God, be merciful to me, a sinner!*'"

"A man only has to humble himself," said the Elder, "and that humility immediately sets him at the doorway of the Kingdom of Heaven.... Discernment," said the Elder, "cannot be achieved without love and humility, and humility and love cannot be achieved without obedience."

"One woman wanted to wander here and there—to Kiev

and Zadonsk. But an elder said to her: 'This is not to your benefit. You would do better to sit at home and repeat the prayer of the publican.'"

About irascibility the Elder said: "No one should justify his irascibility by an ailment—it comes from pride. *The wrath of man,* according to the words of the Apostle *worketh not the righteousness of God* (James 1:20). In order not to fall into anger and irritation, you should not hurry."

About envy and remembrance of wrongs, the Elder said: "You must force yourself to do something good for your enemies, even if it is against your own will. But mainly do not take revenge on them, and be careful not to offend them with an appearance of contempt and humiliation."

Someone said to the Elder: "How is it that you, Batiushka, not only do not get angry with those who speak ill of you, but even continue to love them?" The Elder laughed at this a long time and said: "Say you had a little son. Would you get angry with him if he said or did something you did not like? Wouldn't you rather try to cover his failings?"

The Elder said of St. Alexander Nevsky that he was a military leader, a tsar, the father of a family, a martyr, a confessor, a monk and, finally, a schemamonk. He was everything, and in everything he was able to display an example worthy of emulation. He told how when he appeared with the others to the Golden Horde and, just as the others, would not bow down to the idol, the Khan punished his co-travellers, but let him go because of his beauty and good bearing. "It follows," said Batiushka, "that beauty and presentable appearance are also gifts of God, talents, the use of which we also should give account to God."

Fr. Ambrose said: "He who does not respect the feasts does not have success."

He also said: "St. Gregory the Dialogist wrote about what

price we have to pay to acquire the Kingdom of Heaven. It has no exact price. Every one has to give everything he has. The Apostle Peter gave his nets and received the heavenly kingdom; the widow gave two mites; whoever has a million dollars, let him give that; and whoever has nothing, let him give his freedom."

"If you do not feel like praying, you have to force yourself," the Elder said. "The Holy Fathers say that prayer with force is higher than prayer unforced. You do not want to, but force yourself. The Kingdom of Heaven is taken by force (cf. Matt. 11:12).

On the book, *Saints Barsanuphius and John,* Elder Ambrose wrote: "Whoever wants to be attentive to himself should read this book attentively, stay at home more, look around less, not go out of his cell, and not invite guests. He should not judge others; he should cry out to the Lord God about his sins in order to receive God's mercy."

About love the Elder said: "Love, in the words of the Apostle, *suffereth long and is kind, ... envieth not, vaunteth not itself, is not puffed up* (I Cor. 13:4)."

"Love covers all things. If someone does something good for his neighbor according to the promptings of his heart and not motivated by obligation, then such a one the devil cannot disturb. But when something is done out of obligation, then he tries to disturb him in one way or another."

"God sends mercy to the laborer and consolation to him who loves."

"Love, of course, is higher than anything. If you find that there is no love in you but you want to have it, then do works of love, although they may have been begun without love. The Lord will see your desire and attempt, and will put love into your heart. But the main thing is to notice when you have sinned against love and immediately confess it to your elder. It may have come from a dense heart, or it may have come from the enemy. You cannot figure this out yourself; but when you confess it, the enemy steps away."

"It is always better to yield," said Fr. Ambrose. "If you insist on fairness, it is the same as a paper ruble, but if you yield, it is a silver ruble."

"Whoever has an unfeeling heart should not despair, because with God's help a man can change his heart. You need only to watch yourself attentively and not miss the chance to be useful to your neighbor, reveal your thoughts to the elder often, and force yourself to give alms. Of course, it is impossible to do this right away, but the Lord is longsuffering. He only cuts short a man's life when He sees either that he is prepared to pass into eternity or that there is no hope for his correction."

"If you accept people for God's sake, then you can believe that everyone will be good to you."

"A man cannot correct himself all of a sudden, but it is like pulling a barge—pull, pull, pull and let go, let go! Not all at once, but little by little. Do you know the mast on a ship? There is a pole to which is tied all of the ship's lines. If you pull on it then everything gradually pulls. But if you take it all at once, you will ruin everything."

"You cannot become passionless all at once. But every time you feel your sinfulness say: 'Lord, forgive me!' Only the Lord is able to put love into a person's heart."

On almsgiving the Elder said: "St. Dimitry of Rostov wrote: 'Even if a man comes to you on a horse and asks you for alms, give it to him. You will not have to answer for how he uses it.'"

Also: "St. John Chrysostom says, 'Begin by giving away what you do not need, what is just lying around unused, to those who are in need. Then you will begin to give what you can according to your means, and finally you will be ready to give away all that you have.'"

"Atheists," said the Elder, "have no justification, for everyone makes his own decision. The Gospels are even preached to pagans. Ultimately, from birth we all by nature have a sense of the knowledge of God—this means that we ourselves are at fault. You ask if you can pray for such people. Of course, you can pray for anyone."

"Batiushka," someone asked, "it seems that people cannot experience total blessedness in the future life if they have close relatives who are tormented in hell." The Elder answered: "No, there will not be that feeling there—you will forget about everyone. It is just like going to an examination. When you go to the examination it is still frightening, and all kinds of thoughts crowd in. But when you have arrived, you take the ticket and forget everything."

About laziness and depression the Elder said: "Boredom is the grandson of depression, and laziness is the daughter. To send her away, labor actively—do not be lazy in prayer, then boredom will pass and zeal will come. And if you add to this patience and humility, then you will escape much evil."*

On insensitivity and lack of fear (of God), Fr. Ambrose said: "Death is not beyond the hill but beyond your shoulders, and we are very pig-headed."

"They could be hanging people on one side of the village, while the other side of the village keeps on sinning, saying, 'They won't reach us soon.'"

One nobleman who did not believe in demons came to the Elder. The Elder told him: "A nobleman came to a village to visit his friend, and he chose a room to spend the night in. They told him: 'Do not sleep here, there is something wrong with this room.' But he did not believe them and only laughed. He went to bed. Suddenly during the night he felt someone blowing on

---

*This saying rhymes in the Russian.—TRANS.

his bald spot. He pulled the blanket over his head. Then whoever it was went to his legs and sat on the bed. The guest was frightened and bounded out of there, having proven through his own experience the existence of dark powers." Having heard the Elder's story, the nobleman said: "Batiushka, I do not even understand what demons are." At this the Elder answered: "Well, not everyone understands mathematics, but it still exists. How could demons not exist, when we know from the Gospels that the Lord Himself made the demons go into a herd of swine?" The nobleman protested: "But isn't that figurative?" "That would mean," answered the Elder, "that swine are also figurative—don't swine exist? If swine exist, then the demons must also exist."

Condemning false shame and faintheartedness in faith, the Elder related: "One man did not really believe in God. When he had to fight a battle in the Caucasus, he was in the very heat of battle with bullets flying around him. He was afraid and hugged his horse, repeating all the while: Most Holy Mother of God, save us! Later, when his comrades remembered this and laughed at him, he denied his words." Having said this the Elder added: "Hypocrisy is worse than unbelief."

About repentance the Elder said: "What times have come! It used to be that if someone sincerely repented of his sins, then he would change his sinful life and become good. But now, people come and tell their sins in detail, then go back to the same thing."

"One time a demon was sitting in the form of a man and swinging his legs. One who saw him with his spiritual eyes asked him: 'Why aren't you doing anything?' The demon answered: 'Nowadays I have nothing to do but swing my legs; people are doing everything better than me.'"

About the power of repentance the Elder said: "One man sinned but repented, and this continued all of his life. Finally he repented and died. An evil spirit came for his soul and said: 'He's mine.' The Lord said: 'No, no, he has repented.' 'But he repented and then sinned again,' said the devil. The Lord said to him: 'If you, being evil, take him back after he repented to Me, then how can I not accept him if after sinning he has turned to Me in repentance? You forget that you are evil, and I am good.'"

The Elder was asked: "What does it mean to lament?" He answered: "Lamentation means sorrowing. It is not lamentation that comes from tears, but tears that come from lamentation."

"Sins are like walnuts—once you crack the shell it is hard to dig out the meat."

"There are three degrees to salvation. St. John Chrysostom says: a) do not sin; b) after you have sinned, repent; c) whoever repents poorly must endure the afflictions that come."

"It happens that although our sins may be forgiven through repentance, our conscience does not cease to reproach us. The late Elder Fr. Macarius used to show us his finger which had been cut a long time ago as an illustration of this—the pain was long gone, but the scar remained. It is exactly the same with sins—after they are forgiven, scars remain, that is, pangs of conscience.

"God does not create a cross for man. No matter how heavy a cross a man may carry in life, it is still just wood, from which man himself is made, and it always grows from the soil of his heart.

"Take me, for example—I was always a talker and loved to talk to people, to entertain myself. The Lord has arranged that I spend my whole life talking with people. Now I would be happy to be silent, but I do not have the opportunity.

"When a man walks the straight path, he does not have a

cross. But when he begins to step away from one side to another, then various circumstances arise that push him back onto the right path. These pushes comprise a man's cross. They vary, of course, according to what each individual needs."

"Sinful thoughts continually disturb a man. But if he does not cooperate with them, then he is not guilty of them."

"One ascetic woman was besieged for a long time with unclean thoughts. When the Lord came and cast them away from her, she called to Him: 'Where were you before now, O my sweet Jesus?' The Lord answered: 'I was in your heart.' She said then: 'How could that be? For my heart was full of unclean thoughts.' The Lord said to her: 'Know that I was in your heart, for you were not disposed to the unclean thoughts, but strove rather to be free of them; and when you were not able to be free, you struggled and grieved. By this you prepared a place for Me in your heart.'"

"Sometimes afflictions are sent to a person even though he is innocent, so that he would suffer for others, as did Christ. The Savior Himself first suffered for people. His Apostles also suffered for the Church and for people. Perfect love means suffering for your neighbor."

"Why do people sin?" the Elder posed this question, and answered it himself. "Either because they do not know what they are supposed to do, what they are supposed to flee, or they know, but they forget; or if they do not forget, then they are lazy or depressed.... These are the three giants—depression or laziness, forgetfulness and ignorance—that have bound the entire human race in inescapable bonds. After these follow carelessness, together with the whole horde of evil passions. That is why we pray to the Heavenly Queen: 'My most holy Lady, Mother of God, by Thy holy and all-powerful prayers, banish from me, Thy humble, wretched servant, despondency, forgetfulness, folly, carelessness, and all impure, evil and blasphemous thoughts,'* and so on."

Fr. Ambrose advised many people, in letters and in person, not to abandon the short prayer of Jesus: "Lord Jesus Christ, Son of God, have mercy on me a sinner."

Fr. Ambrose counselled that when we are beset by the punishments of men and demons we must have recourse to the Psalms of the Prophet David that he prayed when he was persecuted by his enemies. In particular read the 3rd, 53rd, 58th and 142nd Psalms. We should choose lines from these Psalms appropriate to the affliction and read them in part, turning to God with faith and humility. When depression wars against us or some unaccountable sorrow wearies our soul, we should read Psalm 101 *(O Lord, hear my prayer, let my cry come unto Thee ...)*, the 36th *(Fret not thyself because of evildoers, nor envy them that work iniquity ... )*, then Psalm 26 *(The Lord is my light ... )*, and Psalm 90 *(He that dwelleth in the help of the Most High ... )*. If we read these three times a day in the name of the Holy Trinity and with humility and zeal, giving ourselves over to the all-good Providence of God, *then He shall bring forth thy righteousness as the light and thy judgment as the noonday. Submit thyself unto the Lord and supplicate Him* (Ps. 36:6-7).

It is useful also to read Psalm 39: *With patience I waited patiently for the Lord, and he was attentive unto me.*

Showing that man has nothing to be proud about, the Elder added: "What is there for a man to exalt himself over? A tattered, wretched creature begs mercy: 'Have mercy! Have mercy!' And whether mercy will be given, no one knows."

When people complained to the Elder that unrelated thoughts disturb their prayer, he said: "A man rides through the market; around him is a crowd of people, conversations, noise.

---

*Prayer to the Mother of God from Morning Prayers.—ED.

But he just sits on his horse—gee-up, gee-up! and little by little he passes through the whole marketplace. Let it be the same with you—no matter what the thoughts say, just keep at your business—pray!"

So that people would not remain careless and put all their hope in other people's prayers, the Elder repeated the usual folk saying: "God help us—and man, don't just lie there." He added: "Do you remember how the twelve Apostles asked the Savior about the Canaanite woman, and He did not hear them? But when she herself began to ask, she received her request (cf. Matt. 15:22-28)."

In order to show that God mostly looks at the inward prayerful disposition of a man, Fr. Ambrose said: "Once a man with ailing legs came to Abbot Anthony and said: 'Father, my legs hurt; I can't make prostrations, and that bothers me.' Fr. Anthony answered him: 'Well, it is written in the Gospels, son give me your heart, not your legs.'"

One nun told the Elder that she had seen an icon of the Mother of God in a dream and heard Her say: "Bring me a sacrifice." Fr. Ambrose asked: "Well, did you bring a sacrifice?" She answered, "What should I bring? I don't have anything." Then Fr. Ambrose said: "It is written in the Psalms: *A sacrifice of praise shall glorify me*" (Ps. 49:24).

In a conversation about the pilgrimess Daria, the Elder sighed and said: "The Lord reposes in simple hearts. Gold is visible everywhere and shows up everywhere, despite its roughness. But as for some—no matter how you preen them, they will not become gold." At the remark that she reposed in a good way, the Elder said: "She had a good end because she lived a good life. However you live, that is how you will die."

About the difficulty of uprooting sinful habits in a man and how significant is the example of others, the Elder said: "When a horse is taken from the herd, a bridle thrown on it and it is led away, the horse resists and wants to go off to the side. But when it sees that the other horses are walking calmly, it also joins the ranks. It is the same with people."

Concerning the nets of the devil, Fr. Ambrose said: "A lazy spider sits in one place, puts out a little thread and waits. As soon as a fly gets stuck there, immediately its head gets taken off! And the fly just buzzes." At this Batiushka added very meaningfully: "We buzz ourselves out! The devil too always throws out his nets; as soon as someone lands there, his head is taken off." Then the Elder turned to someone and said: "Watch—don't you be a fly, or you too will buzz yourself out."

Life itself often directs a man to the right path. "One father sent his son to the woods on some business. The son said: 'Father, how can I go there alone? I do not know anything.' 'That's okay, go,' his father said to him, 'necessity will teach you everything.' He went, but in the woods his sledge broke. He remembered his father's words—necessity teaches everything—and he started shouting: 'Nec-essity!' and it answered 'essity!' He waited and waited, yelled and yelled, but no one came to help him. Then he climbed off the sledge, somehow managed to put it back together, returned to his father and said: 'You deceived me, Father. Necessity did not come to my aid.' 'Then how did you fix it?' 'Well, just somehow.' 'Well that you somehow fixed it shows that necessity came to your aid.'"

Father loved sometimes to make the names or surnames of the person he was talking to rhyme, with some humorous reproach; superficially it would be a joke, but there was always some underlying meaning and serious instruction.

"Watch, Melitona," he said to one nun, warning her against haughtiness, "keep a medium tone; if you go too high you'll cry, if you go too deep, it will be creepy. But you, Melitona, keep a medium tone."

# ELDERSHIP

Fr. Ambrose manifested his love and care for people by every available means—material aid and spiritual guidance. The things that people brought him he gave away through his cell attendants to needy monastics; and the money people sent him he divided into three parts: one part he sent to the Skete Superior for the Skete's needs and for commemoration of the benefactors, another part he gave to the poor, and the third and smallest part he set aside for lamp oil and wax candles for his cell Vigils and other services. His alms were distributed daily, also through his cell attendants, to people who came to him with needs. In exclusive cases he gave it away himself. Once he was walking in a rush from the cabin to his cell, and his secretary stopped him as he was passing by, asking: "There is a woman who has come with her orphans—little ones. There are five altogether, and they have nothing to eat. The widow herself is crying bitterly and asking for help. But the littlest one says nothing, only looks me in the eye and holds out his tiny hands. How can I not give him something?" The Elder began to take out some money. His hands were trembling and tears involuntarily welled up in his eyes.

Every year on the great Feasts of the Nativity and Pascha the Elder would send out several dozen letters with money to various places where people were unable to come to him personally for alms. He would send three or more rubles to each. At the end of the Elder's life the number of money letters sent on the great Feasts grew to two hundred. It would happen, although rarely, that Fr. Ambrose would send to one person over a hundred rubles. It could be said that several poor nuns were actually supported by him. He helped many people and materially supported entire families with the money sent by wealthy people who went to him and trusted him.

Finally, the highly populated Shamordino Monastery, with many poor and sick nuns, orphans, invalids and homeless women, received its sustenance from the Elder, or for his sake [people often contributed because of his presence there].

The Elder's love and compassion for people was such that he never left anyone without attention, sympathy and help even in what would seem to be the most unimportant woe, one which would seem silly and insignificant in other people's eyes. One day a peasant woman, who had been hired by a noblewoman to tend the turkeys, stopped him. The turkeys were not staying alive for her, and the noblewoman wanted to let her go. "Batiushka," the woman cried in her tears, "you at least help me. I have no strength left. I myself do not eat for their sake; I keep them as the apple of my eye, but they get sick. The mistress wants to throw me out. Have pity, my own father!" The other people present laughed at her stupidity, wondering why she came to the Elder on such a trifling matter. But the Elder tenderly asked her how she fed them and explained to her how she could take care of them another way, blessed her and bade her farewell. To those who had laughed at the peasant woman he pointed out that those turkeys were her whole life. The woman's turkeys stopped getting sick.

When Shamordino was first built and there were few sisters, one elderly but strong woman asked Fr. Ambrose if she could join the new Monastery. Fr. Ambrose accepted her and sent her to the Rudnevo farmhouse to tend the farm animals. She took to her obedience with zeal and labored well, but gradually she began to feel burdened by the fact that she lived outside the Monastery, far from the church, and had no time to pray as she always had to think about the cows and pigs. She became so depressed that she began to murmur against the Elder, saying: "I asked Batiushka if I could join the Monastery, and he sent me to the pigs." Finally she decided to leave altogether for some other monastery, but she did not say anything to the Elder or anyone else. At that time it happened that Fr. Ambrose came to

Rudnevo, and following him were, as usual, many lay people, amongst whom were some notable individuals. The Elder gave them all a general blessing, and the visitors began to ask the Elder to receive them separately, but he replied: "You are free individuals, but I have come here to be with the local sisters, who labor ceaselessly and see me rarely." With these words he conducted everyone out of his cell and called in the elderly, depressed farm-sister. "You silly," the Elder said to her tenderly, "why do you lament that I do not need you, and you are even ready to leave? I have sent all the visitors away and received you. Well, tell me, how are all your calves and piglets?" These few but paternally warm and loving words were enough to banish without a trace every thought, not only of leaving, but even of dissatisfaction. Not only then but even later on, when the Elder was no more, these words inspired and encouraged her in moments of weakened patience.

One modern writer who was not at all well-disposed toward monasticism but very well-disposed toward Elder Ambrose, informed us of the following example of the Elder's loving care.

"The daughter of one well-known merchant, an educated but modest girl, attracted by one young professor, became a mother.

"The enraged merchant threw her out of the house without a penny. She made her way to the next town, gave her child over to a tradesman's wife promising to pay her, and then, just as all the lost people in the provinces surrounding Kaluga do, she headed for Optina Monastery to Elder Ambrose for 'forgiveness and advice.' The Elder came out to the visitors who stood near the square that was fenced by railings and who waited for their turn to be called on by him. The Elder went inside the fence either immersed in reflection, talking with one person or another, or calling someone into the square. Within the crowd was the young woman. She was preparing herself for a difficult, shameful confession. What was her perplexity and embarrassment when, passing by the others near her, he called to her from far away. No sooner had she come to him and bowed to the ground than he gently and sympathetically asked her where she had left her newborn child. She told him everything in tears. Then he directed her to quickly return, take the child from the woman, go back to her father's town, and 'God will send money to live on….' She did just that.

"Up till now I have told you what I heard—the rest I saw with my own eyes.

"In the second grade of the gymnasium there studied a tall, thin and unusually active boy—constantly getting into mischief, but naive, innocent, so that without his mischief it would have been dull in class. And all of his pranks were delicate, quiet, in a word—clever. He was very nervous, impressionable, and at the same time open. He possessed none of the insolence and importunity that, unfortunately, you find in almost all Russian children at thirteen years of age. I marked a grade in his notebook and saw that for the previous week's 'witness of review of grades' was signed not his surname but another. 'Why didn't you give this to your parents to sign?' I asked mechanically. 'That is Mama's signature.' 'How could it be your mama's?' I pointed out the difference in surnames. On his face was a look of surprise: obviously this had never occurred to him. 'It must be that your mama married a second time and has this name (different from that of the boy) from her second husband.' 'No, I know for sure that my mother has not married a second time.' Only then did I begin to guess that there was some abnormality in the boy's family situation. Having marked the grade and sat down, I then took advantage of the pupil's cheerfulness and openness, and, as I had a habit of doing with almost all my students, I began to ask him where and how he lived with his parents. All of his answers were, I might say, surprising and all together comprised the continuation of my story presented above, which I had heard not long before my conversation with this boy. 'My mother draws, but only icons and nothing else, but she will not draw you an icon, because she doesn't draw for strangers; and as soon as she draws them she takes them to Batiushka.' 'To which batiushka?' 'To Batiushka Ambrose, in Optina.' 'How does she know him?' 'We have known him for a long time. He is so kind, like no one else.' 'Have you seen him, too?' 'He especially loves me. We go to see him about twice a year. Each time he takes us into his cell and caresses me, and he always gives me a treat. He is jolly, so jolly, always joking and laughing; and he asks me to do things for him, and I feel myself at home.' Incidentally, from other stories I knew that Fr. Ambrose is serious, instructive, and at times even severe.... Obviously there was an exceptional connection here. The Elder had saved the young woman with his counsel; he also saved the boy. He had come to love them with a special love, like his own creation, and he adopted them both. The grateful woman had completely given herself over to a precisely grateful religious feeling, which she expressed by painting icons. As I asked and learned, the strict father gave her a little money to live on, but never let her into his house, and neither he nor his family had any contact with her."*

---

*About the Elder's love for children, it was also related that during his life one family sometimes spent their summers in Optina. There were small children in the family. So that the children would not grow bored, the Elder had a tiny house built for them where they could play. The children themselves were so well-disposed to the Elder that when they drew their pictures they gave them to him for safekeeping. The Elder carefully preserved them. When these children grew up and had completely forgotten about their pictures, the Elder one day showed the pictures to them, asking what to do with them. That is how sacred he held everything entrusted to him, even by children.

To one recently widowed woman who was left with a daughter and grandson and absolutely nothing to live on, no pension or aid, but with a house, the Elder said: "Do not even dare to think about selling the house." She could have received a couple thousand for the house and begun to make ends meet—for a start it would have been enough. But the Elder was considering not the start but the long term. His prohibitions were equal to law. The three orphans lived in a cold, hungry home, but during the first months some relatives helped them out, and then a boarder turned up, and there was enough money to buy the "family feed." The family has now made ends meet for ten years, with difficulty, but without falling into complete financial failure and poverty, which they would not have escaped if they had had no home.

Another incident: "A grown son, already educated in the city school, was lost to drunkenness. His alcoholism was so uncontrollable and so unbearable to everyone that his father and all of his family had long desired not to see the young man, or even let him into their clean, well-ordered house. Only his mother had not given up on him. After his expulsion from the house he would sleep in the garden, in the bathhouse. They also found him drunk on the street, and it was altogether shameful. Otherwise, during rare moments of sobriety the unfortunate man was intelligent, amiable with everyone, bashful and modest. He had been taught to drink in his youth by bad comrades in seminary. His despairing mother brought him several times to 'Batiushka Ambrose,' who rapped this caring and inexhaustibly patient mother on the back with his staff (as stated before, a sign of the Elder's particular affection, and sometimes a special kind of sternly instructive gesture). But the drunkard he treated with unmitigated tenderness and 'vouchsafed him a word.' They had thought about giving the son to the army, which they could have done because of his meek character and because his alcoholism was apparently incurable. But the Elder forbade them, and he commanded the mother to unfailingly preserve him, and foretold for him a 'wondrous fate, that he would become a priest and send up prayers before the Throne of God.' This prediction even cooled the desire to come to Elder Ambrose for advice—the drunken young man was not even ordained a reader, but had been in the teaching course, and mainly he was in such a deplorable state. But the mother continued to take care of him, and he got married. The wife took her alcoholic husband to a doctor.... Later, after the death of his father a deaconate position opened up, he was ordained, and finally became a priest. The mother who told this story lived with him and was in charge of his vast household, looking after his sons and daughter."

Under Fr. Ambrose's loving and attentive guidance the course of people's lives were changed at the very root, as we can see from the following story by Nun N. "I joined the Monastery with Fr. Ambrose's blessing, but earlier my character was far from monastic, although I had received an education from a theological institute. Next to our institute was a convent. We often visited it and became acquainted with the monastic way of life, but we did not like it. Therefore my friends and I gave our word never to join a monastery. After graduation I got a job as a domestic teacher in a secular household and, living thus for six years, was drawn even more into worldly life.

"I hadn't even a recollection of the monastery. But God's Providence, Whose ways are known only to Him, works our salvation. One of my brothers, a priest, was widowed after living two years with his wife. He was all alone and asked me to come to him. I left my teaching position and moved in with my brother. I must mention that my brother was spiritually inclined and even as a seminarian had longed to enter a monastery, but Fr. Ambrose, with whom he kept up a correspondence, told him to first finish his course of study. When he graduated my brother had to help our mother and support his younger brothers, and therefore he first became a teacher and then, at my mother's wish, a priest. The Lord saw his spiritual disposition and sent him a sickly wife, who soon died. During her illness my brother turned to Fr. Ambrose through a pilgrim in whom he had great trust and asked the Elder to pray for the sick one. He received this answer: 'Let him keep vigil; he will plant an orchard, will water it often, and there will be much fruit. July will be sorrowful for him.'

"Truly, his wife died in July. So we came to him—I, my sister and mother. He thought to set one of us up in his place,* and in order to decide *who*, we went to Fr. Ambrose. Fr. Ambrose, at the general blessing, rapped me on the head and said: 'But don't you want to go to a monastery?'

"I was confused and did not know what to say. He took my mother aside, talked with her and told her to come back in a year. He did not bless either me or my sister to get married, and of the younger sister, he said that she was sick, 'How could she get married?' although he had never seen her. The monastic life of the hermits and the chanting made a deep impression on me, and the penetrating glance of the Elder, his ardent fatherly love to all the afflicted and tormented, completely remade me, and I began to think about a monastery. I abandoned my fine dress, merry-making and travels, and started eating only dairy products [that is, she gave up meat]; thus a year passed and I returned to the Elder. This time I talked with him, confessed and received a blessing to join the Monastery. In another year I came for good, although it was hard to overcome all the

---

*That is, marry one of them to a future priest and let the priest have his parish.

obstacles. After living a year in the Monastery, I heard that my brother had contracted tuberculosis of the throat, and the Moscow doctors had pronounced his case hopeless. I came with this sorrow to Batiushka, and he said: 'He needs to join a monastery but his mother holds him back. Go and ask your mother which will be easier for her—his death or his entering a monastery?' When I went home, I passed this message on to my mother. Mother began to cry and said, 'May God bless! Let him go!' In the morning we began to sell all the property. Batiushka blessed us to lock up the house and not wait for buyers.

"Some time passed, and I returned to my Monastery, having taken my sister along as a guest. My sister very much liked monastery life, and she stayed with me; only she contracted some kind of illness and was sick for two years. The doctors could not help her, but Batiushka healed her by giving her comfrey root to drink. When she got well, she was clothed as a novice and given an obedience in the cliros. After our return to the Monastery, my brother also came to Optina. Batiushka took him to himself and gave him an obedience—correspondence and singing on the cliros. My brother was doubtful and said: 'My throat is diseased, it's hard to sing.' 'That is nothing, it will go away!' said Batiushka. And truly, his throat disease did pass without a trace. My brother lived in the Skete twenty-three years after this, was the father-confessor to the Shamordino sisters, and then was appointed Archimandrite of the Borov Monastery.

"Six years after my arrival with my sister at the Monastery, my mother came to visit us and remained. She lived in the Monastery ten years, was tonsured twice by Fr. Ambrose\* and died a schemanun.

---

\* First in the mantia and later in the Schema.—ED.

"That is how great and holy Elder Ambrose was," the nun concluded her guileless story; "how he was able to turn people to the better and establish their soul's salvation and physical well-being."

The Superior of the Kashira Convent, Abbess Tikhona, related how she had experienced the power of Elder Ambrose's spiritual influence and how profitable his guidance was to her:

"After the repose of the ever-memorable Elder Macarius of Optina, our sisters, myself included, began to take our sorrows, confusion and spiritual needs to the reposed Elder's disciple, Fr. Hilarion. Fr. Hilarion was a man of wisdom, strong in faith, and an unwavering adamant of obedience, which he also demanded of his spiritual children. After the repose of this unforgettable spiritual man, I was left in that following year of 1873 without a guide at twenty-five years of age. At the temptation and counsel of the evil hater of our profit and salvation, I agreed at his suggestion to live unabashedly according to my own will and not submit my will to a new elder; especially since the occasional severity of the reposed Fr. Hilarion seemed difficult for a willful and sinful soul, already having tasted the bitter fruit of self-will during the Elder's long illness. Moreover, the now reposed Mother Abbess Paulina, knowing by experience how dangerous it is for young people to live according to their own will, more than once suggested and insisted that I go to Optina to seek the guidance of Batiushka Ambrose. Not wishing to contradict the Abbess' will any longer, I went there during Great Lent, at the very time when most people come to the Elder. Being under the influence of temptation, I counted on the large number of people to prevent Batiushka from having any time for me, and I thought: 'I will just sit here a while, look around, and then go back, thus putting Mother Abbess at rest, who so insisted that I come again to Optina.' But here the full power, spiritual strength and grace that dwelt in Batiushka showed itself. He saw my cool attitude toward him and, pitying a soul that was close to destruction, treated me with particular attention. Without keeping me long, he took me to confession. When I went into his cell, Batiushka went into his sleeping room, leaving me alone. It was completely dark, only the lampada brightly illuminated the face of the Mother of God. I remember that when I entered, coldness and emptiness filled my soul. But that is not all—I regarded maliciously and ironically everything surrounding the Elder and came to the confession with a sort of aversion. This was not hidden from Batiushka: his spiritual eyes penetrated my sinful soul and leaving me—as I think—had gone to pray in his cell.

"Not suspecting this at the time, I stood in expectation of the Elder and then—it is difficult to convey in words what happened in my soul—some kind of light, some kind of warmth, came over me and illuminated me. I fell on my knees before the icon of the Heavenly Queen; tears streamed forth of themselves—they were peaceful, special, joyful tears, and when Batiushka came in with a candle, I arose from my prayer and turned to him with the words: 'My Father! Save me! I want to open my soul to you; I want to speak sincerely and sincerely repent. I want to be obedient and devoted to you—guide me to salvation, I beg you!' From that moment everything within me was transfigured: horribly repugnant seemed my former state. In order to reveal my soul to the Elder in confession, I briefly told him about my life and the recent temptation—the desire for self-will, so strongly deceiving my young heart! What could this be if not the grace-filled power of the Elder's prayer for me?!

"Departing from Optina I was entirely happy and at peace. Everything in me was ecstatic: the same road, the same pine forest, but it all seemed different to me!… My heart felt the nearness of God, so that in His creations I came to know the greatness of God the Creator; and from that time on I became a sincere and devoted spiritual daughter of Fr. Ambrose until his very repose. More than once did I experience the grace-filled power of the Elder's prayer and influence. Compared to Frs. Macarius and Hilarion he was much more condescending. I remember hearing the remark of a person experienced in spiritual life that if it was appropriate to call the above-mentioned reposed elders fathers and wise instructors, then it would also be appropriate to call Fr. Ambrose a tender, loving mother. Batiushka's gentleness accomplished much; without even mentioning others, I will say about myself that I was ready to do anything in order to fulfill the Elder's wish. I had to sacrifice much, to renounce all the deceptive pleasures and smallest entertainments that are not always allowed in monasteries. If I could express it this way: Batiushka had a particular tactic—he never spoke severely against anything and never forbade anything. If you confessed to him that you had allowed yourself fish on a Wednesday or Friday, precisely those days when the rule does not allow fish, Batiushka would only say: 'I see that you miss being healthy; well, go ahead and eat fish when you are not supposed to!' Of course, after these words, from the fear of angering God and attracting the punishment of illness, you would not allow yourself fish. This impression would remain in your memory for the rest of your life.

"Batiushka acted in this as in many other situations with gentleness, but at the same time so powerfully that his word remained as a law that could not be transgressed. One day I was repenting to the Elder in confession that I had bought some things in a market, and when the merchant counted the change, the latter made a mistake and gave me one thing instead of another, and what he gave me was of greater value. At the time I did not notice it; when I came home, I saw it but thought that it was not worth returning and left it where it was. Nevertheless, this misdeed burdened my conscience and I, realizing my sin, repented before the Elder. At this the Elder told me a story from his life. 'When I studied at the seminary,' the Elder said, 'several of us went to the store to purchase various study materials. When the merchant counted the change he overpaid us by a ruble or more. At that time we schoolboys were overjoyed and divided the money between us. Having completely forgotten about this, I came to Optina, and there I remembered the incident, and my conscience began to bother me. Then it began to bother me more and more, and in order to quiet it, how much did I do! How many alms I gave to the poor, donated to the churches, to various God-pleasing organizations, and all with the aim of paying back what I had unjustly taken, although it was essentially a trifling amount. But to this day I would give anything if someone would show me the heirs of that merchant, whose name I do not remember, so that I could return that money I had unjustly taken from them. Therefore I advise you,' he continued, 'go home and immediately take back what you received to the store and tell the merchant that by mistake you have such and such.' Batiushka also said, 'Debts also weigh heavily on the soul after death—we must avoid them! God is infinitely merciful and forgives repentant sinners, but people are not the same—some forgive, but others do not forgive debts; they complain and grumble about their deceased debtors, and the soul gets weighed down by this after death!'

"He also said: 'People have to answer greatly for not keeping the rules of the Church with respect to the fasts. People justify themselves by saying that they never considered it a sin to eat dairy products during the fasts. They repent and consider themselves sinners in every other respect, but they do not think to repent about not keeping the fasts. Meanwhile, they are transgressing the commandment of our holy Mother, the Church, and, according to the teaching of the Apostle, they are as the heathen and publicans because of their disobedience.'

"I remember some young, worldly noblewomen once came to the Elder for his blessing, motivated solely by curiosity. Having waited for Batiushka's arrival with us at the hut, they grumbled about the conditions and, speaking to one another in French, whispered to each other about us and about the Elder, saying: 'What are we waiting for? What interesting thing can we hear from Fr. Ambrose? What could he understand?' Then the door of the hut opened up and Batiushka walked in with his characteristic smile, directing his attention first of all on the newly arrived, above-mentioned visitors. Having blessed them, he did not ask them anything about who they were or where they were from. Instead, he immediately began to occupy himself with their accessories, began to arrange their parasols, lace and feathers in their hats and carried on a conversation with them on the theme of ladies' fashion. He talked this way for a long time. We listened and the ladies became confused, realizing the emptiness of their usual conversations with which the Elder had so cleverly reproached them; and they humbled themselves, afterward regarding with great respect the Elder from whom they had not expected anything special.

"Living in the monastery in Belev, I had an obedience to serve on the cliros; and they sent me many times to the monastery dacha to teach singing to the sisters living there, since they had built a church and services were occasionally performed there.

"Three years in a row I greeted Pascha at the (monastery) dacha, and there was this incident: a poor, old village woman came and asked for some farmer's cheese for Pascha. The steward was a generous, good nun, but she was too economical and refused the woman. Soon afterwards the sisters went to get some farmer's cheese for the pascha cheese and were stunned when they saw that in the large, full vat of farmer's cheese a rat had rummaged through to the bottom and died right there in the vat.

"When I saw Batiushka I told him about all this and he replied meaningfully: 'Remember this and know that this will be useful to you and will serve as a lesson when you yourself become an abbess. In a monastery where the steward is generous there is always abundance; and to the contrary, where the steward is stingy, there are always chastisements from God, just as it happened on your dacha with the farmer's cheese.'

"Batiushka many times after this also foretold my abbacy, which did come to pass. Only concerning this the Elder told me: 'If thoughts or the desire to be in charge ever arise, you must oppose them as much as you can.'

"Batiushka said: 'I know from experience that the heavy cross of leadership becomes twice as heavy for those who desired to be leaders, and it is altogether difficult to bear for those who willfully obtained it.'

"Once when I came to Optina, already in the rank of Abbess, I asked for the Elder's instruction as to how I should conduct myself with the sisters of the monastery. He told me: 'Within your soul be deeply aware of your own nothingness; mentally throw yourself at the feet of your sisters, but do not show this—remember that it is the rod that has been entrusted to you, not some kind of toy. Therefore guard against joking, guard against any familiarity on their part, guard against having any especially close ones; behave so that they will fear you, love you and obey you. Know that you will answer to God not only for yourself, but for your sisters. Mainly, strive not so much with words but with your own example to impart the fear of God to them—in church, in trapeza, and on obediences.'

"Truly this abbatial yoke was heavy for me, an infirm one, and at that time beyond my strength. My spirit was despondent, being far from the Elder, and because of my inexperience I was in constant need of his counsel and instruction.

"I remember how bitterly I cried to Batiushka, telling him that I was perishing and not serving for the salvation of others. Batiushka comforted me, saying: 'That is how Fr. Archimandrite Isaac cried for a whole year and desponded, also fearing for his own salvation. The late Fr. Hilarion told him about this once: "Why are you so fainthearted, making the devil rejoice?! Just look at all the other 'holy ones'—who of them is a saint?! The bishops and the abbots—everyone prays for them, the flock, the brothers; and they will be saved by these prayers." You, too, don't be timid! You too will be saved by the prayers of the sisters, only humble yourself more; consider yourself mentally beneath everyone, not worthy of them.'

"When I first began my abbacy, during the building of the catholicon and other monastery matters I had to travel and do business, and sometimes it was very difficult. I had to ride horses very far in all kinds of weather, riding even in the rain. When I was at Batiushka's I wept bitterly over my lot, asking his holy prayers. The Elder replied: 'Many times have I noticed that when anyone has some kind of outstanding weakness in youth, he is punished for it in his older years.' And taking himself as an example, he continued: 'When I was young, I loved to talk and makes jokes. I was Fr. Macarius' cell attendant. They would send me on some errand and I would start talking and forget that they were waiting for me. They would wait and wait, and even send someone after me. And now in my old age what do I have? My tongue barely moves, I slur my words and am barely coherent—but people are waiting for me all around—they grumble, and I have to talk whether I like it or not. And now you—in your youth you were always eager to travel somewhere; do you remember how you longed to travel! For that, now you have to wander around whether you want to or not.' Thus Batiushka always encouraged people by telling some example from his own life, or by a parable, and it would be so consoling that it was as if he had just wiped the sorrow away with his hand.

"I remembered all my life the guidance of the Optina Elders. Now I would not dare to begin any matter without calling upon the help and prayers and blessing of our reposed holy fathers and guides.

"May their powerful, mighty prayers at the Throne of the Lord of glory, always preserve our Monastery!"

B<small>EFORE BECOMING</small> acquainted with Elder Ambrose some people out of ignorance and prejudice sometimes regarded him antagonistically. It even seemed strange to some that anyone would advise them to go to Optina. "What would we have in common with him? He is probably some hypocrite, who only seeks his own glory. It is an old hook—only simpletons get caught on it." Thus did some people reason and not want to go to Optina. In order to soothe their conscience they chose not to believe in the good things said about the Elder. Of those who went to Optina out of curiosity, the majority began with judgment. In Optina it was the custom among the monks out of humility to stand on their knees before the Elder. Some of the lay people voluntarily did the same. The Elder himself always invited lay visitors to be seated in the chair opposite his, sometimes even asking them not to stand on their knees before him. Even so, how much negative talk there was on this account! "Why should I kneel before any monk! Where is his humility?" It was as if some, being offended that people went to the Elder, tried to sow trouble.

When the moment of the first meeting arrived, some looked at the Elder with displeasure in their hearts and with the desire to unmask the old monk. But sometimes this mistrust would disperse in one visit and give place to the warmest feeling.

The Elder had the most people during the summer days. One young woman, who had been persuaded to visit Fr. Ambrose, was in an irritated state because she was being made to wait. Suddenly the door opened wide. The Elder appeared with a clear face in the doorway and loudly pronounced: "Whoever here is impatient, come forth." He came closer to the woman and took her aside to talk. After this talk with him she became a regular visitor to Optina and Fr. Ambrose.

One sister in a large, aristocratic family, who often came to Fr. Ambrose, tried for a long time to persuade her favorite sister, who had a very vivacious and impatient character, to go with her to Optina. She finally agreed just to please her sister, but the whole way there she loudly complained. When they came to the Elder and sat in the waiting room, she became upset about something. "I am not going to stand on my knees! Why this humiliation?" She was walking rapidly around the room from one corner to the other. The door opened in such a way that it closed her into the corner where she stood. Everyone went to their knees. The Elder walked right to the door, threw it back and gaily asked: "Who is this giant standing here?" Then he asked the young girl: "It's Vera, come to see the hypocrite!"* The acquaintance was made. Vera got married, became a widow, then returned to live under Batiushka's wing, in Shamordino.

There was one young girl with a good education and good aspirations who was worn out by her inner conflicts, doubts and the empty life and interests of the world surrounding her. Influenced by the stories she had heard about the Elder, she unaccountably went to see him in Optina, not having any

---

*In Russian this is a rhyme: *Eto Vera prishla smotret litsemera.*—TRANS.

particular purpose. In the Elder's cell the All-Night Vigil was being served. There were many people. Standing amongst the other people, the girl felt an inexplicable trembling. A grace-filled warmth encompassed her heart. Looking at the large icon of the Mother of God "It is Truly Meet," she seemed to feel the caresses of the Heavenly Queen Herself, and without even noticing she began to weep bitterly. Suddenly the Elder came out of his cell and, with an expression full of compassionate love and sympathy, he asked: "Who is crying so bitterly here?" Everyone answered: "No one is crying, Batiushka." "No," the Elder repeated, "someone is crying here." Seeing the Elder's sensitive, sincere love, responsive to every human suffering, the girl was deeply moved, and she herself began to love the Elder. At that moment her fate was sealed. She asked the Elder to accept her at Shamordino. Her mother came, as she put it, "to tear her away from this horrible monastic world." The mother went to Fr. Ambrose with grief and castigations. The Elder offered her a seat. The conversation lasted a few minutes, and the outraged mother involuntarily, without even understanding why, rose from the chair and fell to her knees before the Elder. The conversation continued for a while. Within a short time the mother was united with the daughter—both of them as nuns.

One young girl lived with her mother, a very religious and pious woman. Her faith was as they say, "like the old way," firm and unbending. She raised her daughter in the same spirit, and this daughter was in her childhood just as religious; but when she went to high school she gave in to the influence of her girlfriends, and her faith grew completely cold. When she finished her schooling and became a teacher, she became acquainted with one young man whom she was later preparing to marry. He was a good man, but a Catholic, and that was enough to incite her mother to categorically refuse. The young people's mutual inclination went so deep that they did not want to stop at this obstacle, and the young girl persuaded him to accept Orthodoxy, which he soon did. But the religious mother in her simplicity did not acknowledge this conversion and again refused to give her consent to this marriage. The daughter was in a very difficult situation—on the one side she was attached to her fiance and felt uncomfortable about inadvertently deceiving him, and on the other hand she was afraid to upset her mother. Her close friends, who knew what inner turmoil she was experiencing, advised her to go to Fr. Ambrose. The girl had already heard about the wisdom and holiness of Fr. Ambrose and had experienced the power of his prayers. (She used to suffer from severe headaches and wrote to Fr. Ambrose, after which her headaches disappeared forever.) Thus, she decided to accept this advice, determined in her soul to submit strictly to the Elder's decision. Soon she received an answer, in which the Elder counselled her to distance herself as much as she could from her fiance, but not to refuse him entirely. Nine months passed after this. The unsurety and awkwardness of the situation began to weigh the girl down, and she again wrote to the Elder, asking him to decide this question somehow. The Elder wrote to her to come to him in person. Fr Ambrose lived at that time in Shamordino. When she entered the reception room and saw the Elder sitting on the couch, she was stunned by his appearance—he was as if emitting rays [of light]. She was stunned and threw herself to her knees before him and sobbed. She could not say a thing, and the Elder dismissed her, also without saying a word. The young girl lived in Shamordino for a few days, seeing the Elder only at the general blessings, and the Elder did not even pay her any attention. Meanwhile, some forceful work was taking place in her soul, and an incomprehensible breakthrough was preparing itself. She began to form a specific decision to enter the Monastery, and she realized that she could not leave that place, but she decided to keep silent about it. Finally her vacation period was coming to an end, and the Elder called her to his cell. Looking at her with his deep, penetrating glance, he quickly and decisively asked her this question: "Well, speak your desire." Not expecting such a direct question, she said: "Batiushka, at the present time my desire is to remain at the Monastery." "Well, then stay," the Elder said simply, just as he always simply resolved complicated issues. "All of the weight just fell from my shoulders," she said. "I felt so light and joyful, only I could not understand how Batiushka could take me into the Monastery so unprepared. I was also disturbed by the thought that I was not behaving in good conscience towards the man who for my sake had even denied his own religion. When I told this to Batiushka, he replied: 'Was what you did for him evil?'"

So she remained in the Monastery completely at peace, and though she never had any personal means, by the Elder's prayers she never wanted for anything.

One day the Elder was walking through the Skete, leaning on his walking stick. A large number of men walked up to him. A little ways behind him was his cell attendant. One hieromonk led two young men to the Elder. They were very well-dressed and had a very educated air. But the elder brother was completely indifferent to the Faith, while the other had judged the Elder when people talked about him, and now he was very displeased that the Elder had been unable to receive them for several days. They watched the Elder even more now, trying to figure out what sort of man he was. The hieromonk asked the Elder to bless them. He blessed them quickly, without a glance, and kept on walking. Several peasants from a distant province were waiting for him. "We greet you with a deep bow," they said. "We heard that your legs are in pain, so we made you a pair of soft boots. Wear them in good health." The Elder took their boots, and talked with each of them. The younger of the two young, educated men saw all this. Suddenly he was able to imagine the Elder's laborious life and all the burdens of others that he bore, the faith with which all these people looked to him, and the love of the peasants who had brought him those boots. The doubt that had lain like a stone on his heart disappeared. He came again closer to Batiushka and said timidly: "Batiushka! Bless me!" The Elder turned around, looked at him cheerfully and began to speak to him about his studies and about life. He thought all the way home about the Elder. The next summer he came again to him, this time at the call of his heart.

A tormented man came up to Fr. Ambrose; he had lost his foundation and could not find the purpose of life. He looked for it in a wide range of works, including the discussions of Tolstoy, and he had run from it all. He told Fr. Ambrose that he had come to have a look at him. "Well, have a look!" the Elder answered. He stood up from his bed, straightened to his full height, and peered at the man with his clear gaze. From this gaze a sort of warmth, something similar to a peacemaking, poured into the man's sickened soul. The unbelieving man settled close to Batiushka and talked with him every day for a long time. Much time passed. One morning he said to Father: "Now I have faith."

The irresistible influence of Elder Ambrose's personality could also be seen in a very interesting story told by a Muscovite, V. V. Yasherov: "My acquaintance with Fr. Ambrose," he wrote, "came about under rather peculiar circumstances. In 1882, during my vacation from southern Bulgaria, living in Moscow, I met and became acquainted with one woman, the relative of a family that was very close to me. The woman was the cause of my acquaintance and close contact with the righteous Elder, for he was her constant spiritual father over the course of several years. I must note that she was a remarkably religious person; during the fasts, for example, she would daily attend all the church services, arriving first before everyone in the church and leaving last. To me, a man with an entirely different disposition, all of this seemed to be sanctimoniousness, and even an emotional illness. But soon I was to change my way of thinking.

"Incidently, the lady of my acquaintance became so drawn to obey the then unknown-to-me Optina Elder, that she was ready to fulfill his slightest requirement or wish. On one October day this person showed me a penciled note she had received from Elder Ambrose through a certain nun, which ordered her to drop everything and come immediately to him in Optina. What especially troubled her was her legal documentation, whether she should bring her pension book with her. 'It seems that Batiushka has been calling me to be there for a long time,' she said sadly. In vain did I try to persuade her not to trust any 'elders' or 'fools-for-Christ' and to stay home. The next day I received a note from her by municipal mail, saying that she did not dare disobey Batiushka and was leaving for Optina. In eight days she informed me again by mail that Fr. Ambrose had told her to remain in Optina for the entire Nativity fast, but for the present he was sending her to the convent in Belev.

"This letter irritated me greatly, to say the least. Considering my friend's behavior to be the fruit of a final emotional breakdown and blaming Elder Ambrose exclusively for this, I took two sheets of stationery and wrote him a long letter, in which in the most polite and respectful terms I expressed a good deal of criticism, justifying each one with lines from the Holy Scriptures and explaining these quotes from my own point of view. Without even re-reading what I wrote, I sent it off right away. And what do you think? Within five days my acquaintance returned to Moscow. She told me that to her bewilderment Fr. Ambrose not only was pleased with my letter, but even ordered her to return to Moscow right away. He sent me a prosphora and asked her to convey to me his desire to see me in Optina. I was touched by such an outcome from my letter and decided to fulfill the Elder's wish at the first opportunity, feeling guilty before him for the unrestraint of my pen.

"On the fourth week of Great Lent, 1883, I travelled to Optina through Tula and Kaluga; from the last town I had to travel forty miles by post chaise.* I departed from Kaluga on Monday morning and arrived in Optina late that evening. Exhausted by the trip, I quickly had some tea and went to sleep. When I sat down to tea the next morning, Fr. Ambrose's cell attendant appeared to me inviting me, 'If you please, come to Batiushka.' I was not at all surprised at this, assuming that they informed him of every arrival. Optina consists of two parts: the Monastery itself with its churches, monastic quarters and cattle and horse stables, which, incidentally, are kept in exemplary order. It is thus with the buildings as well as the animal stables, the guest houses and various functional buildings. The other part is the Skete, where the more austere ascetics lived. Women are not allowed to enter the skete gates. The cell attendant and I passed by the catholicon, through the orchard, crossing the entire length of the Monastery, and finally left the boundaries. Before us stretched the forest, sadly denuded by the winter, and the path stamped out between high snowdrifts by the masses of people who came to see the holy Elder. It led through the forest to the Skete, about a quarter-mile from the Monastery. We went out to the field and saw there the white skete wall. To the right of the entrance gate could be seen a small, white stone wing, one side of which faced the outside, the other side hidden

---

*At that time there was no railway system to Optina. Now [1912] people travel by rail to the Kozelsk station, two miles from Optina Monastery.

Elder Ambrose.

within the wall. In front of the porch of the outside portion of the building, which the women for some reason call 'the hut,' stood a crowd of about fifty women of both high and simple calling, waiting to see Fr. Ambrose. The majority of them had walked or ridden from far away, and amongst them all there reigned a firm belief that they would find here consolation in their sorrows and good advice in their difficult situations, even healing of their ailments. But it happened that one pilgrimess who had stood outside the cabin for several days in a row without success, not having been received by the Elder, was going to have to leave in great distress, without having seen him.

"Entering through the gates of the Skete, we turned to the right to the inner portion of the wing, which turned out to be more spacious than it seemed from the outside. The door opened directly into the corridor that divided the wing in half. To the right was a room that was small but neatly furnished and a reception room for men. To the left was Fr. Ambrose's living quarters, and further on were the cell attendant's rooms and the women's reception room. The cell attendant, having taken my coat, invited me to the reception room on the right while he informed Batiushka of my presence. In a minute he came out and said that Batiushka asked me to wait a little, while he finished his talk with a visitor. I started looking over the reception room. The cell attendant's invitation to come to see Batiushka cut short my examination of the room, and I followed him along the corridor, which had benches along each wall, where sat several dozen visitors.

"Turning to the left, I passed through a small anteroom and through a narrow doorway and found myself in a chamber about 10 by 7 feet, with a rather low ceiling. Right across from the door was a small window, and under it was a desk with drawers and a cabinet; what was on the right I do not remember, for the left side of the desk drew my attention. On a bed, about 6½ feet long and just less than 2 feet wide, made out of boards and covered with a thin padding of two carpets or a mattress (I didn't notice), a little old man half-reclined, wearing an old, worn black cassock and the same sort of scoufia, leaning on one elbow on a pillow and counting the knots of a prayer rope with his right hand. He had a small, spiky beard, penetrating, kind eyes, and an extraordinarily attractive face. It was a decisive contrast to the elder I had imagined! I stopped, waiting for an invitation to come closer. The Elder attentively and motionlessly gazed at me for a minute. Finally, he raised himself a little, smiled and motioned for me to come closer. I approached and involuntarily fell on my knees to receive his blessing. Having blessed me, Fr. Ambrose took my hand, not ceasing to look at me in the eyes, and with a gentle, cheerful voice said: 'So this is that fierce defender of his own happiness!' I mumbled something by way of an apology, but he stopped me and, pointing at my letter that lay on the desk, continued: 'No need to apologize! I am very pleased with that letter, the proof of which is my desire to see you. What is that uniform that you are wearing?' I answered that I command the southern Bulgarian military detachment, and this was the uniform of the Eastern Rumelian Corps. 'The first name is good, but the second one it would be better not to be!' the Elder pronounced seriously. 'I am very pleased, Batiushka, to hear that your views are in perfect agreement with the late Skobelev and all true-Russians!' I answered with a respectful bow. 'S. tells me that you were a volunteer in Serbia. By the way, how is her health? I heard that she was ill after her trip to Petersburg.' 'Glory be to God, she is well,' I said. The Elder smiled again and said: 'I shall not keep you any longer. You saw how many people are waiting for a word of consolation. Go, we will talk later. Have you come for long?' 'I plan to go and have a look at your famous Kozelsk and to depart from Optina on Thursday.' 'That's excellent! It means that you can prepare for Holy Communion here.' 'Fr. Ambrose! Today is Tuesday, when will I have time to prepare for Communion? Thursday is the day after tomorrow!' I protested in a somewhat surprised tone. 'For true repentance not years nor days are needed, but only an instant,' he pointed out seriously, almost sternly. 'Today you will come to the evening service, tomorrow the morning services and Presanctified Liturgy, and after Vespers you will come to me to have confession. On Thursday you will receive the Holy Mysteries, and in the evening you can depart for Moscow.'

"Leaving the Skete, I directed my attention to a particular animation in the group of women. Curious as to what was going on, I stepped closer to them. One rather elderly woman with a sickly face, sitting on a stump, was telling everyone that she had walked with sick legs from Voronezh, in hopes that Elder Ambrose would heal her. As she was passing the beehives about five miles from the Monastery, she got lost, lost her strength and found herself on a snow-covered path; she fell in tears on a fallen log. But some old man came up to her in a cassock and scoufia, asked her why she was crying and with a key pointed her in the direction of the road. She headed in that direction and, turning at the bushes, saw the Monastery right there. Everyone agreed that it must have been the monastery forester or one of the cell attendants. Then suddenly the familiar servant appeared on the porch step and asked loudly: 'Where is Avdotia from Voronezh?' Everyone was silent, looking around. The servant repeated his question more loudly, adding that Batiushka was calling for her. 'My little doves! Why, Avdotia from Voronezh is me, myself!' exclaimed the woman with the ailing legs, who had told the story, and she rose from the stump. Everyone silently made way for her, and the pilgrim, ambling to the doorway, disappeared within. It seemed strange to me that Fr. Ambrose should already know her name and where she came from. I decided to wait for her return. In about fifteen minutes she came out of the house all in tears and, at the questions pouring on her she nearly sobbed, replying that the little old man that had shown her the way in the woods was none other than Fr. Ambrose, or at least someone very much resembling him. I returned to the guest house lost in thought. 'What can this be?' I thought. 'Let's say it was a resemblance; but firstly, there is no one in the Monastery that looks like him, and secondly, here were two strange coincidences: Fr. Ambrose, as everyone knows, because of his sickness could not go out of the house during the winter or until the warm, summer days, and now he appears in the woods in the cold to show a pilgrim the way to the Monastery. Then within a half hour, almost at the minute of the woman's arrival at the 'hut,' he already knows about her in detail.'

"I decided to fulfill my short preparation for Holy Communion according to all the rules of the Church—I kept the fast as in the Monastery and went to all the church services. On Wednesday evening, after Vespers, I went directly from the church to the Skete. The Elder received me only a half hour after my arrival. Entering the chambers, I found him in the same position as before and, standing on my knees, I received his blessing. 'Well, now I can talk with you a little longer. Come a little closer,' said the Elder to me tenderly. I supposed that I would really get it during confession, for I had not confessed for six years, and I prepared to bear the threats. Fr. Ambrose began to ask me about my childhood, my education, service, about the more notable individuals whom I had met during my life, about my unhappy marriage, about Serbia, Bulgaria and Turkey, sprinkling the conversation with remarks and smiles. I who had never even been able to stand on my knees in church because of the pain in my legs, did not even notice that our conversation went on for an hour and seven minutes—that is how nice the

Elder's conversation was, interesting and wisely instructive! With every phrase I felt that I was growing closer and closer to him in heart and soul.

"'Give me the epitrachelion and cross,' Fr. Ambrose suddenly said to me, after a silence of a couple of minutes. I gave him these things. Putting on his epitrachelion, he began to read the prayer of absolution. I briskly stuck my head out from under the epitrachelion and exclaimed: 'Batiushka! What about the confession? After all, I am a great sinner!' The Elder gazed at me with, as I might express it, a tender-stern expression, again covered me with the epitrachelion and, having finished the prayer, gave me the cross to kiss. 'Now you can go, my son! Tomorrow, come to see me after the Liturgy!' Then he dismissed me affectionately.

"Never in my life did I have a more marvelous walk than I did then, from the Skete to the Monastery. It was as if some enormous relief was felt throughout my entire being; and around me the rays of the full moon played in a myriad of diamond-like sparkles upon the snow on the field and the fantastical flakes that magically clung to the branches of bare trees here and there. I did not notice how I came to my room or how I fell asleep there.

"The next day, after receiving the Holy Mysteries and the Liturgy being over, I set off to see my new spiritual father. The Elder greeted me affectionately, blessed me with a prosphora and granted me a half-hour talk, during which he gave me several instructions and directions on my life's path, which I will never forget and which to this day often serve as a consolation to me and a support in difficult moments. Saying goodbye, he again blessed me and kissed me, and gave me a prosphora wrapped in paper for his spiritual daughter....

"When I returned to the guest house, I found a wonderful mushroom dinner prepared for me. Having made arrangements for a horse, I took my dinner in the company of the father-guestmaster and, after attending Vespers, boarded the post troika [a three-horse carriage] headed for Kaluga, bringing with me the most positive recollections of the amiable Optina Monastery; and in my heart was love and respect for Fr. Ambrose, that great instructor and healer of human hearts and souls."

Here is another example of the remarkable influence of the Elder's personality. The father of one nun from Shamordino was, in her own words, not a believer. When he came to Optina to stay at the guest house, he suddenly felt within his soul such an uneasiness and aversion toward Fr. Ambrose that he decided to return home immediately. Because of the late hour, the guestmaster persuaded him to stay until morning, promising to send for a horse. In the morning the visitor, still in the same anxious mood, hastened to leave; but the guestmaster, who was experienced in such matters, offered to show him around the Monastery and Skete. Out of impatience the guest agreed. In the Skete, the guestmaster invited him to take a look at the Elder's cabin, but the man categorically protested, saying that he did not wish to see the Elder. "I am not suggesting that you see the Elder, I am only offering to show you his cells, his habitation," answered the guestmaster.... They went into the reception room. There they accidentally began a conversation with one of the other visitors. At that time the Elder came out for the general blessing. Everyone present drew close to the Elder, but the visitor, taken unawares, intentionally moved over to the opposite corner and glared resentfully at the Elder. Meanwhile the clairvoyant Elder, passing all the others by, went directly to him and silently placed his hand on his head. "I cannot say or explain how or why it happened, but I only know that I fell to my knees before the Elder," the man related later. "Then Batiushka, having taken me by the hand, led me to his cell and, sitting on the bed, asked me whether I went to confession. I answered that I did not believe in anything, and therefore I considered confession unnecessary. After this a miracle occurred which, as they say, made my hair stand on end. The Elder began to ask me questions, going over my life step by step, penetrating and revealing with authority all the secrets of my heart, bringing to the surface everything that only I knew. This confession was so peculiar that it shook me to the core. After it was over, the Elder blessed me and told me to go home. In the evening of the same day I went to Fr. Ambrose myself and told him, 'I want to be a believer, and I want to prepare for Holy Communion.' The two months of vacation he took for the sake of his health he spent without leaving Optina, going to every church service and carrying on long discussions with the Elder. From that time he became a deeply religious Christian, cherishing to the very end a reverent love for the Elder, and was vouchsafed a peaceful Christian repose.

Fr. Ambrose made a strong impression on Count Leo Tolstoy, whose visit to Optina was mentioned earlier in this chapter.

Tolstoy recounted his impressions from his conversation with Fr. Ambrose: "This Fr. Ambrose is absolutely a holy man. I talked with him, and my soul felt light and joyful. When you speak to such a man, you sense the nearness of God." This was spoken by Count Tolstoy in 1881. In 1890 when he left the Elder, he said to the people surrounding him, "I am deeply, deeply touched."

Not only during his life, but even after death, the Elder's personality made an indelible impression on many.

One young girl, very religious and serious, longed with all her heart to enter a monastery. When she finished high school she became a teacher, but meanwhile began to look over and read all available reading material on women's monasteries, yet she just could not decide on one. She read much descriptive and

Elder Ambrose.

interesting literature on monasteries and their foundresses, but something always told her that this was not the place for her, that she would not be here, but where—she could not clearly tell. In 1891, leafing through the latest issue of the *Niva*, she saw a portrait of Fr. Ambrose of Optina with a very brief notation about him saying that the Elder had reposed in the Kazan Convent he had built. In spite of the fact that the image of Elder Ambrose in the magazine was a rather bad one, it stunned the young girl. Even from the picture, the gaze of his penetrating and at the same time infinitely kind eyes penetrated her very soul, and she felt right away that she should be in the Monastery founded by this Elder. In the magazine notation there was nothing written about the Elder himself, nor about the Monastery, but in her soul she had come to a firm decision. Soon, unknown to her mother she went to Optina, and from there to Shamordino, where she remained permanently.

Fr. Ambrose's conduct with everyone who came to him was most amiable, as we have already shown. But to each one he gave just as much as his spiritual state would allow. People who did not need his spiritual advice, but were obligated to see him on one business or another, remarked about him: "A very intelligent man!" The Elder was able to speak about any issue, continued a conversation for as long as decency required, and then departed from such visitors. Here he was very restrained, polite to the highest degree, and only polite.... But with those devoted to him Batiushka was entirely different. He always remained kind and gentle, but to these relationships he added a most sincere intimacy. The Elder did not have the custom of directly or sharply rebuking someone in front of other people; but he would rebuke so deftly that his rebukes, despite the presence of so many people, were understandable only to the person concerned. He was able not so much with threats as with love to bring people to correction, implanting faith in their souls that all is not lost and that perhaps with God's help they could conquer the enemy. The Elder preserved to the end his natural vitality, which was an expression of his multi-faceted, kind and caring personality. When people who knew the Elder came to him with their sorrows and displeasures, their souls would quickly become light and free. Everything sort of cleared up and became inexpressibly consoling. Nothing can be compared to the joy that his spiritual children would experience upon seeing him again after a long separation. They were moments that cannot be described but must be experienced. We shall say a few more words about Fr. Ambrose.

He was an Elder of noble appearance, a little taller than average height, and slightly stooped with age. From his youth he was very handsome, as people who knew him personally then have said, and even in old age he did not lose the pleasant appearance of his face, in spite of his paleness and sallowness. He had a small bald spot on the front of his head which, incidentally, did not at all detract from but even added to his good appearance. On the back of his head were several tufts of not very long, darkish-blond and graying hair. He had two or three wrinkles on his forehead that smoothed out completely at times. His eyes were light-brown, lively, penetrating and saw the soul through and through. His lips were ordinary, his beard rather long, but thin and gray, divided at the end.

Elder Ambrose's facial expression constantly changed with his liveliness. First he would look at you affectionately, or laugh with you with his young, vivacious laugh, or joyfully sympathize with you if you were pleased, or quietly incline his head if you were telling him something sad. When you would want him to tell you what to do in some situation, for a minute he would sink into contemplation, or decisively begin to shake his head when he gave advice about something; or he would

The catholicon of Shamordino Convent.

intelligently and precisely begin to explain something to you, looking up at you to make sure you understood.

You could feel that those eyes saw everything in you, bad or good. You would rejoice that it was so, and that you could not keep the least secret from him.

# 9

# *The Last Podvig of Love of Elder Ambrose*

## THE FOUNDING OF THE SHAMORDINO-KAZAN CONVENT AND HIS CARE FOR IT

> *For though ye have ten thousand instructors in Christ, yet have ye not many fathers; for in Christ Jesus I have begotten you through the gospel. Wherefore I beseech you, be ye followers of me.*
>
> I Corinthians 4:15-16
>
> *Protect us all, O Lady, Queen and Mistress!*
>
> Troparion of the Kazan Icon

WHAT KIND of payment do you think someone might receive who, having gathered a hundred virgins in a monastery to serve God, would enable them to remain there and not be forced to scatter to various places or return to the world? It is good to help people made homeless by fire; but here there is only grief which, for the most part, brings benefit to people, for which reason the fire is allowed by Providence from on high; but a hundred times greater is he if he preserves many, or gives them the opportunity to be preserved, from obvious danger to the soul...." Thus wrote Fr. Ambrose to one of his spiritual daughters, trying to persuade her not to refuse to donate a certain sum for the building of a convent; and in these short words he showed the lofty, vital and spiritual meaning of such a sacrifice.*

---

*We will present here an excerpt from a recently found and as yet unpublished letter of the Elder to Constantine N. Leontiev, in which he states his opinion about monasticism, with regard to attacks that had then appeared in print against this ancient institution...."The opinion that monks and hieromonks in monasteries should be educated would have some plausibility if the twelve chosen disciples of Christ the Savior had been educated. But the Lord, in order to disgrace human pride and arrogance, chose for Himself disciples, simple fishermen, who simply and quickly came to believe in His teaching. And in order to convert and bring to the Faith the educated Saul, He had first to punish him with blindness. For educated people have difficulty believing and do not easily humble down, being clouded by scientific learning.

"It is true that in monasteries there are bad personalities, but evil is always and everywhere mixed with good and even, as it were, runs ahead. Cain was born before Abel, Esau before Jacob. Among the three sons of Noah who saw the Flood was the hated Ham. Among the chosen disciples of Christ the Savior was Judas the traitor. Evil people have always driven out good people but have not overcome them, and the evil ones have always been put to shame and humiliated. Worst of all is when evil ones are from among the educated, as, for instance, the Arian heretics. How much evil and abuse they committed against right-believing Christians and the Church of Christ in general.

"If this pompous preacher against monasticism would spend even three months in any desert monastery and would attend all the church services, getting up daily at 2:00 in the morning and earlier, then he would know from experience whether monks in monasteries do not do anything or not.

"No matter how bad monasticism is, the evil satan wants to destroy even bad monasticism any way he can. Obviously it grieves him and greatly hinders his wiles and evil tricks. Therefore he stirs up the educated people who are submissive to him against monasteries.

"Monks, according to the words of St. Dimitry of Rostov, are the dry stakes

# THE LAST PODVIG OF LOVE OF ELDER AMBROSE

From all ends of Russia, monastics and laymen hastened to Elder Ambrose for both written and oral counsel. One sought spiritual consolation, another asked for a resolution of doubts about the Faith, another for instruction on how to live. Those who wished to consecrate themselves to monastic life asked a blessing from the Elder to tell them which monastery to enter and how to live there, how to behave towards their relatives and how to organize their domestic affairs. But especially many were the cares of the Elder for women—widows, poor girls, and orphaned children. There were very, very many such women and girls who, wishing to lead a pious life, did not have the means to enter a monastery and did not know where to lay their heads.

Almost all women's monasteries in Russia accepted into their ranks only those who were in a position to buy a cell for themselves, make even a small deposit to the monastery, and support themselves by their own means or labor, since the monasteries were unable to provide full support for monastics. Very rarely was there a monastery that would accept a woman without a monetary deposit, counting only on her physical strength, health and capability of fulfilling difficult monastic obediences. Therefore, many of these women who did not

---

which hold up the grapevine of the Church of Christ. Grapevines that are not held up by stakes are unable to bring forth fruit, being choked by the weeds below.

These pompous windbags try to convince you that monks do nothing and eat their bread for free. However, none of them has shown any desire or zeal to enter a monastery for the free bread. Many would rather live by begging in the world. There is an anecdote about a gypsy who wound up living in a monastery during the first week of Great Lent. He secretly ran away and, seeing a peasant who was leading a dog to the forest to strangle it, said to him: 'Take him out to the monastery—that will kill him.'

"In every society there are needed educated people, average people and simple people. If all were educated, who would do the lesser task?..."

have the opportunity to enter monasteries lived in cells in villages and labored to feed themselves, while those who were successful at finding a places in monasteries lived in uninterrupted labors. For the healthy, however, such a life was still not very burdensome; and they themselves were even convinced that God loves labor and that their labors would procure eternal salvation for them. Another matter was a woman in poor health. Nowhere would they accept her into a convent, even if she had modest means, out of fear that she might burden the monastery in case of a prolonged illness and her inability to work. These were the kind of poor and destitute ones that Elder Ambrose accepted into his care, trying somehow to find a place for them.

For this he persuaded certain pious, well-to-do people to organize women's communities, and he himself, as much as he could, cooperated in this holy matter. By his counsel and directions, the St. John the Forerunner Women's Community was formed in 1879 in the city of Kromi, in the Orel Province. He took particular care in the '70's for the founding of the Akhtyrsk Gusev Women's Community in the Saratov Province. By his blessing the Kozelschansk Community in the province of Poltava and the Nikolo-Tikhvin Community in Voronezh Province were founded by philanthropists. The Elder not only had to scrutinize the plans, give advice and bless people to act, he also had to protect both the philanthropists and the inhabitants of the communities from a variety of mishaps and obstacles on the part of unfriendly lay people. On account of this he sometimes even entered into correspondence with diocesan archbishops and members of the Holy Synod. But in all these cases, the Elder only blessed others to act and gave guidance through others during the founding of the communities; he himself did not participate directly in these matters.

# THE LAST PODVIG OF LOVE OF ELDER AMBROSE

By the special ways of God's Providence, there came a time when he had to take upon himself the work, close to his heart, of caring for shelterless (in the material and spiritual sense) women who wished to lead a pious life and who were seeking his help and support. The circumstances of this affair took shape slowly and gradually. Everything proceeded as if by accident.

It began when a well-to-do man from St. Petersburg asked the Elder to buy a small dacha for him not far from Optina, so he could reside there with his family. Seven miles from Optina, along the main Kaluga road, a little to the left, stands the town of Shamordino. A short distance from the town there lived an old landowner named Kalygin, together with his aged wife. During a personal meeting with Kalygin (who occasionally visited the Skete), in the midst of the conversation Fr. Ambrose asked if he would sell his estate. Kalygin agreed, under the condition that he and his wife be permitted to live the remainder of their lives in Optina, in the guest house. However, the gentleman from St. Petersburg soon declined to buy the Kalygin estate for personal reasons. Then a spiritual daughter of the Elder, Mrs. Klyuchareva, who likewise wanted to acquire an estate close to Optina, reserved it for herself with joy. At this time the Elder said to her: "Well, mother, it has fallen to your lot to take this estate for yourself. Live there as on a dacha with your granddaughters, and I will come and visit you." We must remark that Klyuchareva had an only son whose first wife, after giving birth to two daughters, twins, died soon afterwards. Their father married another woman, but these half-orphans remained under the care of their grandmother and lived with her. By the wish of their grandmother, their godfather was Fr. Ambrose, who cared a great deal for them. For the future security of these granddaughters, Klyuchareva bought the Kalygin estate.

Schemanun Ambrosia (Klyuchareva).

## THE LAST PODVIG OF LOVE OF ELDER AMBROSE

The purchase of the Kalygin estate was completed in autumn of 1875. It is remarkable that a year before the sale of his estate, the elderly Kalygin had a certain vision—he saw a church in clouds on his estate. Kalygin's property consisted of 135 acres of land. On the top of a steep, high hill there stood the more-than-modest, single-storied wooden house of the Kalygins, 180 feet long and 84 feet wide. One half of the house was occupied by the aged owners, and the other part, which had no floor, served in place of a storehouse. The thatched roof on the house had become blackened by time, and the corners had rotted in places. For all that, the view of the surroundings from there was beautiful.

The whole huge slope of the hill was covered with a thick hardwood forest. And there, deep, deep in a dale at the foot of the hill, amidst the emerald green, wound the silvery ribbon of the small river Serena. Beyond that were meadows, and further on the right, to the southwest, a hilly area blending with the azure sky. All of this became green in the summer and abounded with a multitude of tiny flowers, strewn about by the generous hand of the Creator. On the left, to the southeast, through the peasant fields planted with various bread grains, the eye of the curious observer could scan a distance of six miles, if not more. And there in the remote distance, the Optina farm could be seen over the river Zhizdra, and beyond it the ancient pine forest, dimmed by the transparent, airy, blue expanse.

The first summer after the purchase of the estate, in July of 1876, Elder Ambrose came to Shamordino to have a look at the location. Upon entering the house, he said to those present: *Follow peace with all men, and holiness, without which no man shall see the Lord* (Heb. 12:14). While inspecting the place, he gave a blessing to build a new house here for Mother Ambrosia and her granddaughters, right on the very spot over which Kalygin had once seen a church in the clouds, and then said:

"We will have a monastery here!" The house was finished the following year, and the Elder himself sprinkled it with holy water.

It is noteworthy that by the order of the Elder a large hall occupied the eastern portion of the house, and the rooms of the granddaughters had to be on the north side, despite the fact that Klyuchareva herself was not pleased with the arrangement. The Elder more than once recalled this later, saying: "She built a house for the children, but we needed a church." Having thus prepared the house, Klyuchareva settled her granddaughters in it, together with novices (her former serfs) who had long served her. After some time, to these women were added their female relatives, even young ones, who were seeking quiet and prayer. Klyuchareva's pious frame of mind had an effect on all who were close to her. Even then, an almost monastic life was already flowering at the new estate. Klyuchareva continued to live as before in the guest house at Optina Monastery, though she was almost inseparable from her granddaughters. First she would stay for a long time at the estate, then she would take them with her. Concerned for the welfare of her granddaughters, Klyuchareva obtained, with the blessing of Fr. Ambrose, a dacha called Rudnevo, which was desirable due to its proximity to the Kalygin estate. She likewise fixed a portion of her capital for her granddaughters, with the condition that, in case of their unexpected repose, there would be a women's community built on the Kalygin estate; and that the nearby dacha she had bought, along with the capital, would be for its support. How good it was for the inhabitants of the Kalygin house to live in quiet and prayer! Only one thing was lacking—a temple of God—since the village church was far from Shamordino. Then, through the blessing of the Elder, Mother Ambrosia began to seek permission to build a church in her house. This was in 1881. Archbishop Gregory reacted sympathetically to Klyuchareva's request, but a soon-to-occur event—the martyric death of Emperor Alexander II—and the repose of Archbishop Gregory which followed soon after, hindered the realization of this request. In the meantime, Klyuchareva herself became ill and, having been sick all summer, she reposed on August 23, 1881.

Her granddaughters with their nurses and tutors continued to live for some time in Shamordino, where the main person in charge after the death of Mother Ambrosia was one of her closest coworkers, the elderly Nun Alipia. But they did not live here for long. At the Elder's blessing they were moved to the Orel boarding school, which belonged to one of his spiritual daughters and where they remained until 1883. In the spring of that year, after finishing their studies the girls came to Optina for a meeting with Elder Ambrose, whom they ardently loved; and there they both suddenly came down with diphtheria on the very same day—May 31. The girls were separated; their disease progressed quickly. They were given the last rites of Confession and Communion of the Holy Mysteries of Christ. While they still had strength, they constantly wrote notes to the Elder begging his holy prayers and blessings. On June 4, one of them, Vera, reposed. The novices who were caring for the sick girls did not speak of this to Lyubov, who was still alive, so as not to alarm her. But, while in a light sleep, the girl suddenly awakened and asked the sister who was sitting next to her: "Has Vera died?" The sister was about to say that she was alive, but Lyubov quickly objected: "How can she be alive? The nurse just told me that she died." But there was no nurse there at all. On June 8, Lyubov died as well. Both sisters, who tenderly loved one another, were buried side-by-side in the Optina cemetery, near the grave of their grandmother, Mother Ambrosia, and not far from the spot where Elder Ambrose would subsequently be buried. The life and fate of these girls were remarkable. Having been born on the same day and receiving the names Vera and Lyubov, they lived all of their short lives with faith and love.* Quiet and meek, they were warmly attached to one another and never parted. They never misbehaved and dressed simply. They loved to listen to the long monastic services, and loved the quiet, solitary monastic life. They were not afraid of death. More than once they said to those around them: "We do not want to live longer than twelve years; what good is there in this life?" And in fact, death overtook them in their twelfth year. As they entered into life together, so did they leave it, in a bright aura of youthful purity, tender mutual love and profound faith.**

After the death of the Klyuchareva girls, a women's community arose on the former Kalygin estate, in accordance with the last will and testament of Mother Ambrosia. Immediately after the repose of the child-heirs and before the opening of the community, work on the estate began to pick up speed. The applications for permission to build a church on the Kalygin estate, and also for the opening of a women's community, were again intiated by the Elder. The petitions were granted. Not much was needed to do for the building of the church. An altar was built onto the large hall, which faced east. The old iconostasis from the Optina Church named for Righteous Anna and

---

*In Russian, Vera means faith and Lyubov, love—TRANS.

** To illustrate the character of one of these sisters, Lyubov, we present the following account of her nurse, who later lived in the almshouse of the Shamordino Convent, the 80-year-old Alexandra: "When Lyuba was still four years old, on Wednesday of Passion Week, when the Presanctified Liturgy was still going on in the Monastery (we then lived near Optina), I had the desire to drink a little coffee. (Normally, we neither eat nor drink tea before the end of Liturgy.) I began to boil coffee for myself and prepared a cup. Lyuba sat and watched, but said nothing. I boiled the coffee and began to pour it, but Lyuba suddenly said: 'Nursie, that's a sin, you know.' At this, I was dumbfounded."

## THE LAST PODVIG OF LOVE OF ELDER AMBROSE

St. Mary of Egypt was renovated and installed, and a new iconostasis was built in Optina at Fr. Ambrose's behest.

In the middle of the 1870's, when Fr. Ambrose entered the newly rebuilt Klyuchareva house, he saw in the hall a large Kazan icon of the Mother of God. Stopping before it, he looked at it for a long time, and finally said: "Your Kazan Icon of the Mother of God is without doubt miracle-working: pray before it and preserve it." It was in the name of this holy icon that the first house-church in the Klyuchareva home was consecrated; and that is why the women's community that was opened here began to be called the Kazan Community.

In 1882 a middle-aged widow named Sophia Michailovna Yankova, a landowner from Tula, came to the Elder. With the blessing of the Elder, she was soon to enter into a second marriage with an aged landowner who lived near Optina, Nicholas Ivanovich Astafiev, also a widower. Astafiev became ill soon after the marriage and reposed after a year and two months. Sophia Michailovna, seeing in this an indication from God, dedicated herself from this time entirely to the service of God, becoming Elder Ambrose's dedicated novice. As she was a smart, capable woman and a gifted speaker, the Elder sent her everywhere on errands concerning the business of the soon-to-be-opened community, and she was later assigned as the first Superior. The consecration of the church and the opening of the community were accomplished on October 1, 1884, by Bishop Vladimir of Kaluga. On that day, the Elder secluded himself in his cell and prayed.

Mother Sophia was Fr. Ambrose's indispensable assistant in organizing the young Monastery—his right hand, as they say. Unfortunately, her management did not continue for long. Intelligent, understanding well both spiritual life and household matters, dedicated to the Elder with her whole soul, she entered onto the path of monastic life under his direct

Superior of Shamordino, Schemanun Sophia.

guidance. Taking on the most difficult obedience in the Monastery, that of superior, she began to struggle with great zeal. She had always lived in comfort from her earliest years and was entirely unacquainted with physical labor, but she now labored untiringly and in no way pitied herself. In the damp, cold autumn weather, it often happened that for the whole day, from morning until evening, she would walk through the entire Monastery looking after all the work; only at night would she return to her cell, all wet and chilled to the bone. These labors and cares, combined with a strict ascetic life, soon broke her robust health. She gradually began to waste away and, little by little, melted like a candle. Finally, on January 24, 1888, she fell asleep in the eternal sleep of the righteous, receiving from the Lord a reward corresponding to her great and holy zeal and labors. The Elder, when recalling her later, would often say with a special feeling of contrition: "Oh, mother! She obtained mercy from God."

At the direction of Elder Ambrose, after the repose of Matushka Sophia, a nun of the Belev Convent, Mother Euphrosyne (Rozova), was named as Superior of the Shamordino Community. She was, from 1860 until the Elder's death, his dedicated and sincere disciple and assistant.

Selecting as superiors of the Shamordino Community zealous and experienced ascetics and his devoted spiritual daughters, Fr. Ambrose did not cease to be the chief director and inspirer of the whole life of the young Monastery. He sought the means for its existence, which was not easy considering the enormous number of sisters he accepted. Without his counsel and blessing, nothing was undertaken in the Monastery; sisters were accepted at his direction.... As a result of this huge collection of sisters, he did not have the opportunity to be the spiritual father of each of them, and therefore he gave them over into the hands of one of his closest disciples, the Skete Superior,

Hieroschemamonk Anatole, who treated them with the most considerate, fatherly love, as is seen from his *Letters to Nuns.*\*

In the meantime, building after building was constructed. But those who wished to enter the newly opened community flocked to it so suddenly that scarcely had they built a house than twice as many were already waiting for a new dwelling. And whom did the Elder accept and settle in the community he built? The greater part were in dire poverty: widows and orphans, and also the blind, the lame, the sick and, in general, the women and girls left most destitute by fate. There came to the Elder, for example, a young woman who was left as a sick widow in the family of her in-laws. Her mother-in-law chased her out and said, "You luckless creature; if you hanged yourself it wouldn't be accounted as a sin for you." The Elder attentively heard her out, took a good look at her, and finally said: "Go to Shamordino." Here is another example: the former blagochinny\*\* of Optina, Hieroschemamonk Hilarion, relates: "My married sister was subject to a serious ailment, and her husband left her to the mercy of fate. They brought her, sick, to Optina, to the Elder. It was summer. Batiushka went out to the sick one; he took a look at her and, having blessed her, he jokingly said to me: 'Well, this flotsam will do for us; take her out to Shamordino!' She lived for about ten years there in the almshouse and died; before her repose she was tonsured into the schema in her cell." Another: A pauper arrived from Siberia and gave his very young daughter over to Batiushka: "Take her," he said. "She has no mother, and what am I going to do with her?" And the Elder sent her to Shamordino. From such orphaned girls, a children's orphanage was created. Among the orphans was one accepted

---

\* *A Collection of Letters to Nuns* was collected and published in Russian through the labors of Fr. Sergius Chetverikov. It is now available in English.

\*\* The person in a monastery responsible for keeping good external order, including church services, etc. He is usually second in rank to the abbot.—TRANS.

by the Elder at the age of two. He then asked her: "What will you be?" The child, barely able to speak, clearly pronounced: "A true nun." "See that you don't let me down," concluded the Elder. From the poor girls and women there was formed an almshouse, which sheltered fifteen people. And if there were that many per cell, then how many more in all the cottages of the community! "Batiushka, you have a real monastery," the Elder's confessor, Fr. Theodore, once said to him. "What do you mean?" "Well, whatever cell you go into—there's a blind one, a lame one, and here one altogether without legs—involuntarily they are all secluded."* Elder Ambrose also had a special house in Kozelsk for the care of women who were not in full possession of their senses.

However, it was not only those women and girls who were simple, needy, sick and lowly who found themselves in the Elder's refuge. Under his protection there also came women who were well-to-do, educated, sometimes of high position in society; they came because life had not given them moral satisfaction. Here, under the guidance of the Elder, they began to comprehend the true meaning of life and true happiness of the soul.

Beginning in 1888, the Elder had the custom of coming to Shamordino each year in the warm summertime, so as to personally have a look at what there was in the Monastery and what was lacking. These visits were great feasts for the sisters. This is how they themselves describe one of these visits, which occurred in 1888. We present this description in its entirety as a portrait of Fr. Ambrose's life in Shamordino:

"Back in the first days of July a rumor spread among us that Batiushka was preparing to visit us after the feast day of the Kazan Icon [of the Theotokos] (July 8). But it seemed to us to

---

*Monk means secluded, alone.

be a vain dream, so that we feared to rejoice, feared even to speak about it. Finally, a week before Batiushka's arrival, this rumor was repeated more and more frequently by those who had heard of it from him personally. But we still did not dare to believe it. Finally, on Monday the 18th, visitors began to stream to us from all directions to meet Batiushka. Troika after troika raced along to Shamordino. All the rooms in the guest house were full. We had to place some arriving monastics in special cells. Now our doubts ceased, and we began to be convinced that great joy awaited us....

"At last, Tuesday came. Right after Liturgy, at 7:00 in the morning, we began to arrange accommodations for Batiushka in the church house, in a large room from which he could hear and even see the services and go out into the church when he wanted. By 9:00 Batiushka's room was ready. It was all covered with rugs, a small iconostasis was made, and blinds were placed in the window; and all this in less than two hours, since it was all done in common, amicably, and with great animation....

"The church was likewise transfigured. They covered the floor with rugs, and the pillars and columns with ferns and live flowers. But an even more festive sight was imparted to it by the joyful, radiant faces of the sisters, who were constantly running there to find out—had anyone arrived from Optina, had anyone heard anything about our dear Batiushka. At last, at 4:00 in the afternoon, one of our sisters came with the joyful news that Batiushka had intended to leave Optina at 3:00, and that we should expect him any minute. In an instant, this news flew around the whole Monastery, and everyone was ready. At 5:00 they came at a gallop on horseback with the news that Batiushka had passed through Poloshkovo. Everyone immediately assembled in the church; the chandelier was lit. From the porch of the church to the holy gates of the Monastery a carpet was placed on the path, on both sides of which the sisters were arrayed, all dressed formally. At the holy gates the priest, Fr. John, waited for Batiushka with the holy cross; Matushka Superior, with the miracle-working Kazan Icon of the Mother of God; the treasurer, Mother Eleutheria, with a large loaf of bread and a prosphora on a plate adorned with live flowers; and all the singers.

"Sisters! Matushka asks you not to converse!" Our blagochinnaya repeated Matushka's order, arranging the sisters in a line. But they were not thinking of conversations anyway. Each waited and strove to be concentrated within: to collect her thoughts, as they say. A profound, reverent quiet reigned. The feelings which filled each of us, which went through us in those minutes, we never again experienced; they do not repeat themselves—they are rare guests on earth and cannot be conveyed. The pealing of the bells resounded and, finally, the long-awaited carriage arrived and pulled up to the gate, but the door remained closed and Batiushka could not be seen. Three or four minutes went by, and Batiushka appeared at last from the opposite side of the carriage in full schema—in his mantia and crosses. They sang: "Today the grace of the Holy Spirit has gathered us together, and we all take up our cross and say: blessed is he who cometh in the name of the Lord!"* Batiushka, meanwhile, made three prostrations to the ground and, kissing the cross and the icon of the Heavenly Queen, took the icon in his hands and, accompanied by the Mother Superior and treasurer, who helped him carry the icon, moved towards the church. We all prostrated ourselves to the ground before him, but no one approached him or crowded him. There were tears in Batiushka's eyes. And the majority of those present wept, but quietly, so as not to disturb the tranquility and the harmonious singing of the welcoming hymn. When Batiushka entered the

---

*Sticheron from the Vespers service for Palm Sunday.—ED.

An early view of the Shamordino Monastery.

church they sang, "It is truly meet ..." after which there followed a litany, and so on, as is customary when important visitors are met. Batiushka, meanwhile, entered the altar, venerated the icon, and then went out through the south door to the grave of the reposed Matushka Sophia. One had only to see the expression on Batiushka's face when he venerated the icon of the Heavenly Queen at the holy gates, went with it into the church and prayed at the grave; it would never be erased from his memory! Serious, concentrated, somehow inspired; and it seemed that his gaze penetrated even to Heaven. After he returned to church and after they sang "Many years" to him, Batiushka went up to the elevated spot specially set up for him, sat in an armchair and began to bless all those present. After blessing them he rested for a while, but later that day he went several times into the church to look it over, and blessed everyone who happened to be there at the time. There was a Vigil in the evening, and on the next day Liturgy and a Moleben....

"After the Moleben there was a procession around the church and around the whole Monastery.... Batiushka himself took part in the procession and blessed all of our sick and feeble ones and cripples to take part as well. And so, behind the crowd of sisters and laymen there followed another train of the sick, crippled and feeble—some on foot, some in a wagon, some in other conveyances.... When everything had ended, Batiushka went out to venerate the icon. Then he went to Mother Sophia's grave and to the bell tower; everywhere he prayed for a long time with full prostrations. That same day Batiushka drove to Matushka's house, to the Chapel of St. Ambrose of Milan, and even walked on the terrace. Then he went to the Chapel of St. Tikhon [of Kaluga], and from there he came on foot to the 'hut.' Batiushka prayed with prostrations everywhere and inspected everything attentively. In the hut, stopping before a large portrait of Mother Sophia (in schema), Batiushka said, 'Mother sees everything that is done here,' and then, glancing at the bookshelves, added: 'Read—and understand what you read!' From the hut Batiushka went out the door to the terrace, walked through the gallery, and sat down on the steps where dear Abbess Sophia loved to sit. Then, coming down from the staircase, he took a few steps down the slope of the hill. 'What a spot the Abbess chose for her hut!' From there, Batiushka proceeded to the 'hesychastarion.'\* He liked everything here: 'I did not expect that it would be so nice here with you,' he said; 'it seems like I should just stay here and live with you.' Then, going up to the window and gazing through it into the ravine below, he said: 'Yes, it is simply better than Mt. Athos here, better than Mt. Athos.' From the hesychastarion Batiushka returned home and went nowhere else that day.

"On Thursday after Liturgy there was a Pannikhida for Abbess Sophia and Mother Ambrosia and then a general blessing. While Batiushka was bestowing blessings, the choir sang the usual church songs for him: 'O Fervent Intercessor' (the troparion for the Kazan icon of the Theotokos), the troparion to St. Ambrose, etc. They also sang, 'Exult ye, O our Monastery....' After several other sacred songs they sang the Paschal Canon. Meanwhile, Batiushka had already finished blessing the sisters; he listened and prayed. When they finished the Canon, Batiushka blessed them to sing, "Let God Arise"; after the end of this hymn, he quickly went up to his room and disappeared behind the door. Singing always affected Batiushka so powerfully.... Later that morning, after a short rest Batiushka drove to the farmyard, inspected the construction, dropped into the 'little orphanage,' and remained there

---

\* Evidently, this was a separate cell in which Mother Sophia would spend time in silent prayer, apart from her usual duties as Superior.—Trans.

for a long time. He went into each small room, blessed all the children, and conversed with them. The eldest girl read a poem to Batiushka composed by the overseer, reciting it very nicely. Here is the poem:

> Holy Father, Father dearest!
> To show our thanks, we know not how.
> Thou hast clothed us, thou hast reared us.
> From want we are delivered now.
> Perhaps we'd still have had to roam
> Across the world so desolate,
> And never to have known a home,
> Pursued and routed by our fate.
> But to our Maker do we pray
> And glorify Him for thy sake.
> We to our Lord and Father say
> His orphans please do not forsake.

"These lines were later set to music by one of the sisters. Subsequently, each time the Elder visited the orphanage community, the children sang this chant for him. The Elder listened to these children's supplications seriously, pensively, and often large tears rolled down his hollow cheeks. What he thought in those moments remains unknown. But one may suppose that he turned in his heart to the Queen of Heaven and earth with the prayer that she not abandon, after his death, the orphans gathered by him, but keep them through her all-powerful protection.

"Batiushka's relationship with children was always the most tender, fatherly, and kind. One of his close spiritual disciples writes: 'I was a witness to the fact that Batiushka, despite his weakness, rode every day to the hospital to call on the sick children. How he pampered them—he would give one candy, another honey-squares; he would caress them and joke with them.'

"From the orphanage Batiushka rode down to the gardens. He visited the cabin where our gardeners live, strolled uphill, and blessed all the wells. He visited the pumphouse, made them pump water before him, inspected the construction, and came right home for the Vigil. The next day after Liturgy and the general blessing, Batiushka, having rested awhile, went to the grave. After praying and blessing it three times as always, he proceeded to the place where water is blessed and to the bell tower, praying earnestly and at length everywhere. From the bell tower he went straight to the refectory. After he prayed here before the icon of the Heavenly Queen, he went over to the Superior's chair, sat down, and blessed them to give him lunch in its sequence. He blessed each course, tasted a little, then rang the bell, as Matushka usually does, thus giving a signal to the kitchen workers to bring him the next dish. Later, they poured food from the cup blessed by Batiushka into pots and buckets, from which they distributed it by the cup to all the sisters in the refectory. From there, Batiushka went to the kitchen and inspected the arrangement of the oven, the stove, and the pots, and gave orders concerning changes that he found it necessary to make—such as the widening of the refectory, as well as the bread bakery, which he visited right after the refectory. After looking over all of our household institutions and having sat for a few minutes in the middle of the small courtyard around which these buildings were situated, Batiushka sat in his open carriage and rode to the porch so as to deliver Matushka from having to bustle about, constantly ordering people not to put pressure on Batiushka and not to crowd him, so he could have a free passage from the bread bakery to the church. The Elder, sitting close to the bakery and examining the layout of the building, turned repeatedly to the sisters with the request to stand aside so that he could better inspect it. 'You I have seen more than once, but the building I still have not seen,' he said.... After lunch that day, he went to the guest house, visited several persons, and returned home after 6:00 in the evening.

"The whole time that Batiushka was with us, on those days when Vigils were not appointed, Matins was served in the evenings following Vespers, in order not to interrupt his rest in the morning. He spent the day thus: after Liturgy he went out to venerate the icons, then to the grave, or he would begin to bless everyone.... Having rested for a short while, Batiushka began to receive visitors, sometimes in his room, sometimes in church, where he sat on a bench near the candle-seller's box. At 11:00 Batiushka was given a horse, and he rode around the buildings and construction sites, accompanied by Mother, who helped him get out of the carriage and protected him from the crowds, and to whom he often gave specific instructions concerning the resettling of sisters, alterations, renovations, etc. He was also accompanied by a crowd of sisters and lay folk who ran after his carriage. The Elder returned home at 2:00 in the afternoon, ate, rested, and then again went for a ride around the buildings until the Vigil or Vespers. During his stay with us, Batiushka visited all the buildings, not omitting a single cell, and went into all the sheds and barns.... They brought litters to Batiushka, which were made for the sisters to carry stones for the building of the church. He blessed them and tried one himself to see if they were well made.

"Finally, the day of Batiushka's departure arrived.... After Liturgy, a Moleben and the general blessing, he received many sisters and lay people; then they gave him something to eat. Almost all of us dispersed to our cells with the idea that he would probably rest; but then we set out for the church again to watch for him to come out, to gaze upon him one more time, when suddenly someone came running up and said, 'Quickly, quickly, gather in the church in your church clothes; there's going to be a farewell Moleben for Batiushka right now.' We all assembled, and it was impossible to recognize that these were the same faces which were still glowing on the day before. Heads were lowered; some wept, others could barely restrain their tears. Profound silence reigned. The Moleben to the Heavenly Queen and for travellers began.... Afterwards Batiushka, in a serious and concentrated state, venerated the icons and went out to the grave, where he blessed it thrice for the last time. Then he returned to his room.

"He changed his clothes and again came out and went on foot to the hesychastarion where, by his blessing, some sort of building was being constructed which greatly interested him. Here Batiushka conversed for a few minutes with our fortunate Cosmas, and, changing his clothes again and blessing us, he went back to the church. Here he blessed everyone for the last time and entered his room.

"The sisters were again arranged in two lines from the church porch to the holy gates, where again, as when we met him, Matushka awaited him with the icon of the Heavenly Queen, along with the choir. Once again it became so reverently quiet, as before, but with a tinge of hidden sadness.... When Batiushka appeared and the choir began to sing "It is truly meet," almost everyone began to weep. Batiushka walked quickly and blessed us on both sides. As he passed by the sisters, they bowed to his feet. When he had made three full prostrations before the icon of the Heavenly Queen and venerated it, Batiushka took it in his hands and, standing at the holy gates, he blessed the sisters and the Monastery with it for the last time, as if entrusting them to the divine protection of our Fervent Intercessor. All together, we prostrated to the ground and wept bitterly. Meanwhile Batiushka, having allowed Matushka to venerate the icon, again placed it in her hands and quickly disappeared into the carriage. The door slammed, and the carriage sped away. Long, long afterwards, standing at the holy gates, we gazed after the disappearing carriage and were unable to move from the spot. A kind of quiet sadness filled our souls, and it was a pity to part with it. How empty it suddenly felt in Shamordino, and for a long time we could not get used to this emptiness, until we again settled into our usual routine."

In the summer of the next year, 1889, the Elder again spent a few days in Shamordino. As in the previous year, he was occupied here for entire days, first with the disposition and inspection of various construction projects and quarters, then with the reception of monastics and lay people. Concerning his way of life and occupations here in this year, one can judge by the following account of a lay woman who was visiting him at that time:

"After his arrival at Shamordino," she wrote in the magazine *Soul-Profiting Reading*, of 1899, "I was struck first of all by the huge crowd of people which surrounded the accommodations in which Batiushka was located from the early morning, in the hope of seeing him and receiving his blessing. The love of the people for him was so great, the desire to see him and receive his instructions and consolation so strong, that among these people—strangers to fatigue who had come from far-off places—were those who had waited for two weeks and had not lost hope of being received by Fr. Ambrose. When I approached more closely, I realized that they were waiting for Batiushka to come out. He was going at once to visit the almshouse, the orphanage and the other philanthropic establishments built by him with the cooperation of benefactors. Being unable to squeeze through to see his departure, I stood farther off. Now the door opened; the people became restless, and the cry was heard: 'Batiushka, you are our own, Batiushka!' And there he was, beloved Batiushka Ambrose, the already stooped-over but magnificent Elder: simple, kind, approachable. Only his clairvoyant eyes radiated with wisdom and pierced to the very depths of one's soul. Having blessed those closest in the crowd, the Elder sat in the carriage and slowly rode through the Monastery. The people did not leave him—at his side, before him and behind him they ran, catching his glance and his blessing hand and, joyously, yielding their place to others. I followed this sight, new to me, from afar with contrition of soul.

"In the evening of that day, in the small home church of the Shamordino Convent the All-Night Vigil was served. The nuns sang and read harmoniously and piously. The worshippers prayed earnestly. In the dark, small corridor that adjoined the church the visitors again crowded, having suffered since early morning, and patiently waited for the opening of the cherished door to Batiushka's cell, which was illuminated by a lampada burning before an icon. Some stood, and some sat. At the door itself, leaning her head against the wall from weakness, sat a young, sick nun; and here too was a young woman, sobbing hysterically. Now the door opened. Everyone roused themselves. Batiushka was all in white and, keenly casting his eye around at everyone, took the sick nun by the hand and led her in after him. The door again closed. At this point the weeping woman cried out, 'Batiushka, take me too! I'm going to die from grief!' and she began to sob even more strongly. Suddenly the door opened again. Batiushka glanced at her with a kind smile and said: 'Who is getting ready to die here? Then we would have to bury you. Well, come on, come on.' The door again closed behind them. When that woman, sorrowing in soul, came out, her face was aglow. Though tears were still rolling down her face, these were not her former tears, and something joyful and peaceful shone in her eyes. When I asked her with sympathy if Batiushka had consoled her, she said: 'Oh, how he consoled me! Just like my own father! Only my grief is very great—you won't cure it soon!'

# THE LAST PODVIG OF LOVE OF ELDER AMBROSE

"At that moment, from the church the hymn was heard: 'Praise ye the name of the Lord; O ye servants praise the Lord!' (Ps. 134). Deeply touched by everything I had seen, I prayed, imploring a great mercy from God—to be received by the great Elder. A few minutes passed, and again the door to the cell was opened. Batiushka himself appeared in the doorway and called me by name. I started with joy and, making the sign of the cross, went after him into his small cell, half-lit by the setting sun...."

She revealed her grief to the Elder—that she was soon to undergo a terrible operation—and she received his blessing not to be afraid of anything, not to have the operation, and to pray to God. At this point the Elder reminded her of some serious sins that she had forgotten. Then the narrator continues: "It is not possible to describe and express in words that which I felt in my soul. This was both a reverent trembling before the righteous one, who by his clairvoyance pierced through my sinful and suffering soul, and a kind of unearthly, ecstatic joy from contact with and breath from the spiritual world.... When, late in the evening, we gathered in the monastery guest house, people congregated in a circle in the corridor, people who had come from varied and distant places, unacquainted until then with one another; but here they made one another's acquaintance openly, in a brotherly way, sharing their joy and their impressions with regard to the consolation, teaching, or wise counsel given them by Batiushka....

"Early in the morning, I had barely opened my eyes when that same joyful state embraced my soul, that same reverence towards the serene Elder and fervent selfless love for him. Leaving the guest house, I glanced with contrition at the window of the modest, humble cell, in which our dear Batiushka could then be found. I made a prostration to him, begging from afar for his holy prayers for my sinful soul. A joyful and fortunate one, I left the still-young Monastery, which I would not have exchanged for all the treasures of the world. Upon returning home, I scrupulously fulfilled all that the Elder had commanded me. By his prayers, my illness has not returned since that time, which was nine years ago."

The year 1890 came, the last year of Fr. Ambrose's stay in the Optina Skete, since in that year he made his last trip to Shamordino and was not able to return to Optina before his repose.

Many were the rumors and suppositions of various kinds concerning this last stay of Elder Ambrose in Shamordino. According to the word of his biographer, Archimandrite Agapitus, "Concerning the Elder, each had his own opinion—many judged and condemned him. Throughout all parts of Russia, wherever the mere name of Elder Ambrose was known, malicious talk was spread about him."

They condemned him, both for abandoning the Skete and for staying in a women's monastery. They pointed to persons on whose account the Elder was supposed to have forsaken Optina. Of course, none of these rumors and suppositions were worthy of any trust. Having lived in the Optina Skete for fifty years, during this time the Elder had certainly experienced no small amount of every kind of grief and unpleasantness; however, he never found it necessary to move away from the Monastery. Now in his declining years, having attained to the height of experience and wisdom in dealing with all the possible ways of God's Providence in human life, having grown accustomed to relying entirely and in everything upon the good and all-perfect will of God—now, would he fail to endure new sorrows and faintheartedly flee from them?! This seems to us to be absolutely unbelievable, inconsistent with the whole life, with all the instructions, of the Elder, and with the precepts of eldership, of which he was a vigilant preserver. Such a suggestion could only have sprung up in the minds of those people who neither knew nor understood in any way the great Elder.

More likely is the suggestion that the Elder moved to Shamordino with the aim of more closely and directly looking after the progress of matters there and the carrying out of construction and work, as well as for the direction of the spiritual life of the newly founded Monastery.

In Shamordino, from the very opening of the community, a great deal of construction was being carried out. Therefore, a multitude of workers were there, but there was no adequate supervision for them. The new Superior herself was of weak health and did not have the appropriate managerial experience. Neither did she have experienced assistants. In addition, neither the Monastery nor the Elder himself had any kind of material means, although no one knew this. Everyone was convinced, on the contrary, that the Elder's means were inexhaustible. Be that as it may, at the completion of all the construction projects in Shamordino, the Elder conceived the idea of raising a huge stone church in the community, the erection of which was begun in 1889. All these complicated and diverse domestic and spiritual undertakings and cares prompted the Elder, as some said, to move to Shamordino for personal, on-site management. Nevertheless, one should understand that the Elder's move to Shamordino and his prolonged stay there depended not so much on the will of the Elder himself, as on the "special Providence of God," as the Elder put it.

There is a basis for the idea that the Elder, leaving the Skete, had a premonition that he would not return again. In the past years, when leaving for Shamordino in the summer he always took with him his senior cell attendant, Hieromonk Joseph; this time he left Fr. Joseph in the Skete, as if foretelling his future calling, and took with him his younger cell attendant, Fr. Isaiah.

## ELDER AMBROSE OF OPTINA

There was another noteworthy incident. Not long before Fr. Ambrose's departure from the Skete, he was sent a large, beautifully painted icon [of the Mother of God], "Surety of Sinners," which was placed in the cell of Fr. Joseph, adjacent to the Elder's. As he left for the last time for Shamordino, the Elder ordered Fr. Joseph to place this icon over the head of his own bed and to light a perpetually burning lampada before it, which Fr. Joseph did after the Elder's departure. Thus leaving the Skete, Fr. Ambrose, as it were, entrusted it, and with it the whole of Optina Monastery, to the Mother of God! There was one other incident. On the very day of his departure, after ordering the brethren to serve a Moleben for travellers before the Kazan icon of the Mother of God in the Catholicon, Fr. Ambrose sent one of his spiritual daughters to Kozelsk to have a Moleben served there as well, before the miracle-working Akhtyrsk icon of the Mother of God, which he had likewise never done before.

Finally, the second of July arrived and the Elder left the Skete, setting out for the Shamordino dacha, Rudnevo.* On the day of the Elder's departure the weather was most pleasant. The day was clear and warm. A large number of people saw him off. Although the Elder, according to his blessing, was accompanied only by his cell attendant, Fr. Isaiah, who also prepared him for the road and carried all his necessities, on the next day a crowd of his admirers appeared in Rudnevo, among whom were Optina monks with their spiritual needs.

In general, during the Elder's stay in Shamordino, Optina brothers from the eldest to the youngest visited him daily. They were unable to remain without his spiritual nourishment and, in addition to corresponding, at the first opportunity they

---

*Rudnevo is located four miles from Shamordino by the main road and two miles by the shortest route on foot.

## THE LAST PODVIG OF LOVE OF ELDER AMBROSE

hastened personally to Shamordino. Neither did those monks who were going to pray at the St. Tikhon [of Kaluga] Monastery bypass Shamordino, wishing to receive the blessing of the Elder beforehand.

Why, however, did the Elder not go straight to Shamordino, as had been done earlier, but to Rudnevo? This was for the following reason. Not long before the Elder's departure from the Skete, a letter reached him from an anonymous "lover of piety." In this letter it was said that many years ago, on the landowner's estate known as the Rudnevo dacha that now belonged to the Shamordino community a well had been dug by some ascetics which alleviated the thirst of many travellers, but that now this place was in a state of neglect. Even before this letter was received, in the autumn of 1889 the Superior of the Shamordino community, Mother Euphrosyne, while once in Rudnevo overseeing the work near the fish-pond, felt that her feet were sinking into the earth.... She related this to the Elder, by whose order they began to dig and soon came across the framework of the well. A spring was discovered; but it was strange—everyone said the same thing—when they gave this water to demon-possessed people, their suffering increased. Having set out on July 2, 1890 for Shamordino, the Elder personally decided to go first to Rudnevo. Arriving there, the Elder inspected a spot close to the dug-out well, a little lower. He first began to pray and ordered everyone who was with him to pray. After the prayer he himself began to dig, and then told others to dig. When water appeared, the Elder commanded them to build a second well there.

The well was brought to a satisfactory state of construction, and then Fr. Ambrose sent a few sick people to be splashed with water from it. He also gave out water and clay from it, which turned out to have healing properties. Later, near the healing well a small shed was built and adapted for the purpose of bathing in the water. Having spent one day in Rudnevo, the Elder went from there to Shamordino.

The arrival of Fr. Ambrose in Shamordino called forth the usual joy of the sisters, who met him as their own dear father. Day after day went by. The Elder's stay in the Monastery continued. Instead of the ten days proposed by the Elder, he had already been living in Shamordino for four weeks. According to persons close to him, he was constantly preparing to leave, but first one matter detained him, then another. He was clearly in a hurry: he was tirelessly present at all construction sites and received the people who were streaming to Shamordino in huge numbers—monks, nuns, and lay people. The guest house was not sufficient for the visitors; at night the people occupied the whole square opposite the guest house.

Finally, at the end of July, the Elder prepared to leave for Optina and gave orders that all be made ready for his departure on the morning of the appointed day. This became known even in Optina. Therefore, towards 6:00 in the evening people had already begun to gather at the Skete; others went out to the ferry, and a few went out across the river to meet him.

However, at 8:00 in the evening news was received from Shamordino that the Elder would not be coming that day; everything was all ready for his departure, but he had suddenly felt such weakness that not only was he unable to leave, he could not even receive anyone. They awaited him in Optina Monastery on the next day. But on that day the same thing was repeated: in the morning the Elder received visitors to Shamordino, then prepared to leave, but towards evening, at the very same time as the day before, he felt very poorly. He had to put off his departure for an indefinite time.

The Dormition Fast arrived, during which the Elder confessed everyone without exception, beginning with the Archimandrite and monks of Optina and ending with a multitude of lay people. By August 29, the feast day of the Skete [the Beheading of St. John the Forerunner], the Elder again began to prepare to go to the Skete. They served a Moleben for travellers for him. However, all over again, he felt so faint that he had to give up any thought of departure. They even said that they had found the Elder lying on the floor in a state of extreme exhaustion. It is interesting to note that the Elder, who had fallen into a state of utter sickness and exhaustion during attempts to go to Optina, made repeated trips at the same time to Rudnevo and felt absolutely vigorous.

After the Elder's last unsuccessful attempt to return to the Skete for the Feast of the Beheading of St. John the Forerunner, it became clear to all that the Elder had to remain all winter in Shamordino. The weather at that time had already changed to autumn, and the Elder could not go outside when the temperature was below 60 degrees.

The Optina monks became alarmed and upset by the long absence of the Elder. The Superior, Fr. Isaac, was greatly grieved. The Elder consoled him, persuading him to humble himself under the mighty hand of God; and to the Optina brethren he sent a letter by his own hand in which, among other things, he said: "I have been detained up to now in Shamordino by the special Providence of God; but why—this must become evident later." This letter was read in the monastery refectory, in the hearing of all the brothers.

In the meantime, winter quarters were prepared for the Elder in Shamordino. Convinced that he would remain with them all winter, the sisters were in ecstasy.

Remaining in Shamordino for an indeterminate time, Fr. Ambrose established the same manner of life for himself there as he had in the Skete. As in the Skete, he listened to the prescribed prayers daily. Also, for feast days he had the All-Night Vigil served in his cell, which he himself served the first time—that is, he read the exclamations and the Gospel at the appointed time; the sisters sang and read the prescribed prayers. Wonderful were those minutes, noted the Shamordino witnesses, when in the middle of the room the stooped-over Elder came out in a short mantia and epitrachelion, with his gray head uncovered and with a kind of childlike, weak elderly voice, clearly read the words of the good news of Christ, of which he himself was a zealous fulfiller and preacher.... However, it was not like this for long. The sickly Elder did not have strength to serve. For the most part, his former secretary, Hieromonk B. [Benedict], came from the Skete for this.

Elder Ambrose always had a special reverence towards the Mother of God, which is why he never let a single feast of the Theotokos go by without serving a cell Vigil before Her holy icon. In 1890, a special icon of the Mother of God, painted at the direction of the Elder, was sent to him at the Skete by the superior of the Bolkhov Convent. The Heavenly Queen was depicted sitting in the clouds. Her arms were outstretched for a blessing. And below, amidst grass and flowers, there stood and lay sheaves of rye. The rye sheaves were painted according to the wish and description of Fr. Ambrose, who gave this icon the name "She Who Ripens the Grain." The Elder sent up fervent prayers before that icon; he instructed and urged the spiritual children gathered by him in the community to pray before it. In the last year of his life he made copies of this icon and sent them to many of his outside admirers. Not long before his last illness he composed a special refrain in honor of it to be sung in the usual Akathist to the Theotokos: "Rejoice, Thou full of grace, the Lord is with Thee! Grant even to us unworthy ones the dew of Thy grace and show us Thy mercy!" The sisters sang this refrain with the blessing of the Elder when the Akathist to the Mother of God was read in his cell. He directed his spiritual children to celebrate the feast day of this icon on October 15.

Fervent prayer before this icon of the Mother of God was accompanied more than once by miracles, by the mercy of the Most Holy Theotokos. Thus, a copy of this icon was sent to the St. Paraskeva Women's Monastery in the Voronezh Diocese. Due to a severe drought which threatened inevitable famine, supplicatory prayers were conducted before it, after which it soon began to rain, and the Monastery and its surroundings were saved from famine. It is said also that in the spring of 1897, or thereabouts, the priest of the village of Ozersk came to Rudnevo to serve, and, due to a dearth of rain, served in the fields there a Moleben with an Akathist to the Mother of God before Her holy icon, "She Who Ripens the Grain." While the Moleben was being served, the rain that for so long had not fallen began to drizzle down. After the Moleben they also served a Pannikhida for Elder Ambrose, and the rain poured down in abundance.

In addition to the unceasing prayer of the Elder, there were also the various cares for the establishment of the internal arrangement of his young Monastery: for the well-ordered carrying out of church services, for understandable and clear reading and singing, for the proper attitude of the sisters towards their Superior and towards one another, and so on. The Elder, as before, entered into all matters of management. All construction was carried out according to his plan and direction. Having summoned several monks from the Skete who understood construction and management in general, the Elder carried out his orders through them. In addition, Elder Ambrose continued to receive people from morning until evening and occupied himself with correspondence with those who requested his advice and instructions.

Thus, time flowed by unnoticed until December 7, Fr.

Interior view of the cell where Elder Ambrose reposed.

Ambrose's nameday. The Shamordino Convent celebrated this day with special solemnity. On the eve of this day several hieromonks arrived from Optina, at the head of which was the Superior, Archimandrite Isaac. They served the Vigil and on the next day they concelebrated the Liturgy, with a Moleben to the Saint, followed by the singing of "Many Years" to the nameday celebrant. Then all who had served came to congratulate the Elder. His face at that time seemed very pale and exhausted. Receiving with gratitude the congratulations from the monks, he only humbly repeated, "This is all too much." After the brethren, all the sisters also came to congratulate their dear Elder. Each of them brought him some kind of gift of her own making—one, a prayer rope; another, socks; another, a sweater; another, an icon.... He accepted the gifts from them with a joyful face, thanked everyone, joked, and presented them with pie and sweets. Despite his visible joy, however, Fr. Ambrose was profoundly sorrowful inwardly.

At the New Year, when they came to congratulate him, he did not come out for a long time and did not receive anyone. Finally, they called everyone into the waiting room. The Elder sat on the couch and, instead of congratulations and greetings, told one of his spiritual daughters who had come from Optina to read the *Trinity Leaflet*\* which ends with the prayer of a pastor for his spiritual children, where he says to the Lord, "Behold, me and my children ..." and says farewell to his flock. All present became sad. Tears welled up in the eyes of many. The Elder himself wept.

During Passion Week of 1891, one woman close to the Elder brought him an icon of the Savior with a crown of

---

\*The *Trinity Leaflets*, instituted by Archimandrite Leonid (Kavelin) and published by the Holy Trinity-St. Sergius Lavra, were very popular, short, edifying periodicals.—ED.

thorns, which she had found at his instructions. He accepted the icon with great joy and said, "What could be better than this crown of thorns!"—and he kissed the icon. Then he added, "It is good to be at the Cross of Christ, but even better to suffer for Him on this Cross." When the Elder pronounced these words, his face was somehow special: something unearthly shone in his eyes.

Holy Pascha arrived. On the first day of the Feast, after Liturgy the Superior came as usual to congratulate the Elder with the radiant Feast; and following her were all the sisters and some lay people who had come to share the "Paschal kiss" with the Elder. He gave each one a red egg and a piece of kulich and pascha cheese. Truly, remarked the Shamordino sisters, this Feast was radiant. Each one had joy in her soul. And how could it have been otherwise? Pascha—and the great Elder was sharing this great celebration with them. Each day throughout Bright Week, the sisters sang Matins, the Hours, and Vespers in his cell. Fr. Ambrose himself sang along; sometimes he gave the tone to the choir, corrected mistakes and made various comments. At the end of the week, when the singers began to thank the Elder for the consolation he had afforded them this Pascha, he said to them kindly, "The Lord save you." Then he added, "You will reminisce about this Pascha." No one understood, nor could they understand, these words by which the Elder was hinting at his approaching repose.

With the onset of summer, Fr. Ambrose resumed his outings. He walked around the building sites and rode to Rudnevo, where he occasionally stayed for two weeks. If some feast or other occurred, he returned without fail to Shamordino—"home," as he would say.

That summer there came to the Elder in Shamordino a man of God by the name of Gavrusha, forty years old, one of those whom the Lord likened to children, saying *of such is the kingdom of God* (Luke 18:16). He lived in the Livensk district of the Orel Province. He was palsied; his whole body trembled, and he could barely speak or take food. His legs did not function; he lay and prayed to God. It was noticed that much was revealed to him. The previous spring Elder Ambrose had appeared to him and said, "Come to me in Shamordino; I will console you." At that very time he got up on his feet and stated that he was going to Shamordino. But since his feet were extremely weak and his gait uneven, they wanted to take him by railroad; but he refused this favor. Near Shamordino he met the Elder as he was quietly riding from somewhere. People surrounded him. "Batiushka!" yelled Gavrusha in his difficult-to-understand language, "You called me, I've come." The Elder immediately got out of the carriage, went up to him and said, "Greetings! Dear guest! Well, you can live here." And he added to those around him: "I have never had one like this." Fr. Ambrose was very kind to Gavrusha. He arranged a corner for him in Shamordino and later also in Rudnevo. Gavrusha wanted very much to go there. "Batiushka! I don't want to be in Shamordino; let's go to Rudnevo; I want to go to Rudnevo." The Elder calmed him down, saying that when quarters for Gavrusha were prepared in Rudnevo, they would go there. It was touching to watch how he spent time conversing with Gavrusha and how they walked around the cell—one hobbling on crooked legs, and the other, bent over, leaning on his cane.

We have already mentioned that Fr. Ambrose experienced great sorrow of soul in Shamordino, which he expressed to those around him, sometimes obliquely by hints, but sometimes directly as, for example, once to the sisters around him: "Mothers and sisters! I am on the cross here with you!" Truly, according to what people close to him said, his life at that time was impossibly difficult. He had no rest, day or night, either from the discomfort of his accommodations (which, up to his very repose, were still being built and prepared), or from the multitude of things to do, or from the crowds around him. His heart ached for the Optina monks, who were left without their spiritual director. When one of them came to him, the Elder would not make him wait long and received him with special love and consoled him.

But very often after such visits he became exceedingly anxious and troubled. They would bring him lunch and it would sit in the cell, and they would carry it back out—he hadn't touched a thing.

With the passing of time the Elder's health began to weaken to the last degree, and murmuring against him by visitors increased, especially now, in the face of the enormous flow of people, many of whom had to wait quite a long time to be received by him. The Elder would have been happy to satisfy everyone, but his strength had altogether failed him. It often happened that one would see him, as the Shamordino sisters said, lying flat on his back, utterly exhausted. His pale, weary face expressed suffering; his voice had completely left him, and his eyes were closed. Gazing upon the half-alive Elder, one's heart would constrict with pity. Quite often he himself said with sorrow: "You know, they don't believe that I'm weak—they grumble." However, this more-dead-than-alive, 79-year-old Elder not only never lost his presence of mind, he was also always calm and happy, as if in the midst of the most pleasant circumstances. By his joyful and humorous stories he was able to chase away the gloomiest despondency from those around him. During this, his last winter in the Shamordino community, because of the extreme weakness of the Elder and various other troubles, all the sisters in the Monastery were once in a particularly dismal state of mind. The sickly Elder gathered his last strength and with a cheerful countenance went out into the room where the sisters were gathered. At first he said something to some individually to console them, at which all of their faces little by little brightened up. And finally he made them all laugh so much that he chased away even the last traces of despondency. Another time the sisters who were with the Elder began to say to him with grief: "How fortunate we are to live in your presence and have you, Batiushka! But the time is coming when you will no longer be with us. What will we do then?" Batiushka smiled, gazed at everyone present with such love, as only he knew how, and, shaking his head reproachfully, told them: "If I have fussed around with you so much here, then surely I will not leave you there."

After Pascha of 1891, a new, unexpected woe befell the Elder. Mother Euphrosyne, his chosen Superior of the Monastery, his closest assistant and fulfiller of his plans, fell gravely ill. Entering his cell once on some kind of business, she suddenly felt very poorly. Her face became deadly pale, her breathing stopped, and she almost fell. The Elder was disconcerted. Barely able to move his feet, he approached the apparently dying woman, then called the sisters, who laid her on a nearby couch. Then the Elder, looking at her as if begging her not to leave him, depressed with sicknesses and sorrows, said with a voice trembling with agitation: "Mother, take a breath!" And soon, by the prayers of the Elder, her breathing resumed and she was given Communion of the Holy Mysteries. After this incident, Mother Euphrosyne began to go blind. Towards the middle of summer she could no longer see—she could only distinguish light from dark. Burdened by the loss of her sight and by her duties as Superior, she asked the Elder to permit her to hand in a request for retirement, but the Elder did not bless her, saying: "Do not hand it in yourself, but if they tell you to hand it in, then do so." During all of this he tried in every way to console and encourage her, saying: "Mother! Endure and do not despair!"

To complete the Elder's sorrows, which became worse towards the end of his life, even the diocesan authorities assailed him. In 1890 a new hierarch was assigned to Kaluga, Bishop Vitaly, who had been transferred from Tambov. He arrived at the diocese in autumn when the Elder was already staying in the Shamordino community. Bishop Vitaly wished very much to see Elder Ambrose, who was well-known to the entire Orthodox world, but when he learned that the Elder was living in a women's monastery, he delayed going to Optina and awaited the return of the Elder to the Skete. Meanwhile, time passed and the Elder did not return. This was not pleasing to the Bishop, even more so since the Elder had moved to Shamordino without the permission of his diocesan authority.

The spreading of absurd rumors by people unfriendly to Fr. Ambrose in connection with his stay in Shamordino also reached the Bishop and disconcerted him even more, so that he even said with alarm: "What is going on with them over there?" Several times he entrusted the diocesan head of monasteries with the task of demanding the Elder's immediate return to his Skete. The sickly, dying Elder, of course, could not carry out this order, but in Kaluga they did not believe this and took his words as merely an empty excuse. They began to threaten to take the Elder to Optina by force, to which he answered: "I know that I will not make it to Optina; if they take me out of here, I will die on the way."

Personally speaking, the Bishop had no reason to be troubled and could have conducted himself towards the Elder with the same trust and reverence with which, for example, the great man of prayer, Fr. John of Kronstadt, did, who said to some Shamordino sisters who had come to him: "Ah, this is from Elder Ambrose; O, great Elder! A prostration to the ground to him from me!" But, obviously, someone had to darken the last days of Fr. Ambrose's earthly life, to increase the weight of the cross he bore, so that in him were fulfilled the words of the Lord: *Blessed are they which are persecuted for righteousness sake: for theirs is the Kingdom of Heaven. Blessed are you when men shall revile you and persecute you and shall say all manner of evil against you falsely, for My sake. Rejoice and be exceeding glad: for great is your reward in Heaven: for so persecuted they the prophets which were before you* (Matt. 5:10-12). Having loved his last and most beloved offspring, the Shamordino Monastery, with his last and most powerful love, the Elder, enduring great sorrow for this Monastery, showed by this that *having loved his own which were in the world, he loved them unto the end* (John 13:1). He loved them, not *in word, neither in tongue, but in deed and truth* (I John 3:18). In the spring the rumor spread that the Bishop, upset by various rumors and reports, had said: "I myself will go to Shamordino, seat the Elder in the coach, and take him to Optina!" When one of the Elder's spiritual daughters conveyed these words of the Bishop to him, Fr. Ambrose answered: "The Lord my God liveth, and my soul shall live. You should know that over all masters is the Master on High; I am not going to go to Optina. How could I go anywhere now, unless it be to the...." The Elder spoke the last words so quietly that they were unable to hear them. Another nun, also worried by the rumors going around, turned to the Elder: "Batiushka! They say that Vladyka's coming here; what will you say to him?" "I will say," the Elder quietly answered, "I will say: 'Seek first the will of God....'"

Now Fr. Ambrose began to hint to many concerning his imminent repose, though they either did not understand, did not want to, or were afraid to understand. Constantine N. Leontiev, his spiritual son who was living in Optina, came to receive his blessing to go to Moscow for treatment. Saying farewell to him, the Elder repeatedly embraced him, saying, "Forgive me, forgive me!" Such a farewell seemed unusual to Leontiev. And, in fact, it was the last.

In 1891, all summer in Shamordino they awaited their new archpastor. The Superior and the sisters, becoming worried and troubled, turned to the Elder with various questions: "Batiushka! How should we meet Vladyka?" The Elder replied: "We won't meet him, he will meet us!" "What should we sing for Vladyka?" The Elder said, "We will sing alleluia for him!"* They asked him further: "They say that Vladyka wants to ask you a great deal." He answered: "I will speak to him very quietly—no one will hear!" By such replies the Elder obviously alluded to his approaching repose, but no one around him at that time understood.

Certain sisters had a premonition concerning his repose, but they did not want to believe it, thinking, on the contrary, that the Elder could not possibly die so soon. Here are the kind of lines we read in the diary of one of the sisters close to the Elder: "Despite the great happiness that Batiushka was with us, some kind of terrible premonition gave me no rest; and the thought—aren't these days that Batiushka is spending with us his last—spoiled it. I feared to speak about it with anyone, so as not to hear from others that the same thought had occurred to them. Once in a conversation with Matushka I decided to ask what she thought about this. Matushka also said that she was afraid to rejoice too much—God knows how long it will be. This thought probably came to many. From Batiushka we never heard a clear indication of his approaching death. Certain of his orders apparently pointed at this, but then everything was explained in some other way and only after the Elder's repose was it all understandable."

---

*The singing of a Pannikhida begins with "Alleluia."—Ed.

# THE LAST PODVIG OF LOVE OF ELDER AMBROSE

A few months before the Elder's repose an artist from St. Petersburg, who occasionally turned to him for financial help, sent him a Kazan icon of the Mother of God, a copy of Her miracle-working icon, and with it the names of his family, asking the Elder to pray for them. Fr. Ambrose gave the order to place the note in the case behind the icon and said: "The Heavenly Queen Herself will pray for them." One poor family man, whom the Elder had helped many times, wrote a letter to him before his final illness with the request to help him buy warm clothing. The Elder sent him as much as was necessary, and added at the end of his letter: "Remember, this is the last help you will get from me." The nun to whom it fell to write this note said that "the last words somewhat confused me. I explained to myself that this had to be written as a warning, so that he would not get his hopes up."

Once an arriving abbess sitting in the reception cell waiting to be received by the Elder saw drops that looked like myrrh that had appeared on the icon of the Savior with a crown of thorns, which had stood for a long time on the table of his reception room, and she communicated this to Mother Euphrosyne. When they brought the icon to Fr. Ambrose and told him about the miraculous drops that had appeared, he looked at it for a long time and said: "There will be sorrows for the one who first saw this and for those living here." A few days after the departure of this abbess, the Elder received a letter from her in which she informed him that immediately after her return to her monastery, she had had to undergo a great, unexpected misfortune. This was in the beginning of September; and after a month the Shamordino Convent had to undergo the loss of their unforgettable great Elder, father and benefactor.

That autumn the Elder said in a joking tone to the sisters around him: "Look—here and there it will be autumn; ducks and geese, we'll sure have caught 'em." After having a laugh, he added: "The geese will haul, and the ducks will bawl."*

One may judge concerning the physical appearance of the Elder in this last time of his life by the following excerpt from the letter of a doctoral candidate of the Moscow Theological Academy, who visited the Elder at the end of August, 1½ months before his repose: "When I went into the room—I must confess—not without a certain trepidation and a sinking heart, I saw the little Elder (once he had been tall), just under 80 years old, in a simple, warm podrasnik and a monk's cap, sitting in an armchair, pale and weak to the last degree. His skin barely covered his bones, and his lower lip trembled so that you would think he was just about to die that minute. If there was something alive in that almost dead body, it was his eyes—not large, light brown in color, radiant, kind, observant, and penetrating. It was as if his whole life was concentrated in them, and they presented an amazing contrast with the deathly pallor of his face and the astonishing weakness of his body. Truly—the spirit was willing, but the flesh was weak."

And, truly—how necessary it was to have vigor of spirit to bear that difficult situation in which the Elder then found himself! In the community he had organized there were more than 300 sisters, an orphanage, an almshouse, and a hospital. It was a year of famine, and therefore bread was expensive. The Monastery had incurred a large debt. The Superior was blind. The Elder was in disgrace with the authorities, defamed, on the edge of the grave.... Only the grace of God upheld the Elder in the face of such circumstances!

---

*Evidently, by geese the Elder meant monks, and by ducks, nuns. The monks would bear his coffin, and the nuns would weep.—TRANS.

# 10

# *The Last Days of Elder Ambrose*

## HIS REPOSE AND BURIAL

> *For I am now ready to be offered, and the time of my departure is at hand. I have fought a good fight, I have finished my course, I have kept the faith.*
>
> II Timothy 4:6-7

WE SHALL NOW give a day-by-day account of the last days in the life of Fr. Ambrose in as much detail as possible, based on the written accounts and stories of the Shamordino sisters.

September 21 was a Saturday. According to custom a hieromonk arrived from the Skete to serve a Vigil in the Elder's cell, but Fr. Ambrose had felt weaker than usual since the morning. Towards the end of the day he weakened so much that he could not listen to the prayers and felt a chill. "Batiushka's weak, Batiushka's sick," was heard in all ends of the Monastery. Everyone grew very worried, knowing well that for the weak, nearly eighty-year-old Elder it would take little to cut short his life. On the other hand, the thought that Batiushka might die was so terrible and seemed so unbelievable that no one dwelt on it. Everyone calmed themselves by saying, "God is merciful; Batiushka cannot die—he is still so needed."

On the twenty-second, a Sunday, the Elder began to complain about a pain in his ears; in spite of this, he continued to take part in monastery activities, even receiving a few visitors, joking, and in general being cheerful.

On the following day, the twenty-third, pain in the Elder's ears intensified. He began to hear poorly and received very few visitors, as it was difficult to speak with them. Everyone begged him to rest, but the Elder would arise, walk around in his cell and give a few people his blessing. In the evening the Elder told them to read aloud to him. When asked whether it would be difficult to listen due to the pain in his ears, he answered nothing, thought for a few minutes and said, "This is the last test—I have lost my hearing and my voice." The Elder's voice had already begun to weaken long ago, so that towards evening he sometimes spoke entirely in a whisper. The next two days the Elder was in that state and received almost no one, since he had completely lost his hearing and voice. The people did not leave the porch of his cell from morning until evening. How much sorrow there was, how many tears were poured out. Some could not wait for long. They asked through the cell attendant for blessings and answers to their questions. In order not to burden the Elder with conversation, written questions were posed to him as a last resort.

On Thursday the twenty-sixth, the Elder felt even worse—he complained of a severe pain in his ears, head, face, and in all of his body. An abscess appeared in one of his ears. The deterioration of the Elder's health was very disturbing to everyone. It was decided to summon by telegram the Moscow doctor, Babushkin, who had treated Fr. Ambrose earlier. The Elder agreed to this.

On the twenty-seventh, the abscess in his ear broke open and the pain subsided a little. In the evening the Moscow doctor arrived, and, having examined the patient, he put everyone at ease, saying that there was no danger, that this was influenza. He prescribed complete rest for the patient and gave him a few sleeping medications. Incidently, this doctor always said: "I came here for the sake of form—if this were a usual patient, I would have said that he would live for a half hour, but after all, this is Fr. Ambrose—he could live for years."

On the twenty-eighth, the condition of Fr. Ambrose's health continued to improve. On Sunday the twenty-ninth, the Elder suddenly walked out of his cell and said that he had forgotten to pray before the icon of the Heavenly Queen "Joy of all who Sorrow." According to his wish, a Moleben was served in his cell before this icon. The sisters and lay people crowded at the door, in order to pray for the recovery of their dear father.

On October 1, the Elder said to one of his spiritual daughters: "I cannot do anything for you anymore; I have entrusted you to the Heavenly Queen." The doctor, having remained with the Elder until October 2, left for a time. The Elder himself accompanied the doctor to another room and spoke much with him. The first two days after that, the Elder felt fairly well. The pain in his ears did not decrease, and small abscesses appeared first in one ear and then in the other, but the fever left him. The Elder continued to use the medication prescribed by the doctor, and all were calm in the Monastery.

On Friday the fourth, the Elder said that the pain in his head had gotten worse, and towards the evening there was a fever. From that point on he had a fever every other day, and he spent the greater part of the day semi-conscious. Despite his extreme weakness he was occasionally able to rise from his bed without outside help, walk around his room, and even summoned several necessary people to give orders concerning construction. On this day one of the Elder's closest disciples, Hieromonk Joseph, was in Shamordino and desired to confess to him; but seeing that the Elder was very weak he feared to disturb him. Meanwhile, as soon as he made a small hint that he desired to confess, the Elder put on his epitrachelion and cuffs and personally gave him the confession book. Fr. Joseph had the good fortune to confess to him on this day for the last time; after this, having taken leave of the Elder, he left for the Skete. On the following night, according to the account of Fr. Joseph, for some reason he could not fall asleep for a long time, and it was as if he heard someone say, "The Elder will die." He heard these words clearly.

On the eve of October 6, there was a Vigil in the Elder's cell. In the middle of the Vigil he felt faint and began to breath with difficulty: all the doors were opened wide. Everyone was terrified, and a difficult time began. The spiritual children of the Elder did not leave the reception room and silently held their breath, awaiting news. Akathists were read in turns almost all the time. On October 6 a remarkable event happened. After dinner the Elder summoned his cell attendant and said to him as he entered: "Go, take a look. Someone is on the porch, asking to come to the Monastery again." When his cell attendant said that there were many people, the Elder again said to him sternly: "Go immediately, you will find out." After a few minutes the cell attendant returned and said that the former Optina novice, Brother M., who had left Optina for Mt. Athos was actually there, but was now in lay clothing. He came to ask the Elder which monastery he should enter now. Fr. Ambrose immediately ordered to call him in, spoke with him for a few minutes, and blessed him to go to the Glinsk Hermitage.

On October 7 the Superior of Shamordino experienced unbearable sorrow. Her soul was in such a dismal state that nowhere and in nothing could she find the least consolation. This, as she expressed it, was as if a foretaste of the tortures of hell. Entering into the sick Elder's cell, she revealed to him her terribly grievous state. It turned out that the Elder himself was

## THE LAST DAYS OF ELDER AMBROSE

going through such an inexpressibly agonizing temptation. He probably was allowed providentially to experience for a short time an abandonment by God, as it were, in order to give him a complete understanding of the poverty and weakness of human nature. Having listened to the Superior, the Elder said: "I feel something I have never experienced in my life."

According to the explanation of Elder Joseph, the Elder suffered the sorrows and sins of his multitude of spiritual children at this time. On one of the last days before the Elder's repose, his confessor, Fr. Theodore, said to him: "Batiushka, you are dying, who are you going to leave the Monastery to?" The Elder answered him with the following words, "I am leaving the Monastery to the Heavenly Queen; but I have gilded my cross."

On October 8, at six in the morning the Elder said that he felt very chilled, and his face had changed a great deal. After a few minutes it became feverish, and he became unconscious. After an hour he asked for fish soup, but he had weakened so suddenly that it was difficult to say what he wanted. His fever increased and he began to be delirious. Immediately the Skete Superior Hieromonk Anatole and Hieroschemamonk Joseph were sent for. The latter soon arrived, and after his arrival he immediately hastened to see the Elder. Coming out after a few minutes, he said to those present: "You are crowding in here for nothing: after all, the Elder cannot speak, and there is no hope for his recovery." Soon afterwards Fr. Anatole also arrived. The Elder grew weaker and weaker all day, so that he could no longer speak. His fever increased, rising to 104 degrees, and the Elder probably experienced such agonizing pain in his body at this time that it would not allow him to lie peacefully in his bed. He motioned to Fr. Joseph and his cell attendant Fr. Alexander, who were present, to lift him; but having barely lifted him, he again motioned them to lay him back down on the bed. He was shaking, as with a fever. Toward evening the Moscow doctor returned, but he found the Elder's condition to be already hopeless. Suddenly it got so bad that they thought that he was already dying, therefore Fr. Joseph read the Canon for the Departure of the Soul from the Body. Finally it was decided to perform an Unction service for the Elder. It was already 11:00 in the evening when the preparations for Holy Unction began. The Skete Superior Fr. Anatole, with Fr. Joseph and the Elder's confessor Fr. Theodore, began the rite of Holy Unction, during which the Elder already lay unconscious. His heavy, hoarse breathing was audible two rooms away, probably due to accumulated phlegm that the Elder had no strength to cough up. The sisters stood in the reception room and prayed. When the Unction service was finished, the sisters who were standing there entered into the Elder's cell by three's to gaze on their fading luminary and to bid farewell forever to their dear, loving father, to whom they had always run in every sorrow and who had always consoled them and encouraged them. Scarcely refraining from sobbing and fearing to disturb the quiet, the sisters silently bowed down to the Elder's feet and kissed his motionless hand, which was burning like fire. They gazed at his face, desiring to imprint his dear features more clearly in their memories; then they immediately left through the opposite door. Certain people still entertained a feeble hope that perhaps this was still not the end, perhaps these eyes would open once again and would affectionately look on them, perhaps this hand would make the sign of the cross over them, or with fatherly love slap the head of a guilty one. But no—this was a vain hope.

After midnight he began to sweat, and his temperature began to drop. This encouraged everyone somewhat. Then he regained consciousness, and they seized this moment to give him the Holy Mysteries of Christ. This was about 2:00 in the morning. Fr. Joseph gave him Holy Communion.

# THE LAST DAYS OF ELDER AMBROSE

One of the Elder's closest disciples entered his room a few times that night with another nun to look in on him, and they both were struck by the unusually bright expression of the Elder's face. His eyes were intently gazing into the distance, and he conversed, as it were, with someone seen only by him. The Elder did not lose consciousness the whole next day. Drinking a few sips of coffee, he arose from his bed when it was necessary to move the bed away from the wall and even took a few steps toward his table. But this was only for a short time. When the Mother Superior came up to him, he was already lying down again, and, having looked affectionately at her, he quietly uttered: "It's bad, Mother!" To all who surrounded him and who looked after him, or who especially labored for the fulfillment of his orders, he expressed the most touching gratitude at this time. Thus, while he still had strength, he once lovingly embraced Fr. Joel, who was helping in the construction of the Monastery; and he spoke to him for a long time, but so quietly that Fr. Joel was unable to understand anything.

Having learned of the Elder's extreme weakness, the Superior of Optina, Archimandrite Isaac, arrived with Hieromonk Macarius on this day (October 9) to bid him farewell. At the sight of the extremely helpless Elder, they both wept. The Elder recognized them, and having directed his deep, intent gaze at them, he raised his hand and removed his cap. The entire day, as in the previous days, the sisters continuously prayed with tears in church before the wonder-working icon of the Mother of God. They served continual Molebens standing on their knees, and all admirers of the Elder, as one man, with cries asked for healing for their dear Elder. But the Lord judged otherwise!...

On this day, so sorrowful for Shamordino, they suddenly received a telegram from the Kaluga governor stating that on October 10 Bishop Vitaly of Kaluga would leave from Kaluga for the Shamordino Monastery. The aim of this visit was known to all of the sisters, and this knowledge brought extreme embarrassment to all the sisters in the Monastery. [The aim was to force Elder Ambrose to return to Optina.]

It became more difficult for the Elder. Toward evening a high fever returned, and from 6:00 on he did not raise his head, lying in one position. All night his breathing was difficult. His eyes were fixed upwards and his lips were moving quickly. It was clear that the Elder was whispering prayers throughout the night until morning. The tenth of October arrived. Towards morning on this day, the Elder's strength left him entirely. He lay without moving. His eyes were lowered and fixed on some point. His lips ceased to move. His pulse became weaker and weaker. His breathing was sporadic but peaceful.

Seeing that the Elder had approached the time when his soul would depart, Fr. Joseph hastened to set out for the Skete in order to take from there the things that had been preserved in the Elder's cell for his burial—his old woolen mantia in which he had once been clothed at his tonsure, a hair shirt, and also the canvas shirt of Elder Macarius, for whom Fr. Ambrose had a profound devotion and respect all of his life. On this shirt was an inscription in Elder Ambrose's own hand—"After my death, clothe me in this without fail." It is needless to say that in these last days of the Elder's life, the Optina brethren, alarmed at the Elder's worsening condition, gathered in an even greater number than previously. Many were ready to stay continually, had it not been for their obedience and the shortness of the time permitted them. When the Elder was departing, in the cell where he lay were: Fr. Isaiah (later the vestry keeper in Optina), Fr. Alexander (later Fr. Anatole the Younger, the confessor of both Optina and Shamordino), Fr. Joel and others. When news had been received at Optina concerning the departure of Bishop Vitaly from Kaluga, Fr. Xenophont, who was then the treasurer and later the Superior of the Monastery, was assigned to meet him. Having left Optina, he learned on the way that the Bishop had stopped to spend the night in the Holy Trinity-Liutikov Monastery. Making use of the free time, Fr. Xenophont rushed to Shamordino. Here the most dismal news awaited him—the Elder was dying. Having joined his fellow brethren of Optina, Fr. Xenophont did not leave the dying Elder until the last minute, and was vouchsafed to witness his blessed repose.

At 11:00 in the morning the Elder's confessor, Fr. Theodore, read the Canon to the Mother of God for the Departure of the Soul for the last time and blessed him with the sign of the cross. The face of the Elder was veiled in a deathly pallor. His breathing became shallower and shallower. Finally, he took a deep breath. This was repeated after two minutes. Then, according to the witnesses, he raised his right hand, joined his fingers together and made the sign of the cross on his forehead, his breast, his right shoulder, and then on his left, striking his left shoulder powerfully, since this obviously cost him a great deal of effort. Then he took a third and last breath. This was exactly a half hour before noon.... The earthly life of the Elder had ended.

For a long time everyone stood quietly around the bed of the reposed Elder, afraid to disturb the solemn moment of the separation of his righteous soul from his body. Everyone was as if numb, not believing their own eyes, not comprehending what this was—a dream or reality. But his holy soul had already flown to another world, to stand before the throne of the Most High God, in the effulgence of that love with which he was filled on earth. His elderly face was radiant and peaceful. An unearthly smile lit his face.

Scarcely had everyone recovered, when a terrible wailing and sobbing was raised. The news of the Elder's repose flew as

Hieroschemamonk Ambrose on his deathbed.

# THE LAST DAYS OF ELDER AMBROSE

swiftly as lightning throughout the entire Monastery, and the heart-rending cries from the souls of the Shamordino community blended into one common, terrible groan of hopelessness and helplessness. This first outburst of fearful anguish later calmed somewhat and changed into quiet sorrow.

Fr. Xenophont went out to the adjoining rooms directly after the Elder's repose. His trembling voice could scarcely be heard as he informed the Elder's admirers, who were gathered in a crowd here, about this great sorrow; and then he hastened without delay to bring the sad news to Optina. The doleful sound of the great bell announced the grievous event to Optina, and, bringing the brothers to unspeakable sorrow, it drew them into church for the first "alleluia" for the newly departed Elder Ambrose. Fr. Joseph, taking everything necessary for the preparation of the body, immediately departed and hurried to the body of his dear instructor, to serve him for the last time and to kiss his hand while it was still warm.

Meanwhile, in Shamordino the preparation of the Elder's body for burial had begun. Just then, Hieroschemamonk Joseph returned from the Skete with the necessary items, accompanied by Monk Gabriel, whose duty it was to prepare the body of the reposed. Following the Elder's testament, they dressed him first in the canvas shirt of Elder Macarius, then in the hair shirt, and finally, according to custom, in the remaining monastic clothes and schema. While the monks prepared the body, the Psalter was read beside them. The prepared body was carried out on a straw mattress into the Mother Superior's hall in the arms of the Elder's disciples. At the sight of the lifeless, cold body of their dear father, the sisters again gave themselves up to loud sobbing. In the hall the body was placed on a table, and at once the first Pannikhida was served for the repose of the newly departed Hieroschemamonk Ambrose.

Immediately after the repose of the Elder a multitude of telegrams were sent to the far corners of Russia, to all the Elder's closest admirers and to his spiritual children.

A telegram was sent also to Kaluga to the local Bishop, the Most Reverend Vitaly, but it did not find him in Kaluga. At the very moment of Elder Ambrose's repose the Bishop had left Kaluga, heading towards the Shamordino community. Being a sickly man, he had gone only seventeen miles from Kaluga when he stopped for a rest and spent the night at the Holy Trinity-Liutikov Monastery, which was on the way. Here he received the news about the Elder's repose. His Eminence was sitting in the hall with the Superior of the Monastery, conversing about various subjects; among them, the Bishop stated his dissatisfaction that the Elder was—according to his expression—not obedient to higher authority. Just then, the cell attendant gave the Superior a telegram. He opened the telegram in the presence of the Bishop, not expecting anything in particular. But as soon as he read that Hieroschemamonk Ambrose had died, his hands shook and tears flowed from his eyes. Looking at him, the Bishop asked, "What is it?" "Such sorrowful news, Your Eminence!" "But, what is it?" Instead of an answer, the Superior gave the Bishop the telegram. Having glanced at it, the Bishop said, "What is this? The Elder has died?" "As you see," answered the Superior. The Bishop was astounded. He turned to the icons, clasped his hands and exclaimed, "My God! What can this be? Unfathomable are the ways of the Lord!"

In the morning, instead of going to Shamordino, the Bishop went to Optina. Here he learned that the Elder had died a half hour before noon, at the very time that he was sitting in his carriage to leave Kaluga.

"Now I see," said the Bishop, "that this Elder invited me for the funeral. Bishops do not serve funerals for simple hieromonks, but this Elder was so great that a bishop must certainly perform the funeral service for him. My doctor dismissed me under the condition that I not serve anywhere; but now I consider it my obligation to perform the funeral for the Elder."

Meanwhile, in Shamordino the body of Elder Ambrose was transferred into a simple coffin, lined with plain black material, and covered half-way with the same simple covering used for all reposed monastics. The sisters alternated reading the Psalter, and any time they pronounced the words "the newly reposed, our father, Elder Hieroschemamonk Ambrose," everyone who was in the hall made a prostration to the ground. On the following day, October 11, in Shamordino, in Optina, and in many other places, Liturgies were performed for the repose of Elder Ambrose. At 2:00 in the afternoon, the last Pannikhida was served in the cell over the body. Then the coffin with the body of the reposed was carried from the Mother Superior's building to the church, where the reading of the Psalter continued and Pannikhidas were sung continuously in the presence of the spiritual children and admirers of the deceased Elder; inconsolable lamentation filled the church.

As a result of the telegrams that were sent and the spreading of the news, the Elder's admirers began to arrive in Shamordino from everywhere, wishing to be present at his funeral. In all, by the day of the funeral, up to eight-thousand people had gathered in Shamordino.

Meanwhile, out of love and respect for the reposed Elder, a misunderstanding arose between Optina and Shamordino concerning the question of where to bury the body of the reposed one, who was dear to both monasteries. By order of the Holy Synod the body was to be given over to the earth in Optina.

On the following night of October 11, Pannikhidas were sung uninterruptedly over the coffin of the reposed at the behest of the sisters and the guests. During the entire time that the body was uncovered, the people brought handkerchiefs, pieces of canvas and other things, requesting that they be placed by the body of the Elder; and they received them back with faith and reverence as holy objects. Some mothers touched their little children to him.

On Saturday, October 12, the Superior of the Likhvin Pokrov Dobry Monastery, Abbot Agapit,* the Elder's former secretary and disciple, arrived for the funeral and served a Moleben with an Akathist before the miracle-working icon of the Kazan Mother of God,** then served the Liturgy and a Pannikhida over the coffin of the Elder. After this, requested Pannikhidas continued all day and night.

Bishop Vitaly appointed Sunday, October 13, for the funeral service for the reposed in God, Hieroschemamonk Ambrose. The day was clear and warm, as rarely happens in October. The brilliant morning sunbeams poured into the Shamordino Convent and passed through the windows of the church, playing gaily upon the golden ornaments of the iconostasis and the large candlestands that stood by the coffin. The entire church and the square in front of the church were filled with a thick crowd of people. Everything had the appearance, not of a funeral, but of a kind of unusual, joyous, spiritual celebration.

Finally, at 8:30 in the morning, the ringing of the bells announced the approach of the archpastor, who had spent the night in Optina. Approaching the building where the preparations for his lodgings had been made, he asked, "Where is the body of the reposed Elder?" Having learned it was in church,

---

\* At the time of this writing he was an archimandrite living in retirement in Optina.

\*\* This Moleben was served in the Monastery weekly, on Saturdays, according to the directive of the Elder.

the Bishop wished first of all to make a prostration before him and, not entering the house, he went on foot to the church. Meanwhile, in church they were not expecting the Bishop at this time and were singing a Pannikhida. The Bishop unexpectedly entered the church just at the time when the Seventeenth Kathisma was finished and they were singing "alleluia," thus fulfilling the words of the reposed Elder, who had answered the sisters' question about what they would sing to the Bishop as he entered the church: "We will sing alleluia for him."

The sisters, seeing the Bishop in church and unable to endure the shock of this recollection, loudly burst into tears. Then, coming to themselves, they began to sing the entrance hymn to the Bishop. The Bishop went into the altar and venerated the Holy Table and the holy icons. Then he went up to the coffin, made a prostration, blessed the deceased thrice with the sign of the cross and withdrew from church.

After a while, the Bishop again came to church to serve the Divine Liturgy, and this time he was properly received according to the rubrics: by two archimandrites, two abbots and four hieromonks who were to concelebrate with him. During the Liturgy, the Bishop's choir sang on the right cliros, and on the left, the sisters of the Convent. After the communion verses, with the blessing of the Bishop, Hieromonk Gregory (Borisoglebsky), a distinguished student of the Moscow Theological Academy who had come from Sergiev Posad for the funeral of Elder Ambrose, ascended the ambo and delivered a beautiful homily. He clearly portrayed the significance of the reposed Elder—for Optina and Shamordino in particular, and for monasticism and Russia in general. The preacher's words were often drowned out by the sobbing of the listeners. He began:

"You should not be amazed at this great throng of worshippers.... In this poor community there lived a man, whom all of Holy Russia knew, and to whom, for a long time, there came innumerable crowds of people from all quarters.... The name of this man was known both in royal palaces and in village huts. This was Batiushka Elder Ambrose, the great pastor and man of compassion of the Russian land. It was he who drew this great crowd of his admirers here today.... In what do the merits of this man consist? He returned the image of God to fallen people and taught repentance. This protector of the Russian land knew how to compel those, who from their very childhood had forgotten how to cry, to pour out tears of contrition, tears of repentance, tears of rebirth towards new spiritual life.... And thus, Holy Russia, grieve! In losing this hermit, humble of spirit and body, you have been deprived of your great benefactor, who loved you with all the power of Christian love, who gave his whole life for you and, one may say, who brought it to you as a sacrifice. You can no longer come to Fr. Ambrose with your grief and afflictions for consolation, and cannot send to him your Dostoyevskys and Tolstoys to be taught by the simple monk a higher science—the ability to live as a human being and as a Christian. Weep bitterly, holy Optina Monastery! You have been deprived of your Elder, who was the bearer of the holy tradition of eldership, who adorned you for so long....

"O monks of Optina—in those moments when the weight of the monastic cross more mightily constricts the powers of your spirit, when your soul becomes grieved and anguished more deeply than usual, you will no longer be able to go for sure healing to your dear Fr. Ambrose. Weep bitter tears also, O you of Shamordino! You have been deprived of your spiritual father, who loved you with all the power of his self-denying pastoral love. He begot you spiritually in the light of God. He, like a

Elder Ambrose's coffin in the church at Shamordino.

tender mother, daily cherished you in your infancy. He gave you all the donations that flowed to him; he built this holy church for you; he gave you all the last days of his much-suffering life, which he spent within your walls, so as, in the sunset of his days, by his presence, with his eyes and words, to more powerfully inspire those who are laboring over your spiritual and bodily health."

Then the preacher called to the remembrance of his listeners the precepts of the Elder and prevailed upon them to follow them. Turning to the Orthodox lay people, he said:

"And so, Christian world who has forgotten God! Come here and see how you must set your life in order. Come to your senses! Forsake the vanity of the world and realize that on earth one must live only for Heaven.... Do not think that to live on earth only for God is impossible. Behold the coffin which convicts you.... Having forsaken the world, his relatives and acquaintances, Fr. Ambrose while still young went to the Monastery, where he lived in a poor cell and was nourished on the most meager food. And when he had become sufficiently strong in the struggle against the carnal man, he gave himself entirely to the service of his neighbor. From morning until night he lived only for the benefit of his neighbor. Never and to no one did he refuse counsel. He treated everyone kindly. Often by evening the sick Elder's tongue was so weary that he was no longer even able to speak. And how much good he did! How many people he set back on their feet—not only by counsel, but even by financial assistance. And look at this Monastery—his love created and reared it. He lived the lives of others; he rejoiced and mourned with the joys and sorrows of his neighbors. One might say that he had no life of his own. And so, Christians—come to this coffin and learn that on earth one must live only for Heaven; that such a way of life is possible and realizable, and that the foundation of this life is full, active self-renunciation for the good of one's neighbor."

Then, turning to the monks, the preacher at first described Fr. Ambrose—how he was a great ascetic and man of prayer.

"His narrow cell," he said, "would tell you how this constantly sick, almost perpetually dying Elder—burdened with tiresome daily conversations with visitors, his pastoral conscience tormented by the sins of the penitents—would sometimes arise from his bed and tearfully and attentively listen to the all-night cell Vigil. How many solitary, fervent supplications, bitter tears, and prostrations these walls have seen! This is their secret! Yes, this was an ascetic, such as can rarely be found. Now his dead lips speak aloud to all monastics about the strict, hard work of keeping the monastic vows and rules."

But Fr. Ambrose had yet another trait—an exalted trait of Christian asceticism which has been somewhat forgotten in recent times, but which monks must learn from the reposed one.

"Living away from the world and fleeing it, he was able to live for the sake of it.... You may believe that not in a single reception room of any lay person, pastor or statesmen, were there as many people as there were in the narrow, lowly cell of this hermit. Believe! This whole world, which lies in evil, has not received from anyone as much counsel and instruction, both written and oral, as this reposed one has given it.... He was able, by the power of his faith and love, to widen the narrow walls of his cell into a vast expanse. He, as a pastor, knew that there were many in the sinful but God-seeking world who hungered and thirsted for Christ's words, for love and faith. He loved this world and gave his whole life to it.... From the world there came to him all who labored and were heavy laden, and he gave them rest."

In this service of love, monks must imitate the Elder....

"And you, monastics, serve—serve sincerely and unrestrainedly, as the reposed Fr. Ambrose served people in the world. Celebrate the church services piously, with fervent feeling and tears of love. Where will the layman hear real services celebrated according to the rubrics, if not in a monastery? Where is he to hear real, ancient, Russian church singing, if not in the churches of the holy monasteries? Monastics—preserve the rubrics and church singing in holiness, and by this, serve the world. Where can a layman become attuned in regards to religion? Again, in a monastery. He walks within the walls of a holy monastery, where the relics of saints repose, where there are miracle-working holy icons. He walks and his soul is filled with reverential fear. He listens to each sound, he is edified by every inscription, every holy picture. Know this, monks, and reverently protect this religious attunement of the layman. Serve him in the Monastery in every way you can. Preach to him tirelessly; believe that he will retain the sermons he hears in the Monastery for a long time. Go through all your sacred treasures with him, through all the churches; show him and tell him everything. Receive under your protection the poor, the sick and the orphan. When you, monk or nun, stand at prayer, do not forget to pray earnestly for the sinful world—it needs your prayers. And so, Russian monastics, remember and keep sacred the posthumous testament of Elder Ambrose: love even sinful people, and serve them as much as possible."

Turning finally to the pastors of the church, the preacher invited them to learn from the Elder, and to study first of all his lofty spiritual state, which cannot always be found in contemporary pastors.

"Compare the attitude of parishioners to any priest with the attitude of those who came to the reposed Elder. In the first instance, each one of them is aware of his own station and calling—the peasant comes after the nobleman, the rich before

# THE LAST DAYS OF ELDER AMBROSE

the poor. You come to a priest with a family as to an acquaintance; often you will sit through the entire evening and not hear a single word about spirituality, about the church, about Heaven. All these conversations are about worldly things, like those you have among yourselves.

"It was not so with the Elder. Before him every man felt he was only a layman; princely titles and the dignity of counts, glory and riches, distinction and the advantage of higher education—everything was left at the threshold of his cell.... Everyone spoke with him, and he spoke with everyone only about spiritual things; anything worldly that was said to him, he would unfailingly interpret as something spiritual.... They looked at Batiushka only as a servant of God.... He was a physician for the sick conscience."

But even more, must one study the Elder's universal pastoral love, that love which, according to the Apostle, *suffereth long, and is kind; ... envieth not; ... vaunteth not itself, is not puffed up, doth not behave itself unseemly, seeketh not her own, is not easily provoked, thinketh no evil; rejoiceth not in iniquity, but rejoiceth in the truth* (I Cor. 13:4-6).

Having said a few more consoling words to the Shamordino sisters concerning the fact that they would not have the grave of their beloved Elder, he counseled them: "Carefully preserve in its entirety and purity the spiritual image of the reposed, which will be pleasing to him and useful for him." Then the preacher concluded his sermon, having made a powerful impression upon all the listeners.

After the conclusion of Liturgy, Bishop Vitaly and twenty-eight concelebrants, all in white vestments, came out into the middle of the church for the funeral service.... Magnificent and touching was this holy sight. The reverent serving of the archpastor, the harmonious singing of both choirs, the touching hymns of the monastic funeral, the multitude of those praying with burning candles in their hands, and, finally, in the midst of this resplendent setting, the poor coffin containing the body, clothed in the schema, of the reposed Elder, who was dear to all present—all of this made a tremendous impression upon everyone. Many sobbed. Before the singing of "With the Saints Give Rest," a student from the Moscow Theological Academy, Hieromonk Tryphon,* who personally knew the reposed one and was his former novice and disciple and who, together with Hieromonk Gregory, had come especially for the burial of the Elder, delivered a brief, but deeply heartfelt speech. He first made note of the amazing fact that although the Elder was constantly at the point of death, he was continually resurrecting the deadened spirit of his neighbor. Then, after speaking about his own relationship with the reposed, the preacher vividly and unaffectedly outlined the fundamental characteristic of the inner state of the Elder—his Christian love towards all.

This is—"not that passionate, pagan love, which loves only those who love it and does good only to those who are in some way useful or pleasant for it; but that love which sees in all people the image and likeness of God, and loves it and mourns over it's distortions if it notices them. And it does not meet human weaknesses and infirmities with proud words of reproach, but takes them upon itself. There can be nothing higher than that love which lays down its life for its neighbor, as is attested to by the Word of God! It is that love which compelled one saint to call to God in his prayers with boldness: 'Lord, if I have acquired grace before Thee, if I have attained the Heavenly Kingdom, then command my brothers also to enter with me—

---

*At the time of this writing, Bishop of Dimitrov, senior vicar of the Moscow Diocese.

but without them, even I will not go there....' It is with that love that Batiushka's whole existence was permeated...."

Fr. Tryphon pointed out Fr. Ambrose's love for children as one of his characteristic moral traits. "Let those who were close to this matter tell you in what terrible condition children sometimes came to the orphanage he founded. They received them all and gave them all a true Christian education, and some of them have already become brides of Christ.

"One had to see our Batiushka among the children who surrounded him; he hugged and caressed him—how especially touching he was then, how often we saw his tears of contrition of soul...." Fr. Tryphon concluded his talk with a prostration before the reposed Elder's coffin.

Finally the time came for the customary farewell to the deceased. There resounded the sad, melodious notes of the sacred hymn, "Come give the final kiss, brethren, to him who has died...." Wailing and sobbing again filled the church.

The Bishop was the first to go up to the coffin. He took the Kazan Icon of the Mother of God that rested on the analogion before the coffin, and with deep, prayerful feeling, he blessed the reposed with it three times, made a prostration before him, kissed his head and hands, and blessed him thrice with his episcopal blessing. After the Bishop, the clergy, the Abbess, the sisters and the people bade farewell to the Elder.

This heartfelt, tearful, last farewell lasted a long time. Finally, at about 3:00 in the afternoon, the Bishop gave the dismissal. They sang "Memory Eternal" for the Elder. The Bishop poured oil and wine which had been sanctified at an Unction service on the body of the reposed Elder in the form of a cross, and then earth was sprinkled on his body according to the rites of the holy Church. Directly after this the lid of the coffin was nailed shut. Everything was over in three hours. The clergy, headed by the Bishop, and the remaining guests set out for the Superior's rooms. The coffin remained in its former place, and continual Pannikhidas began again....

The whole night, from Sunday to Monday, the Shamordino church was filled with people. As before, a multitude of candles burned by the coffin of the deceased Elder. Incense swirled, Pannikhidas were sung, and the reading of the Psalter proceeded on the side. The Elder's admirers continued to venerate the coffin.

On Monday the fourteenth, the Liturgy for the reposed was celebrated by the Superior of the Skete, Hieromonk Anatole. The Liturgy and Pannikhida ended at 11:00 in the morning. The coffin was lifted by the sisters, placed on a bier and, with the holy icons and banners proceeding, it was first carried around the church and then through the Monastery, past the Superior's building and the stone church which had been built by the Elder. Then the procession set out on its way to Optina.

The weather on this day was rainy. A cold autumn wind pierced right through the travellers, and the constant rain would first lighten and then grow stronger, thoroughly drenching the earth.

The coffin was carried alternately by the sisters of the Convent, by the Optina monks, and by lay people who wished, to the very end, to show their love and devotion towards their deceased instructor. A crowd of thousands of people, stretching out for more than a half mile, walked and rode behind the coffin. The procession was slow. Often, despite the rain and cold, they stopped to serve a Lity for the reposed. As they drew near to the villages that lay along the way, the bells of the churches began their funeral toll. The priests in their vestments, with banners and icons, came to meet the procession. The villagers came forward and prayed, and many of them kissed the coffin of the deceased, afterwards joining the funeral procession. In this way, as they came closer to Optina, the crowd grew

## THE LAST DAYS OF ELDER AMBROSE

and grew. It was remarkable that the burning candles carried alongside the body of the deceased Elder did not go out along the entire way, despite the strong rain and wind.

Evening drew near and it was already a little dark when the Elder's coffin was carried through the last village, Stenino, located a half mile from Optina. Melancholy was the sound of the great thirteen-ton Optina bell which was struck at long intervals, shaking the air and carrying for a great distance the sorrowful tidings of the approaching moment of the final parting with the deceased great Elder. From the town of Kozelsk, the local clergy and many townspeople came to meet the funeral procession. High above the heads of the people, through the semi-dark evening the black coffin could be seen mysteriously illuminated by the bright flames of the candles. As it swayed from the stride of those who were carrying it, the coffin seemed to float in the air. Truly this touching, sadly triumphant translation of the body of the deceased Elder, according to the remarks of many, resembled the translation of relics and made a moving grace-filled impression upon everyone present.

The narrow river Zhizdra which flows below the Monastery is usually crossed over by ferry, but this time a temporary bridge was set up. Here a procession came out from the Monastery to meet the deceased Elder. At its head were two archimandrites, accompanied by a multitude of monastics and lay people.

Majestic was the sight, when the Elder's coffin was carried across the bridge, among the ranks of a great assembly of priests in resplendent vestments and an innumerable crowd of people who joined them from both sides. The funeral toll of the bells, the singing of the choirs, the banners blowing in the wind, the immeasurable number of people, both in front and behind, far, far beyond the river, and finally this poor coffin which attracted the eyes of all present—all of this struck the hearts of everyone who had gathered to pay their last respects to the Elder. All of

The arrival of Elder Ambrose's body in Optina.

this drew heartfelt sighs from everyone, with fervent supplications for the repose of his departed soul in the heavenly abodes, with secret sorrow of heart over the loss of their dear father, and with entreaties for him to intercede before the throne of the Most High Heavenly Father.

It was 5:00 in the evening. The procession headed towards the holy gates of the Monastery. The coffin with the body of the reposed Elder was brought into the Monastery and placed in the unheated Catholicon of the Entrance of the Theotokos, which shone with festal radiance. The Superior of the Monastery, Archimandrite Isaac, with several concelebrating hieromonks, sang a Pannikhida over the deceased. After a little while the solemn All-Night Vigil service in the heated Kazan Church began. Meanwhile, in the Catholicon where the body of the Elder remained, Pannikhidas were served one after another all night, and the people continued to bid farewell to the reposed.

On the following day, October 15, the coffin was carried into the Kazan Church. The Liturgy began at 10:00 in the morning, which Bishop Vitaly served again in spite of his poor health, along with two archimandrites—Moses and Isaac—three abbots and five hieromonks. The Bishop's choir sang on the right cliros and the monastic choir on the left.

At the end of the Divine Liturgy, the Bishop turned to the people and delivered a beautiful, touching sermon in which he portrayed the essence of eldership and vividly depicted the moral features of the heroic guardian of the precepts of eldership—Hieroschemamonk Ambrose.

At the end of Liturgy the Bishop served a Pannikhida in which forty priests took part, all in white brocade vestments. At the end of the Pannikhida, after the ninth ode had been sung, Hieromonk Gregory (Borisoglebsky) once again came forward with a short farewell sermon to the Elder. In this sermon he expressed the final farewell to the Elder from the Moscow Theological Academy, with which the Elder had a living, spiritual relationship and for which he was always an exalted example of faith and life and spiritual guidance. "We, students of the theological schools," said Fr. Gregory, "who are preparing to be pastors, as well as our instructors, looked upon you as upon an image and example of pastorship. During your life, the leaders and instructors and pupils of our Moscow Academy were all permeated with a sense of reverential respect towards you, and many of us benefitted from your counsels; and you, loving spiritually minded youth, were able to instill in those who turned to you the true spirit of pastorship—ascetical, self-denying, and breathing love. Believe that your memory will always be preserved in holiness and reverence by the Russian clergy and the spiritually minded Russian youth."

These words of the young preacher-student concluded the earthly farewell to the reposed Elder.

A<small>FTER THE PANNIKHIDA</small>, the coffin of the deceased was lifted in the arms of the priests, and, with the holy icons and banners preceding, the funeral procession set out towards the prepared grave. Behind the coffin walked the Bishop in his full vestments with the remaining priests. The mournful funeral toll, blending with the singing of the funeral hymns, accompanied the body of the reposed holy Elder to his final resting place on earth. Elder Ambrose's grave was prepared beside that of his great teacher, Elder Hieroschemamonk Macarius, near the southeastern wall of the summer church of the Entrance of the Theotokos. After the Lity for the repose of the soul, which was celebrated by the Bishop, and the singing of "Memory Eternal" to the deceased, the coffin was lowered into the grave.

When the Elder had been buried, one observer from among the lay people remarked that one of the monks closest to the

# THE LAST DAYS OF ELDER AMBROSE

Elder,* standing by the grave, put his arms on his chest in the form of the cross and closed his eyes. Everyone set out for the refectory. Two hours went by. That same monk was still standing in the same position by Fr. Ambrose's grave.

This observer said that it was remarkable that in both monasteries (Optina and Shamordino) the grief over the Elder, though it was both deep and sincere, was at the same time bright and not without hope. It was possible to speak to those closest to the Elder about him. Everyone was calm, reserved, and went about their business. Only sometimes would pain appear on the face of a monk, or would you find him in a deeply pensive state. And sometimes, in the midst of conversations about the Elder, someone would suddenly quietly utter with a sigh, "Ah, Father, Father!" Such sincere grief was heard in these short words. With whomever you would speak about him, everyone loved him, everyone benefitted from him.... "But whom did he not love?"—these words were on everyone's lips.

We will present here an excerpt of a poem dedicated to the memory of the reposed Elder by one of the nuns of the Shamordino community:

> Our Elder's gone! His words have ceased!
> His lamp's extinguished here on earth!
> But there his light will be increased
> Because it is his heav'nly birth.
>
> > He 's laid aside the heavy burden,
> > Of his pastoral loving care.
> > His earthly fetters now for certain
> > Are happily no longer there.
>
> But woe to us—we are no longer
> Under his ever-seeing eye,

---

*This was Fr. Isaiah, the Elder's cell attendant.

And pain within grows ever stronger.
Forsaken, we are left to die.

> But we believe: you'll not abandon,
> Nor forsake us to the end,
> Your children, gathered not at random.
> To God you'll lead us by your hand.

Is it not you whose voice we're hearing,
That echoes in us as a call.
From higher realms, wherein you're living,
An invitation to us all?

> It is your deed of patient caring,
> While seeing us from azure heights,
> That cleans our conscience overbearing
> And sends us heavenly delights.

So ended the earthly pilgrimage of the ever-memorable Optina Elder Hieroschemamonk Ambrose! His earthly pilgrimage has ended, but his true, eternal and, we believe, blessed life in Heaven has not only not ended—it has just begun.

We believe this because, even while he was here on earth, it was obvious to everyone that in him there shone a reflection of heavenly, blessed glory—it shone in the features of his moral character; it shone in his ineffable joy and peace of soul, which he poured out upon the soul of every person who came to him who had a close or distant contact with him; it shone in that deep, moral renewal and rebirth which was accomplished in people, sometimes under the influence of only one word or glance from Fr. Ambrose; and finally, it shone in the special, grace-filled gifts of clairvoyance and miracle-working which, according to the unanimous testimony of witnesses, were manifest in Elder Ambrose. Now that we have ended our narrative about the earthly pilgrimage of the Elder, we would like to speak about these gifts, because they lead us into the

Elder Ambrose's closest disciple, Elder Joseph.

domain not of the temporal and earthly, but of the eternal and heavenly life of the Elder. They assure us with particular clarity that Fr. Ambrose, who warmed so many by his love here on earth, will not cease to care for us after his translation to the heavenly abodes. For this reason we are able to beg with great hope and boldness his holy prayers for us before the throne of God, especially in any grievous and difficult circumstances of our life!

The well of St. Ambrose of Milan near the Skete.

# II

# *The Special Manifestations of the Grace-filled Power of God in Elder Ambrose*

> *And He said unto me: My grace is sufficient for thee: for My strength is made perfect in weakness.*
> II Corinthians 12:9

A<small>LL WHO KNEW</small> Elder Ambrose spoke unanimously of his characteristic gift of clairvoyance. For him there were no secrets. A stranger could come to him and be silent, but the Elder knew his life and his circumstances, his spiritual state, and why he had come. Fr. Ambrose questioned his visitors, but to an attentive man, it was clear by the kind of questions he posed that the matter was known to the Elder. Thus, a young man from the gentry once came up to him with his hand bandaged and began to complain that he could in no way be healed. With the Elder there were another monk and a few laymen. He had not managed to finish saying, "It hurts, it hurts a lot!" when the Elder interrupted him. "And it will hurt—why did you offend your mother?"

The Bishop of Kaluga, Macarius, passed on the following concerning himself: When he was still a married priest and a teacher of religion in the Orel Institute for Girls of the Nobility, it happened that he was in Optina with Elder Ambrose, together with the rector of the Orel Theological Seminary. Having conversed with his guests, upon bidding them farewell the Elder presented them both with books of identical content, namely, on monasticism. "I, as a priest," said the Bishop, "thought then: 'Why did he give me such a book?' And the Elder, as if coming to his senses, said, 'Yes, that wouldn't be right for you'; but then he added: 'well, yes, that's how it will be.'" In time, having become a widower, the former priest and teacher of religion became a monk, as is well-known.

Hieromonk Dorotheus of Optina said that he once came to the Elder and waited a long time to be received. It was already 10:00 in the evening. He sat and thought: "Here everyone calls the Elder a saint. And what kind of sanctity is this, when he forces me to wait so long for him to come out? Because of this I'll have to omit the evening rule, and I'll sleep through Matins. It will be his sin for all this." Suddenly at this moment he heard the voice of the Elder from his cell: "Right away, right away!" He looked; out came the Elder. Having blessed him, he grabbed him by the beard and, lightly striking him on the cheek, he said: "Look, nuns sometimes live in the guest house for a month; they wait until I can receive them. Another one, perhaps, came hundreds of miles and is also patient and waits. I have to dismiss them first. Because of them I sometimes refuse admission to the brothers. I can't receive everyone immediately. And you don't want to wait even a little! This will be my sin alone for all this?!" Brought to reason by the words of the Elder, Fr. Dorotheus calmly and joyfully left him for his own cell and never again dared to murmur against him, even if he sometimes had to wait a long time for him to come out.

# THE GRACE-FILLED POWER OF GOD

Hieromonk V. told the following story: "After graduating from the Smolensk Theological Seminary, I held the position of priest in the village of Chebotovo in the Dorogobuzhsky district. My name was Victor Dyakonov. Soon my wife became ill, but apparently not dangerously. About this time a pilgrim who was on his way to Optina Monastery stopped by our house. I sent a ruble with him to give to Fr. Ambrose, asking him to pray for my sick wife. After the pilgrim came to the Monastery the Elder asked him during their meeting: 'Are you going back by the same way?' The other answered: 'The same way.' 'Stop in again at Fr. Victor's, Batiushka said to him, 'and thank him for remembering me. Tell him that I also won't forget him.' I will note at this point that when I was still a student at the Seminary, I went personally to Fr. Ambrose for a blessing. After becoming a priest, I always commemorated him at the proskomedia. The Elder even remembered this. 'A podvig awaits him,' continued the Elder. 'Let him restore the garden and water it often—there will be much fruit. The month of July will be sorrowful for him; we will see each other.' On July 29 of that year my wife reposed, and I set out for Optina. I came to the Elder, and he gave me a prayer rope and the book *The Royal Path of the Cross of the Lord* and ordered me to prepare to become a monk—to sell all my belongings and to give a request to the bishop for me to retire due to illness, which I did. Afterward I came to Batiushka in the Skete, and in a short time I was tonsured into the mantia."

The same Hieromonk V. told about another graduate of the Smolensk Theological Seminary, Paul Semyonovich Sokolov. After finishing the Seminary he held the post of village teacher and several times personally asked Elder Ambrose's blessing to become a priest. But the Elder always put aside his request, advising him to wait. Two years went by that way. Paul

Semyonovich once again turned to Elder Ambrose by letter, expressing the desire to take the position of priest in the city of Vyazma. This time the Elder answered him: "Over you there hangs a crown of thorns, and soon it will descend upon you—wait." And so it happened. After two months Paul Semyonovich became ill and reposed.

Monk I. recounted: "When I lived in the world, I was married, but after four years I became a widower. At this time my brother set out for Optina to Elder Ambrose, and I wished, through my brother, to find out how the Elder would bless me to live. When he had returned, my brother gave me the Elder's answer: 'Let him wait a year before getting married and come to us.' I thought: 'Do they want to make me a monk?' At that time I had no intention of entering a monastery. A year went by, and I entered into a second marriage, without having gone beforehand to Optina and without having received a blessing for this from the Elder. But 3½ months went by and my second wife died. Two months after this I went to Optina. I came to the Elder, and he said to me: 'Come here. Where's your wife? Why didn't you obey me?' I answered, 'Forgive me, Batiushka. I have come now to ask you whether I should get married or enter the Monastery.' At this, Batiushka said, 'There are no third marriages. Your immediate duty is to remain in the Monastery and be a monk.' After this I returned home and two months later came for good to Optina and was numbered among the skete brotherhood."

According to the words of the skete monk G. there lived in the Skete an ecclesiarch, Hieromonk Palladius. Once, on a Sunday, he finished serving Liturgy in the skete church, feeling healthy. But the Elder that very day sent his cell attendant to him and ordered him at once to receive Unction and be tonsured into the Schema. Fr. Palladius was quite surprised at this and told the cell attendant that he was healthy. Batiushka again, a second and third time, sent his cell attendant with the same proposal, but the other continued to refuse. Monday came. In the morning Batiushka, for the fourth and last time, sent his cell attendant to Fr. Palladius with the same suggestion. But while he was making preparations for the Unction service, he had a stroke. However, although his tongue was paralyzed, he was still conscious. They managed to complete the Unction service and give him the Holy Mysteries of Christ. In the evening of that same day he reposed.

Monk Gennadius relates: "I was once greatly troubled by blasphemous thoughts. I came after this happened to Fr. Ambrose late in the evening—it was already dark. Batiushka came out of his cell into the corridor and began to bless, in order, the brothers who were kneeling. He came up to me as well. In the darkness he could not see my face, but suddenly he turned to me and said, 'What are you thinking?' And he began to wipe his hand across my face, as if washing dirt from it and then blessed me, having said nothing to me. But suddenly I sensed that everything felt light in my soul. The blasphemous thoughts had left me, and joy filled my heart."

The nun Barbara Englehart of the Belev Convent recounted this remarkable incident: "In 1875 my brother, having graduated from the Michailov Artillery School, entered the service as an artillery officer. Then after two years, in 1877, he was assigned to the staff of the front-line army against the Turks. At that time he was about twenty years old. I myself was then in the Zosima Hermitage, in the Verey district of the Moscow Province. Once I received a letter from one of my brother's companions, in which he communicated to me the horrible news that my brother had shot himself. In terrible grief I set out for Optina to Elder Ambrose. I appeared before him in tears and told him everything. Batiushka tried, as much as he was able, to console me. To my question—was it possible to pray for my brother—Batiushka answered that the Church does not pray for suicides, but that he would give me a prayer which I could use in my cell for my brother.

"I came to him on the next day. Batiushka met me joyfully and declared that my brother was alive and well. To my question—would I see him?—Batiushka answered that I would find out about him after ten years. Batiushka's prediction came to pass. After ten years I received a letter from America from my brother, informing me that he was alive and well and begging my forgiveness that he had not sent any news about himself for so long."

One of the devoted spiritual daughters of the Elder, A. A. Shishkova, recalls the following: "During one of my visits to the Elder he blessed me with the book, *The Royal Path of the Cross of the Lord, Which Leads Unto Eternal Life,* adding: 'Read it more often.' I said to him: 'You already gave me this book last time.' 'And did you read it?' the Elder objected. 'It seems to me that I read it,' was my answer. 'It seems, does it? You gave it away without unwrapping it.'

"Then I remembered—that was exactly what I had done, and I begged his forgiveness. Batiushka, with his usual kindness, gave me the book again, and said: 'Read this one more often.'"

To the same A. A. Shishkova, Fr. Ambrose clearly predicted the death of the granddaughters of Mother Ambrosia Klyuchareva seven years before it occurred. When she, on an errand from Klyuchareva, asked the Elder for permission to hire a French teacher for the girls, he answered: "No, don't do that; the children do not need a French teacher. I have placed an excellent, pious Russian woman with them, who will instruct and prepare them for the future life. You know, the children will not live long, and on the place where their estate is they will be prayerful intercessors. Only, do not tell this to Mother Ambrosia."

## THE GRACE-FILLED POWER OF GOD

Once two sisters came from St. Petersburg to the Elder. The younger one was a prospective bride in a joyful mood; the older one was quiet, thoughtful and reverent. The first asked a blessing to be married, the other to go to a monastery. The Elder gave a prayer rope to the fiance and said to the elder sister: "What kind of monastery? You'll get married—but not at home; that's what you'll get!" And he named a province, to which she had never travelled. They both returned to the capital. The bride learned that her bridegroom had betrayed her. This brought about a terrible change, for her emotional attachment was deep. She comprehended the vanity of all that had occupied her before; her thoughts turned to God, and she soon entered a monastery. Meanwhile, the elder sister received a letter from that distant province from an aunt she had forgotten about, a devout woman who lived close to a women's monastery. She was summoning her to have a look at the life of the nuns there. But it turned out otherwise: while living with her aunt, the niece became acquainted with a man no longer young but quite suited to her by his character, and she married him.

A rich merchant once proposed marriage to a poor woman of the gentry because of her beauty. But the Elder said to her mother: "You need to refuse your bridegroom." The mother threw herself at him: "What do you mean, Batiushka?! Such a thing was beyond our wildest dreams; God sent him to an orphan, and you tell us to refuse!" But Fr. Ambrose answered, "Refuse this one; I have another bridegroom for your daughter, better than this one." "But what do we need a better one for? She's not going to marry a prince, is she?" said her mother. "I have such a great bridegroom that it is difficult to express; refuse the merchant." They turned the merchant down, and the girl became ill and died. Then they understood what kind of Bridegroom the Elder was talking about.

A young peasant from near the St. Tikhon of Kaluga Monastery conceived the idea of getting married, since his old mother was getting weak and there were no other women in the house. He went to the Elder on the Feast of the Dormition, but he advised him to wait until the Feast of the Protection of the Theotokos. Meanwhile, his mother was very dissatisfied with the Elder's advice. The Feast of the Protection arrived; but Batiushka said, "Wait around until Theophany, then we'll see." The old woman was greatly upset; the young man had no peace from her: "The Elder's only rambling—stop loafing!" The young man came to the Elder on Theophany and declared that he could no longer endure his mother's scolding. But Batiushka answered him: "I am afraid that you will not obey me; but my advice is—there is no need for you to get married; wait a bit." The peasant left and got married, and two months after his wedding he died.

A resident of Kozelsk by the name of Kapiton had an only son, a grown-up youth, clever and handsome. He decided to send him off to work and brought him to the Elder to obtain a blessing from him for this notion. They were both sitting in the corridor, and near them were several monks. The Elder came out to them. After he and his son had received a blessing, Kapiton stated that he wished to send his son off to work. The Elder approved his intention and advised him to send his son off to Kursk. Kapiton began to argue with the Elder: "In Kursk," he said, "we don't know anyone; but bless, Batiushka, to send him to Moscow." The Elder, in a joking tone, answered: "Moscow will knock his socks off and smack him with boards; let him go to Kursk." But Kapiton nevertheless did not obey the Elder and sent his son to Moscow, where he quickly found a good job. The employer into whose service he had entered was at this time constructing a building. Suddenly, several boards fell down from the top of the building and crushed both legs of the young man. His father was immediately informed by telegram. With bitter tears he came to the Elder to inform him of his sorrow, but it was already impossible to help his grief. The injured son was brought back from Moscow. He ailed for a long time, and though the wounds healed, he remained a cripple for good, unable to do any kind of work.

Once a brother in the Skete asked Elder Ambrose for a blessing to go to Mt. Athos. The Elder, as was his custom, said to him, jokingly: "Go to Athos and you'll be Agathon."* This brother wandered for a long time from monastery to monastery and finally reposed in St. Tikhon's Monastery, being tonsured into the mantia before his death with the name Agathon. Another monk related: "My relative, an old maid, came to Optina to pray and to ask Batiushka what she should do: should she enter a monastery or live at home with her family? Batiushka answered: 'Go home; your father has bought you some kind of corn kiln. Place it in the garden and there you will live.' When she returned home her father, greeting her, said: 'I bought you a corn kiln; I'll put it in the garden. There you can live, like in a monastery.'"

On August 6, 1883, a woman from the Belev district arrived in Optina and sought to see Fr. Ambrose; but due to the large number of people, she was in no way able to get to the hut in which Fr. Ambrose received women. Finally, she sought out a monk from her own hometown and implored him to ask the Elder how he wanted her to pray for her son—as for one living, or one dead? She had a grown son who was deaf and dumb; he could not even beg bread for himself. On July 8, on the Feast of the Kazan Icon of the Theotokos, he had gone to the village church and disappeared. They had not found him either in the forest or in the surrounding area. The Elder answered: "Why

---

*This rhymes in Russian.—Trans.

commemorate him as dead? You must commemorate him among the living—he will be found! Maybe they'll even bring him back soon." Then he added: "Her son, her son; but how does she herself live? She'd better change her life!" When these words of the Elder were passed on to the woman, she began to sob and confessed to a grievous sin.... Her son, in fact, was found after a while in the Odoevsky district.

In 1874 a young clerk from the city of B. prepared to go to Moscow to look for a job, but he went to visit Fr. Ambrose beforehand to ask for advice and a blessing. Receiving him, the Elder said: "It's not for everyone to live in Moscow—go to Voronezh." "But I don't know anyone there!" answered the young man. "That's nothing, you will get to know people!" said the Elder. In accordance with the blessing of the Elder, he went to Voronezh, lived there for a week and, not finding a job, set out on his return trip with bitterness. Having reached Tula, he stayed in a hotel and here became acquainted with a flour merchant from Voronezh, who hired him. After three years he got married and continued to live in the Voronezh Province, carrying on a large bread business.

The widow of an archpriest turned to the Elder for advice: Should she marry off her son, who had finished his studies at the seminary, or leave him to continue to study? The Elder blessed him to continue to study. But they did not obey his counsel. Enticed by a good position and by a rich and beautiful bride, the seminarian took a position as a priest. However, he was not happy for long. His family life unfolded very sadly, and after seven years he died of consumption in his parents' home.

The Priest S. reported concerning a priest whom he knew that when he was still a young man he thought to marry his second cousin. His father, a pious elderly priest, did not approve of a marriage with a relative and did not give his blessing. The mothers of the prospective bridegroom and bride, on the contrary, very much wanted this marriage. In view of the difference of opinion, it was decided to turn to the counsel of Elder Ambrose. They wrote him a letter, in which they laid out all the particulars of the matter and asked his blessing for the proposed marriage. The Elder answered: "According to the Church rules the marriage is allowable, but it will be unhappy."

The mothers, who very much wanted to arrange this marriage, paid no attention to the last words of the answer and even said: "The Elder is not a prophet; and, after all, he himself writes: 'The marriage is *allowable.*' Then, what more do we need to think about?"

The marriage took place. The young husband soon found a job as a public school teacher and left with his wife for the place where he would be working. Some time passed and it was learned that his wife would be a mother. At that time the inspector of public schools arrived for a review and demanded that the teacher's wife be sent away from the school quarters. Not knowing what to do, the teacher decided, finally, to send his wife to the city, to the public hospital where she, by mistake, was placed in the ward for infectious diseases. Here, right before her eyes a woman sick with typhus died giving birth. All of this so shook her, that she became insane, and then gave birth to a healthy child. From that time she never completely came to her senses. With time she became better, but once a month fits of wild behavior were always repeated, during which she had to be watched carefully, so that she would not cause harm to herself or to others. But once when the sick woman was left alone in the house through carelessness (at this time a fireworks expert was living in their apartment), she took a bottle of gunpowder that was in the pyrotechnician's room and threw it into the hot oven. A terrible explosion was heard. The house was destroyed, and fragments of the house severely wounded the sick woman. The husband of this unfortunate one later became a priest and, remembering the prediction of the Elder and his disobedience, bore his heavy cross with patience, seeing in it the special action of God's Providence, leading him to salvation through sorrows.

One nun conceived the idea of moving from a rich monastery in the western regions to the poor Shamordino Convent for Fr. Ambrose's sake. But later, fear fell upon her: what would happen to her after the Elder's death? With such thoughts she came to the hut for a blessing and stood there behind everyone. Suddenly the Elder, as if answering her doubt, said: "Remember that Elders, even after their death, do not abandon their monasteries." These words of the Elder calmed her completely.

The following incident happened with another Shamordino sister. She needed to turn to the Elder for the clarification of certain important questions concerning her interior life. This was during the Dormition Fast, in the last year of his life. There were many people. The Elder was extremely tired, and, having no hope of reaching him for a conversation, she wrote him a letter. After two days she was with the Elder and he gave complete answers to all the points in her letter, recalling himself what else had been written in it. The sister left the Elder consoled and calmed, not suspecting, however, what a miracle of clairvoyance the Elder had performed for her. In October the Elder reposed and, after six weeks, while sorting through the papers in his cell they found a still-sealed letter with his name on it. Since on the envelope there was also written who it was from, it was returned to her. What was the surprise of that sister when she saw her own letter—which she had written during the Dormition Fast and about which she had received such detailed answers—still sealed.

THE FORMER Abbess of Kashira Monastery, Tikhona, relates: "After the repose of Elder Macarius, Abbess Paulina and the sisters of the orphaned Belev Convent began to turn to the two closest disciples of the reposed Elder—Hieroschemamonks Ambrose and Hilarion." The person writing the following account about Fr. Ambrose at first turned to Fr. Hilarion with her spiritual needs, but after his repose she gave herself over in complete obedience to Elder Ambrose. The present narrative was written by her back in 1870, before she was the spiritual daughter of Elder Ambrose, and therefore her impartial attitude is even more trustworthy towards the wondrous clairvoyance of the Elder, who at that time amazed the whole Belev Convent:

"There entered into the Convent two aged sisters in their 70's—Paraskeva and Maria. They were born of a middle-class family of Orel, and so they were called Orlovskaya, since the sisters of the Monastery did not know their surname. At that time Abbess Paulina began the construction of a church. Due to this matter she travelled more than once to St. Petersburg to see Bishop Nicander, who had been summoned, in his turn, to the Holy Synod. During one of their absences, the elder sister, Paraskeva Orlovskaya, came down with pneumonia and died on the third day. Because of the absence of the Abbess, however, she was not tonsured into the mantia, as had always been done earlier in Belev Convent. For the younger sister, Maria, who remained among the living, this event was exceedingly sorrowful. She poured forth bitter tears and with her sorrow went to Optina, to Elder Ambrose. The Elder consoled and calmed her concerning the fate of her reposed sister, citing an example from the *Kiev Caves Patericon,* in which there is a narrative concerning a monk who received the tonsure from the invisible hand of an angel of God. Maria began to feel more at peace over her reposed sister. Her thoughts and cares shifted to the renovation of her cell, which needed repair and, at the general blessing at the Elder's cell, she spoke to him and asked his blessing for this endeavor. But Batiushka, in front of everyone—and many from Belev were present—answered her: 'Don't worry about your cell. Your cell will be a simple coffin. Put all your effort into the passage to the life beyond the grave.' And, turning to the Belev sisters who were there as choir singers, he said to them: 'Leave off confessing; you need to be dismissed to go home quickly to bury Masha!' They returned home right away. To the questions of the Belev sisters: 'Why did you come back so soon?' they replied that Batiushka had urged them to leave for the burial of Maria Orlovskaya, who in full vigor and health had remained by the blessing of the Elder for an additional week in Optina. She was told to prepare for Holy Communion, together with Unction, and for tonsure into the mantia. Maria obeyed the will of the Elder without contradiction. He tonsured her himself and changed her name to Marionilla. Sending her off to Belev, he personally wrote to Abbess Paulina, saying that he found it unavoidable to tonsure Maria and begged forgiveness for acting in this way, without contacting her earlier. Maria returned in full health; it was easy to understand how the sisters met her, amazed by the news in advance of her impending repose. And what happened? After her arrival, she appeared before the Abbess, gave her the letter from the Elder and, having asked forgiveness for all that had happened with her, she returned to her cell. That very night she fell ill with encephalitis, was unconscious for three days, and on the fourth she reposed peacefully and calmly—she just fell asleep. The repose of Maria made an astonishing impression on everyone."

FR. GEORGE Kosov, the now-famous priest of the village of Spas-Chekriak, of the Orel Province, related the following: "When I arrived at my parish, I was seized with panic: What am I supposed to do here?! No way to live, no way to serve! The house was old—delapidated; the church—you go to serve and you might fall through the floor boards. There was almost no income; the parishioners were far from the church and from the clergy. The people were poor; in the best of times they could barely feed themselves. What could I do here? I was then a young priest, inexperienced; on top of that my health was weak, and I coughed up blood. My matushka was an orphan, poor, without any dowry. Consequently, neither from here nor from there was there any support, and I also had younger brothers on my hands. It remained only to run away. That's what I contemplated. At that time the glory of Elder Ambrose was great. Optina Monastery was thirty-six miles from us. Once in summer, on a sleepless night I raised myself up from my pillow. It was neither light nor daybreak; I put my knapsack on my shoulders and off I went to him for a blessing—to leave the parish. At 4:00 in the afternoon I was already at Optina. Batiushka didn't know me, either by sight or by having heard about me. I went into his 'hut' and there were already people there—a crowd, waiting for Batiushka to come out. I stood on the side to wait. I look, and out he comes, and straight at me through everyone he beckons me to come to him: 'You, priest! What on earth are you contemplating? to abandon all? Eh? Don't you know Who assigns priests? And you want to leave?!.. His church, see, is old; it has started to fall down.... But you—build a new one, a big, stone one, and warm; and the floor—make it wooden. They'll bring sick people there, so it will be warm for them. Go home, priest, go; and kick that nonsense out of your head. Remember—a church; build a church, like I'm telling you. Go, priest; God bless you!'

"But I had no sign of priestly garb on. I couldn't utter a word. I went home right away. I'm walking and thinking: what on earth is this? I have to build a stone church? At home you're almost dying from hunger, and now build a church. How skillfully he consoles; there was nothing to say.

"I came home and somehow dodged my wife's questions; well, what was I supposed to say to her?! I said only that the

Elder didn't bless me to ask for a transfer. What was going on in my soul then, you can't even put into words....

"A nagging depression came over me. I want to pray but no prayers go on in my mind. I didn't talk with people, not even with my wife. I became lost in thought. And I began to hear, both night and day, mostly at night, some kind of strange voices: 'Get out,' they say, 'quick! You're alone and there are lots of us! How are you going to fight with us?! We'll be the death of you altogether!....' Hallucinations, it must be.... Well, whatever it was, it finally got to the point that not only was I unable to pray, now blasphemous thoughts began to pop into my head.... Night comes. I can't sleep—and some kind of power throws me right off the bed onto the floor, and not in a dream, but right when I'm wide awake. It just picks me up and tosses me from the bed to the floor. And the voices, even more dreadful, more terrible, more persistent: 'Get away, get away from us!'

"Terrified, barely remaining sane from the fear I was going through, I again rushed to Fr. Ambrose. Fr. Ambrose, as soon as he saw me, straightway, without questioning me at all, says to me:

"'Well, what are you scared of, priest? He's one, and there are two of you.'

"'How is that, Batiushka?' I say.

"'Christ God and you—see, that comes out to two. And the enemy—he's one. Go home,' he says, 'and do not be afraid of anything that's before you; and the church, the big stone church, and warm—don't forget to build it. God bless you!'

"And with that, I left. I come home, and it's as if a mountain had fallen from my heart. And all fear fell away from me. Right then I began to pray to God. I put an analogion in the church behind the left cliros before the icon of the Heavenly

Queen, lit a lampada, lit a candle; and I began, all alone in the church, to read a Canon to Her. I began to add some of the other prayers.

"I look and, after a week, someone else came alone, stood by himself in a corner, and together with me prayed to God. Then another, a third, and already they began to gather and fill the church...."

We will add to this that now, by the care of Fr. George, a large stone church, a hospice, orphanages and schools have been built, and from all the ends of Russia worshippers come for advice, a blessing, prayer and consolation.

HERE IS YET another striking occurrence. A master iconostasis builder from K. conveyed the following. "Not long before the repose of the Elder, about two years, I had to go to Optina for money. We were building an iconostasis there, and I was due to receive a fairly large sum of money from the Superior for this work. I received my money and before my departure visited Elder Ambrose to be blessed for the return trip. I was in a hurry to go home; I was waiting to receive a large order on the next day—ten thousand rubles—and the customers were to be, without fail, at my place in K. on the next day. That day, as usual, there was a swarm of people at the Elder's. He knew about me, that I was waiting, and he told me through his cell attendant to visit him in the evening for tea.

"Even though I needed to hurry home, the honor and joy to be with the Elder and have tea with him was so great that I decided to put off my trip until evening, in full confidence that, even if I had to travel all night, I would manage to get there on time. Evening came, and I went to the Elder. He received me so gladly and so joyfully that I didn't even feel the ground under my feet. Batiushka, our angel, kept me for a pretty long time—it was beginning to get dark, and he said to me: 'Well, go with

God. Spend the night here, and I bless you to go to Liturgy tomorrow; and from Liturgy, stop by to have tea with me.'

"'How can this be?!' I thought. But I didn't dare contradict the Elder. I spent the night, attended the Liturgy, went to the Elder for tea, but I was grieving over my customers and thought to myself, 'Maybe I'll make it to K. at least by evening.' But it didn't work out that way! We finished tea. I wanted to say to the Elder: 'Bless me to go home,' but he didn't let me utter a word: 'Come to me today to spend the night,' he says. My legs were giving way, but I didn't object.

"The day passed, the night passed! In the morning I had already become bolder, and I thought: 'No matter what, I am leaving today; maybe my customers waited for me with the money.' No, you'll never make it! Again the Elder didn't give me a chance to open my mouth. 'Go to the All-Night Vigil,' he says, 'and tomorrow to Liturgy. Spend the night here again today!' What a strange thing! At this point I really began to get upset and, to confess, I sinned against the Elder: 'Well, here's a clairvoyant! He just does not know what's going on with me; by his mercy a profitable business has now gone right out of my hands.' And I was so agitated at the Elder that I can't even express it to you. I wasn't able to pray at the Vigil that time—there just knocks around in my head: 'Here's your Elder for you! Here's your clairvoyant!... Now your wages are whistling by....' Ach, how annoyed I was at that time!

"But my Elder, as luck would have it, well, just as if—Lord forgive me—in mockery of me, meets me so joyfully after the Vigil!... I became bitter and hurt: 'And what,' I think, 'is he so happy about?' But all the same I did not dare to express my grief aloud. I spent the third night sort of well. During the night my sorrow eased somewhat: 'You can't bring back what has floated away, and it floated off right through your fingers....' In the morning I come from Liturgy to the Elder, and he says to me,

'Well, now it is time for you to go home! Go with God! God bless you! But after a while, do not forget to thank God!!'

"And right then all my grief fell away. I left Optina for home, and my heart was so light and joyful that I can't describe it.... Only, why did Batiushka say, 'After a while, do not forget to thank God?...' It must be, I thought, for the fact that the Lord made me worthy to be in church for three days in a row. I went home in no hurry, and I didn't even think about my customers; I was so gratified that Batiushka had treated me so well.

"I arrived home, and what do you think? I'm at the gate, and my customers are right behind me; they were three days later than our arrangement. Well, I think: Ach, my grace-filled little Elder! This is the real thing—*Wondrous are Thy works, O Lord!* However, this all didn't end here. You listen to what happened next! A little time went by after that. Our Fr. Ambrose died. Two years after his righteous repose, my senior foreman became sick. He was a trustworthy man; not just a worker, but real gold. He lived with me continually for more than twenty years. He was sick unto death. They sent me for a priest, to confess and commune him while he was still conscious. Only, I look and the priest comes to me from the dying man and says, 'The sick one is calling for you; he wants to see you. Hurry, before he dies!' I come to the sick man and he, as soon as he sees me, raises himself up somehow on his elbows, looks at me, and now he begins to cry: 'Forgive my sin, boss! I actually wanted to kill you!...'

"'What are talking about; God be with you! You're delirious....'

"'No, boss, I really wanted to kill you. Remember, once you were three days late coming home from Optina? Well we—there were three of us—by my arrangement, we lay in wait for you on the road three days in a row under a bridge; we were envious of the money you were bringing from Optina for the iconostasis. You would not have been alive at this time but the Lord, by someone's prayers, saved you from a death without repentance. Forgive me, the wretch; for God's sake, let my soul go in peace.'

"'May God forgive you as I forgive you!'

"Right then my sick one started wheezing and began to die. May his soul be granted the Kingdom of Heaven! Great was his sin, but great was his repentance!"

On one occasion, the Elder insistently detained one of his spiritual daughters, Mrs. B., and her son in Optina Monastery for an entire day and night, and thereby protected them from leaving on the very train with which the Kukuevsky catastrophe occurred.

HERE IS a noteworthy incident which took place with Constantine N. Leontiev, who was then residing in Optina Monastery.* After the Elder's move to Shamordino, he began

---

*C. N. Leontiev, the famous writer and publicist, was at one time the Russian Consul to Turkey. At first utterly cold and indifferent to the Faith and to religion, he was completely reborn spiritually and became a profoundly believing Christian on one of his visits to Mt. Athos, under the influence of conversations with the Elders Jerome and Macarius who lived there. Then, after his return to Russia he became acquainted with Optina and Elder Ambrose.

Fr. Ambrose had a strong influence on Leontiev in the last years of his life. In one of his letters, Leontiev himself related that for the first five years of his acquaintance with the Elder he was in no way able to go up to him, become close with him, or receive any spiritual benefit from him. However, the constant and softening effect of the Elder exerted its influence on Leontiev, and in 1879 a sharp change took place in his relationship with the Elder. He began with love to be obedient to him in all things, and from this time up to the end of his life, for eleven years, he remained his faithful and dedicated disciple:

to think of leaving. In August of 1891, two months before the Elder's repose, he came to him at Shamordino, and, having received a blessing from him to move to Sergiev Posad, he bid farewell to him. The Elder blessed him with special love and then said: "We will soon see each other." Leontiev at first did not attach any particular significance to these words, but when after two months he learned of the Elder's repose, he became agitated and began to say: "That means that I will die soon, too!" And, in fact, forty days did not even pass before Leontiev came down with pneumonia and reposed in November of that same year. It is further noteworthy that Leontiev, suffering from a very grievous internal illness, thought with fear that his death from this disease would be quite agonizing. But the Elder always

---

"In 1874 I arrived from Turkey infused with the Athonite air and soon went to Optina. I took an extreme liking to Elder Ambrose; but all the same, for five years I did not receive from him such consolation as I had received from the more severe Fr. Jerome of Athos. And my emotional life was very complicated, difficult, very tangled—both in matters of the heart and matters of the home, etc. The most terrible thing of all was the fact that I had to speak so briefly with Fr. Ambrose; he would only give me the final conclusion, without any explanation. This was torture—after Fr. Jerome, who talked with me, questioned me, talked about himself, explained, blessed, etc. Every time [with Elder Ambrose] I heard, 'Speak more succinctly, I'm tired. I am very weak; tell me without a preface. An abbess is waiting; a merchant's widow has been waiting for three days: faster!' etc.

"Fr. Clement [Sederholm] helped out, of course; he made every effort to accustom me to him. I tried—for five years I went to Optina and greatly loved to go there, but much more because of Fr. Clement than Fr. Ambrose.

"When Fr. Clement died and I was sitting in Fr. Ambrose's corridor, waiting for him to call me in—I prayed before an icon of the Savior and said: 'Lord! Instruct the Elder that he be supportive and consoling. Thou knowest my struggle!' And sure enough, Fr. Ambrose on this occasion kept me for a long time, calmed me and taught me; and from that minute everything went differently. I began to heed him with love, and he clearly loved me and consoled me in every way!...."

comforted him and said, "No, you will not die from this illness." That is how it turned out: Leontiev died from pneumonia, one of the least painful ailments.

In one of his letters, Leontiev communicated the following instance of the clairvoyance of Elder Ambrose: "Near my former place, Kudinovo in the Meshchevksy district, is the village Karmanova of the city of Raevsk. In Karmanova there is a young peasant, George; he was a soldier and he, among fifteen others, once had to choose lots to see who could have a ticket to return home. He prayed: 'Prophet Elijah! Fr. Ambrose! Dormition of the Mother of God! Help me to go home!' The lot fell according to his wishes. George promised to go to Optina. Having returned home, he began, as usually happens, to put it off, to forget. Suddenly he became gravely ill. He lay in bed for a long time, but was conscious. Of course, he began to repent and to pray again. Once he was lying there and saw—an old monk entered in a short overcoat and an old cap, approached him and said: 'God will help you, but you have to fulfill your promise.' And he left. His family was in the house, but no one besides him saw it. Since this was not a dream (and his relatives testify that he was not sleeping), this greatly amazed him, of course. Soon after this he got better and told his relatives about his vision. He had not only never seen Fr. Ambrose himself, he had never even seen his portrait, but when he heard that the landowner had a small photograph, he went to Raevsk and saw that it was the same old man! The other day he came here [to Optina] and the Elder received him. When he had related everything to him, Fr. Ambrose said: 'This is according to your faith. God sent it to you because you are not a drunk, you live well with your family, and you never use bad language.' This especially surprised both George and us. George really is that way, and never curses or uses foul words! Fr. Ambrose, of course, had no idea about him before this visit. (His village is forty miles from here.)"

ONE OF THE LAST incidences of the Elder's clairvoyance was the following: During the commemorative meal at Shamordino, right after the funeral service for Fr. Ambrose, there occurred an event that made a strong impression on everyone present. One of those at the meal, a spiritual daughter of the Elder, together with her husband, had once asked the Elder's advice and blessing to adopt a child. In 1890, in almost the middle of October the Elder had replied to her request: "Wait a while; after a year I myself will point out a child for you to adopt." During the funeral meal the couple remembered the words of the Elder with sorrow and regretted that his repose did not grant them the fulfillment of his promise. But they did not even manage to finish the meal when a rumor spread that in a wing of the Superior's building, where the guests were having lunch, they had found an abandoned infant. When the childless woman heard that, she rushed to the little one with a feeling of deep contrition and cried out: "It was Batiushka who sent me a daughter." And the child was taken by her and subsequently adopted.

Besides the instances of clairvoyance, there are also many known cases when by the prayers of the Elder sick people received healing. Such occurrences happened both during the life of the Elder and after his repose. During his life many turned to him with requests to pray for the healing of severe illnesses. And the greater part were as a last resort, when the skills of physicians proved to be powerless. In such cases the Elder most often counseled them to make use of the Mystery of Unction, and he would explain, both by letter and personally, that by means of this Holy Mystery a person receives absolution of all forgotten and perplexing sins and that many incorrectly postpone this Sacrament until their repose is imminent.

Sometimes the Elder prescribed the serving of a Moleben before local wonderworking icons, or he sent people to the St. Tikhon Hermitage (eleven miles from Kaluga) to pray to St. Tikhon of Kaluga and to bathe in the healing spring. But sometimes, by the grace given him by God, he would heal through his own direct prayers, as the following incident will show. The aforementioned spiritual daughter of Fr. Ambrose, A.A. Shishkova recounts: "In 1877 I was very sick for almost a year with a severe throat ailment, the result of a cold. I was barely able to swallow only liquid food. At that time I was living and undergoing treatment in the country. The doctors, seeing that the illness was worsening, advised me to go to Moscow, call for a consultation, and live abroad in a warm climate. At that time there arrived at the neighboring Troekurovo Convent Mrs. Klyuchareva, who was living with her granddaughters on her estate near Optina.

"Upon learning that I was so sick, she suggested to the nuns that they give me her advice—to write to Optina Elder Ambrose and ask his prayers. At the beginning I did not pay attention to these words, but seeing the worsening of my painful condition, I decided to write to the Elder (although I did not know him), requesting his prayers for me. Batiushka soon answered me: 'Come to Optina without doubting for a moment; only have a Moleben served to the Savior, the Mother of God, St. John the Soldier, and St. Nicholas the Wonderworker.' The suggestion to go to Optina greatly frightened me, since I knew how long and difficult a trip lay before me. Meanwhile, from the illness my strength was exhausted and I was unable to get up. 'How would I leave?' I thought. But the emphasized words 'without doubting for a moment' fortified my spirit and my strength. Despite the plea of my children not to go and the persuasions of the doctor, I invited a priest, had a Moleben served and left the next day, at first in a coach, then by railroad and then again by horse. Upon my arrival in Optina, I sent to learn from Batiushka in the Skete when I could come to him. He sent word that I should immediately rest and that on the next day I should attend the Liturgy and go to him from there.... And that is what I did.... When I went into Batiushka's room with Mrs. Klyuchareva, she, kneeling before him, began to beg with tears: 'Batiushka, heal her, as you are able to heal.' The Elder was greatly angered at these words and ordered Mrs. Klyuchareva to leave immediately. To me he said: 'It is not I who heal, but the Heavenly Queen; turn to Her and pray.' In the corner of the room there hung an icon of the Most Holy Theotokos. Then he asked where my throat hurt. I pointed to the right side of my throat. The Elder, with a prayer, made the sign of the cross three times over the painful spot. Right then, it was as if I received some kind of strength. Having received a blessing from Batiushka and thanked him for the kind reception, I withdrew. I came to the guest house, where my husband and an acquaintance, Lady V.D. M.-P. were waiting for me. In front of them I tried to swallow a piece of bread, to determine whether I had become better by the prayers of the Elder. Previously I had been unable to swallow anything hard. And suddenly, what joy I had! Without pain, very easily, I was able to eat anything, and up to this time the pain has not returned once—and fifteen years have already gone by!"

WE WILL NOW present the account of Mrs. V.D. M.-P. concerning the miraculous recovery of her son: "On May 27, 1878, our fourteen-year-old son Dimitry came down with an incomprehensible ailment. He suffered from pain in his ear, head, and jawbone, with a strong discharge from his right ear and a fever that reached 104 degrees. In the midst of this he lost his hearing. At night he groaned and cried out from the pain and was delirious. His sleep was not restful but interrupted, and he often spent entire nights without sleep. We attributed these sufferings to an internal abscess in the ear and greatly feared what would happen. Dr. Belaev, the invited doctor who was a specialist in diseases of the ear, declared to us after a careful examination of the patient that our son had a very serious case of catarrh of the ear which had occurred as a result of an inflammation of the middle ear, and that this persistent catarrh would produce a perforation in the eardrum. This illness was considered to be untreatable. Dr. Belaev began to console us, saying that there was hope in the youth of the patient, that in this illness great patience is necessary, that in the remote future it would be possible to hope for recovery, and so on. He categorically denied the presence of an abscess. After two weeks, during which the suffering sometimes increased and sometimes lessened, the doctor advised us to take our son to the country for fresh air, since he was manifesting severe anemia, terrible paleness, and loss of strength. Heeding the advice of the doctor, we carefully took our son to the village (in the Mozhaisk district of the Moscow Province), hoping in the salutary influence of a change of air. On the very day of our arrival, the sufferings of our son increased so much that his face became distorted, and he could open his eyes only with difficulty. Quite often, anguished cries could be heard throughout the entire house.... With each day, his suffering and weakness increased, so that it was difficult for him to raise his head from the pillow, and the smallest noise or sound caused him extreme suffering. In general, his condition seemed hopeless, but the Lord is great and merciful. On June 24, my husband arrived from Moscow and suggested that the whole family go to Optina, to pray and prepare for Holy Communion, and to ask for the blessings and prayers of Fr. Ambrose. When we left, we entrusted our sick son to the care of his teacher and his old nurse, both of whom loved him and in whom we were confident.

"Having arrived at Optina on June 26—my husband, two daughters, a nephew, an adopted girl, a maid and I—we set out for Fr. Ambrose at the Skete and told Batiushka about the condition of our sick son, begging his prayers for him. Batiushka calmly answered us, smiling amicably: 'It's nothing, it's nothing; be at peace, all will pass—only pray to God.' We began to visit Fr. Ambrose every day, and Batiushka was so kind that he conversed with us at length and supported all of us, saying, 'The prayers of parents reach God; only believe in His mercy and pray, and the Lord will console you.' We told him that we did not hope in our sinful prayers, but in his intercession and holy prayers. He led us to understand that the Lord would grant us joy. At the advice and blessing of the Elder, we stayed in Optina for another three days in order to prepare for Holy Communion. Confession with him left a deep impression on us.

"On July 1, having received news of our son that his unbearably painful condition was getting worse with each day and that, evidently, we must expect the end soon, we decided without delay to receive the blessing of Fr. Ambrose and immediately set out on the return trip. But Batiushka blessed us to leave only on the following day. On July 2, we all came to the Elder after the early Liturgy, at 9:00 in the morning. He blessed us all with kind departing words and, turning to my husband and me, said: 'Don't worry and don't be distressed; go in peace and hope in God's mercy, and you will be consoled. Pray to God; pray to God! You will be made happy.' Then he gave me two small crosses hung on little belts with prayers woven into them—one to St. Tikhon of Zadonsk and one to St. Nicholas the Wonderworker—one for me and one for our son, with the words: 'Give your son my blessing.' As we left we once again earnestly begged his prayers. 'Alright, alright,' he answered quickly, and immediately added, 'and you pray to God.' Having blessed everyone, he dismissed us.

"After an hour we headed home to our son. We arrived at the station (five miles from our estate) on July 3 at 4:00 in the morning. The coachmen who were waiting for us with the carriage told us that our son's suffering had greatly increased since our departure and that his health had worsened with each day. Especially on July 2 he suffered unbearably, and his cries pierced the soul of each person that they reached. He had not slept the entire day, nor did he sleep on the two previous nights, and his strength had completely left him. The teacher and nurse were just about to send to Moscow for the doctor when our telegram concerning our return from Optina was received. With inexpressible trepidation and depression of heart we left the station.... Suddenly, almost a mile from our property, my thoughts were interrupted by the sudden halt of our carriage. Our son's teacher rode up to us at a gallop, and at this moment I thought that all was surely over and that Dimitry was no longer in this world. But the teacher explained to us with great joy that some kind of unusual occurrence had happened with our son, or a crisis (as he put it), and that at the present time he was completely well. 'Well?' We did not believe our ears. 'Yes,' he repeated. 'Dimitry is completely well.' He told us, in short, how his miraculous recovery had occurred. After the agonizing last day, July 2, the dying boy, exhausted and broken, suddenly fell into a sound sleep at 11:00 at night, and his sleep was quiet and calm. He slept in this way until 4:30 in the morning. When he woke up he was completely well, cheerful and strong. The discharge from his ear had ceased, and his hearing had returned; only his paleness remained. 'Now he is up,' added the teacher, 'and dressed, and wants to meet you on his feet.' It is difficult to convey what we felt at this news. Tears of joy and deep gratitude to the Lord flowed from our eyes. In our souls we fervently glorified and thanked God and the loving intercessor, Fr. Ambrose....

"We hurried home. We didn't ride, we flew. When we entered the hall of our home, the door of Mitya's room opened; and on the threshold there appeared our still terribly pale, but healthy and happy son. His head was still wrapped in white kerchiefs, and at that moment he reminded us of the resurrected Lazarus. He joyfully threw himself at us to embrace us, and there was no end to our mutual interrogations. I gave him the cross I had brought, sent to him by Fr. Ambrose, and Mitya kissed it and put it on with reverence. From that day his strength increased more and more, and his appetite returned; the discharge from his ear never reappeared, and his hearing became equally good in both ears. After a week he was already capable of taking on studies and riding horses.... Later that year we invited doctors for a consultation, and after a long examination of our son Dr. Belaev was unable to determine in which ear the eardrum was perforated. Only after we indicated the right ear to him did he notice a small scar and had to admit that this was a supernatural matter. This is an absolutely true though, perhaps, inept description of the miraculous event accomplished in our family through the prayers of the dear, loving Elder of Optina Hermitage, Batiushka Ambrose, the memory of whom will never be erased from our grateful hearts."

Once in the summer," related the Optina monk, Fr. P., "I had to be in Kaluga. On the return trip to Optina I was overtaken by a priest with his wife and eleven-year-old boy. Conversing about Batiushka Ambrose, the priest, Fr. John, said that his parish was not far from the Podborky station and that this boy, his son, had been born through the prayers of Elder Ambrose. The priest's wife confirmed the words of her husband.

'It is the absolute truth,' she said. 'We had no children. We longed for one and often came to Batiushka, who consoled us, saying that he would pray to God for us. And this very boy was born to us. Besides him we have no other children.' The priest then told us the following story: 'One time our son's eye began to hurt. My wife and I went to Kozelsk with him to the doctor, but we stopped beforehand at Optina and came to Fr. Ambrose. The Elder, having blessed the child, began to lightly strike the sick eye. My hair stood on end from the danger that the Elder would injure the boy's eye. His mother started crying. And what happened? We left the Elder and came to the guest house, and the boy declared to us that his eye was better and the pain in it had subsided; later it passed altogether. Having thanked Batiushka, we returned home, glorifying and thanking God.'"

**INTERESTING ALSO** is the account of the skete monk, Nestor. "On December 1, 1873 I was tonsured into the mantia, together with several of the brothers. I was received under the spiritual direction of the ever-memorable Elder, Fr. Ambrose. In May of the following year I had the intention of visiting my birthplace. After having prayed at the graves of our ever-memorable Elders, I went to the Superior, Fr. Isaac, and explained my request to him. Having heard me out, he then said: 'Have you been to the Elder?' I answered: 'No, Batiushka, I haven't been there yet.' 'Well then, go to him—see what he says. I, brother, have decided once and for all: If he blesses and finds that this trip will not be to your detriment, then I will not keep you; only don't stay there for too long. The sooner you are back in your cell, the better. For a monk to live for long in the world is—you know—not beneficial. It is good there, only not for our brother.' I went to the Elder filled with enthusiasm, but I was unable to see him that day, since there were many people with him, both lay people and nuns. Certain that the Elder would not keep me from going, I informed certain of the brothers that I would soon go home. Meanwhile, more than a week passed, and I was still completely unable to get to the Elder. Finally I succeeded in catching him alone. I went into Batiushka's cell, prayed before the holy icons, and then bowed before him to receive a blessing. Blessing me, he said, 'God bless you to do good.' I still had not managed to say anything to him, but he already answered my thoughts: 'You came for a decision concerning your trip?' I said, 'Just so, Batiushka.' 'Really, brother—it hasn't come to me to let you go like you want; you see, it is better not to repent afterwards, when it is already too late.' I was extremely bewildered by this unexpected development. I said to him: 'What is it, kind Batiushka; is it likely that something unfavorable will happen to me on the road?' Batiushka said: 'I, brother, do not have the gift of prophecy; I do not know what might happen with you, but whatever has been given me to know about you, I have said. To tell the truth, something makes me hate to let you go.' Batiushka spoke these words in so kindly and fatherly a way that I was even unable to keep myself from tears. For some reason my heart began to ache, and I couldn't bear to part with the Elder.

"I said: 'Batiushka, I have decided to stay—I won't go.' 'And it will be good for you,' said the Elder; 'your home won't go anywhere; maybe next year you can visit, if we will be alive and well.' I said to him: 'Forgive me, Batiushka, for my frankness; it will be awkward for me before the brothers. I am ashamed that I prepared myself for so long, went to the Abbot to say goodby, and now I'm staying.' To this Batiushka said seriously, 'So what? Shame is not smoke, it doesn't get in your eyes. It is shameful, brother, for a monk to do his own will; it is better to be the disciple of a disciple than to live by one's own will. The writings of the Holy Fathers speak about this. One should be ashamed not before others, but before

God and one's conscience, which is an uncorruptible and impartial judge. To be obedient to the counsel of one's spiritual father is not shameful, but soul-saving and necessary; and he who is not obedient to good counsel is punished. No one will ask you, no one has any need to; but if someone does ask, say that it is probably not the will of God for you to travel.' After these wise and loving words of the Elder, how joyful in soul I became. I was ready to thank the Elder for not letting me go, as though he had guarded me from some misfortune.... What happened after that? Suddenly, after a week, I unexpectedly came down with typhoid fever. The disease progressed quickly in me and did not respond to treatment. There was a rapid loss of strength. I became worse and worse. I was between life and death. The doctors, Fr. Niphon of the Monastery and Dr. Kustov of Kozelsk, declared that there was no hope for recovery. I was given Unction and received the Holy Mysteries every day. Then, with the blessings of the Superior and the Elder, I was tonsured into the Schema, as is usually done for monks who are close to death. I was then only twenty-eight years old. The fathers and brothers came to bid me farewell.

"My mental faculties did not fail me—I recognized everyone, but was so weak that I could not open my eyes and it was extremely difficult to speak.... Finally, our Abbot came to say farewell and to bless me to go to the world beyond the grave. Our doctor, Fr. Niphon, was there. Although weakly, I heard what the Abbot said to the doctor: 'Behold our life, father! Was it so long ago that he came to me in perfect health, asking for a blessing to go home? It's good what the Elder so wisely did—surely at the suggestion of God—that he talked him out of going. And I had a mind to let him go. You see, I would have dismissed him to the other world, and later it would have been on my conscience!'

## THE GRACE-FILLED POWER OF GOD

"The doctor said: 'He would, without fail, have gotten sick on the road and died, only probably more quickly. Here we could at least treat him. And, of course, communing of the Holy Mysteries greatly strengthens the severely ill. But on the road he would not have had this. Now he receives Communion every day, after which he becomes more joyful.'

"The Abbot came up to me and, having blessed me, said: 'Forgive me, Fr. Nestor! You are prepared as much as is possible, so now let the will of God be done! We all have to die sometime—it is an unavoidable path, only may the Lord lead you to death with pure repentance.'

"During the course of my illness, I had mentally called upon the help of the prayers of the Elder, my spiritual father, Batiushka Ambrose. In the hours of my unbearable sufferings I had even sent to him to beg his holy prayers—that I would either die or have just a little relief, since I could not endure it. But as it happened, each time they came from the Elder and said: 'Batiushka is praying for you and sends you his blessing,' I felt a little better, and even joyful. I remember one time—it was early in the morning, and the Elder was probably resting after his morning rule—it became so difficult for me, that I decided to disturb him, that is, to beg for his holy prayers. The person I sent quickly returned and brought me a small, sealed vial of holy water from Pochaev, which Batiushka sent with instructions: to pour it into a bottle, adding clean water until it was full, and to give me a little to drink and moisten my head with it. The good brothers who were taking care of me zealously fulfilled his order and, by the prayers of the Elder, from that time I became better. The fever gradually subsided and I began, little by little, to come back to life, to the amazement of many, especially the doctors, who had given up on me entirely. Of late, they had even stopped treating me and had left me to the will of God.... Our doctor, Fr. Niphon, bewildered after this, asked the Elder: by what miracle had I remained alive? To this the Elder answered him: 'That which is impossible for man is possible for God, Who gives life and takes it away.... Upon such hopelessly sick ones is fulfilled the word of the ancestor of God, David, who said: *With chastisement hath the Lord chastened me, but he hath not given me over unto death* (Psalm 117:18).'"

THE NUN A. of Shamordino gave the following account about herself: "In the spring of 1882, at Pascha, my throat began to hurt; a sore appeared, and I was able neither to eat nor drink. The doctor stated that I had tuberculosis of the throat and that I would certainly die. I set off to see Batiushka. He said to me: 'From the well that is behind the Skete, take some water into your mouth and rinse your throat three times a day.' After three days he himself summoned me. Taking three eggs from under his pillow and taking out the yolks, he poured the whites all together. Then he blessed Fr. Joseph, his cell attendant, to bring water from the well. He blessed the water and ordered that I be massaged with it in my cell, and that I eat the egg whites. When I came to my cell, I was massaged and was given the egg whites, which I swallowed without pain. After this I slept for an entire day and night, and after awakening I felt that my illness was gone and that I had completely recovered. Without delay, I went to the Elder. The nuns did not recognize me and thought that it was not I, but my own sister. Batiushka met me and blessed me, saying that St. Tikhon of Kaluga had healed me. From that time I have not suffered from throat pain. When I announced my healing to the doctor, he said that a miracle had been performed over me and that my illness could not have been cured by natural means."

IN IMITATION of one of his predecessors in eldership, Hieroschemamonk Leonid, Fr. Ambrose sometimes liked to conceal his miraculous help with humorous words or gestures, to divert the attention of witnesses. For instance, a monk once came to the Elder with a terrible toothache. Walking past him, the Elder hit him in the teeth with his fist with all his might and merrily added: "Well done, eh?" "Well done, Batiushka," the monk answered, to general laughter, "but it really hurts." However, upon leaving the Elder he felt that the pain had gone, and it did not return afterwards.

Peasants noticed well this characteristic of Fr. Ambrose, and those who suffered from headaches would say to him: "Batiushka Abrosim, hit me; my head hurts."

There were even more amazing cases. Though he never went anywhere out of the Monastery due to his sickliness, he would, however, appear to people hundreds of miles away, who had never seen him and had never even heard of him. At these times he either warned them against some sort of danger, or gave instructions to the sick as to how to be delivered from their illness, or healed them right then.

Thus, the skete hieromonk V. related: "Mrs. A.D.K. was severely ill and lay in bed for several days, unable to get up. One time she saw that Elder Ambrose entered her room, came up to the bed, took her by the hand, and said: 'Get up, that's enough of being sick!' And then he vanished from her sight. At that point she felt so strong that she rose from her sickbed, and the next day she set out on foot from Kozelsk to Shamordino (where Batiushka was then residing) to thank him for the healing. Batiushka received her, but did not bless her to make this known before his repose."

The nun Hilariona Ponomarieva of the Kashira Convent in the Tula Province conveyed the following in writing: "Once when I was severely ill, two days before the Feast of St. Nicholas (December 6, 1888), I grieved and wept over the fact that due to my sickness I would have to sit in my cell for the Feast, being unable to go to the temple of God. And I became so very ill that at 9:00 in the evening I went to bed and fell asleep. Then I saw a dream: Batiushka Ambrose came up to me and said: 'What are you grieving in advance for?' With these words he hit me so hard on my right ear, that blood flowed from it. 'Go to church for the Feast, you fool!' he added. Having awakened, I saw that the pillow on which I lay and the robe that I was wearing were covered with blood. But from that hour I felt completely well, and not a trace of the illness remained.

We will now present excerpts from the remarkable account of one of the Elder's spiritual daughters, Mrs. N.

"Since I was a worldly woman who had married early, I knew nothing aside from my family life. Concerning monasteries, monks, and their elders, though I had heard of and seen them while still a child, I had only the most vague and even incorrect understanding, which was imparted to me by the same sort of people as myself, who knew nothing. And I did not consider it necessary to learn anything more detailed about them—in short, I thought nothing at all about it.

"During my whole harmonious life with my husband, the Lord often visited me with various sorrows—sometimes through loss of children, sometimes through sickness. But in all the many years of my married life, it was never so miserable, so bleak for me, as in 1884 and the years following…. The loss, as a result of a barefaced fraud, of the material means gathered by my husband through many years of labor so affected him that he became ill with a gradual form of cerebral palsy and, at the same time, angina pectoris. His and my suffering were inexpressible. Besides that, the situation in society, his job, and our daughter, a young girl, demanded, as it seemed to me then, the help of acquaintances and of secular life. To this was added not a little grief and worry caused by the man who was planning to marry our daughter; he had been chosen with our parental love in concord with our daughter. This matter, evidently not without reason, dragged on and was put off from year to year. The young man's occupation demanded his constant presence at the place of his residence and promised him a brilliant future, which he chased after as a mirage, delaying both himself and us....

"But all of this was the will of God. If it had not happened, I would not have run into dear Batiushka Ambrose, and never would have seen or known the life opposed to the one I had led up to that time.

"Once," she continued, "I returned from a grand ball just before morning (this was in the beginning of winter, 1884, exactly two years before I met Batiushka), with emptiness in my heart and a weight on my mind, as always happened with such entertainments. Having barely said my prayers, I threw myself, fatigued, into bed and immediately fell asleep. And this is what I saw in a light sleep: I found myself in a thick, ancient forest—of a type I had seen only in panoramas. I walked alone along a trampled-down little lane, which soon led me to some sort of building; and I found myself before holy gates, not large, with depictions of saints on both sides. The gates opened and I went into a beautiful garden. I walked straight along the sand-covered path. There were flowers on both sides. Soon this path led me to a small wooden church. I went up some steps into the portico. The green-painted iron door of the church was locked from the inside. When I approached it, someone moved aside the bolt from the inside and opened the door for me. I saw before me a tall, bare-headed elder in a mantia and epitrachelion. He took me firmly by the right hand, led me into the church, turned sharply to the right towards the wall, placed me before an icon of the Mother of God (the 'Fyodorovskaya' as I later learned), and tersely and strictly said: 'Pray.' Even in the dream, I remember, I was struck by the appearance of the Elder and asked him: 'Who are you, Batiushka?' He answered me: 'I am the Optina Elder Ambrose.' And, leaving me alone, he left by the opposite door of the church. Standing there, I prayed before the icon of the Heavenly Queen, before which the Elder had placed me. Then I glanced to my left and saw a tomb or burial shroud. (In fact, the plashchanitsa is located here the whole year round, except for Great Friday and Saturday.) I walked up to it, prayed, and then looked back at the whole church. It was a wonderful, small church, with a pink curtain over the Royal Doors, and all bathed in sunlight. Then, strangely, I suddenly found myself in the middle of it, in a white shirt, barefoot, and with my hair loose; and I prayed and wept like I never had when awake. After this I awoke. My whole pillow was drenched with tears. This strange, unheard-of dream made a profound impression on me and caused me to ponder. The thought of going to see the Elder or writing to him did not enter my mind then. But the dream I had seen did not leave me and was not erased from my memory.

"Two more years passed of my husband's physical suffering and my emotional torment. But the Lord wished to test us to the end, so as to bring us to our senses. My husband came down with typhus. The illness became complicated. From an unknown cause, the upper part of his leg began to hurt and became swollen, with sharp pain at times, especially during the nights which he spent without sleep, tossing from side to side from the pain. Then his leg became much more swollen and red. For this reason they decided to bandage his whole leg, and a surgeon was summoned for this. During the examination of the leg, the latter diagnosed an internal abscess and found that the leg was full of pus. An incision over five inches long was made and the pus cleaned out. My husband felt some relief but was far from recovery. After a few days the same thing began again. His leg again swelled up, and a cut had to be made in a different place. This happened several times. The incisions, after the pus was removed, healed over. It got to the point where it was impossible to make any further incisions.

"Despite painstaking care, all the wounds festered. He lay on his back for three months in a row. His leg was like a log. The nerves were so sensitive that the touch of the bed sheets caused him pain.

"The swelling of his leg went higher and higher. I could not endure it and again sent for the doctor. But, after examining the leg, he took all hope from me for his recovery.

"Now the thought of turning to the prayers of the great Elder entered my mind for the first time, and I did not delay in fulfilling it. To one of my relatives, a spiritual daughter of the Elder who was staying as a guest in Optina at that time, I wrote a letter with a detailed description of the condition of my sick husband, begging her to report everything to Batiushka and ask for his holy prayers.

"A few days after the letter was sent, when changing the position of his leg I saw with horror that the swelling had already spread to his lower abdomen. Furthermore, his suffering was so great at that moment that, not knowing how to relieve it, I suddenly took it into my head for some reason to make a bandage and tie it near the groin. My hands were trembling. I was afraid to make it tight. And, of course, the idea of this bandage, which had come into my head for some reason, was only to console myself. But, three hours did not go by when my husband loudly called me, saying, 'Take a look, something is all wet around my leg.' Uncovering the leg, I saw that the very first wound—that is, the first incision, made by the doctor three months earlier, had opened to its entire former depth and a fountain of pus was gushing out. For three full days the discharge came out continuously, after which he began to noticeably recover his strength. Having written to my relative about this in as much detail as possible, I learned, to my extreme amazement, that the day and hour of the opening of the wound in my husband's leg corresponded with the day and hour of the reading of my letter to the Elder by my relative.

"Spring arrived. My husband's health recovered to such an extent that he was able to go outdoors.

"This was the second time Elder Ambrose brought himself to my mind. There soon followed a third as well.

"Struck by a distressing family misfortune (an unscrupulous act of my daughter's fiance), I conceived the idea of going on a pilgrimage by foot to the local Saint [Tikhon of Kaluga], in the hope of killing my anguish of soul by tiring out my body.... But, from being unaccustomed to walking and from nervous shock due to grief, my strength failed me. Towards evening my head, arms and legs began to ache, and I was barely able to drag myself to the monastery. My whole body became feverish, and my right arm became numb from the top down—something which had never happened before. Coming to the monastery where the relics of the Saint were located (under a reliquary), I fell upon the first stone I reached. Having no strength to move myself further, I sent the maid whom I had taken with me to find a place for us in the guest house. But she soon returned and said that due to the large throng of people there was not a free corner anywhere.

"We had to go to the village by the monastery to seek shelter. There, in a common lodging with other worshippers, a corner was found for me. A bare bench fell to my lot, but the hostess out of pity for me, since I was so sick and weak, gave me her pillow. Almost unconscious from the pain, I threw myself on the bench, dressed just as I was. But the shouts of the people strolling in the streets and the noise of the guests who were coming to my hostess gave me no rest all night. Added to this, the inexpressible pain in my entire body did not allow me to lie comfortably. Towards morning the street cries diminished and I fell into a light sleep, which transported me back home. It seemed to me that I was in my parlor on the couch. But my sleep was so light that I felt the pain in my whole body even in sleep. Suddenly the doors of the room opened, and an elder-monk came up to me. Extending his hands he lifted me up, sat me down and solicitously said: 'What's hurting you?' I remember well, I answered him: 'My arms and legs, Batiushka, but most of all, my head,' which I placed in his hands. The Elder with his own hands grasped my ailing arms and legs; then, across my head, across the painful spot, he struck me three times. I asked someone who was standing behind the Elder: 'Who is this?' And I received the answer: 'Why, this is Elder Ambrose of Optina!' Suddenly, the voice of my hostess awakened me: 'It's already 5:00; they are ringing the bells for Liturgy—are you going, madame?' I leapt to my feet. I felt no pain, either in my head or in my body; I was healthy and strong—somehow completely renewed. I crossed myself and, splashing cold water in my face, went to church. I stood through the Liturgy, through a Moleben with an Akathist to the Saint, and was already preparing to go strengthen myself with tea for the trip home. 'What?' said my maid. 'Is it possible that we, being here, are not going to bathe in the holy spring of the Saint?' I was at the point of refusing but, remembering my wondrous healing by the Elder that night, I went. We bathed, and then we set out on the return journey, which I completed so easily and with such vigor that I surprised everyone with my early arrival. Right then I decided not to allow any obstacles, but to go to Elder Ambrose, who had summoned me, the sinner, in such a wondrous way."

Once there came to the Elder a peasant of the Tula Province who suffered from drunkenness and, since he was unable to quit this pernicious habit, several times he had wanted to kill himself. He came to the Elder, unable to say anything. But the Elder, exposing him, stated that he suffered from drunkenness because when he was still a boy, he stole money from his grandfather, a church warden, and with that money had bought wine. He gave him herbs to drink at home. The peasant was delivered from drinking and became completely well.

The St. Petersburg resident Alexei Stepanovich Maiorov, excessively addicted to smoking tobacco, sensed the danger to his health from this. He wrote a letter to Elder Ambrose, asking for his advice on how he could be delivered from this passion.

In answer to this request, the Elder sent Maiorov a letter on October 12, 1888 in which the following was written: "You write that you cannot stop smoking tobacco. That which is impossible for man is possible with the help of God. Only stand firm in your decision to quit, realizing the danger from it for soul and body, since tobacco debilitates the soul, increases and strengthens the passions, darkens the mind, and destroys bodily health by a slow death. Irritability and melancholy are the result of the infirmity of soul that comes from tobacco smoking.

"I advise you to make use of spiritual treatment against this passion: confess in detail all the sins of your whole life from the age of seven, receive the Holy Mysteries, and read the Gospel daily while standing, one chapter or more. And when depression attacks, then read it again, until the depression passes. If it attacks again—read the Gospel again. Or, in place of this, when alone make thirty-three full prostrations in memory of the earthly life of the Savior and in honor of the Holy Trinity."

When he received this letter, Alexei Stepanovich read it through and then began to smoke a cigarette, but he suddenly felt a strong pain in his head together with an aversion to tobacco smoke, and that night he did not smoke. The next day, by habit, he attempted four times to smoke a cigarette, but he could not inhale the smoke due to the severe pain in his head. Thus he quit smoking easily, while in the previous two years when he had tried to force himself to cease smoking, he could not. And though it had made him ill, he had smoked seventy-five cigarettes a day all the same.

In the Borisov Convent of the Kursk Province, among the sisters of the Monastery there was one young novice who had developed such a passion for visiting a worldly family that often, despite the prohibitions of the Abbess and even against her own wishes, she would go to them. At the advice of certain sisters she wrote to Fr. Ambrose, revealing her weakness and asking for his holy prayers. Soon she saw a dream in which a magnificent Elder led her to an icon of the Mother of God and said: "Pray to the Heavenly Queen!" With these words of the Elder the novice woke up and related the vision to the sisters. They explained to her that it was Elder Ambrose who had appeared to her, whom she had never seen up to that time. Soon after that she received an answer to her letter from Batiushka, which greatly calmed her. When after this the desire again came to her to go for a visit to the above-mentioned family, she always reread the Elder's letter and the desire passed. She was subsequently entirely freed from this habit and began to live according to the monastic way, cutting off close acquaintanceship with worldly people.

Fr. Ambrose also protected his spiritual children from temptations of the enemy. Thus Hieromonk Dorotheus related the following about himself: "After my entrance in 1874 into Optina Monastery, the obedience of working as cook was entrusted to me. A half year passed, and then I began to have fears at night in my cell, induced by the enemy. It seemed to me as though some old man came to me and pronounced the prayer indistinctly. Dishes began to rattle in the cell for no reason. My bed shook, and the enemy attacked me. And when, in the midst of this fear, I would begin to cry out or take a breath, then I would clearly hear a voice and the words: 'There's nothing worse than this, ach!' At first I went to Fr. Anatole and told him about these enemy-induced frights, but he sent me to Batiushka Ambrose. The Elder, having heard me out, said that I must not be afraid and that for the chasing away of demonic fear I must pronounce the Prayer of Jesus. After this, all fear ceased and I always remained peacefully in my cell."

Something similar occurred several times in Shamordino; knocking was heard at the doors and windows, etc. When they communicated this to the Elder, he said: "Well, he won't knock anymore." "But, who is knocking, Batiushka?" they asked him. "He who was knocking won't knock anymore," the Elder answered again.

Now it remains for us to speak about how Elder Ambrose did not cease to help those in need even after his repose.

IN THE OCTOBER issue of *Soul-Profiting Reading* for 1897, there was published the letter of a certain Nicholas Yakovlevich Shirokov, of Vyatka Province, Glazov district, to the Optina Elder Hieroschemamonk Joseph, with the following contents: "I was extremely ill: I suffered from pain in my legs and head. On November 26 of last year (1896), my father brought from our village priest the anthology *Soul-Profiting Reading*, in which I found an article about Fr. Ambrose. After reading it and meditating on it for a while, I began to pray mentally to Fr. Ambrose for the healing of my ailments, and, having finished praying, I fell into a light sleep. I had only just managed to fall asleep when suddenly an unusual light began to shine before me, which soon disappeared; only one trace of it remained in the form of a cloud. Suddenly I heard a man's footsteps. I soon saw before me a man adorned with gray hair, in a mantia, with a cross on his chest. At this point I will attempt to describe his appearance: he was not tall, his face was exhausted from fasting, and therefore bright. He had a hooked nose, gray hair which was not very thick, and his voice was quite resonant. In addition, he had in his left hand a prayer rope and in his right a staff. He approached my bed and said: 'Child, Nicholas! Arise, hasten to church; have a Moleben served to St. Ambrose of Milan, and you will receive quick relief.' He took me by the hand, blessed me and touched his staff to my leg, which immediately felt better. He gave me something like a prosphora to eat, and suddenly I began to hear a noise in my head. I became terrified and thought that my head was no longer on my shoulders. But this Elder covered it with his mantia, and I felt relieved. The Elder blessed me once again, and I was vouchsafed to kiss his radiant hand. At this point I ventured to ask him: 'By what name shall I call you?' He answered me: 'He to whom I commanded you to serve a Moleben is the one whose name I bear; I am Hieroschemamonk Ambrose from Optina Monastery.' Having said this, he became invisible. When I awoke, I greatly rejoiced that I had recovered, as did my relatives. Yet, I did not soon inform them about this appearance, but only wrote it down in my diary. But then this phenomenon was repeated. Fr. Ambrose appeared to me, lying in his coffin and clothed in the schema, and said: 'Who do you think you are, slave-of-God Nicholas, that you keep silent about the deeds of the mercy of God—that is, you have not told Optina about your healing?' Only because of this have I dared to inform your saintliness concerning the above-mentioned account; and now I beg you, Fr. Joseph, not to leave my account without attention, but to publish it in the biography of Fr. Ambrose for the benefit of others."

A SIMILAR CASE is related in the letter of February 23, 1898 to L.O.R., who lived in Shamordino: "Yesterday V. arrived and related that a woman, a relative of L., wrote to him from Moscow that her husband was very sick. The doctors refused to treat him, and he was dying. One night he saw an Elder by his bed who prayed over him and said: 'Have a Moleben served to St. Ambrose of Milan,' and disappeared. The sick man told his wife, and they had a Moleben served. He received Holy Communion and from that time began to improve, and even got up from his bed; but he told no one about the appearance of the Elder. When he began to feel completely well, the same Elder again appeared to him (the formerly sick man recognized him), and said: 'Now you are completely healthy; why do you hide your healing and not speak about it? You need to report it, and the Elder before you is Ambrose of Optina.'" And he disappeared.

"When V. told us about this incident," continued the author of the letter, "I became envious, but my soul somehow became joyful—I don't know how to express it. Our dear one will, perhaps, not abandon us either."

A novice of Shamordino, under the influence of some grief and unpleasantness that had overtaken her, wanted to leave the Monastery. At this time the reposed Elder Ambrose appeared to her in a dream and said: "Do not go anywhere, but live in one place. Do not run from sorrows; you will not find anything better. You need to endure!" The novice calmed down and remained in the Monastery.

HERE IS ANOTHER unusual account by S.A.M.: "In 1880 I finished my studies at the institute. On February 3, 1881, I opened a school with a boarding house for both sexes. My mother and I opened the school without any means, since my married brother had refused to give us anything. My mother was a deeply believing elderly woman and when I asked her whom she placed her hope in, opening a school with no means, she meekly answered me, pointing to a large image of the Savior: 'There's the One upon Whom I hope! He will help me!' I was greatly irritated by her answer and said sharply: 'What? Has He said something to you?' She again answered me meekly: 'Yes, He will tell me!'

"And so, despite my protest and that of my sisters, my mother still energetically set about organizing the school. From the first month our work proceeded with great success, so that by the end of the year the quarters were insufficient for the number of students, and we were forced to take a large apartment. I was not to work with my dear old mother for long. In 1882, she suddenly became ill, and in three days she died. I was left alone and continued to work. Matters went even better, and I began to try to organize a preparatory high school. But God judged otherwise: an upheaval occurred in my life, both unexpected and terrible for me.

"In 1887, on August 26, having finished studies in the school, I went to the estate of my friend for her nameday. On that day, in full health and contented, I was unusually happy. After lunch, one of my friends asked me to do an experiment in suggestive thought with her. Though I very much liked to engage in such things, this time for some reason I began to refuse persistently. They tried for a long time to convince me, and I finally agreed. We had to take some sort of object and force someone, through suggestion, to move it from one place to another. I went up to the dresser, where there were many different items; right there stood a 'nine-ordered' prosphora,* which the priest had brought for the nameday celebrant. Well,

---

*So-called because during proskomedia the nine categories of saints are commemorated using it.—ED.

after thinking a bit, I took the prosphora and transferred it to the washstand and said to those present: 'All right, Zhenia (my friend) has to take this prosphora and transfer it to the dresser.' All agreed. I called Zhenia from the other room, blindfolded her, took her by the hand, and began in earnest to suggest that she go up to the washstand, take the prosphora, and carry it over to the dresser. She quickly went up to the washstand but, having stood for a little while, she began to spin and fell senseless. Her hand had not even touched the prosphora. We picked her up, carried her to the balcony, and quickly brought her to her senses. But I went to the dining room, sat at the table, and only said: 'Lord, how terrible'; and with these words I fell into a violent fit, which recurred up to twenty times an hour, so that I became completely weakened. They laid me on a bed and sent for a doctor. All night, until four o'clock in the morning, I had fits. Finally, I asked to be carried home.

"After my arrival at home, the attacks began again and despite whatever treatment and painstaking care I received, the illness intensified more and more, so that at the end of September, after a consultation the doctors urgently demanded that the school be closed and that I be settled in the country. But even with complete isolation in the country, it was no easier for me. On the contrary—to the fits there was added severe depression. I spent three years in this condition with my nephew, a public doctor. Finally, he went to Moscow and left me with his mother. Then I became worse and worse. Once, I remember, it was especially severe; depression tormented me to such a degree that I decided to commit suicide. In such a state I went to my sister, wept, tossed about in bed, and said that I could live no longer. My sister began to persuade me and, among other things, implored me to receive Holy Communion, since for three years (i.e., since I had become ill) I had not been to church and had not received the Holy Mysteries.

But I did not even want to hear about Communion. I don't know how, but they still persuaded me to receive Communion. They brought me on the next day to the Holy Trinity Monastery, where I stood through the Liturgy. After Liturgy a hieromonk, whom my sister had asked, approached me and suggested that I go to his cell for confession. I confessed, but afterwards said to him: 'Well, Batiushka, tomorrow I am not coming for Communion.' He began to persuade me, but I did not want to listen. But, all the same, the next day I came to Matins and Liturgy. I stood calmly through Liturgy, but when they began to sing 'Our Father ...' I was unable to cope with it and wanted to run from the church. But the hieromonk stood near me and did not let me. I turned completely pale and began to tremble. They had only just brought out the Holy Gifts when I had a demonic fit, and the priest with the Gifts went back into the altar, fearing that I might upset the chalice. Eight monks could barely handle me, and they brought me up and communed me, but I remember nothing—only that afterwards I calmed down. The hieromonk, seeing what had happened with me, advised me to receive Communion as often as possible, which I did.

"Every time I received Communion I was attacked by demonic fits, and I was terribly tormented. Finally, I went to Voronezh, to St. Mitrophan. There, before Communion, I had such a severe attack that I almost pushed the Chalice, ran from the church, and tore my blouse. In Voronezh a hieromonk performed an exorcism over me, but when he began to read the Gospel it became so difficult for me that I broke up the armchair I was sitting on and tore the cross from the hands of the hieromonk. After my arrival from Voronezh, seeing that prayer did not seem to help me, I became utterly cold towards God and even began to blaspheme. I turned again to doctors and by their advice entered a psychiatric hospital, where my health became even worse. In one month I had ninety attacks. I became so weak that I was no longer able to walk.

"Having spent three months in the hospital, I was moved to the ward for the chronically ill—to the asylum. The attacks became more and more rare, but they were replaced by bouts of depression. The depression was so severe that I attempted suicide more than once; I always thought about taking my life and would try to do it, but my attempts never succeeded.

"Thus I suffered for eighteen years, but I finally began to receive the Holy Mysteries without fits. The last attack of horrible depression was on June 3, 1905. The depression was so powerful that I began to strangle myself, and it was only thanks to one of the patients that I did not succeed. After this I wrote a letter to my sister in which I asked her to take me out of the asylum and fix me up somewhere in the country. It seemed to me that my depression was due precisely to the conditions in the hospital and that with a change of place the depression would pass. My sister came to me, but instead of the country she suggested that I go to Optina Monastery, which stands in a forest and is famous for its beautiful surroundings. A pine forest, which would be beneficial for me, stretched around the Monastery for many miles. Complete seclusion and life in the forest tempted me very much, and I decided to go there with the aim of staying for a month, like at a dacha. When the time came to go to Optina, I became terribly angry at my sister, that she was sending me to a completely unfamiliar location; I began to get agitated and said to her: 'You and your husband want to finally finish me off; well, where am I going, alone and sick?! I'm not going anywhere.' My sister became angry at me and we argued. But despite this, I went anyway.

"I arrived at Optina on July 7, 1905. In the morning I went to the Skete to the Elder [Joseph], who soon received me and said that to be their guest for a long time was not allowed and that there was nothing for me to do in Optina. A day passed—then another, but I was not feeling well, and nothing pleased me. I would drop into the church for a minute, but could not stand there for long. On the 12th I very much wanted, for some reason, to read the biography of Elder Ambrose; I requested this book from the guestmaster and read far past midnight. While reading I began to experience an extraordinarily pleasant state of soul, such as I had never in my life experienced. And at the time that I was reading I decided to have a Pannikhida served over the grave of Elder Ambrose. The next day I hastened to the early Liturgy, and after Liturgy I requested the serving of a Pannikhida. I had to wait a long time for the hieromonk, who was serving Pannikhidas at other graves. While waiting, I remained at the grave of Elder Ambrose and began to weep—and so bitterly that it was as if I had opened a spring of tears. During the Pannikhida I wept the whole time, and the tears continued all day. On this day I was supposed to confess. The Elder sent me to the confessor. I came to him in tears and began to speak about my aching soul. He gently treated my pained soul, which was worn out by suffering. After confession he read a special prayer over me, during which I began to feel faint, and I asked him to finish it more quickly. After the end of the prayer, I felt an unusual weakness. When I left his cell, I calmed down and ceased to weep.

"The next day I received the Holy Mysteries peacefully, and that same day left for St. Tikhon's Hermitage. When I arrived at the train station from Optina, something extraordinary happened to me: my whole emotional state immediately changed. It seemed such a terrible pity to leave Optina, so that if a choice had been proposed to me: either all the treasures of the world or Optina, I would have taken the latter. And it is already a year since I was reborn; a year in which I have not had a single bout of depression, in which I have become less irritable, in which there has appeared in me faith in God, in life beyond the grave; I have understood the aim of life. The thought of suicide has entirely left me, and I now consider myself to be a fortunate person, though the circumstances of my life have not changed a bit. I believe that the Lord healed me from the terrible ailment from which I suffered for eighteen years through the prayers of Elder Ambrose.

"My physical health is poor, and this does not allow me to leave the asylum; but what is physical sickness compared to that of the soul? It is impossible even to compare. After my first trip, a kind of inexplicable power attracted me to Optina, and the Lord led me again to be at the grave of Elder Ambrose that same year in September, then again on Pascha of 1906, and now.

"A year has gone by since I have been psychologically well, and I do not know how to thank God and Elder Ambrose for such great mercy."

As a supplement to what has been set forth, we may add that in the summer of 1911 we saw the healed woman in Optina and she, confirming the truth of all that has been set forth above, with joy and profound gratitude to God and to Elder Ambrose announced that during the past six years after her miraculous healing the previously terrible condition of unbearable depression and fits had not once returned. She feels calm and is filled with the joy of life, despite the difficult external circumstances of her existence. The doctors who had treated her earlier, seeing her present condition, told her that she was healed by means of suggestion, but this is absolutely untrue. When they had treated her through suggestion in the hospital in Moscow she not only did not get better, but was made worse, so that when she left Moscow to go back they had to carry her to the railroad car in their arms, whereas when she had set out for Moscow for treatment she was still in a condition to walk herself. Nor could the favorable climate in Optina have exerted an influence over her, since she spent, in all, only five days there. S.A. has the firm and unshakable confidence that Fr. Ambrose, who healed her from her grave illness, even now does not leave her bereft of protection. From the moment that she received healing in Optina, as she said in her letter, this Monastery became extremely dear to her and an indispensable source of moral strength and spiritual inspiration, so that she has begun to feel the need to be there each summer for spiritual renewal and strengthening. But, in view of her complete lack of material means, she has no possibility of undertaking such a trip. And right there the solicitude of Fr. Ambrose towards her is again manifest. Each time summer has come, circumstances have developed in such a way that the necessary means for the trip have appeared for S.A.; and this is already the sixth year that she has been able to be in Optina and spend some time here, through the mercy of the loving Elder Ambrose.

The above-mentioned S.A. further related the following incident: "In September of 1908, a nurse at the St. Elizabeth Asylum at the hospital of T. Province, L.G., came down with a severe form of recurrent typhus soon after her return from Optina. Her temperature remained high all the time, and she complained in particular of an extremely painful headache. On the night of the ninth of October (the eve of the repose date of Batiushka Ambrose), she fell unconscious and saw clearly that she was lying in the hall on the floor in the apartment of Mrs. N. Through the door came Batiushka Ambrose, who approached her and, giving her a prosphora, ordered her to eat it; but the sick woman answered him that she was unable to eat because her tongue had become dried out and cracked. Batiushka Ambrose said to her: 'Go home quickly (to the asylum) and there, from a tall lady who often comes to me, take artos and water from my well; soak the artos in this water, and eat it up!' After this she regained consciousness, but her temperature reached 105.8 degrees and she felt very bad. That day her coworker, the nurse E., came to visit her; the sick woman had been waiting impatiently for her. She had only just arrived when L. begged her to quickly go to me and take the artos and water from me; then she related her dream.

"The nurse E. came to me and conveyed the patient's request. I, of course, immediately gave her artos and water but was quite surprised, since besides me, no one knew that I had artos and water from the skete well, which I had brought back from Optina in August.

"After the sick woman had eaten the artos, she fell into a sound sleep. When she awoke, she no longer felt the pain in her head, her temperature had dropped to normal, and she was sweating intensely, after which she began to improve. Having been released from the infectious disease ward, L. resumed her work as a nurse and personally told me about her dream. I asked her if she had known that I had artos and water from Batiushka's well. She said that she had not known, and it's true—she couldn't have known, since I had not told anyone."

WE WILL PRESENT one more account, of the ryassophore-novice Xenia Alexeyevna (Shershova) of the Kraishev Holy Trinity Convent, Saratov Province, Atkar district: "I consider it my sacred duty to inform you," she wrote to the Superior of Optina Monastery, Archimandrite Xenophont, "about the healing I received through the prayers of the reposed-in-God Elder Ambrose. Until July 30, 1906, I had been sick for a month with head pain that was sometimes accompanied by a fever. On the morning of July 30, while working at my obedience as a dairymaid, I was boiling milk in a pot in the oven. Having boiled the milk, as I remember, I began to close the oven and suddenly fell to the floor; I had a fit. I remember nothing further. When I regained consciousness, I was unable to answer the questions of those who surrounded me, was unable to pronounce a single word, and became absolutely mute. The doctor in the settlement of Yelan, in the Atkar district nine miles from our Monastery, to whom I had gone twice, stated that hope of a full recovery was small and that even if there was some recovery, it would be insignificant: I would speak barely understandably and irregularly, and not as I spoke formerly.

"With the blessing of our Abbess, I set out in the company of our nuns to Optina to venerate the grave and beg the holy prayers of Elder Ambrose; I arrived on August 19, 1906. Once there, on the very day of my arrival, I had a Pannikhida served at Batiushka's grave. Afterwards I confessed and received the Holy Mysteries and Unction. At first I was unable to bend over for the prostrations due to pain in my neck. I took a little soil from Fr. Ambrose's grave and swallowed it. Then dropping some in a bottle of water, I drank this water and moistened my head with it. I often went to Pannikhidas at Batiushka's grave. On the twenty-first and twenty-second, I drank oil from the lampada before the icon at Batiushka's grave on an empty stomach. On August 22, after lunch I went to the Skete, and along the road near Batiushka Ambrose's well I had a coughing fit, during which something broke loose in my throat and I swallowed. At the advice of my companion, a nun, I went up to the well and drank some water from it. Then, to a question that she addressed to me, I suddenly began to answer her clearly and distinctly, being surprised at this occurrence. I began to weep at this unexpected joy, and the nun with amazement stepped away from me, hearing me speaking. From that time I speak absolutely fluently, just as I had before the fit, without any speech impediments. With deep gratitude I attribute my healing to the prayerful assistance of Batiushka Ambrose, to whom I ran for help, being often at his grave and begging his prayers for me, the sinner. Those who accompanied me to

The chapel over the grave of Elder Ambrose.

Optina Monastery can attest to my illness and the sudden and miraculous healing that happened to me in the Monastery: Nun Angelina (treasurer) and Nun Euthemia; Ryassophore novices Euthymia, Domnica and Maria. August 29, 1906, Optina Monastery. Ryassophore-novice Xenia."

## MORE ACCOUNTS OF THE ELDER'S LOVE*

A formerly very rich man, owing to various fortuities of life, was ruined, in the most exact sense of the word, and went through one of those torturous periods that inevitably follow the loss of a large fortune. He had to find work, but some people did not think he had the spirit to apply himself, while others turned him down, feeling that a man who had himself once been an employer, and even a rich one, could not become a worker. It must be noted that this man and his wife were very charitable, never refusing anything to anyone; and in view of the fact that their house stood not far from a major road, they never refused any pilgrim who passed by them and turned to them for comfort and a night's lodging.

Then, on one unpleasant, rainy autumn evening, the unfortunate man was sitting by his window and thinking oppressive thoughts: "No means, no job—might as well lie down and die of starvation." Suddenly he saw an old man, obviously a pilgrim, turning from the big road and heading straight for his window. Since a fine rain was drizzling down outside, he opened the window and said to him, "I have no money, old man, and nothing to give you, but if you want to take shelter from the rain, then come in and have a seat here." The old man went in, took a seat opposite his host, and began to question him about various things; among others, about his business. His host sadly related his difficult experiences. When he had fin-

---

*From V. P. Bykov, *Quiet Havens for Storm-tossed Souls,* pp. 176-7.

ished his tale, the pilgrim said to him, "Well, sir, what are you waiting for? Not far from you, not more than seven miles away, is a man like Elder Ambrose, and you do not go to him for advice? How many people go to see him, and everyone receives something, each what he needs.... They come from a long way off.... He is a man with many acquaintances and lots of connections—he will help you quickly." The pilgrim won over his cordial host to such a point that the latter began to question him as to how he could make his way to Elder Ambrose and see him. He made up his mind to go by horse the next morning and unfailingly visit the Elder. During this conversation the host's wife came by the room several times. When their conversation had ended, the pilgrim glanced out the window and hurried to leave, since it was already getting dark. His host did not detain him. The pilgrim quickly got his things together and left. Right after his departure the man's wife came in and, not seeing the pilgrim, asked her husband where he had disappeared to. He told her that the pilgrim had left. She expressed very great dissatisfaction: "How could you let that man go, with night coming and in such bad weather, without having put a glass of tea before him?...We couldn't show kindness towards the man in any other way, but we could have poured him some tea and warmed him." Hearing this, the landowner was straightway appalled—how was it that he had not had the good sense to do that which he had always done with regard to almost every passerby? Supposing that the pilgrim was still not far off since he had only just left, he darted outside to bring him back. But, alas, though the area before him was wide open, no matter how much he looked around, the old man had simply vanished into thin air. Morning came, and the man harnessed his horse and rode to Optina. He arrived and located the Elder's cell, as the pilgrim had indicated to him; he expected to stand in line. When he entered the cell he did not believe his eyes—before him stood the pilgrim of the previous day. The landowner was on the verge of crying out in astonishment, but Batiushka Ambrose ordered him not to say a word about what had transpired. Then he went into the neighboring cell and said to someone, "Well, my dear, I have found the very best manager for you." He returned to the impoverished rich man with some gentleman, introduced them, and after a half hour he who had fallen into despair now had a wonderful job.

The beloved older brother of one lady had suffered from alcoholism for many years. There was nothing the man had not tried and no one he had not turned to, but nothing had come of it. Meanwhile, the unfortunate man's health and resources had been ruined. The matter finally reached the point that the doctors who had been treating him stated that if he did not cease drinking he would die of a heart attack. The poor woman lost her head and, not knowing what to do, recalled that in Optina Monastery there was a great and righteous Elder who could do anything through his prayers. She squinted her eyes and, though she had never seen Fr. Ambrose, tried to imagine him, mentally begging him to help her brother. Since it was evening, she soon fell asleep. In a dream she saw an old man coming towards her and instantly understood that this was Elder Ambrose. He said to her, "Go to the pharmacy and buy twenty-five kopecks' worth of the herb 'chernogorki-staronos,' finely chopped, and boil two tablespoons of it in five teacups of water. Let the teapot stand in the stove for a half hour, then take it out and let the sick man drink all five teacups at one sitting, either hot or cold—it makes no difference. Since this herb is quite bitter, he can drink it with sugar or honey. After taking it there may be vomiting, but do not be frightened by this—it means that the remedy has worked. If after this dose he again has the desire for vodka, then you must repeat the dose. After this treatment he will lose his appetite, but this is not dangerous.

The chapels over the graves of Elders Macarius and Ambrose, before the Revolution.

Then he has only to take twenty-five drops of Witte's stomach elixir and ten drops of Hoffman's in a shot glass of water each time before taking food."

The woman instantly woke up and copied down this recipe during the night. When she arose in the morning she sent to the city for the herb. By the time they went to the city, looked for the herb and brought it home it was already evening. Not wishing to lose precious time, the compassionate sister prepared the remedy and night had already fallen by the time she gave it to her brother to drink. To her great horror, before he was to go to sleep her brother began to vomit to such an extent that the poor woman was confounded. And, as usually happens, all kinds of thoughts began to lead her mind astray, such as, "How careless I am; how could I trust all kinds of dreams? This is some kind of terrible poison!" In a word, the poor woman could not sleep all night, and dozed off only when it was almost morning. Again she saw the same old man, who approached her and said, "Do not be frightened, Matushka; do not be frightened, I tell you. This is harmless, and the vomiting is the root of the wine being destroyed."

In those days there were no theories of autosuggestion, the subconscious, and the like. The woman calmed down and, indeed, from that moment her brother's urge for alcoholic beverages was taken away as if by a touch.

Many years later this woman went to Optina, and how delighted and gratified she was when she saw Elder Ambrose, exactly as she had seen him in her dream.

Processing with St. Ambrose's icon inside the Skete in 1989.

Veneration of St. Ambrose in Optina Skete on the same day, October 10th, a year later.

# Conclusion

*O Lord, in Thy light shall we see light!*
Great Doxology

We have finished our narrative concerning the life, exalted asceticism and grace-filled gifts of Elder Ambrose. Taking a last general glance at his spiritual understanding and his holy, ascetic life, we see that the most characteristic feature of his spiritual makeup was his life-giving, active, salvific love. He was not an indifferent observer of human sufferings; he responded warmly to them, received them into his generous heart and, with his mind consecrated to God, he sought the means for their cure. The woes of people are varied—there are material ones: deprivations, physical sicknesses.... There are spiritual ones: torment of soul from the recognition of one's corruption, one's inability to live [righteously], lack of understanding of the meaning of life, and spiritual confusion.

There are people, especially many among educated youth, who are not indifferent to the sorrows of their neighbors, but who do not see further than material sorrow—the sorrow of poverty. They are ready to go selflessly to the aid of their suffering neighbor, but their aid is exclusively external in character: to deliver him from material need, to change the external circumstances of his existence. This is not true, all-embracing Christian love.

Christian love also co-suffers with external grief, but it sees and feels infinitely deeper; it pierces to the very soul of a man and there sees its fundamental suffering—that suffering which is not cured by external measures, but demands the spiritual influence of sincere, revivifying, salvific love in the name of the God of love. Fr. Ambrose possessed this gift to a high degree. As we have seen, he also relieved material human sorrow with external methods, but together with this he embraced the whole soul of a man with his loving feeling. He knew how to comprehend one's innermost spiritual sorrow and precisely upon it pour out the healing oil of his compassionate solicitude and kindness, raising it up to Heaven, to God. This is why people who came to him with shattered souls and, as it seemed, dead forever, came away from him resurrected, revived, joyful, saved and believing. We have seen in the pages of this biography many examples of such spiritual rebirths. And we would hardly be mistaken if we say that a significant majority of the inhabitants of Shamordino, and many of those of Optina, were indebted precisely to the salvific love of Elder Ambrose at the beginning of their spiritual life.

Russian society understood this feature of the spiritual makeup of Elder Ambrose. It understood that he was neither a strict hermit, nor a rigid exposer of human shortcomings and weaknesses, nor an abstract theologian. He was *living love* itself, having the ability to stand in the immediate proximity of any grieving and burdened soul, take upon himself his infirmity and sorrow, warm him, console him, and call him to a new, vigorous, pure and joyful life. And that is why he became a spiritual center, attracting to himself not only simple people who flocked to him as to a man of God, a man of holy God-pleasing life, but even the educated came seeking in him a guide of life who

## CONCLUSION

would indicate the path to true happiness of soul, who would teach them to know and love God.

Fr. Ambrose solved for Russian society its long-standing and difficult-to-solve question of *what to do*, how to live, and for what to live. He also solved for Russian society the fatal question of how to unite the educated classes with the simple people. He said to Russian society that the meaning of life consists of love—not that humanistic, irreligious love which is proclaimed by a certain portion of our intelligentsia, and which is expressed by outward measures of improvement of life; but that true, profound Christian love, which embraces the whole soul of one's neighbor and heals by its life-giving power the very deepest and most excruciating wounds. Fr. Ambrose also solved the question of the blending of the intelligentsia with the people, uniting them in his cell in one general feeling of repentant faith in God. In this way he indicated to Russian society the one saving path of life, the true and lasting foundation of its well-being—in the first place spiritual and then, as a result, material.

One may ask now on what basis did this wondrous teacher of life in our times grow? He grew on the ground of Orthodoxy; he was cultivated by the Orthodox Church. And involuntarily, one wishes once again to repeat what was written by us in the foreword. Whatever the enemies of the Church have said, however they have defamed this, our national sacred treasure—the Orthodox Church and, in particular, our Russian Church—by the grace of God she has still not been depleted! This grace is still active in her, still raises up great lamps of faith and piety for our edification, for our consolation. We declare this greatly momentous and joyful fact, not with a feeling of pride and vainglory, not for empty bragging about our righteous ones, but with humble gratitude towards the Lord, Who is merciful and saves us. We declare it so as to love and value even more our holy Orthodox Church, with all its saving order;

so as to become firm in sincere, child-like and rationally conscious obedience to her; so as to fear more than anything to consciously or unconsciously fall away from her, from her ancient ways and precepts! By his lofty example, Fr. Ambrose clearly indicates to us that only in the Church of Christ is the fullness of true Christian perfection attained, is the straight and true path to eternal salvation found; and therefore, for whoever wishes to be made perfect and grow in Christ, for whoever wishes to attain to eternal life, there is no other way than the indicated Church of Christ, the bearer of eternal truth and grace.

Let us also wish that that spirit of humble faith, holy simplicity and sincere brotherly love with which Elder Ambrose was permeated, as were also his great instructors, would not lessen, but would, on the contrary, brightly burn in our holy monasteries—among them Optina Monastery and the Kazan-Ambrose Monastery [of Shamordino]; so that they, watered by this spirit, would be revealed as mighty, indestructible spiritual supports to the Russian people, who are tumbling in the waves of life's cares, and would give them, according to the testament of Elder Ambrose, spiritual enlightenment, reassurance and consolation whenever they come, tormented by life, with their devastated and shattered souls under these holy and grace-filled shelters to seek spiritual help and inward peace! In this, precisely in this, consists the lofty, vital significance of our holy monasteries. Remote from the world, they serve the world by the fact that, guarding within themselves the very image and truth of Christ, they reveal this when necessary to the wayward world, isolated from Christ! Monasteries were always centers of the spiritual life and Christian growth of the Russian people. Let us hope that they will remain such in the future, following, together with the whole Orthodox Russian Church, Christian truth in

The first icon of St. Ambrose in Optina
prepared for his canonization.

all its purity, unmixed with human fantasy and vain human wisdom, in all its untouched Tradition of the Apostles and the Holy Fathers, as a precious treasure received from ancient times by the Russian people for careful preservation and transmission to the last generations.

For the wise and loving Optina Elder Hieroschemamonk Ambrose, who showed us a living example of lofty Christian life and who warmed the hearts of so many with his fatherly love, may there be eternal and grateful memory in the Russian people!

ST. AMBROSE OF OPTINA
*Canonization icon of 1988.*

# AKATHIST

## TO OUR HOLY AND GOD-BEARING

# *Elder Ambrose of Optina*

*Whom the Church Commemorates on October 10/23*

### KONTAKION I

Chosen God-pleaser and wonderworker, great Elder Ambrose, / boast of Optina and and wondrous instructor of all Russia, / glorifying thy superlative life of labors we offer unto thee a hymn of praise. / As thou hast boldness before the Lord, pray for all of us, thy children, who with contrition cry out:

> Rejoice, O venerable Father Ambrose, divinely wise teacher of faith and piety!

### IKOS I

Emulating the angelic life, thou didst reject all the beautiful and fleeting things of this corruptible world and didst direct thy steps to the spiritual teacher and clairvoyant elder Hilarion, that he might instruct thee on the path of true life and bless thee for the work of salvation. He, foreseeing thy future God-pleasing life, did send thee to Optina Monastery, and there thou didst find for thyself a good haven. Seeing God's preference for thee, we say to thee thus:

Rejoice, divinely chosen offspring of pious parents!

Rejoice, beloved of the Lord from thy childhood!

Rejoice, thou who didst have zeal for the wisdom of books from thy youth!

Rejoice, thou who didst come to know the Spirit bearing teachings of the Holy Fathers!

Rejoice, renunciation of the quickly perishing goods of this world!

Rejoice, unremitting love of incorruptible treasures!

Rejoice, seeker of God's will for the salvation of thy soul!

Rejoice, thou who didst receive a blessing for the monastic path!

Rejoice, O venerable Father Ambrose, divinely wise teacher of faith and piety!

## KONTAKION 2

Seeing the good intention of thy heart, Christ did foreordain the narrow and thorny path of thy salvation, and when thou wast suddenly on the death-bed of infirmity, thou didst make a promise to the Lord if he would heal thee: to give thyself over entirely to the labor of monasticism. Having risen from thy bed of sickness through the mercy of God, thou didst straightway glorify the All-generous God, the Physician of souls and bodies, crying out: Alleluia!

## IKOS 2

Having acquired understanding of the Divine Scriptures, with fear of God thou didst contemplate how thou wouldst embark upon the greatly difficult and sorrowful path of monastic life. We, amazed at thy good intention, praise thee thus:

> Rejoice, thou who didst place all thy hope in God the Provider!
> Rejoice, thou who didst seek for His good will alone!
> Rejoice, thou who wast ready to bear any trial for the salvation of thy soul!
> Rejoice, thou who didst follow the dictates of thy conscience!
> Rejoice, thou who didst despise the pleasures of the world!
> Rejoice, thou who didst not love earthly riches!
> Rejoice, thou who didst move thyself entirely to work for God alone!
> Rejoice, thou who didst wish to please only Him!
> Rejoice, O venerable Father Ambrose, divinely wise teacher of faith and piety!

## KONTAKION 3

Confirming thyself in the Faith through the power of love, thou wast zealous to acquire the evangelical life according to the model of the Holy monastic Fathers of the ancient Church. When the Lord gave thee understanding of this pleasing work, thou didst sing with contrition: Alleluia!

## IKOS 3

Having strong faith in the good Providence of God for the salvation of man, thou didst hasten to the honorable icon of the Most Holy Theotokos of Tambov, which was a blessing to thee from thy parents, and didst humbly beseech our Lady to direct thy path. We, seeing thy steadfast hope in the mercy of the Heavenly Queen, sing to thee:

> Rejoice, faithful and beloved child of the Mother of God!
> Rejoice, mystical comprehension of the power of her sacred protection!
> Rejoice, thou who didst respectfully preserve thy parents' blessing through her icon!
> Rejoice, thou who didst reverently honor our Fervent Intercessor!
> Rejoice, thou who didst often tearfully offer up prayers to her in the night!
> Rejoice, thou who didst unashamedly receive heavenly help from her!
> Rejoice, thou who didst thus find sweet consolation in thy heart!
> Rejoice, for thou didst receive tranquil contrition!
> Rejoice, O venerable Father Ambrose, divinely wise teacher of faith and piety!

## KONTAKION 4

Moved by a storm of thoughts thou didst come to the Monastery of St. Sergius of Radonezh, that the Wonderworker of All Russia and teacher of monastic activity, who poureth forth from his honorable relics drops of grace-filled help, might strengthen thy heart for the labors of monastic endeavor that lay before thee. Touched in thy heart there, thou didst cry aloud with joy: Alleluia!

## IKOS 4

Hearing of the great life and piety of the divinely wise fathers and Elders of Optina Monastery, thou didst secretly leave the world and all that is therein, and didst come boldly to this monastery in humility of soul, that thou mightest save thyself and please God. We, seeing the great zeal of thy soul, offer thee a hymn of praise:

> Rejoice, thou who didst regard the corruptible goods of this world as nothing!
> Rejoice, thou who didst come to know the sweetness of the Church!
> Rejoice, thou who didst settle in the holy monastery!
> Rejoice, thou who didst give thyself over wholly to God!
> Rejoice, unslothful fulfiller of the commandments of God!
> Rejoice, thou who didst sweetly taste of the fruits of Christ's teachings!
> Rejoice, emulator of the ascetic labors of the Holy Fathers!
> Rejoice, unflagging preserver of purity of soul!
> Rejoice, O venerable Father Ambrose, divinely wise teacher of faith and piety!

## KONTAKION 5

The divinely created monastery received thee as into the Father's embrace, and thou didst meekly settle therein, and didst take up thy first labor of obedience in the cell of the great and divinely enlightened Elder Leonid, by whom thou wast instructed in spiritual activity. Having come to know the sweetness of the renunciation of thine own will, thou didst cry out: Alleluia!

## IKOS 5

Beholding thy progress in monasticism, the fathers of the monastery clothed thee in the raiment of the great schema. And Christ, the Founder of the struggle, vouchsafed thee to be a partaker of the grace of the angelic rank; for this reason we cry to thee:

> Rejoice, thou who didst love God with all thy heart!
> 
> Rejoice, thou who wast obedient to Him with all thy soul!
> 
> Rejoice, thou who wast immutably confirmed in faith through many labors!
> 
> Rejoice, thou who didst arm thyself with hope in help from on high!
> 
> Rejoice, treasury of evangelical love!
> 
> Rejoice, receptacle of the Holy Spirit!
> 
> Rejoice, valiant warrior of monastic labors!
> 
> Rejoice, most wondrous emulator of the life equal to that of the angels!
> 
> Rejoice, O venerable Father Ambrose, divinely wise teacher of faith and piety!

## KONTAKION 6

Thou didst reveal thyself to be a preacher of the Orthodox Faith and of the true life in Christ Jesus, repudiating teachings opposed to the Gospel and the Church, and turning many from the path of delusion to Christ the Giver of life, singing in thanksgiving: Alleluia!

## IKOS 6

Thou didst shine forth as a brightly burning candle in the Russian land, enlightening every man who came to thee with the light of truth. People burdened by sins and many sorrows found in thee an instructor of piety filled with the knowledge of God and a kind father to all the infirm, suffering, and humiliated, who cry out thus:

> Rejoice, luminary of Orthodoxy of the Russian land!
> Rejoice, mirror of divine love!
> Rejoice, pillar of the apostolic Faith!
> Rejoice, rock of hope in life eternal!
> Rejoice, divinely inspired instructor in all circumstances!
> Rejoice, zealous preacher of repentance!
> Rejoice, physician of bodily afflictions!
> Rejoice, healer of infirmities of soul!
> Rejoice, O venerable Father Ambrose, divinely wise teacher of faith and piety!

## KONTAKION 7

Wishing to follow Christ Himself, thou didst emulate Him with all zeal, taking His yoke upon thyself and, having learned from Him meekness and humility, thou didst find rest for thy soul, ever calling out: Alleluia!

## IKOS 7

Thou wast revealed as a new and wondrous star of holiness in the firmament of the Church when thou didst ascend the spiritual ladder towards angelic perfection. Thou didst extend the rays of thy love across the face of the whole Russian land, and thou didst draw to thyself the prominent and those of low estate, the wise of this age and the unlearned, all of whom cry to thee thus:

> Rejoice, thou city standing high upon a hill!
> Rejoice, luminary, banishing the darkness of ignorance!
> Rejoice, healer of all infirmities!
> Rejoice, deliverer from the dangers and enticements of the enemy!
> Rejoice, consoler of the sorrowing!
> Rejoice, giver of spiritual drink to those who thirst!
> Rejoice, reprover of the falsely eloquent wisdom of this age!
> Rejoice, thou who didst return many who had gone astray to the true path!
> Rejoice, O venerable Father Ambrose, divinely wise teacher of faith and piety!

## KONTAKION 8

Thou wast a wanderer and a stranger in the earthly world, a seeker after the heavenly city, and thou didst bear the burdens and infirmities of thy neighbors who sought help of thee; and thus didst thou fulfill the law of Christ, singing with thanksgiving: Alleluia!

## IKOS 8

Wholly filled with the flame of divine love, thou didst bear the arduous cross of bodily sicknesses throughout thy whole monastic life, in patience possessing thy soul, according to the words of the Gospel of Christ; and thou didst teach us all to bear our cross without murmuring, crying out to thee:

> Rejoice, leader of those seeking salvation!
> Rejoice, model of true obedience!
> Rejoice, thou who didst thyself endure grievous infirmities to the end!
> Rejoice, teacher of patience to those who came to thee in sickness and sorrow!
> Rejoice, goodly guardian of the souls of thy flock!
> Rejoice, feeder of those hungering for life eternal!
> Rejoice, protector of the offended!
> Rejoice, thou who didst bring to their senses those disobedient to the will of God!
> Rejoice, O venerable Father Ambrose, divinely wise teacher of faith and piety!

## KONTAKION 9

Thou didst experience all of human nature in sickness and bodily infirmities, having crucified the flesh with the passions and lusts; by unceasing prayer thou didst drive off the attacks and temptations of the evil spirits, and by this thou didst teach all to oppose the wiles of the devil, crying out with faith: Alleluia!

## IKOS 9

By the Word of God and by thy pure life thou didst sweep aside the eloquence of the vainly wise who knew not the power of the Orthodox Faith; and thou didst truly shine forth as a resplendent pillar of piety and a preserver of the patristic traditions, zealously translating the ancient writings of the Fathers into works easy to comprehend. We, marveling at thy labors, cry out thus:

>Rejoice, thou adamant of the right Faith!
>Rejoice, stronghold of life according to the Faith!
>Rejoice, planter of the spirit of piety!
>Rejoice, sower of Christian virtues!
>Rejoice, thou who didst progress in the labors of eldership!
>Rejoice, spiritual enlightenment of a multitude of monks!
>Rejoice, thou who didst lead them to salvation!
>Rejoice, thou who didst turn many sinners to repentance!
>Rejoice, O venerable Father Ambrose, divinely wise teacher of faith and piety!

## KONTAKION 10

Assisting those seeking the Kingdom of Heaven to be saved, thou wast revealed to be a sure guide, directing them in mundane and spiritual matters; at the end of thy years thou didst exert much labor, building the Shamordino Convent for those of low estate, that the sisters therein might find rest for their souls and salvation, singing a hymn of praise: Alleluia!

## IKOS 10

Thou wast a wall and a haven to thy spiritual children, preserving them from the calumnies of the demons by thine untiring prayers. Thou didst rouse them to unseen warfare with evil spirits, abolishing pride and ambition through humility; therefore, rejoicing, we call unto thee:

> Rejoice, thou who didst extinguish the darts of the enemy!
> 
> Rejoice, conqueror of the regiments of the demons!
> 
> Rejoice, thou who didst set free those held captive by evil spirits!
> 
> Rejoice, thou who didst lead many souls out of the prison of the passions!
> 
> Rejoice, thou who through love and prayers didst convert to God those gone astray!
> 
> Rejoice, good guardian of orphans and widows!
> 
> Rejoice, God-bearing founder of the guidance of monks and nuns!
> 
> Rejoice, mellifluous preacher of humble-mindedness and meekness!

Rejoice, O venerable Father Ambrose, divinely wise teacher of faith and piety!

## KONTAKION 11

We offer unto thee a contrite hymn, O speedy helper of all in need and sorrow who have recourse to thee with faith and love to the end of their days. Thou wast a child-loving father of the suffering and burdened, who hoped for consolation of soul. Therefore, thou dost truly glorify God, Who is wondrous in His saints who cry out unceasingly: Alleluia!

## IKOS 11

All the ends of the earth see in thee a luminary of the virtues, O our Father Ambrose, for thou didst end thine earthly wandering in patience and humility, and didst fulfill all that Christ commanded us in His holy teachings; and thou didst pass from earth to heaven, entering into the joy of thy Lord as a faithful servant of Christ. Therefore, rejoicing, we sing to thee thus!

>Rejoice, zealous servant who didst fulfill the will of thy Lord!
>
>Rejoice, warrior of Christ who didst abandon life's vanity!
>
>Rejoice, thou who didst serve God alone!
>
>Rejoice, fulfiller of all the commandments of God!
>
>Rejoice, thou who wast made worthy of the heavenly habitations!
>
>Rejoice, thou who hast become a communicant of the glory on high!

Rejoice, heir of life eternal!
Rejoice, all-praised God-pleaser!
Rejoice, O venerable Father Ambrose, divinely wise teacher of faith and piety!

## KONTAKION 12

Thou didst inherit the treasury of the grace of God that cannot be stolen and didst find a quiet, tranquil refuge in the heavens. By the action of the knowledge of God, in the days of the celebration of the thousand year anniversary of the Baptism of Russia, thou wast glorified and numbered among the choir of the saints: Glorifying thy holy memory, we all sing: Alleluia!

## IKOS 12

Hymning thy glorification by all of Russia, we offer up to thee, as sweetly scented incense, our humble prayers. Forget not thy children, who honor thy holy name and call out to thee in thanksgiving:

Rejoice, O Ambrose, namesake of divine immortality!
Rejoice, honorable boast of the Orthodox Church!
Rejoice, partaker in the choir of the holy saints of God!
Rejoice, sharer of the mystery of the assembly of the venerable Fathers!
Rejoice, our steadfast defender before the throne of the Most High God!

Rejoice, our fervent intercessor before the judgment seat of God!

Rejoice, guide of us who wander in this vale of tears!

Rejoice, untiring man of prayer for all the Russian land!

Rejoice, O venerable Father Ambrose, divinely wise teacher of faith and piety!

## KONTAKION 13

O wondrous saint of Christ and wonderworker, our venerable Elder Ambrose: receive now this small supplication from thine unworthy children. Do not abandon us in sorrows and sicknesses; come and stretch forth thy helping hand. Instruct us on the path of repentance and salvation, that we might be delivered from eternal torment; through thee may we ever glorify God, crying out: Alleluia! *(thrice)*

## IKOS I

Emulating the angelic life, thou didst reject all the beautiful and fleeting things of this corruptible world and didst direct thy steps to the spiritual teacher and clairvoyant elder Hilarion, that he might instruct thee on the path of true life and bless thee for the work of salvation. He, foreseeing thy future God-pleasing life, did send thee to Optina Monastery, and there thou didst find for thyself a good haven. Seeing God's preference for thee, we say to thee thus:

Rejoice, divinely chosen offspring of pious parents!

# AKATHIST

Rejoice, beloved of the Lord from thy childhood years!
Rejoice, thou who didst have zeal for the wisdom of books from thy youth!
Rejoice, thou who didst come to know the Spirit bearing teachings of the Holy Fathers!
Rejoice, renunciation of the quickly perishing goods of this world!
Rejoice, unremitting love of incorruptible treasures!
Rejoice, seeker of God's will for the salvation of thy soul!
Rejoice, thou who didst receive a blessing for the monastic path!
Rejoice, O venerable Father Ambrose, divinely wise teacher of faith and piety!

## KONTAKION I

Chosen God-pleaser and wonderworker, great Elder Ambrose, / boast of Optina and wondrous instructor of all Russia, / glorifying thy superlative life of labors we offer unto thee a hymn of praise. / As thou hast boldness before the Lord, pray for all of us, thy children, who with contrition cry out:

Rejoice, O venerable Father Ambrose, divinely wise teacher of faith and piety!

# Prayer

## To Our Holy Father Ambrose, Elder of Optina

O ALL-HONORABLE ELDER of the most glorious and wondrous Optina Hermitage, our holy and God-bearing Father Ambrose! Good adornment of our Church and grace-filled lamp who illuminest all with heavenly light; beautiful and spiritual fruit of Russia and all under the sun, who abundantly delightest and makest glad the souls of the faithful! Now, with faith and trembling, we fall down before the healing shrine of thy holy relics, which thou didst mercifully grant for the consolation and help of the suffering. We humbly entreat thee with heart and lips, O holy Father, as the instructor of all Russia and a teacher of piety, as a shepherd and physician of our infirmities of soul and body: Look down upon thy children who have greatly sinned in word and deed, and visit us with thy great and holy love, in which thou didst gloriously prosper while still on earth, and even more after thy righteous repose, instructing us in the rules of the Holy and God-enlightened Fathers, giving us understanding of the commandments of Christ, in which thou wast zealous until the last hour of thy laborious monastic life. Entreat for us, who are infirm of soul and endangered in sorrows, propitious and salvific time for repentance, true correction and renewal of our life, in which we, as sinners, have grown idle in mind and heart and have given ourselves up to dissolute and evil passions, vices, and iniquities without number. Accept, watch over, and shelter us with the protection of thy many mercies; send down upon us a blessing from the Lord, that we might bear the good yoke of Christ with longsuffering to the end of our days, hoping in the future life and kingdom, where there is neither sorrow nor sighing, but life and joy everlasting, abundantly flowing forth from the One, All-holy and blessed Source of immortality, worshiped in Trinity, God the Father, the Son and the Holy Spirit, now and ever, and unto the ages of ages. Amen.

The reliquary of St. Ambrose in the main
church of Optina Monastery.

## TROPARION
### Tone 5

We hasten to thee, O Ambrose our Father, * as to a healing spring. * For thou dost faithfully instruct us on the path of salvation, * preserving us from misfortune and calamity by thy prayers, * consoling us in sorrows of body and soul, * teaching above all humility, patience and love. * Pray to Christ, the Lover of mankind, * and to our Fervent Intercessor * that our souls may be saved.

## KONTAKION
### Tone 2

Having fulfilled the precepts of the Shepherd of shepherds, * thou didst inherit the grace of eldership, * having pain of heart for all who have recourse to thee with faith. * Therefore we, thy children, cry out to thee with love: * O holy Father Ambrose, * pray to Christ God that He save our souls.

# *Glossary*

*akathist:* a service to Jesus Christ, the Mother of God, or a saint during which one should stand; literally, "not sitting."

*all-night vigil:* a service sung on the eve of a special feast; it is usually comprised of Vespers, Matins, and the First Hour.

*analogion:* an icon stand or a stand upon which the Book of the Holy Gospels is placed or read.

*archimandrite:* the highest rank conferred upon a priest-monk.

*batiushka:* an endearing term for a priest or monk.

*canon:* a set of hymns and verses sung to a particular saint or in honor of a feast; a rule or decree of an historic church council.

*canonarch:* the person who during Divine Services chants out verses, one line at a time, which are then repeated by the choir.

*catholicon:* the main church of a monastery.

*cliros:* the place in church where the services are read and sung.

*epitrachelion:* a vestment that hangs from the neck of the priest and is the one indispensable vestment for all priestly ministrations.

*cell:* room or dwelling place of a monastic.

*hermitage (in Russian, pustyn):* a monastic dwelling, traditionally of a solitary monastic, but often used interchangably with the word "monastery."

*hierodeacon:* a monk who is ordained a deacon.

*hieromonk:* a monk in priestly rank.

*hieroschemamonk:* a schemamonk in priestly rank.

*iconostasis:* a screen partitioning the altar area from the nave of the church on which icons are placed; the "Holy Gates" and side doors allow the clergy and acolytes to enter or exit the altar.

*irmos* (pl. *irmoi*): the opening stanza of each canticle of a canon.

*kathisma:* one of the twenty sections into which the Psalter is divided for use in Church services.

*klobuk:* head covering with a veil worn by monastics.

*kontakion* (pl. *kontakia*): a hymn used in the Divine services in honor of a particular saint or feast.

*lampada:* an oil lamp hanging before an icon.

*lavra:* a large coenobitic monastery.

*litia:* a procession and solemn intercession at Vespers for special feasts, taking place in the narthex of the church, or another place, such as the shrine of a saint. Also, the shortened Office of the Dead.

*mantia:* a mantle; the pleated outer garment worn by tonsured monks and nuns.

*Matins:* one of the daily services which takes place late at night or early in the morning. (According to the daily cycle it is scheduled at 3:00 AM) This service is comprised chiefly of psalms and a canon of hymns which differ from day to day.

*matushka:* an endearing term for a priest's wife or for a nun.

*moleben:* a prayer service in which the faithful ask for heavenly help or give thanks to God.

*obedience:* in addition to its ordinary meaning, it signifies a duty assigned and carried out as part of one's relationship to the superior or elder.

*pannikhida:* a service of prayer for those who have reposed.

*Pascha:* the Feast of the Resurrection of our Lord Jesus Christ.

*patristic:* of or relating to the Holy Fathers of the Church.

*Philokalia:* an anthology of classic ascetic writings compiled by St. Nikodimos of the Holy Mountain and St. Macarios of

Corinth, based upon the previous patristic labors of St. Paisius Velichkovsky.

*podrasnik:* the basic robe worn by all monastics, including novices.

*podvig:* an ascetic feat, spiritual labor or simply, Christian struggle.

*prelest:* spiritual deception or delusion; not seeing reality the way it is.

*prosphoron* (pl. *prosphora*): a small round loaf of bread prepared especially for the Divine Liturgy.

*ryassa:* the outer robe worn by tonsured monastics.

*ryassaphore:* a monastic who wears a ryassa but has yet to be fully tonsured a monk or nun.

*schemamonk:* one who has taken on the highest and strictest monastic discipline, leading a life of seclusion and prayer. He wears the "schema," a special cowl and stole.

*semi-uncial script:* mixed upper-lower case script which employs a half cursive style, used for centuries in copying liturgical and Patristic books.

*skete:* a small monastery; usually a close-knit "family" with the abbot or abbess as its head.

*sticheron* (pl. *stichera*): verses of liturgical poetry which are sung in the Divine Services.

*Symbol of Faith:* the credal statement of the Councils of Nicaea and Constantinople, also commonly referred to as the Nicene Creed.

*synaxis:* gathering, host or multitude, such as a gathering of saints.

*Theotokos:* the Greek word for the Mother of God; literally, "the God-birthgiver."

*tonsure:* the rite whereby a novice takes vows to renounce the world and becomes a monk or nun.

*trapeza:* the monastery refectory; also the communal meal in the refectory.

*troparion* (pl. *troparia*): a hymn used in the daily cycle of services and also at Divine Liturgy in honor of a particular saint or feast.

*Typica:* a service usually chanted in lieu of the celebration of the Divine Liturgy, consisting of the "Typical Psalms" (Psalms 33, 102, and 145, and the Beatitudes) with other hymns and prayers.

*Unction:* the Sacrament of anointing, usually for the sick or dying.

*Vespers:* the evening service, celebrated according to the daily cycle at 6:00 PM. It consists of psalms and verses to the saint or feast of the day.

# Select Bibliography

Agapit [Belovidov], Archimandrite. *Elder Ambrose of Optina* (in Russian). Moscow: Optina Monastery, 1900. Reprinted as *The Biography of Optina Elder Hieroschemamonk Ambrose.* Harbin, 1941.

Andronik, Abbot. *Elder Ambrose of Optina* (in Russian). St. Petersburg: Valaam Monastery, 1993.

Bykov, Vladimir P. *Quiet Havens for Storm-tossed Souls* (in Russian). Moscow, 1913.

Chetverikov, Archpriest Sergius. *Description of the Life of Optina Elder Ambrose of Blessed Memory* (in Russian). Shamordino Convent, 1912. 2nd Russian ed. Platina, California: St. Herman of Alaska Brotherhood, 1980.

Dunlop, John. *Staretz Amvrosy: Model for Dostoyevsky's Staretz Zosima.* Belmont, Massachusetts: Nordland Publishing Co., 1972.

Kontzevitch, I. M. *Optina Monastery and Its Era* (in Russian). Jordanville, New York: Holy Trinity Monastery, 1970.

Nilus, Sergius. *On the Bank of God's River: Notes of an Orthodox Man* (in Russian). Vol. 1. 2nd ed. Moscow, 1916. Reprint. Forestville, California: St. Elias Publishing, 1975.

Nilus, Sergius. *On the Bank of God's River: Notes of an Orthodox Man* (in Russian). Vol. 2. San Francisco and Platina, California: Orthodox Christian Books and Icons, 1969.

Poselyanin, Eugene. *Elder Ambrose of Optina* (in Russian). Moscow, 1904.

Stanton, Leonard J. *The Optina Pustyn Monastery in the Russian Literary Imagination.* New York: Peter Lang, 1995.

Vereshchagin, Evgenii Mikhailovich. "St. Ambrose, the Great Optina Elder, as the Interpreter of Church Hymnography" (in Russian). Manuscript, 1990.

# Index

Abramius, first Abbot of Optina, 60–61, 85

Agapit (Belovidov), Archimandrite of Optina and Abbot of Likhvin Pokrov Dobry Monastery, 13, 354, 354n

Akhtyrsk Gusev Women's Community, 298

Alexander Nevsky, St., 249

Alipia, Nun, of Shamordino Convent, 303

Ambrose, St., Elder of Optina,
  Akathist to, 441–55
  canonization of, 11
  cell of, 198 ill., 330 ill.
  childhood of, 44–45
  clairvoyance of, 229–30, 321, 373–92, 394–95
  coffin of, 198 ill., 330 ill.
  compassionate love of, 215–18, 259–61, 362, 436
  correspondence of, 157–63, 167–71, 174–87
  counsels of, 206, 230–44, 246–49, 251–58
  eldership of, 139, 143, 145, 150
  final illness of, 341–49
  funeral of, 353–56, 358–61, 363
  grave of, 39, 65, 423, 427, 428 ill., 432 ill.
  handwriting of, 205 ill.
  healings of, 395–418, 420–27
  illustrations of, 4, 10, 30, 36, 38, 134, 156, 245, 283, 291, 350, 439, 440
  kontakion to, 458
  love for children of, 315, 363
  pastorship of, 39, 41, 215
  prayer to, 456–57
  procession for, 12 ill., 434 ills.
  reliquary of, 30 ill., 457
  repose of, 348–51, 350 ill.
  sermons of:
    on Nativity, 187–89
    on Pascha, 190–95
  troparion to, 458
  upbringing of children, on, 163–66
  "Vision of Eternal Rest," 22–30

Ambrose (Konavalov), Archimandrite 13–16, 14 ill., 15 ill.

Ambrose of Milan, St., 39, 114, 212, 418
  well of, 372 ill.

Ambrosia (Klyuchareva), Nun of Shamordino, 299, 300 ill., 301–4, 314, 378

Anatole I (Zertsalov), St., Elder of Optina, 21, 66, 150, 208, 308, 345

Anthia of Belev, Eldress, 136

Anthony, St., Elder of Optina, 31, 61, 85–86, 89, 89n, 104, 115, 146, 148, 239, 248, 257

# INDEX

Anthony (Khrapovitsky), Metropolitan, 17, 17n
Antiochus, Schemamonk, 122n
*Ascetical Homilies of St. Isaac the Syrian*, 217n
Athanasius, Schemamonk, disciple of St. Paisius (Velichkovsky), 100, 102

Barlaam, Abbot of Valaam Monastery, 119, 120 ill.
Belev Convent, 136, 155, 307, 384–85
Bessarion, Monk, disciple of St. Paisius (Velichkovsky), 80
*Blessed Paisius Velichkovsky* (Schemamonk Metrophanes), 81n
Borisov Convent, 144

Chetverikov, Archpriest Sergius, 13, 16–22, 18 ill., 21 ill., 308n
Chetverikova, Yelena Stratonikovna, 19–20
Clement (Sederholm), Hieromonk, 132, 146, 149–51, 151n, 208, 239, 393n
*A Collection of Letters to Nuns* (Hieroschemamonk Anatole [Zertsalov]), 308, 308n
Cyril of Radonezh, St., 55

Dimitry of Rostov, St., 251, 296n
discernment, 78–79, 228
*Discourses of St. Symeon the New Theologian*, 76, 77
Dosithea of Ivanov Monastery, Nun, 85
Dostoyevsky, Feodor, 11, 11n, 213
Dragomirna Monastery, 81

*Elder Anthony of Optina* (Hieromonk Clement Sederholm), 89n, 151n
*Elder Leonid of Optina* (Hieromonk Clement Sederholm), 91n, 151n
*Elder Macarius of Optina* (Archimandrite Leonid Kavelin), 99n, 150n
eldership, 77, 82, 89, 96, 135–36, 140, 322
Elisha, Novice, 154
Euphrosyne (Rozova), Abbess of Shamordino, 230, 232n, 307, 325, 335

*Father Clement Sederholm, Hieromonk of Optina Monastery* (Constantine Leontiev), 150n

Glebov, S., 22–30
Golubinsky, T. A., 127
Gregory (Borisoglebsky), Hieromonk, 355, 367
Grenkov, Michael Feodorovich (father of Elder Ambrose), 43
Grenkova, Martha Nicholaevna (mother of Elder Ambrose), 43

Hilarion, Recluse of Troekurovo, 31, 48 ill., 54, 104, 118, 199
Holy Fathers, 75–77, 79–80, 82–83, 88, 114, 123, 126–27, 133, 137, 141, 220, 250, 403
Holy Trinity–St. Sergius Lavra, 17, 19, 33, 54–55, 331n
humility, 65, 76, 79, 126, 167–68, 185, 194, 216, 218–23, 227, 234–35, 242–43, 246–48

# INDEX

Ioasaph of Canada, Archbishop, 16
Isaac, St., Archimandrite of Optina, 147 ill., 148, 327, 347
Isaac the Syrian, St., 217, 217n
Isaiah, Fr. (cell attendant of Elder Ambrose), 369, 369n

Jerome, Elder of Mt. Athos, 392n, 393n
Jesus Prayer, 21, 101, 256
John Cassian, St., 78, 79n, 138n
John Chrysostom, St., 251, 254
John Climacus, St., 77n, 79, 79n
John of Kronstadt, St., 19, 336
Joseph, St., Elder of Optina, 65, 65n, 150, 324, 343–45, 347, 351, 422
Jurewicz, Priest Theodore, 36
Juvenal (Polovtsev), Monk, 129n

Kashira Convent, 268, 384
Kireyevsky, Ivan, 65, 65n, 123–27
Kireyevsky, Natalia Petrovna, 125–26
Kireyevsky, Peter, 65, 65n
*The Kireyevsky Brothers—Their Life and Works* (V. Lyakovsky), 125n
Klyuchareva, Lyubov, 303, 304n
Klyuchareva, Vera, 303
Kosov, Priest George, 15, 386–89
Kozelschansk Community, 298
Kozelsk, 62, 282n

*Ladder of Divine Ascent* (St. John Climacus), 77, 79, 168
Leonid, St., Elder of Optina, 31, 65, 85, 91–96, 97 ill., 98, 102–4, 108–10, 112–13, 122n, 123n, 127, 136, 139, 145

Leonid (Kavelin), Hieromonk, 123n, 129n, 150, 150n, 331n
Leontiev, Constantine, 150n, 153, 153n, 213, 296n, 337, 392–93

Macarius, Elder of Mt. Athos, 392n
Macarius, St., Elder of Optina, 31, 65, 79n, 85, 92, 98–99, 99n, 100–104, 112–15, 119, 122, 125, 127, 128 ill., 129, 131–33, 135, 139–40, 145, 150, 368
Maria of Radonezh, St., 55
Mark the Ascetic, St., 78, 78n, 162
Mary of Egypt, St., 137
Mitrophan of Voronezh, St., 421
Moscow Theological Academy, 17, 19, 355, 362, 368
Moses, St., Abbot of Optina, 31, 61, 85–86, 88–89, 90 ill., 92, 104, 144, 146, 148, 241
Mother of God, Most Holy, icons of:
  Akhtyrsk, 324
  It is Truly Meet, 199, 206, 223, 277
  Joy of All Who Sorrow, 155, 343
  Kaluga, 151, 155, 212
  Kazan, 39, 305, 309, 311, 354, 363
  Kiev Caves, 197
  Quick to Hear, 197
  She Who Ripens the Grain, 25 ill., 328–29
  Tambov, 52, 113, 197
Mount Athos, 75n, 122n, 392n, 393n

Neamts Monastery, 81
New Diveyevo Convent, 14, 15 ill.

## INDEX

New Martyrs and Saints of Russia, icon of, 32 ill.
Nicholas, Schemamonk, of Konevits Skete, 21 ill.
Nikolo-Tikhvin Community, 298

Optina Elders, 13, 16, 65–66, 72, 85, 91, 103, 105, 275
Optina Monastery, 11, 13–16, 22, 24, 31, 38–39, 42, 59–62, 64–67, 69, 69n, 72, 88–89, 91–92, 103–5, 107–8, 127, 145–46, 150, 196n, 264n, 282n, 422, 438
  illustrations of, 8, 12, 23, 58, 63, 74
  St. John the Forerunner Skete of, 11, 13, 61, 68 ill., 69, 69n, 70, 71 ill., 72 ill., 89, 106 ill., 111 ill., 112, 121, 282, 322, 327

Paisius (Velichkovsky), St., 11, 20, 73, 75–76, 75n, 80–83, 89, 101, 122, 122n, 123, 125, 130
  disciples of, 84–86
  translations of, 82–84, 127
Pambo, Hieromonk, of Valaam, 21 ill.
Panteleimon, Great-martyr, 155, 197
Pascha, 190–95, 211, 332
Paulina, Abbess of Belev Convent, 268, 384–85
Peter I, Emperor of Russia, 35n
Philaret, Metropolitan of Kiev, 35, 61
Philaret, St., Metropolitan of Moscow, 35, 126–27, 145
*The Philokalia*, 78n, 79n, 138, 140, 210

Platon of Moscow, Metropolitan, 60
Ploschansk Hermitage, 100, 103
Pokrovsky, Paul Stepanovich, 54, 112
Poltava Military Academy, 20
prayer, 199–200, 216, 218, 223–24, 226–27, 231–32, 241, 250, 252, 256
Providence of God, 117, 119, 122, 157–58, 162, 241, 256, 265, 299, 322–23, 327
Pyatnitsa Women's Community, 329

*Quiet Havens for Storm-tossed Souls* (V. P. Bykov), 429n, 463

repentance, 76, 185, 227, 243, 253, 285–86
revelation of thoughts, 76, 82, 92, 98, 105, 114, 137–38, 140, 251
Roslavl Forests, 86
Rudnevo, 302, 324–26, 324n, 332
Russian Christian Student Movement, 20–21
Russian Orthodox Church, 11, 13, 35, 37
Russian Orthodox Church Outside of Russia, 13
*Russky Palomnik*, 22n

St. John the Forerunner Women's Community, 298
St. Tikhon's Hermitage, 423
Serena River, 301
Sergius of Radonezh, St., 54-55
Shamordino Convent, 31, 112, 230, 260, 294 ill., 299,

## INDEX

307–10, 312 ill., 319–20, 322–27, 324n, 331–34, 336–37, 339, 347, 349, 351–52, 364, 384, 438
catholicon of, 294 ill.
orphanage of, 314–15, 319
Shevirev, S. P., 126
Soloviev, Vladimir, 213
Sophia, Schemanun, Abbess of Shamordino Convent, 305, 306 ill., 307, 313–14, 314n
*Soul-Profiting Reading*, 319
Symeon the New Theologian, St., 76–77, 79n

Tambov Theological Seminary, 46 ill.
Theodore of Valaam, Schemamonk, 122n
Tikhona, Abbess of Kashira Convent, 268, 384
Tolstoy, Leo, 214, 290
Trinity Leaflets, 331, 331n

Tryphon, Hieromonk, 362

Valaam Monastery, 21–22, 21 ill., 91, 122n
Vitaly of Kaluga, Bishop, 336, 348, 352, 354, 361, 367
Vladimir of Kaluga, Bishop, 31, 305

*The Way of a Pilgrim*, 221n

Xenia (Shershova), Ryassophore-novice, 426
Xenophont, Archimandrite of Optina Monastery, 426

Yakovleva, Yelena Stratonikovna, *See* Chetverikova, Yelena Stratonikovna
Yankova, Sophia Michailovna, *See* Sophia, Schemanun

Zhizdra River, 61–62, 301

*Other Volumes in the Optina Elders Series*

## Vol. I: Elder Leonid of Optina
*by Fr. Clement Sederholm*

Elder Leonid (†1841) introduced and firmly established in Optina the tradition of eldership as transmitted from St. Paisius Velichkovsky. Possessed with penetrating spiritual discernment, he was at the same time loving and fatherly. He could mystically see into human hearts, knowing when to rebuke, when to exhort, and when to console. Thousands came to him to be healed both in soul and body.

*272 pages, paperback, illustrated, $12.00.* ISBN 0-938635-66-2

## Vol. II: Elder Anthony of Optina
*by Fr. Clement Sederholm*

Through a life of terrible hardships and excruciating physical ailments, Elder Anthony (†1865) acquired perfect spiritual freedom through the careful guarding of his soul and the humble acceptance of God's Providence. He remained joyful to the end, filled with tender compassion for all who came to him and with an unconquerable inner peace.

*269 pages, paperback, illustrated, $10.00.* ISBN 0-938635-51-4

## Vol. III: Elder Macarius of Optina
*by Fr. Leonid Kavelin*

A disciple and co-laborer of Elder Leonid, Elder Macarius (†1860) further established the Optina spiritual tradition by publishing major Patristic texts. He himself was an embodiment of Patristic wisdom, an ancient Church Father come forth in recent times. Meek, gentle, loving, and noble, he was imbued with the power of humility that exorcises evil spirits, chastens the proud-minded, and strengthens the infirm.

*390 pages, paperback, illustrated, $14.00.* ISBN 0-938635-58-1

## Vol. V: Elder Nektary of Optina
### by Ivan M. Kontzevitch

Marked by simplicity, childlikeness, spontaneity and creativity, Elder Nektary (†1928) radiated joy to the thousands of suffering souls who came to him. The last Elder to function as such at Optina, he was there when it was forcibly closed by the Communists in 1923, and spent his remaining years in exile from his spiritual home. At this time of immeasurable sorrow for Orthodox believers, God gave Elder Nektary to Russia as both a consoler of souls and a voice of prophecy.

*520 pages, paperback, illustrated, $19.00.* ISBN 0-938635-59-X

## Vol. VI: Elder Sebastian of Optina
### by Tatiana V. Torstensen

Elder Sebastian (†1966) was a longsuffering, quiet bearer of the vision of the Optina monastic tradition, who preserved Optina eldership through decades of Communist persecution of the Church. After the closure of Optina in 1923, Fr. Sebastian, a disciple of both Elder Joseph and Elder Nektary, spent ten years in the Karaganda concentration camps of Kazakhstan. After his release he spent the rest of his life as a grace-filled pastor to the multitudes of exiles in that area.

*496 pages, paperback, illustrated, $19.00.* ISBN 0-938635-62-X

## Vol. VII: Elder Barsanuphius of Optina
### by Victor Afanasiev

Elder Barsanuphius (†1913), a disciple of Elders Anatole (Zertsalov) and Nektary, was a highly cultured colonel before entering the monastic life at a relatively late age. Due to his purity of heart and spiritual sobriety, he was transformed by God into a grace-filled Elder virtually overnight. In frail health but strengthened by the power of the Lord, Elder Barsanuphius received great numbers of people, directing them to the true path. He was a man of extraordinary spiritual vision, and could see clearly into the hearts of those who came to him.

*840 pages, paperback, illustrated, $23.00.* ISBN 0-938635-61-1

## ST. HERMAN OF ALASKA BROTHERHOOD

Since 1965, the St. Herman Brotherhood has been publishing Orthodox Christian books and magazines.

Write for our free catalogue, featuring over fifty titles.

St. Herman of Alaska Brotherhood
P. O. Box 70, Platina, CA 96076 USA

You can also view our catalogue and order online, at
**www.sainthermanpress.com**